A Complete Guide to Graph Representation Learning with Case Studies

A Complete Guide to Graph Representation Learning with Case Studies

E. Chandra Blessie
Dean – Innovation
School of Innovation
KG College of Arts and Science, Coimbatore
Tamil Nadu, India

Pethuru Raj Chelliah
Principal AI Architect
Infocion Inc., AKR Tech Park, Hosur Road
Bangalore 560068, India

B. Sundaravadivazhagan
Department of Information Technology
College of Computing and Information Sciences
University of Technology and Applied Sciences Al Mussanah
Oman

IEEE*Press*
WILEY

Published by John Wiley & Sons, Inc., Hoboken, New Jersey.

Library of Congress Cataloging-in-Publication Data applied for:

Hardback ISBN : 9781394314843

Cover Design: Wiley
Cover Image: © artida/stock.adobe.com

Set in 9.5/12.5pt STIXTwoText by Straive, Chennai, India

Contents

List of Figures *xxi*
List of Tables *xxvii*
About the Book *xxix*
About the Authors *xxxi*
Preface *xxxiii*
List of Abbreviation *xxxv*

Part I Foundation Learning *1*

1 Introduction to Graph and Graph Representation Learning *3*
1.1 Introduction *3*
1.2 What Is a Graph? *3*
1.3 Importance of Graph *5*
1.4 Types of Graphs *6*
1.4.1 Directed Graph *6*
1.4.2 Undirected Graph *7*
1.4.3 Weighted Graph *8*
1.4.4 Multigraph *8*
1.4.5 Complete Graph *9*
1.4.6 Planar and Bipartite Graph *10*
1.4.7 Hypergraph *11*
1.4.8 Hierarchical Graphs *12*
1.4.9 Homogeneous and Heterogeneous Graphs *12*
1.4.9.1 Heterogeneous Graph *13*
1.5 Overview of Graph Representation Learning (GRL) *13*
1.5.1 Definition of GRL *14*
1.5.2 Benefits of GRL *14*

1.6 Overview of Graph Connectivity *15*
1.6.1 Definition of Graph Connectivity *15*
1.6.2 Importance of Graph Connectivity *15*
1.6.3 Role of Graph Connectivity *16*
1.7 Foundation on Graph Neighborhood *17*
1.7.1 Introduction *17*
1.7.2 Properties of Graph Neighborhoods *18*
1.7.2.1 Properties *18*
1.7.3 Types of Node/Graph Neighborhoods *18*
1.7.3.1 Direct/Local Neighborhood (1-Hop Neighborhood) *18*
1.7.3.2 K-Hop Neighborhood *18*
1.7.3.3 Ego Neighborhood *19*
1.7.3.4 Attention-Based Neighborhoods *19*
1.7.3.5 Structural Neighborhood (Graphlets and Motifs) *19*
1.7.3.6 Graphlets *21*
1.8 Applications of Graph *23*
1.8.1 Traffic Prediction in Transportation *23*
1.8.2 Pattern Recognition *23*
1.8.3 Social Network Analysis *24*
1.8.4 Application of Graphs in Biology *24*
1.8.5 Application of Graphs in Chemistry *24*
1.9 Case Studies of GRL *25*
1.9.1 Case Study in SNA *26*
1.9.1.1 Friend and Connection Recommendations *26*
1.9.1.2 Community Detection and Group Formation *26*
1.9.1.3 Fake Account and Bot Detection *27*
1.9.1.4 Sentiment and Opinion Analysis *28*
1.9.2 Case Study in Fraud Detection for Financial Transactions *28*
1.9.3 Case Study in Molecular Biology *29*
1.10 Conclusion *31*
References *32*

2 Fundamental Concepts of Graph Structure *33*
2.1 Introduction to Graph Structures *33*
2.1.1 Characteristics of Graph Structure *34*
2.2 Node-Level Features *35*
2.2.1 Node Degree *35*
2.2.2 Node Centrality Measures *36*
2.2.2.1 Importance of Node Centrality *37*
2.2.2.2 Types of Node Centrality *37*
2.3 Structural-Level Features *46*

2.3.1 Introduction to Structural-Level Features *46*
2.3.1.1 Clustering Coefficient Measure *46*
2.3.1.2 Closed Triangles *48*
2.3.1.3 Egographs *48*
2.3.1.4 Motifs *50*
2.3.1.5 Definition with Its Types *50*
2.4 Graph-Level Features *52*
2.4.1 Structural Properties of Graphs *52*
2.4.1.1 Graph Degree and Density *52*
2.4.1.2 Graph Eccentricity and Modularity *53*
2.5 Graph-Based Representation Techniques *56*
2.5.1 Graph Clustering Coefficient *56*
2.5.2 Bag of Nodes *58*
2.5.2.1 Approach *59*
2.5.3 WL Kernel *61*
2.5.3.1 Working Process of the WL Kernel *61*
2.5.4 Graphlets and Path-Based Methods *64*
2.5.4.1 Definition of Graphlets *64*
2.5.4.2 Different Types of Graphlets *64*
2.5.4.3 Path-Based Methods *65*
2.6 Graph Representation Matrix *66*
2.6.1 Types of Graph Representation Matrices *66*
2.6.1.1 Adjacency Matrix *66*
2.6.1.2 Incidence Matrix *67*
2.6.1.3 Laplacian Matrix *68*
2.6.1.4 Transition Matrix *70*
2.7 Conclusion *72*
References *72*

3 Overlapping Neighborhood in Graph *73*
3.1 Definition and Its Importance *73*
3.2 Methods for Detecting Neighborhood Overlap *75*
3.2.1 Local Overlap Measures *75*
3.2.1.1 Jaccard Similarity Measure *75*
3.2.1.2 Adamic–Adar Index *76*
3.2.1.3 Resource Allocation Index *77*
3.2.2 Global Overlap Measures *78*
3.2.2.1 Katz Index *78*
3.2.2.2 SimRank *79*
3.2.2.3 PageRank-Based Similarity *81*

3.3 Neighborhood Overlap Visualization Techniques *81*
3.3.1 Venn Diagrams *81*
3.3.1.1 Neighborhood Overlap Analysis *81*
3.3.1.2 Subgraph Comparison *81*
3.3.1.3 Feature Distribution Understanding *82*
3.3.1.4 Analyzing Multi-Relational or Heterogeneous Graphs *82*
3.3.2 Node-Link Diagrams (Graph Representation) *82*
3.3.2.1 Usage of Node-Link Diagrams *82*
3.3.3 Heatmaps *82*
3.3.3.1 Usage of Heatmaps *83*
3.3.4 Edge Bundling *83*
3.3.4.1 Usage of Edge Bundling *83*
3.3.5 Graph Embedding and Projection (t-SNE, UMAP) *83*
3.3.5.1 Usage of Graph Embedding and Projection (t-SNE, UMAP) *84*
3.3.6 Ego Networks (Subgraph Extraction) *84*
3.3.6.1 Usage of Ego Networks (Subgraph Extraction) *84*
3.4 Overlapping Neighborhoods in Heterogeneous Graphs *84*
3.4.1 Introduction *85*
3.4.2 Methods for Detecting Overlapping Neighborhoods in Heterogeneous Graphs *86*
3.4.2.1 Meta-Path-Based Approaches *86*
3.4.2.2 Clustering-Methods *90*
3.4.2.3 Approach: Clustering for Overlapping Neighborhoods *90*
3.4.2.4 Soft Clustering Methods *90*
3.4.2.5 Fuzzy C-Means *91*
3.5 Case Studies on Neighborhood Overlap Detection in Real-World Scenarios *92*
3.5.1 Application of Graph Neighborhood in Healthcare *92*
3.5.1.1 Introduction *92*
3.5.1.2 Healthcare: Community-Based Anomaly Detection in COVID-19 Spread *92*
3.5.2 Case Studies on Social Networks: Overlapping User Communities and Friend Recommendations *94*
3.6 Conclusion *95*
References *95*

Part II Core Graph Representation Learning *97*

4 Graph Machine Learning *99*
4.1 Introduction to GML *99*

4.1.1 Key Features of GML *100*
4.1.2 GML vs Traditional ML *100*
4.2 Types of Tasks in GML *101*
4.2.1 Supervised GML Tasks *101*
4.2.1.1 Node Classification *102*
4.2.1.2 Link Prediction *104*
4.2.1.3 Edge Classification *106*
4.2.1.4 Graph/Subgraph Classification *107*
4.2.2 Unsupervised GML Tasks *109*
4.2.2.1 Introduction *109*
4.2.2.2 Node Clustering *109*
4.2.3 Case Studies and Applications of GML *118*
4.3 Conclusion *121*
References *121*

5 Graph Sampling *123*
5.1 Introduction *123*
5.1.1 Issues Related to Large and Complex Graphs *124*
5.1.2 Definition with Examples *124*
5.1.3 Challenges of Using Sampling *125*
5.2 Types of Graph Sampling *125*
5.2.1 Node Sampling *126*
5.2.1.1 Overview of Node Sampling *126*
5.2.1.2 Types of Node Sampling *126*
5.2.2 Edge Sampling *137*
5.2.2.1 Overview of Edge Sampling *137*
5.2.2.2 Types of Edge Sampling *138*
5.2.3 Neighborhood Sampling *142*
5.2.3.1 Overview of Neighborhood Sampling *143*
5.2.3.2 Types of Neighborhood Sampling *143*
5.2.4 Subgraph Sampling *148*
5.3 Case Studies *149*
5.3.1 Case Study: Sampling Patient Networks for Disease Prediction *149*
5.3.2 Case Study: Sampling in Learning Management System *149*
5.3.3 Case Study: Community-Based Sampling for Efficient Social Network Analysis *150*
5.4 Conclusion *152*
References *152*

6 Graph Pooling *153*
6.1 Introduction to Graph Pooling *153*

6.1.1 What Is Graph Pooling? *153*
6.1.2 Why Is Graph Pooling Important? *153*
6.2 Types of Graph Pooling *155*
6.2.1 Flat Pooling *155*
6.2.1.1 Methods of Flat Pooling *156*
6.2.1.2 Applications of Flat Pooling in Graph-Level Tasks *165*
6.2.2 Hierarchical Pooling *166*
6.2.2.1 Types of Hierarchical Pooling *167*
6.2.2.2 Common Techniques *168*
6.2.3 Comparison Between Flat Pooling and Hierarchical Pooling *178*
6.3 Case Study on Graph Pooling *178*
6.3.1 ContrastPool for Brain Network Classification *178*
6.4 Conclusion *179*
References *180*

7 Graph Neural Networks and Deep Representation Learning *181*
7.1 Foundation of Deep Representation Learning on Graphs *181*
7.1.1 Basic Concept *181*
7.1.2 Challenges and Importance of Deep Learning on Graphs *182*
7.1.3 Approach of Deep Learning in Graph *183*
7.1.3.1 Step-by-Step Process *183*
7.1.4 Characteristics and Benefits of Deep Learning on Graphs *184*
7.2 Introduction to GNNs *185*
7.2.1 GNN Architecture Overview *186*
7.2.1.1 Algorithm Steps *186*
7.2.2 Message Passing in GNNs *187*
7.2.3 Case Study on GNNs *188*
7.3 Fundamentals of GCNs *189*
7.3.1 Core Concepts and Motivation for GCNs *189*
7.3.2 Workflow Process of GCN *191*
7.4 Types of GNNs *194*
7.4.1 Graph RNN *194*
7.4.1.1 Definition with Illustration *195*
7.4.1.2 Working Process of GRNN *196*
7.4.1.3 GRNN Architecture *196*
7.4.1.4 Applications of GRNN *198*
7.4.2 Graph Attention Networks *199*
7.4.2.1 Definition With Illustration *200*

7.4.2.2 Working Process of GAT *202*
7.4.2.3 Architecture of GAT *202*
7.4.2.4 Application of GAT *205*
7.5 Applications of Deep Learning on Graphs *207*
7.6 Conclusion *208*
References *208*

8 Advanced Graph Neural Networks *211*
8.1 Spatiotemporal GNNs *211*
8.1.1 Definition With Illustration *212*
8.1.1.1 Key Features of ST-GNN *212*
8.1.2 Working Process of ST-GNN *213*
8.1.3 Architecture of ST-GNNs *213*
8.1.3.1 Key Components of ST-GNN Architecture *213*
8.1.4 Application of ST-GNNs *215*
8.1.4.1 Case Study on COVID-19 Spread Prediction Using ST-GNN *215*
8.2 Dynamic GNNs *216*
8.2.1 Work Process of Dynamic GNNs *217*
8.2.2 Example: Dynamic Graph—Social Interaction *219*
8.2.2.1 Dynamic GNN Process *219*
8.2.3 Dynamic GNN Models *220*
8.2.3.1 Temporal GAT *220*
8.2.3.2 Dynamic GCN *221*
8.3 Hypergraph Neural Networks *223*
8.3.1 Architecture of HGNN *223*
8.3.2 Working Process of HGNN *224*
8.4 Unsupervised Deep Learning Models *224*
8.4.1 Graph Autoencoder *224*
8.4.1.1 Key Components of GAE *224*
8.4.1.2 GAE—Workflow With Its Architecture *224*
8.4.1.3 GAE Algorithm *225*
8.4.1.4 Applications of GAE *227*
8.4.1.5 Advantages and Limitations of GAE *229*
8.4.2 Variational Autoencoder *229*
8.4.2.1 Variational Graph Autoencoder—Workflow With Its Architecture *230*
8.4.2.2 Advantages and Limitations of VGAE *231*
8.5 Conclusion *231*
References *232*

Part III Advanced Analysis and Techniques *233*

9 Graph Alignment and Matching *235*
9.1 Introduction to Graph Alignment and Matching *235*
9.2 Definition and Purpose of Graph Alignment and Matching *235*
9.2.1 Purpose *236*
9.3 Example for Graph Matching and Alignment *236*
9.3.1 Matching *236*
9.3.2 Example of Graph Alignment *237*
9.3.3 Alignment *237*
9.4 Types of Graph Alignment and Matching *237*
9.4.1 Exact Graph Matching (Graph Isomorphism) *237*
9.4.2 Inexact/Fuzzy Matching *239*
9.4.3 Global Alignment: Aligning Entire Graphs *239*
9.4.4 Local Alignment: Aligning Specific Substructures *240*
9.5 Mathematical Approaches for Graph Alignment and Matching *241*
9.5.1 Graph Embedding + Distance Minimization *241*
9.5.2 Gromov–Wasserstein Distance *243*
9.5.3 Contrastive Learning for Graph Matching *244*
9.5.4 Deep Graph Matching Networks *245*
9.6 Case Studies on Graph Alignment and Matching *246*
9.6.1 Graph Alignment and Matching in Healthcare *246*
9.6.1.1 Method: GW Graph Matching *246*
9.6.2 Benefits *246*
9.6.3 Matching Users Across Facebook and Twitter Accounts in Social Networks *246*
9.7 Conclusion *247*
References *248*

10 Neighborhood Reconstruction Methods *249*
10.1 Introduction *249*
10.1.1 Introduction to Neighborhood Reconstruction in Graphs *249*
10.1.2 Benefits of Neighborhood Reconstruction in Graphs *250*
10.1.3 Importance of Reconstructing Graph Structures *251*
10.2 Neighborhood Reconstruction Techniques *251*
10.2.1 Matrix Factorization *251*
10.2.1.1 Mathematical Definition *252*
10.2.1.2 Application *253*
10.2.1.3 Advantages and Disadvantages *253*
10.2.1.4 Approaches in Matrix Factorization *253*
10.2.2 Embedding Models *255*

10.2.2.1 Mathematical Definition *255*
10.2.2.2 Popular Embedding Models *256*
10.2.2.3 Applications *259*
10.2.2.4 Advantages and Disadvantages *259*
10.2.3 Similarity Measures *259*
10.2.3.1 Common Similarity Measures *260*
10.2.3.2 Applications *261*
10.2.3.3 Advantages and Disadvantages *261*
10.3 Neighborhood Reconstruction Methods *262*
10.3.1 An Encoder–Decoder Method *262*
10.3.2 Factorization-Based Approaches *262*
10.3.3 Random Walk Embeddings *262*
10.3.4 An Encoder–Decoder Method *262*
10.3.4.1 Encoder *262*
10.3.4.2 Decoder *264*
10.4 Applications of Encoder–Decoder in Graph Learning *265*
10.4.1 Link Prediction *265*
10.4.2 Node Classification *265*
10.4.3 Anomaly Detection *265*
10.4.4 Graph-Based Recommendation Systems *266*
10.4.5 Graph Generation and Completion *266*
10.4.6 Knowledge Graph Completion *266*
10.5 Case Study on Neighborhood Reconstruction *266*
10.5.1 Case Study on Urban Road Network Reconstruction Using Neighborhood Inference *266*
10.6 Conclusion *267*
References *268*

11 Transfer Learning on Graph *269*
11.1 Introduction *269*
11.2 Overview of TGL *270*
11.2.1 Key Features of TGL *271*
11.2.2 Benefits of TGL *271*
11.2.3 The Need for TGL and Its Necessity *272*
11.2.3.1 Need for TGLs *272*
11.2.3.2 Necessity of TGL *272*
11.2.4 TGL vs GL *272*
11.3 Types of TGL *273*
11.3.1 Inductive TGL *273*
11.3.1.1 Working Process of ITGL *273*
11.3.1.2 Algorithm: GraphSAGE *276*

11.3.1.3 Key Features and Benefits of GraphSAGE *277*
11.3.2 Transductive TGL *277*
11.3.2.1 Working Process of TTGL *278*
11.3.2.2 Algorithm: Graph Convolutional Network with Domain Adaptation *279*
11.3.2.3 Key Features and Benefits of GCN-DA *281*
11.3.3 Heterogeneous Transfer Learning *282*
11.3.3.1 Working Process of HTL *282*
11.3.3.2 Algorithm: Heterogeneous Feature Augmentation *282*
11.3.3.3 Key Features and Benefits of HFA *283*
11.4 Key Techniques in TGL *284*
11.4.1 Feature-Based Transfer Techniques *284*
11.4.1.1 Transfer Component Analysis *286*
11.4.1.2 Domain Adversarial Neural Networks *289*
11.4.2 Structure-Based Transfer Techniques *292*
11.4.2.1 Overview and Its Definition *292*
11.4.2.2 Algorithm for Structure-Based Transfer Learning *292*
11.4.2.3 Flow Process and Its Diagram *293*
11.4.2.4 Meta-Path–Based Learning *294*
11.5 Technique Comparisons *296*
11.5.1 Inductive vs Transductive TGL *296*
11.5.2 Feature-Based TGL vs Structure-Based TGL *297*
11.6 Case Studies *297*
11.7 Conclusion *299*
References *299*

Part IV Emerging Trends with Case Studies *301*

12 Graph Contrastive Learning *303*
12.1 Introduction to Self-Supervised Learning *303*
12.1.1 Definition With Example *303*
12.1.1.1 Self-Supervised Task Idea: Predict Missing Links *304*
12.1.2 Key Characteristics of SSL *307*
12.1.3 Types of Self-Supervised Tasks *307*
12.1.3.1 Generative Tasks *308*
12.1.4 Application in Graph Domain *309*
12.1.4.1 Node Attribute Masking and Link Prediction in Author Citation Graph *309*
12.1.4.2 Recommendation System in Social Network Analysis *310*
12.1.4.3 Fraud Detection in Financial Transactions *311*

12.2 Comparison with Supervised Graph Learning *311*
12.3 Fundamentals of GCL *312*
12.3.1 Motivation: Why Contrastive Learning for Graphs? *312*
12.3.2 Key Components and Mechanism *313*
12.3.2.1 Anchor, Positive and Negative Samples *313*
12.3.2.2 Encoder Network *315*
12.3.2.3 Contrastive Objective Function (InfoNCE, JSD) *315*
12.4 GCL Frameworks *316*
12.4.1 Components *316*
12.4.1.1 Graph Encoder *316*
12.4.1.2 Graph Augmentation *317*
12.4.1.3 Projection Head *318*
12.4.1.4 Contrastive Objective Function *318*
12.5 Conclusion *318*
Further Reading *319*

13 Multimodal Graph Representation Learning *321*
13.1 Introduction to Multimodal GRL *321*
13.2 Types of Modalities in Graph Data *322*
13.2.1 Text Modality *322*
13.2.2 Image Modality *323*
13.2.3 Audio Modality *324*
13.3 Data Fusion Techniques in Multimodal GRL *325*
13.3.1 What Is Data Fusion? *325*
13.3.1.1 The Importance of Data Fusion *325*
13.3.2 Data Fusion Techniques *325*
13.3.2.1 Early Fusion *325*
13.3.2.2 Intermediate (Joint) Fusion *327*
13.3.2.3 Late Fusion (Decision-Level Fusion) *329*
13.4 Applications *331*
13.4.1 Autonomous Vehicles *331*
13.4.1.1 Graph Representation *331*
13.4.1.2 Modalities *331*
13.4.1.3 Working Process of the Multimodal GRL *331*
13.4.2 Agriculture—Pest Detection Network *332*
13.4.2.1 Graph Representation *333*
13.4.2.2 Modalities *333*
13.4.2.3 Working Process of the Multimodal GRL *333*
13.5 Conclusion *334*
Further Reading *334*

14 Demystifying Graph Embeddings and Industrial Applications *337*
14.1 Introduction *337*
14.2 The Importance of Graph Representation *337*
14.3 Making Sense Out of Graph-Structured Data *338*
14.4 Delineating AI Model Engineering Steps *339*
14.5 Graph Embeddings *340*
14.5.1 The Need for Graph Embeddings *340*
14.5.2 Knowledge Graph Embeddings *341*
14.5.3 The Advantages of Graph Embeddings *343*
14.5.4 Graph Embedding Applications *345*
14.5.4.1 Clustering *345*
14.5.4.2 Anomaly Detection *345*
14.5.5 Types of Graph Embeddings *346*
14.5.5.1 Node Embeddings *346*
14.6 Edge Embedding Techniques *348*
14.6.1 Graph Embeddings *348*
14.7 Applications of Graph Embeddings *354*
14.7.1 Graph Embeddings Challenges *355*
14.8 Conclusion *356*
References *357*

15 Knowledge Graph Foundation, Techniques, and Its Case Studies *359*
15.1 Introduction to KG *359*
15.1.1 History and Evolution *359*
15.1.2 Definition and Core Concepts *361*
15.1.2.1 Core Concepts *362*
15.1.3 Difference Between KGs and Traditional Databases *363*
15.2 Construction of a KG *365*
15.3 Techniques for Building a KG *366*
15.3.1 Named Entity Recognition *367*
15.3.1.1 Working Process of NER in NLP *367*
15.3.2 Entity Linking and Disambiguation *368*
15.3.2.1 Purpose of EL and ELD *368*
15.3.2.2 Step-by-Step Working Process of EL *369*
15.3.2.3 Example of Disambiguation *369*
15.3.3 Relation Extraction *369*
15.3.3.1 Step-by-Step Working Process *370*
15.3.4 Ontology Engineering *370*
15.4 Representation and Storage *371*

15.4.1 Introduction to Representation and Storage of KGs *371*
15.4.2 RDF Triples and SPARQL *372*
15.4.2.1 RDF Triples: The Foundation of Semantic Representation *372*
15.4.2.2 SPARQL: Querying RDF Data *373*
15.4.2.3 Comparison: RDF Triples vs SPARQL *374*
15.5 Case Studies of KG *374*
15.5.1 Supply Chain Management Using KG *374*
15.5.1.1 Introduction *374*
15.5.1.2 Methodology *375*
15.5.1.3 Approach *376*
15.5.1.4 Evaluation Metrics Used *376*
15.5.1.5 Result *378*
15.5.2 DRKG: A KG Approach to Drug Repurposing for COVID-19 *378*
15.5.2.1 Introduction *378*
15.5.2.2 Methodology *379*
15.5.2.3 Approach Used *380*
15.5.2.4 Proposed Methodology *381*
15.5.2.5 Implementation Procedure *381*
15.6 Conclusion *383*
References *383*

16 Graph Representation Learning in Wireless Communication and Tourist Movement Analysis *385*
16.1 A Graph-Theoretic Framework for Analyzing Tourist Flows from Social Media Data *385*
16.1.1 Introduction *386*
16.1.2 Methodologies *386*
16.1.2.1 Data Preprocessing *386*
16.1.2.2 Clustering Analysis *386*
16.1.2.3 Network Analysis *386*
16.1.2.4 Feature Engineering with Weisfeiler–Lehman Algorithm *386*
16.1.2.5 ML with GNNs *387*
16.1.3 Approach Used *387*
16.1.3.1 Feature Engineering *387*
16.1.3.2 ML Modeling *388*
16.1.4 Inference *388*
16.1.5 Conclusion *390*
16.2 Knowledge-Driven Graph Learning for Next-Generation Wireless Networks *390*
16.2.1 Introduction *391*
16.2.2 Methodology *392*

16.2.2.1 GAN Without GCN *392*
16.2.2.2 GAN with GCN *393*
16.2.3 Approach *394*
16.2.4 Experimental Evaluation *395*
16.2.5 Conclusion *395*
16.3 Applications of GRL in Wireless Networks and Urban Tourism *395*
16.4 Other Areas of GRL Applications *397*
16.4.1 Healthcare and Biomedical Informatics *397*
16.4.1.1 Application *397*
16.4.1.2 Drug Discovery *397*
16.4.1.3 Drug Repurposing *397*
16.4.1.4 Patient Graphs *397*
16.4.2 E-commerce and Recommendation Systems *397*
16.4.2.1 Application *397*
16.4.2.2 User–Item Graphs *398*
16.4.2.3 Session-Based Recommendations *398*
16.4.2.4 Social Influence Modeling *398*
16.4.3 Financial Fraud Detection *398*
16.4.3.1 Application *398*
16.4.3.2 Transaction Graphs *398*
16.4.3.3 Anomaly Detection *398*
16.4.3.4 Link Prediction *398*
16.4.4 Cybersecurity *398*
16.4.4.1 Application *398*
16.4.4.2 Network Graphs *398*
16.4.4.3 Attack Graphs *399*
16.4.4.4 Code Graphs *399*
16.4.5 Social Network Analysis *399*
16.4.5.1 Application *399*
16.4.5.2 Community Detection *399*
16.4.5.3 Fake News and Bot Detection *399*
16.4.5.4 User Profiling *399*
16.4.6 Traffic and Smart Transportation *399*
16.4.6.1 Application *399*
16.4.6.2 Traffic Graphs *399*
16.4.6.3 Multimodal Networks *399*
16.4.6.4 Dynamic Graphs *399*
16.4.7 Natural Language Processing *400*
16.4.7.1 Application *400*
16.4.7.2 Knowledge Graph Embedding *400*
16.4.7.3 Document Graphs *400*

16.4.7.4 Dialogue Systems *400*
16.4.8 Supply Chain and Logistics *400*
16.4.8.1 Application *400*
16.4.8.2 Supply Network Graphs *400*
16.4.8.3 Demand Graphs *400*
16.4.8.4 Risk Management *400*
16.4.9 Energy Systems and Smart Grids *400*
16.4.9.1 Application *400*
16.4.9.2 Grid Graphs *401*
16.4.9.3 Sensor Networks *401*
16.4.9.4 Renewable Integration *401*
16.5 Conclusion *401*
References *401*

Index *403*

List of Figures

Figure 1.1 Sample graph example *4*
Figure 1.2 Entrepreneurs working in the healthcare industry *4*
Figure 1.3 Entrepreneurs working in similar fields *5*
Figure 1.4 Directed graph for author citation *7*
Figure 1.5 Undirected graph example for author citation *7*
Figure 1.6 Author citation example using weighted graph *8*
Figure 1.7 Author citation example using a multigraph *9*
Figure 1.8 Example of complete graph *9*
Figure 1.9 Bipartite graph for author citation *10*
Figure 1.10 Hypergraph for author citation *11*
Figure 1.11 Hierarchical graph for author citation *12*
Figure 1.12 Heterogeneous graph for author citation *13*
Figure 1.13 Graph representation learning flow of process *14*
Figure 1.14 Well-connected and disconnected graphs *16*
Figure 1.15 Illustration graph for direct neighborhood nodes *17*
Figure 1.16 K-hop neighborhood example graph *19*
Figure 1.17 Graph used for graph attention networks *20*
Figure 1.18 Different types of motifs *21*
Figure 1.19 Graphlets example *21*
Figure 2.1 Graph representing patient–doctor relationship based on "diagonalized by" factor *36*
Figure 2.2 Healthcare graph with patient-to-doctor relationship *39*
Figure 2.3 Example of betweenness centrality measure *42*
Figure 2.4 Eigenvector centrality measure example *44*

Figure 2.5 Graph for calculating clustering coefficient *47*

Figure 2.6 Citation graph for egograph *49*

Figure 2.7 Types of motif *51*

Figure 2.8 Example graph for calculating graph density *53*

Figure 2.9 Graph for finding eccentricity *54*

Figure 2.10 Cluster community *55*

Figure 2.11 Author citation graph example for calculating clustering coefficient *57*

Figure 2.12 Architecture of bag of nodes and its components *60*

Figure 2.13 Example illustrating working process of the Weisfeiler–Lehman (WL) Kernel *62*

Figure 2.14 Different types of graphlets *65*

Figure 2.15 Path-based method graph example *66*

Figure 2.16 Adjacency matrix illustration graph *67*

Figure 2.17 Graph for incidence matrix *68*

Figure 2.18 Graph for unnormalized Laplacian matrix *69*

Figure 2.19 Graph used for transition matrix *71*

Figure 3.1 Graph for finding common neighborhood *74*

Figure 3.2 Author citation graph for Jaccard similarity measure *76*

Figure 3.3 Family relationship graph for Katz index *79*

Figure 3.4 Graph for finding similarity *80*

Figure 3.5 Heterogeneous graph for finding meta-path *89*

Figure 4.1 Supervised graph machine learning model task *101*

Figure 4.2 Social network *104*

Figure 4.3 Link prediction in recommendation system *105*

Figure 4.4 Graph classification process *107*

Figure 4.5 Node clustering connecting nodes with similarity *109*

Figure 4.6 Weighted and undirected graph *111*

Figure 4.7 Graph illustration for label propagation algorithm *114*

Figure 4.8 Label updated graph illustration for LPA *115*

Figure 4.9 Graph sample for community graph *116*

Figure 4.10 Updated community structure *116*

Figure 4.11 Final community detection output *117*

Figure 4.12 Patient–disease network *118*

Figure 4.13 GML in drug diseases and development *119*
Figure 5.1 Sampling graph example *127*
Figure 5.2 Types of node sampling *128*
Figure 5.3 (a) Original input graph; (b) sampled subgraph using uniform node sampling *128*
Figure 5.4 (a) Original input graph; (b) sampled subgraph $K = 3$; (c) sampled subgraph $K = 4$ using degree-based node sampling technique *130*
Figure 5.5 (a) Original input graph; (b) sampled subgraph using stratified node sampling technique *133*
Figure 5.6 (a) Original input graph and (b) sampled subgraph using snowball node sampling *134*
Figure 5.7 (a) Original input graph; (b) sampled subgraph using random walk node sampling *136*
Figure 5.8 Types of edge sampling *138*
Figure 5.9 (a) Original input graph; (b) sampled subgraph using uniform edge sampling *139*
Figure 5.10 (a) Original input graph; (b) sampled subgraph using weighted edge sampling *140*
Figure 5.11 (a) Original input graph and (b) sampled subgraph using temporal edge sampling *142*
Figure 5.12 (a) Original input graph; (b) sampled subgraph using K-hop neighborhood sampling *144*
Figure 5.13 Sample graph for random walk neighborhood sampling *146*
Figure 6.1 Example of pooled graph *154*
Figure 6.2 Single vector representation of pooled graph *156*
Figure 6.3 Chemical bond example for sum pooling *157*
Figure 6.4 Example for mean pooling *159*
Figure 6.5 Example for max pooling *161*
Figure 6.6 Example for attention pooling *163*
Figure 6.7 Applications of flat pooling *165*
Figure 6.8 Social network illustration in first pooling step (merging nodes) *167*
Figure 6.9 Social network illustration in second pooling step *168*
Figure 6.10 Pooling using top-K pooling technique *170*

Figure 6.11 Final reduced pooled graph using top-K pooling *172*
Figure 6.12 Hierarchical graph structure pooled at various levels *173*
Figure 7.1 Step-by-step process of deep learning on graph *183*
Figure 7.2 CNN and GCN of deep learning model *190*
Figure 7.3 (a) CNN uses pooling layer; (b) GNN uses neighborhood information *190*
Figure 7.4 Graph representation with feature vector *191*
Figure 7.5 Graph representing message aggregation *192*
Figure 7.6 Dynamic graph representation of social network *195*
Figure 7.7 Working process of GRNN *196*
Figure 7.8 Architecture of GRNN *197*
Figure 7.9 Social network example for GAT approach *200*
Figure 7.10 Influential graph *201*
Figure 7.11 GAT architecture *203*
Figure 7.12 Graph representation of molecular structures *207*
Figure 8.1 Flowchart of spatiotemporal graph neural networks *214*
Figure 8.2 Workflow process of dynamic GNN *217*
Figure 8.3 Graph snapshot of social interaction dynamic graph *219*
Figure 8.4 DyGCN architecture *222*
Figure 8.5 Node feature matrix and adjacency matrix for author citation graph *227*
Figure 8.6 Encoder: Learning author embedding *227*
Figure 8.7 Workflow of VGAE *231*
Figure 9.1 Graph example for graph alignment and matching *236*
Figure 9.2 Author citation graph for isomorphic graphs *238*
Figure 9.3 Inexact matching graph example *239*
Figure 9.4 Global alignment example using author citation graph *240*
Figure 9.5 Graph to illustrate graph embedding *242*
Figure 9.6 "Y"-shaped graphs for finding Gromov–Wasserstein distance *244*
Figure 9.7 Contrastive learning for graph matching *244*
Figure 9.8 Graph matching in molecular structure *245*
Figure 10.1 Simple undirected graph for matrix factorization *252*
Figure 10.2 Example for graph embedding *256*

Figure 10.3 Encoder–decoder framework *263*
Figure 11.1 Model graph for transfer graph learning *270*
Figure 11.2 Working process of inductive transfer graph learning *274*
Figure 11.3 Flow of process of feature-based TGL *284*
Figure 11.4 Working process of transfer component analysis *287*
Figure 11.5 Advantages and limitations of TCA *288*
Figure 11.6 Working process of DANN *291*
Figure 11.7 Advantages and limitations of DANN *291*
Figure 11.8 Flow of process in meta-path-based transfer learning *295*
Figure 12.1 Social network graph *304*
Figure 12.2 Graph representing multiple indirect paths *305*
Figure 12.3 Latent similarity graph *306*
Figure 12.4 Core component example using author citation graph *313*
Figure 12.5 Graph contrastive learning frameworks with its components *317*
Figure 13.1 Text modality in author citation graph *323*
Figure 13.2 Early fusion working process *326*
Figure 13.3 Intermediate fusion working process *328*
Figure 13.4 Late fusion working process *330*
Figure 13.5 Autonomous vehicle's multimodal graph pipeline *332*
Figure 13.6 Pest detection network multimodal graph pipeline *334*
Figure 15.1 Flowchart showing the evolution *360*
Figure 15.2 Knowledge graph representation of entities, relationships, and ontology *362*
Figure 15.3 Author Citation Knowledge Graph *363*
Figure 15.4 Multi-stage process of a knowledge graph *365*
Figure 15.5 Supply chain knowledge graph showing optimized travel routes *377*
Figure 16.1 Data exploration of tourist POIs *387*
Figure 16.2 Visualization of grouping POIs into clusters *388*
Figure 16.3 Graph of tourist spots (POIs) with proximity edges *389*
Figure 16.4 Comparative analysis using GAN and its variants *396*
Figure 16.5 Epoch execution for different models *396*

List of Tables

Table 2.1 Shortest path distance for healthcare graph *40*
Table 4.1 Graph machine learning (GML) vs traditional machine learning *100*
Table 6.1 Score calculation for each user *171*
Table 6.2 Influence score for each user in top-K pooling technique *171*
Table 6.3 Advantages and disadvantages of top-K pooling technique *172*
Table 6.4 Feature vector of each node (A, B, C, D, E) *174*
Table 6.5 Influencer table for user nodes *175*
Table 6.6 Comparison Between flat pooling and hierarchical pooling *178*
Table 7.1 GAT assigns attention weights based on David's interactions *201*
Table 9.1 Embedding values for each node *242*
Table 10.1 Advantages and disadvantages of matrix factorization *253*
Table 10.2 Advantages and disadvantages of embedding models *259*
Table 10.3 Advantages and disadvantages of similarity measures *261*
Table 11.1 Inductive vs transductive transfer graph learning *296*
Table 11.2 Feature-based transfer graph learning vs structure-based transfer graph learning *296*
Table 12.1 Example for latent similarity *306*
Table 12.2 Author citation details *310*
Table 12.3 Social network friend recommendation system *310*
Table 12.4 Payment network *311*
Table 12.5 Difference between supervised graph learning and self-supervised learning *312*
Table 15.1 Difference between knowledge graph and traditional databases *364*
Table 15.2 Comparison of RDF triples and SPARQL *373*

About the Book

Graph representation learning (GRL) is a rapidly growing field. It has attracted significant amounts of attention from different domains and consequently accumulated a large body of literature. Thus, it is a promising time to provide a comprehensive overview and distillation of this domain. This book is our diligent attempt to achieve this goal by taking advantage of our teaching and research experience over many years in this field. In particular, we aim to help undergraduate or postgraduate students and researchers acquire essential knowledge of GRL and its wide range of applications, and understand its advances and new frontiers.

Graph Representation Learning is a comprehensive guide that explores the foundations, methodologies, and applications of learning from graph-structured data. The book is organized into 14 detailed chapters, beginning with the basics of graphs and progressing to advanced topics such as GNNs, sampling strategies, deep learning, transfer learning, and industrial applications. Advanced chapters cover cutting-edge topics such as deep learning on graphs, graph pooling, alignment and matching, transfer learning, and graph embeddings. Each topic is enriched with diagrams, mathematical formulations, and algorithms to provide both conceptual clarity and technical depth.

Each chapter blends theoretical insights, enriched by case studies from healthcare, education, social networks, and wireless communication. Special emphasis is placed on techniques such as neighborhood sampling, graph pooling, and knowledge graph construction. Through its structured approach and real-world examples, the book aims to equip readers with the theoretical foundations and technical skills necessary to tackle problems in diverse domains using graph-based learning.

A key strength of this book lies in its application-driven approach. Real-world case studies from healthcare, education (e.g., learning management systems), social networks, urban tourism, and wireless communications illustrate how GRL is transforming diverse industries. The book also highlights industrial techniques, such as knowledge graph construction and domain-specific transfer learning, demonstrating how GRL can be integrated into large-scale systems and decision-making processes. By the end of this book, readers will not only understand the mechanics of GRL but also gain the confidence to apply these concepts in real-world scenarios and research problems.

This book is designed to serve a broad audience—ranging from undergraduate and graduate students to postdoctoral researchers, faculty members, and professionals in industry and government—whether they are new to the field or possess foundational knowledge and wish to deepen their understanding of advanced techniques and emerging applications in GRL.

About the Authors

Dr. E. Chandra Blessie PhD, is Dean of Innovation, School of Innovation, KG College of Arts and Science, Coimbatore, Tamil Nadu, India. She has 24 years of teaching experience. She is guiding Ph.D. research scholars. She has published 6 books; 2 patents; 25 book chapters; 47 papers in reputed journals indexed by Scopus, Springer, IEEE, and Elsevier; and 40 papers in international conference proceedings. Her areas of research interest are deep learning, big data analytics, graph representation learning, knowledge graph, and security. She has organized many faculty development programs, workshops, guest lectures, and webinars.

She has acted as a resource person in workshops/FDPs/symposiums. She has acted as a resource person in six days' AICTE-ISTE Refresher Course/Orientation Programme. She has delivered guest lectures in various colleges and has acted as Chief Guest, reviewer, and chairperson in national and international conferences. She has done IBM certifications in Data Analytics, certification on "Deep Learning," Data Science, and SQL Server Administration. She was honored as "Best Active Participation—Woman Member" by the Computer Society of India. She is the Chief Editor of the *Recent Advancement in Engineering and Management* book. She is a Member of CSI, Institute of Advanced Scientific Research, and Member of IACSIT International Association of Computer Science & Information Technology. She is a member of the Board of Studies in NGP Arts and Science, Coimbatore. She is a member of the Advisory Board Meeting in PPG Institute of Technology. She was the Chairperson of Computer Society of India, Coimbatore Chapter during the academic year 2022–2023, and chairperson of Nomination Committee of the Computer Society of India, Coimbatore Chapter, Tamil Nadu during the academic year 2024–2025.

Pethuru Raj, PhD, is the principal AI architect at Infocion Inc., Bangalore. Previously, he worked as the vice president and chief architect at the AI division of Reliance Jio Platforms Ltd., Bangalore, IBM Global Cloud Centre of Excellence (CoE), Wipro Consulting Services (WCS), and Robert Bosch Corporate

Research (CR). He has gained over 25 years of experience in the IT industry and nine years of research experience. He has finished the CSIR-sponsored PhD at Anna University, Chennai. He continued with UGC-sponsored postdoctoral research in the Department of Computer Science and Automation at the Indian Institute of Science (IISc), Bangalore. After that, he got two international research fellowships (JSPS and JST) to work as a research scientist for 3.5 years in two leading Japanese universities.

He focuses on emerging technologies, including Generative and Agentic AI, AI Model Optimization Techniques, Cloud of Things (CoT), Cloud-native and Edge Computing Paradigms, Platform Engineering, 6G Communication, and Blockchain Technologies, as well as Quantum-safe Cryptography Algorithms. He has authored and edited over 75 technology books, published more than 60 research papers, and contributed to more than 55 book chapters.

Dr. B. Sundaravadivazhagan is an experienced researcher and educator in the field of Information and Communication Engineering. He has more than 21 years of experience in teaching and research and has earned his Ph.D. in Information and Communication Engineering from Anna University in Chennai in 2016. He is a member of various professional bodies such as IEEE, ISACA, ISTE, and ACM, and has published over 40 research articles in SCI and Scopus journals. He has also served as a resource person, keynote speaker, and advisory committee member in more than 20 international and national conferences.

He has received two research grants from the Ministry of Higher Education, Research and Innovation, The Research Council (TRC), Oman. His research interests include IoT, AI and machine learning, deep learning, cloud computing, networks and cybersecurity, wireless networks, and MANET. He has published articles in *Cybersecurity*. He is a reputable journal editor and reviewer and serves on the Doctoral Committee in International Committee Member–Amrita University, Bangalore, as well as an Adjunct Faculty in Saveetha School of Engineering, Chennai.

Preface

The world around us, from social networks and biological systems to transportation grids and the very wide range of the internet, is inherently graphical. This modern world has seen the rapid emergence of graph representation learning (GRL) as a transformative area in the fields of data science, machine learning, and network analysis. However, despite its undeniable importance, there exists a noticeable gap in readily accessible and well-structured educational resources for both undergraduate and postgraduate students. Much of the existing literature is either overly theoretical, written for advanced researchers, or fragmented across various papers and edited volumes—a non-suitable landscape for anyone new to the field.

This book was born precisely to bridge that gap. Watching engineering and computer science students struggle with complex academic texts, we recognized the urgent need for a more pedagogically sound and learner-friendly approach to GRL. Our core aim has been to present this powerful subject, presenting it in a way that is both technically rigorous and easily digestible. You'll find clear explanations, detailed examples, thoughtfully structured chapters, and real-world case studies throughout the book. We've focused not just on the "how" but crucially on the "why" behind each concept, model, and technique.

We genuinely hope this book serves as a comprehensive and inspiring starting point for students, educators, and practitioners alike. Whether you're exploring the fundamental building blocks of graph structures, diving deep into graph neural networks (GNNs), or applying GRL to solve practical challenges in healthcare, finance, or communication systems, this guide is designed to meet you where you are. Our greatest hope is that it encourages more students to venture into the world of graph-based learning and sparks continued exploration in this dynamic and exciting field.

This book, *A Complete Guide to Graph Representation Learning with Case Studies*, is designed to be your necessary companion on this transformative journey. We'll take you deep into the theoretical foundations of GRL techniques, spanning from established methods such as matrix factorization and random walks to the cutting-edge advancements in GNNs, including graph convolutional networks, graph attention networks (GATs), and their many innovative and advanced topics.

Beyond theory, a key strength of this guide lies in its practical application. We've assembled a rich collection of meticulously detailed case studies from diverse domains, demonstrating how GRL can be effectively applied to solve real-world problems. Each case study serves as a tangible example, bridging the gap between theory and practice and offering actionable insights for researchers, practitioners, and students alike.

Our goal is to equip you with both the conceptual understanding and the theoretical skills necessary to learn and interpret GRL models, ultimately empowering you to unlock the hidden knowledge embedded within your graph-structured data.

List of Abbreviation

AA	Adamic–Adar Index
AI	Artificial Intelligence
B5G	Beyond-5G
BERT	Bidirectional Encoder Representations from Transformers
BFS	Breadth-First Search
Cat-GNN	Causal Temporal Graph Neural Network
CDA	Contrastive Dual Attention
CNN	Convolutional Neural Networks
DANN	Domain Adversarial Neural Networks
DDIs	Drug–Drug Interactions
DFS	Depth-First Search
DGMC	Deep Graph Matching Networks
DiffPool	Differentiable Pooling
DL	Deep Learning
DNE	Discriminative Network Embedding
DNMF	Deep Asymmetric Nonnegative Matrix Factorization
DR	Drug Repurposing
DRKG	Drug Repurposing Knowledge Graph
E-GAE	Ensemble Graph Autoencoders
EHRs	Electronic Health Records
EL and ED	Entity Linking and Entity Disambiguation
FCM	Fuzzy C-Means
GAEs	Graph Autoencoders
GAT	Graph Attention Networks
GCC	Global Capability Centres
GCL	Graph Contrastive Learning
GCN	Graph Convolution Networks
GCN-DA	Graph Convolutional Network with Domain Adaptation
GML	Graph Machine Learning

GNN	Graph Neural Networks
GRL	Graph Representation Learning
GRL	Gradient Reversal Layer
GRNN	Graph Recurrent Neural Networks
GRUs	Gated Recurrent Units
GW	Gromov–Wasserstein
HGCN	Heterogeneous Graph Convolutional Network
HIN	Heterogeneous Information Network
HTL	Heterogeneous Transfer Learning
InfoNCE	Info Noise-Contrastive Estimation
IoT	Internet of Things
iPSC	induced Pluripotent Stem Cell
KGs	Knowledge Graphs
KGC	Knowledge Graph Completion
KGE	Knowledge Graph Embedding
KRL	Knowledge Representation Learning
LINE	Large-scale Information Network Embedding
LOD	Linked Open Data Cloud
LPA	Label Propagation Algorithm
LSTM	Long–Short-Term Memory
M-GAT	Multimodal Graph Attention Network (M-GAT)
MAE	Masked Autoencoders
MinCut	Minimum Cut
MLP	Multi-Layer Perceptron
MMD	Maximum Mean Discrepancy
MRR	Mean Reciprocal Rank
MSE	Mean Squared Error
MST-GAT	Multimodal Spatial-Temporal Graph Attention Network
MTS	Multimodal Time Series
NER	Named Entity Recognition
NLP	Natural Language Processing
OWL	Web Ontology Language
PCA	Principal Component Analysis
POIs	Points of Interest
POS	Part-of-Speech
PPI	Protein–Protein Interaction
RA	Resource Allocation Index
RAG	Retrieval Augmented Generation
RBF	Radial Basis Function
RDF	Resource Description Framework
RE	Relation Extraction

RNN	Recurrent Neural Network
SAGPool	Self-Attention Graph Pooling
SGD	Stochastic Gradient Descent
SMEs	Subject Matter Experts
SNA	Social Network Analysis
SSL	Self-Supervised Learning
ST-GNNs	Spatiotemporal Graph Neural Networks
SVD	Singular Value Decomposition
SVMs	Support Vector Machines
t-SNE	t-distributed Stochastic Neighbor Embedding
T2D	Type 2 Diabetes
TCA	Transfer Component Analysis
TGL	Transfer Graph Learning
TPSC	Traffic Prediction using nodes Similarity and Causal Relations
TTGL	Transductive Transfer Graph Learning
VGAEs	Variational Graph Autoencoders
ViT	Vision Transformers
WL	Weisfeiler–Lehman Kernel

Part I

Foundation Learning

1

Introduction to Graph and Graph Representation Learning

1.1 Introduction

In today's rapidly evolving, dynamic, and interconnected world, scientists, researchers, businessmen, government, and all humans need a faster and more efficient way of solving problems and challenges with emerging innovations, discoveries, and opportunities. The graph is the most promising and invaluable tool for visualizing and analyzing the business, communicating the research findings and patterns in the data, and gaining knowledge. This chapter provides insight into graphs and graph representation learning (GRL) along with its benefits, and the application in various domains.

1.2 What Is a Graph?

A graph is a mathematical tool for representing data or objects visually and finding associations among objects or pairs of points. It is defined as the network G with an ordered pair of sets (N, E), where N denotes nodes (or vertices), and the links between the nodes N are termed edges E. The nodes are termed entities/features or variables. These nodes represent the individual entities or objects within the system being modeled. For instance, in a social network, nodes might be people; in a road network, cities; in a biological network, proteins or genes. An edge is typically represented as a pair of nodes (u, v), indicating that node u is related to node v. Examples of graphs are as follows:

Example 1.1 In Fig. 1.1 above, A, B, C, D, and E are the nodes, and the relationship among the nodes is shown by a straight line. They are the edges represented as $E = \{(A, B), (B, C), (C, D), (D, E), (E, A), (E, C)\}$.

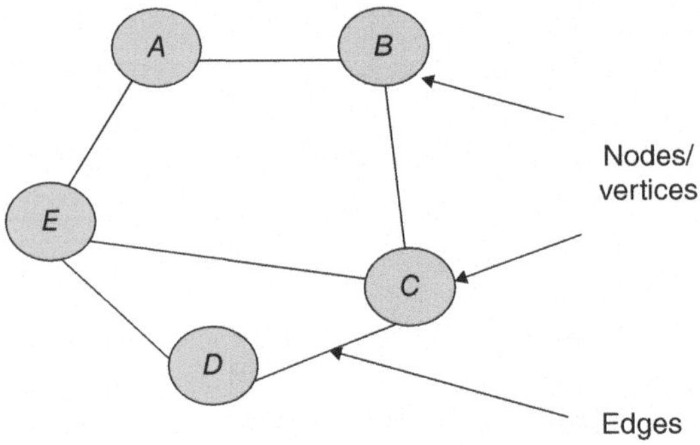

Figure 1.1 Sample graph example.

Example 1.2 ***Entrepreneurs Working in the Healthcare Field***
Entrepreneurs who are working in the healthcare field depend on new technologies, services, and business models to improve patient care, increase accessibility, and reduce costs. They address critical needs in areas such as telemedicine, medical devices, health data analytics, and personalized medicine, driving advancements in the healthcare industry.

In Example 1.2, each node represents an entrepreneur, and edges connect entrepreneurs who work in the healthcare industry. In this graph, each entrepreneur working within the healthcare sector is represented as a distinct node. An edge labeled "health" connects these entrepreneurial nodes, signifying their shared work and impact on the healthcare domain. This is represented in Fig. 1.2.

Example 1.3 ***Entrepreneurs Working in Similar Fields***
Example 1.3 shows the entrepreneurs who share identical fields as given in Fig. 1.3.

Each node represents an entrepreneur. Relationships are represented by edges connecting entrepreneurs who share similar fields (three types of industries such as healthcare, retail, and textile).

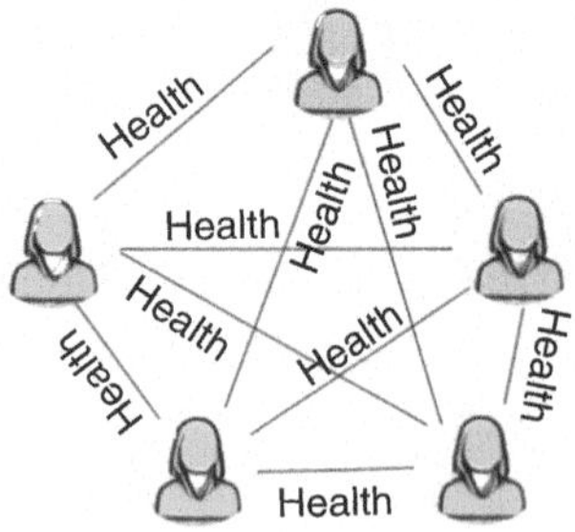

Figure 1.2 Entrepreneurs working in the healthcare industry.

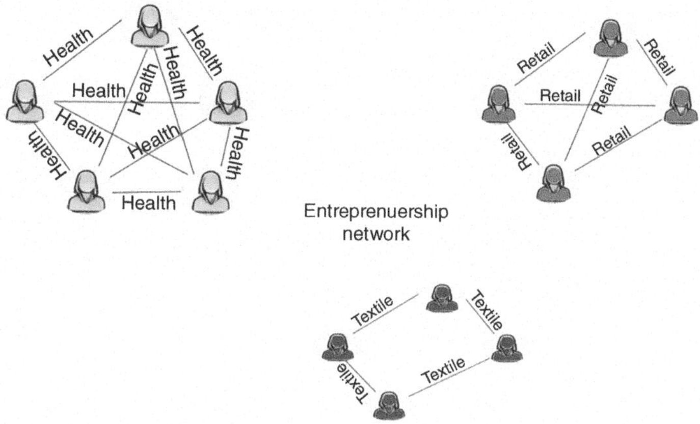

Figure 1.3 Entrepreneurs working in similar fields.

1.3 Importance of Graph

- Before the rise of GRL, traditional machine learning models struggled significantly with complex, interconnected data. These conventional methods relied heavily on manual feature engineering, either by completely overlooking inherent relationships or painstakingly crafting them by hand. This approach severely hampered both scalability and adaptability. While effective for structured data such as tables, sequences, or grids, these methods simply couldn't capture the rich, non-Euclidean structures intrinsic to real-world networks such as social connections, biological systems, and knowledge graphs.
- Graphs are essential tools for making sense of complex, interconnected data.
- They offer a visual framework that simplifies real-time information, serving us to discover patterns, trends, and relationships that remain hidden in raw datasets.
- By effectively representing complicated connections, graphs become crucial for extracting hidden insights, conducting thorough analyses, and clearly communicating outcomes.
- They naturally foster network connections, proving vital for forecasting, predictive modeling, and building robust decision support systems. Furthermore, graphs are an excellent way to share research findings with both experts and the public.
- Their universal utility stretches across numerous real-world applications, from healthcare and finance to social media, computer vision, and recommender systems, solidifying their role as a fundamental data structure for complex systems.

- They help identify patterns, trends, and relationships that might be difficult to distinguish from raw data.
- They allow the users to get connected to the network.
- They are used for forecasting, predicting, and supporting decision-making systems.
- Graphs are a universal framework and a widely used data structure for representing complex systems.
- They provide a statistical technique for finding interactions among the entities and interpreting the connections.

1.4 Types of Graphs

Graphs can be categorized into various types based on their properties [1], structures, and connectivity. Broadly, graphs are classified as directed or undirected depending on whether their edges have a direction. They can also be weighted or unweighted, where weighted graphs assign values to edges, representing costs or distances. Some graphs are simple, with no loops or multiple edges, while multigraphs allow parallel edges. Specific types like bipartite graphs have nodes divided into two disjoint sets, whereas complete graphs connect every pair of nodes. Trees represent hierarchical structures, and planar graphs can be drawn without edge crossings. Other classifications include sparse and dense graphs, cyclic and acyclic graphs, each suited for different applications in network analysis and machine learning. Each type of graph is discussed in this section, and the domain area where they are applied are also discussed.

1.4.1 Directed Graph

A graph where the edges between nodes are represented with arrow lines indicating direction is called a directed graph [1]. In a directed graph, the flow of process or path flows is in the direction of the arrow pointing to the other edge. Consider the author citation graph example: "Author A's Paper is cited by Author B" (Fig. 1.4). This is represented as a directed graph by having nodes as Author A's Paper and edges as a "cited" relationship between papers. An author citation graph can be represented as a directed graph, as shown in Fig. 1.4.

The diagram shown in Fig. 1.4 depicts that Author "A" Paper cited Author "B" Paper and so on. The directed graph provides details about the nodes, edges, and graph properties. Nodes ensure the author's name; edges ensure that the relationship is directional; and weight can be assigned to each edge by simply counting the number of citations. Graph properties such as in-degree and out-degree can be used to find the number of citations received by an author and outdegree to

Figure 1.4 Directed graph for author citation.

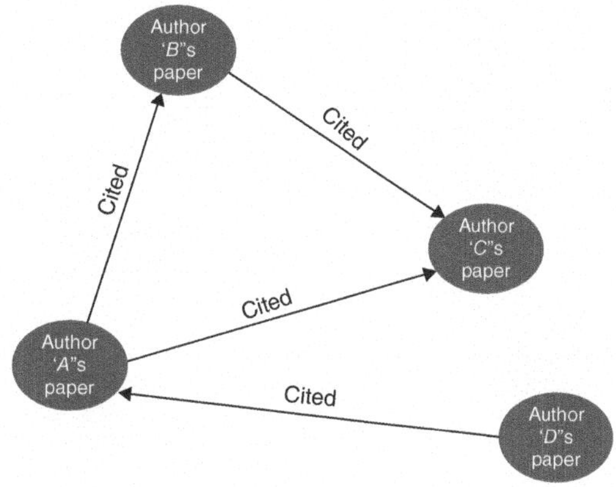

Figure 1.5 Undirected graph example for author citation.

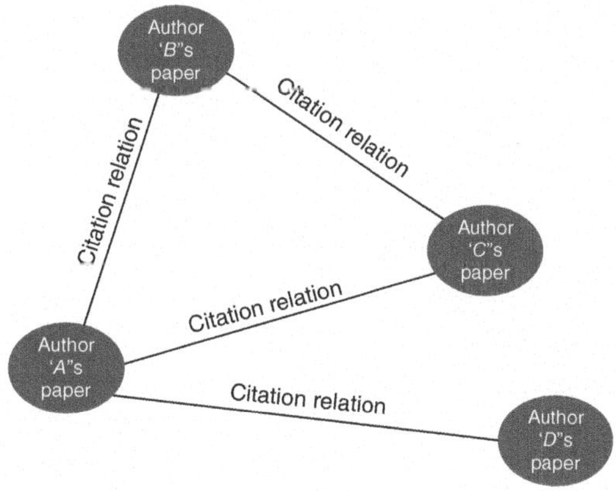

see the number of citations made by an author, respectively. In a directed graph, analysis can be made to identify the authors whose papers are most cited. This can be done by finding the highest in-degree.

1.4.2 Undirected Graph

An undirected graph is a type of graph where edges have no direction. Each edge connects two vertices (nodes) symmetrically. The process flow or path can be done in both directions. Undirected graphs are useful in situations where directions do not matter, and it's simpler to use. For the same example given above, "There is a citation relationship between Author A and Author B." The graph now represents citation activities between authors, but it does not indicate who cited whom. If two authors cite each other, the edge indicates mutual influence or collaboration.

Figure 1.5 shows an example of an undirected graph using an author citation graph with authors and papers as nodes.

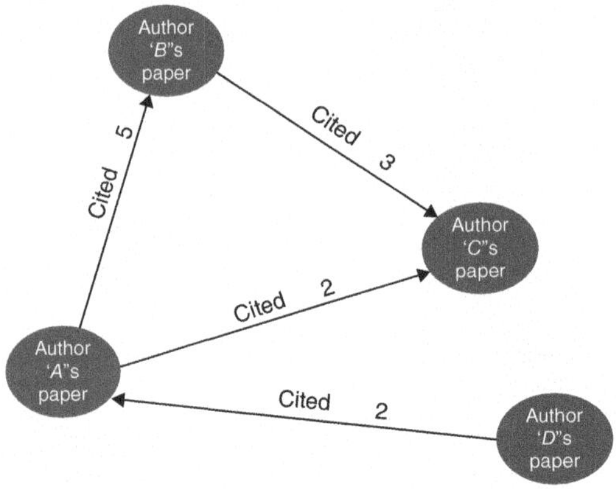

Figure 1.6 Author citation example using weighted graph.

The above undirected graph can be used for identifying clusters of authors that frequently cite each other. It could be used to visualize collaboration or shared research interests, where the focus is on connections rather than specific citations.

1.4.3 Weighted Graph

The other type of graph is a weighted graph, where edges are associated with weights, which represent some kind of value or cost of the connection between nodes. These weights can indicate distances, costs, capacities, strengths, or other quantitative measures. Weighted graphs can be directed or undirected, depending on whether edges have a direction. The main purpose of a weighted graph is that the weights provide additional information about the nature of the connections.

In the context of the author citation graph given in Fig. 1.6, transforming it into a weighted graph adds extra measurable information to the edges, making the representation richer and more meaningful. Weights can signify the strength, frequency, or importance of the relationship between two authors. Let us take the weight information as the frequency of citation between two authors' papers. For example, in the above example, "Author B's Paper has been cited five times by Author A" and "Author C's Paper has been cited three times by Author B." These graphs are used to identify how frequently an author cites another, help to identify influential authors based on their total citation weight, and highlight the quality of the authors' papers. We can group the authors based on their mutual citation.

1.4.4 Multigraph

A multigraph is a kind of graph that allows multiple edges (parallel edges) between the same pair of vertices (nodes). These edges may or may not have associated

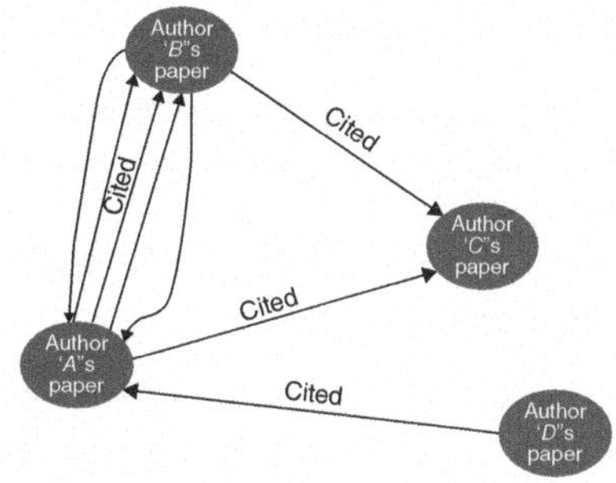

Figure 1.7 Author citation example using a multigraph.

weights. Repeated or redundant interactions between the same entities occur in multigraphs. For the same example of the author citation graph, a multigraph would represent multiple citation instances between the same pair of authors. In Fig. 1.7, Author A's Paper cites three different papers of Author B, and there will be three edges between Authors A and B. Similarly, Author B's Paper cites author A's paper two times.

A multigraph extends the concept of a simple graph by allowing multiple edges between the same pair of nodes. It is a powerful tool for modeling real-world systems with complex relationships. A multigraph may also contain loops, which are edges that connect a node to itself.

1.4.5 Complete Graph

A complete graph is another type of graph where every pair of distinct nodes is connected by a unique edge. In a complete graph, every node interacts with every other node directly. It is an undirected and connected graph where there must be at least one path between any two nodes.

In the author citation graph example given in Fig. 1.8, a complete graph is a graph where every author is directly connected to every other author. Each author cites every other author's paper at least once. The graph is fully connected, which shows that none of the authors is left out of the citation loop.

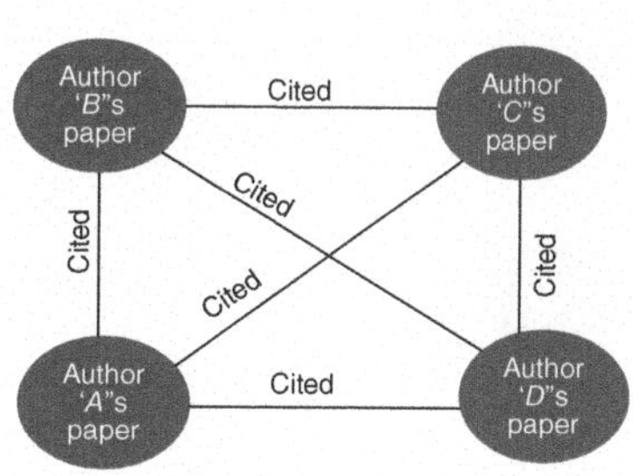

Figure 1.8 Example of complete graph.

1.4.6 Planar and Bipartite Graph

A planar graph is a type of graph that can be drawn on a two-dimensional plane without any edges crossing each other. The key feature of planar graphs is that their edges only intersect at their endpoints (vertices). If a graph can be arranged this way, it is said to be embeddable in the plane.

For example:

- A triangle graph is planar, as its three edges can be drawn without any crossings.
- The complete graph with four nodes with edges connecting every pair is also planar, but higher-order complete graphs with a crossing of lines are not planar.

In the author citation graph, nodes represent a small group of researchers, and directed edges indicate one author citing another author's work within a specialized domain. The graph's simple structure allows it to be drawn on a plane without any citation links crossing, reflecting a clear, nonoverlapping flow of knowledge or collaboration among closely related works. The graph in Fig. 1.8 is nonplanar, as there is a crossing of lines.

Bipartite Graph

A bipartite graph shown in Fig. 1.9 is a two-set graph in which the nodes can be divided into two disjoint and independent sets S_1 and S_2, such that every edge connects a node from S_1 to a node in S_2. Edges only exist between nodes in different sets. This special type of graph is useful for analyzing the relationship between two distinct groups of nodes. Consider the author citation graph as a bipartite graph where the set of nodes in the S_1 and S_2 sets represents authors and papers, respectively. The edges represent relationships between authors who cite papers in set S_1 and papers that are cited by authors in set S_2.

In Fig. 1.9, the authors' nodes ("Author A," "Author B," "Author C") are in set $S_{1,}$ and the Papers' nodes ("Paper 1," "Paper 2," "Paper 3") are in set S_2. The citation relationship is represented as Author A cites Paper 1 and Paper 2, Author B cites Paper 2 and Paper 3, and Author C cites Paper 1. The purpose of using a bipartite graph is to analyze the relationship between different types of nodes more easily

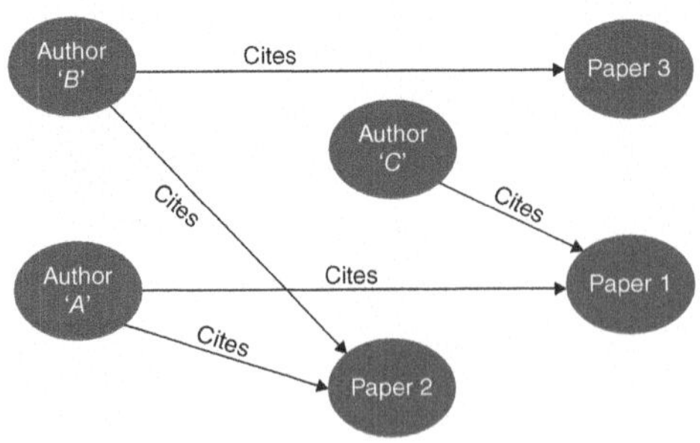

Figure 1.9 Bipartite graph for author citation.

by dividing the nodes into two sets. Also, we can find the shared citation patterns and similar citation behaviors.

The main usage of bipartite graphs in author citation graphs is to recommend papers to authors based on similar citation patterns or topics of interest, to analyze which papers are frequently cited by many authors, and to identify clusters of authors citing similar papers, suggesting shared research interests or collaborations.

1.4.7 Hypergraph

A hypergraph is a generalization of a traditional graph where edges, known as hyperedges, can connect more than two nodes. Unlike traditional graphs, where edges link only two nodes, hyperedges in a hypergraph can connect a subset of nodes, enabling the representation of group relationships. Hypergraphs are suitable for capturing complex, multi-way interactions that standard traditional graphs cannot represent. They are used for tasks requiring group-level relationships. They are also designed to capture higher-order relationships.

For the author citation graph, authors (nodes) are connected by citations (edges). Typically, this could be represented as a directed graph, where an edge from node A (Author A) to node B (Author B) means that Author A cites Author B in their work.

However, in a hypergraph model, we can represent more complex relationships such as a group of authors collaborating on a paper and citing each other. In this case, a hyperedge can represent the citation of a paper written by a group of authors, rather than just a single citation relationship between two authors.

Figure 1.10 represents a hypergraph for the author citation example. Nodes represent the author's paper, and the hyperedge represents collaborative relationships. A hyperedge connects a set of vertices (authors) that are involved in a specific citation or collaboration. One hyperedge $H1$ connects Authors A, B, and C, signifying that they are involved in a collaborative paper or a citation relationship where B and C co-author a paper and cite A. Hyperedge $H2$ $\{A, B\}$

Figure 1.10 Hypergraph for author citation.

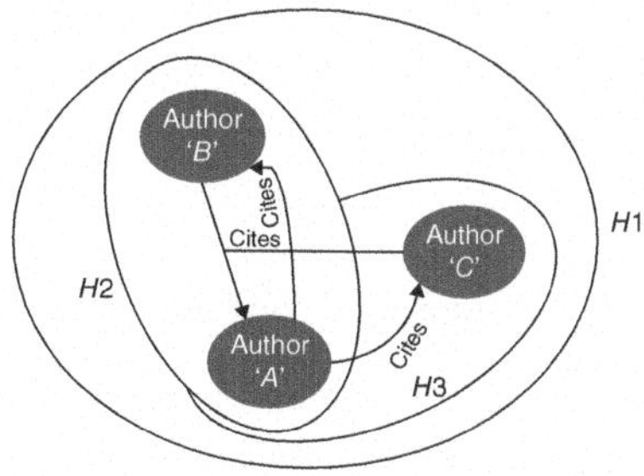

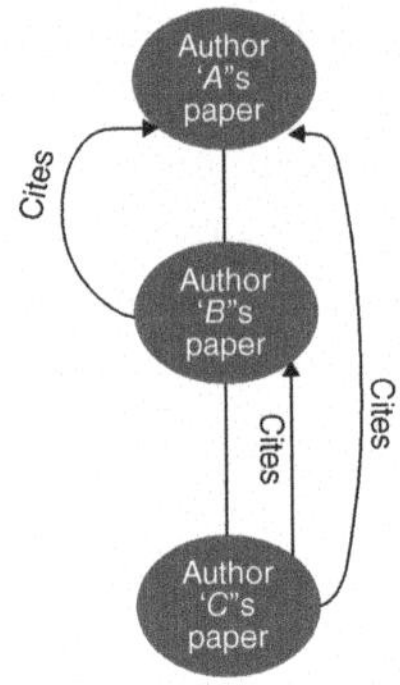

Figure 1.11 Hierarchical graph for author citation.

indicates that Author A cites Author B. Hyperedge $H3$ $\{A, C\}$ indicates that Author A cites Author C.

A hypergraph allows to represent more complex relationships in a citation graph, such as group collaborations or joint citations, which would be difficult to represent using simple pairwise edges. If multiple authors contribute to a paper and cite each other, a hypergraph captures this collaboration better by using a single hyperedge instead of multiple pairwise edges.

1.4.8 Hierarchical Graphs

Another type of special graph is a hierarchical graph, which organizes nodes in layers or levels, forming a hierarchy. Nodes in one layer can be connected to nodes in the adjacent layer. This graph is used to identify the dependencies between nodes in a hierarchical manner. This type of graph helps in the decision-making process.

In the author citation graph shown in Fig. 1.11, the author whose papers are highly cited appears in the top-level node (Author A's Paper is highly cited, as shown in the figure), the author whose papers are moderately cited appears in the next level (Author B's Paper is moderately cited and appears in the middle-level node), and the author whose papers are less cited appears in the bottom-level node (Author C's Paper is less cited, and it is in the lower level).

The graph helps identify influential authors (top-level nodes) and how their work propagates through the hierarchy. It helps the institutions to prioritize the faculty members (researchers) based on their paper publications. This type of graph facilitates analysis of relationships between influential and emerging authors.

1.4.9 Homogeneous and Heterogeneous Graphs

A homogeneous graph is a special kind of graph in which all nodes (vertices) and edges are of the same type. The graph represents relationships or interactions

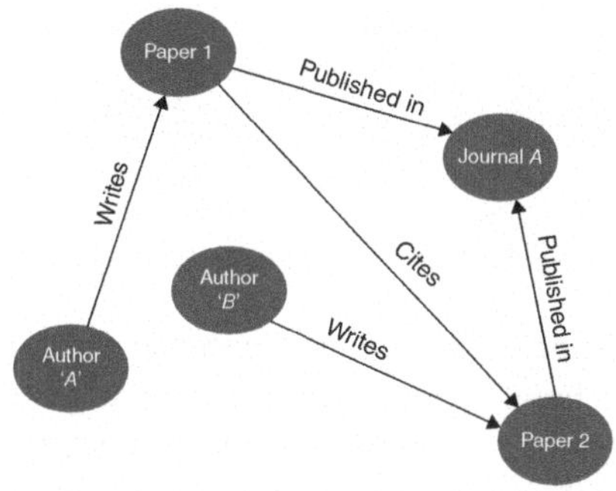

Figure 1.12 Heterogeneous graph for author citation.

between nodes that are fundamentally similar in nature. Homogeneous graphs provide a simpler structure by focusing on one type of relationship or entity. A single type of entity (Author) is represented in nodes. Homogeneous graphs are easier to process computationally because the relationships are uniform. This allows for focused analysis of specific types of interactions or relationships.

In the author citation graph, each node represents an author in the citation network. All nodes represent the same type of entity (authors). All edges represent the same type of relationship (citations). The graph in the figure is a homogeneous graph.

1.4.9.1 Heterogeneous Graph

A heterogeneous graph is also a special kind of graph that involves multiple types of nodes (entities) and/or multiple types of edges (relationships). It is designed to model complex systems where different entities interact in various ways [6]. Nodes are the different types of entities. Here, different types of relationships between entities appear.

A heterogeneous graph given in Fig. 1.12 for a citation graph might include nodes, authors (*A* and *B*), papers (Paper 1 and Paper 2), and a journal (Journal A). The edges in the graph represent relationships like "writes," "cites," and "published in." The relationships can include "author writes a paper," "paper is published in a journal," and "paper cites another paper."

1.5 Overview of Graph Representation Learning (GRL)

Graphs are powerful tools for modeling relationships. However, many graph algorithms are computationally expensive. Large-scale graphs (e.g., social networks, biological networks) have millions or billions of nodes and edges, making storage and processing challenging. Representing different graph structures and their relationships effectively is very difficult. There is no proper method for capturing information and knowledge from various graphs and communication between

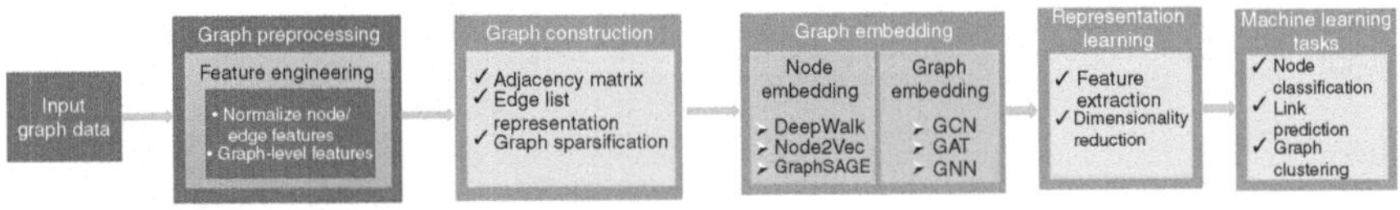

Figure 1.13 Graph representation learning flow of process.

graphs. Traditional graph-based algorithms often struggle with scalability and generalization, requiring manual feature engineering to extract meaningful information. To overcome these challenges, GRL, which represents graph structure in low-dimensional vectors, enables one to learn automatically from complex graphs. GRL has techniques to work on tasks of machine learning models and advanced neural network models. GRL bridges the gap between graph theory and deep learning and helps in easily analyzing the graph data.

1.5.1 Definition of GRL

GRL is the process of converting graph-structured data into low-dimensional [3], continuous embeddings that preserve the graph's structural and feature information.

The flow of the GRL process starts with the input graph (Fig. 1.13), where nodes and edges are defined with data and its attributes. The input data may be noisy, so it needs to be cleaned. The preprocessing step contains a data-cleaning process along with feature engineering. Feature engineering enhances the node and edge representations by normalizing the node and edge features and helps in analyzing the graph connectivity. The next step is graph construction. In this, an adjacency matrix A is created, and the edge list creates pairs of edges with source, target nodes, and weights [2]. In graph sparsification, the less important edges are moved by preserving the overall structure.

GRL techniques embed graph data into a low-dimensional space by preserving the feature information. The techniques are DeepWalk, Node2Vec, graph neural networks (GNN), graph convolution networks (GCN), GraphSAGE, and graph attention networks (GAT). Dimensionality reduction and feature extraction are done during the learning process. Finally, the graph is used for various tasks like node classification, link prediction, and graph clustering.

1.5.2 Benefits of GRL

GRL has key benefits:

1) Helps in automatically learning features of nodes, edges, and graph structures.
2) Facilitates the identification and capture of structural relationships such as neighborhood relationships and community associations.

3) Helps in working with irregular, unstructured, and non-grid-structured graph data.
4) Handles efficiently large-scale graphs by reducing their complexity while maintaining essential information.
5) Preserves the structure and pattern of dynamically growing graphs.
6) Applies techniques to machine learning tasks such as link prediction, node classification, and clustering.

1.6 Overview of Graph Connectivity

Graph connectivity is essential for gathering information about the entities in the domain fields. It plays a vital role in determining the information flow between entities and finding the relationship between entities. In GRL, graph connectivity helps in learning or understanding the meaningful pattern from the entire graph structure.

1.6.1 Definition of Graph Connectivity

Graph connectivity refers to the extent to which edges connect the vertices (or nodes) in a graph. It highlights the strength to navigate between nodes within the graph and represents a core concept in graph theory.

Graph connectivity in an undirected graph examines whether a path exists between any two vertices/nodes. In a directed graph, connectivity considers the direction of edges.

1.6.2 Importance of Graph Connectivity

The main concept of graph connectivity in GRL revolves around how the structural and relational information in graphs can be captured and leveraged to learn meaningful representations for nodes, edges, or entire graphs. Connectivity helps as the foundation for defining the relationships and dependencies among graph components, directly influencing the learned embeddings and their effectiveness in downstream tasks. Graph connectivity is so important because it ensures that communication or flow is possible between nodes, even if some nodes/edges fail. Any fault or failure can be detected, as it may indicate malicious attacks and help in evaluating critical points or bottlenecks.

Example ***Author Citation Graph***
In an author citation graph, nodes represent authors and edges indicate citations between them. Graph connectivity is crucial for determining how research knowledge spreads across academic communities.

For example, suppose an author publishes an innovative paper. In that case, its impact is higher if the citation graph is well-connected, meaning researchers from

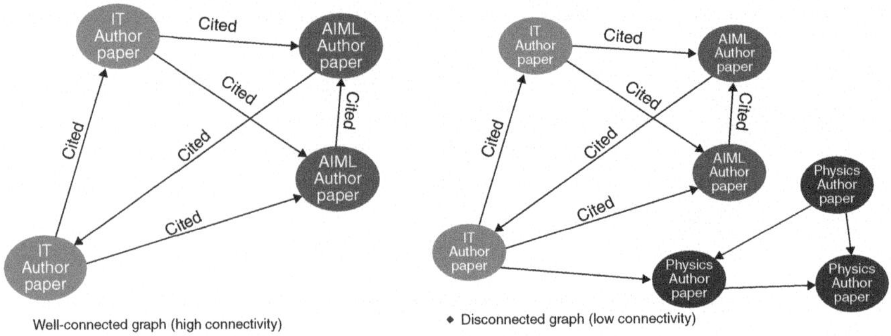

Figure 1.14 Well-connected and disconnected graphs.

different fields can reference and build upon the work. However, if the graph is disconnected, knowledge remains trapped within isolated groups, limiting interdisciplinary collaboration.

A well-connected citation network:

- Enable more sharing of research insights across domains.
- Enables authors to gain more recognition and have a greater impact.
- Allows better collaboration opportunities between research groups.

In a well-connected citation graph (high connectivity) as shown in Fig. 1.14, authors actively cite each other's work, ensuring seamless knowledge transfer across research communities. This fosters innovation, accelerates discovery, and enhances the impact of scientific contributions. For example, a researcher in IT citing work from Artificial Intelligence and Machine Learning can lead to AI-driven healthcare advancements, where deep learning techniques improve disease prediction models. Such interdisciplinary connections drive technological progress and enable novel applications.

Conversely, in a disconnected citation graph (low connectivity) as shown in Fig. 1.14, research communities remain isolated, limiting the exchange of ideas and slowing innovation. Citations are often confined within small, specialized groups, restricting the broader adoption of valuable insights. For instance, researchers in the physics stream may rarely cite work in IT or AIML, missing out on computational breakthroughs. This lack of connectivity reduces the potential for cross-pollination of ideas, delaying scientific progress and innovation.

1.6.3 Role of Graph Connectivity

Graph connectivity plays a vital role in various real-world applications, ensuring efficient communication, robustness, and network reliability. It provides network reliability even if some parts of the network fail. A well-connected internet backbone ensures users can access websites even if some servers go down. A strongly connected graph provides strong connectivity between nodes with its neighborhood nodes and within the community network. Graph connectivity allows the transmission of data/information by optimizing information flow and communication within and outside the network. It ensures that the network can be secured from cyberattacks or any failure in the network. It is important to support efficient navigation. It plays an important role in finding the shortest route between locations using Google Maps.

Graph connectivity helps in identifying the identical patterns in the network, which facilitates customers' similar buying patterns, and friends in social media, and connects people around the world. Some of the applications where graph connectivity is so important are social media, finding the shortest route for traveling salesman problems, fraud detection, cybersecurity, stable infrastructure, banks to find the suspicious transaction patterns, and electrical connections to ensure good connectivity and identify power failures.

It helps in connecting the patients with the doctors, which will facilitate the immediate and proper treatment.

1.7 Foundation on Graph Neighborhood

1.7.1 Introduction

In GRL, a set of nodes that are directly or indirectly connected within a graph is referred to as neighborhood nodes. Consider a graph $G = (V,E)$, where $v_i \in V$ and $e_i \in E$. The neighborhood [2] is defined as $N(v_i)$ of a node v_i such that

$$N(v_i) = \{v_j \in V \mid (v_i, v_j) \in E \text{ and } i \neq j$$

where v_j is the adjacent node to v_i and (v_i, v_j) is the direct edge between v_i and v_j.

In Fig. 1.15, the dark black-color node at the center has direct neighborhood nodes, which are colored in dark gray shade and indirect neighborhood nodes, which are colored in light gray. Neighborhood nodes help in understanding local structures and connectivity patterns and influence propagation within a network. We can gain knowledge about the neighbor nodes and their relationship or association in various situations.

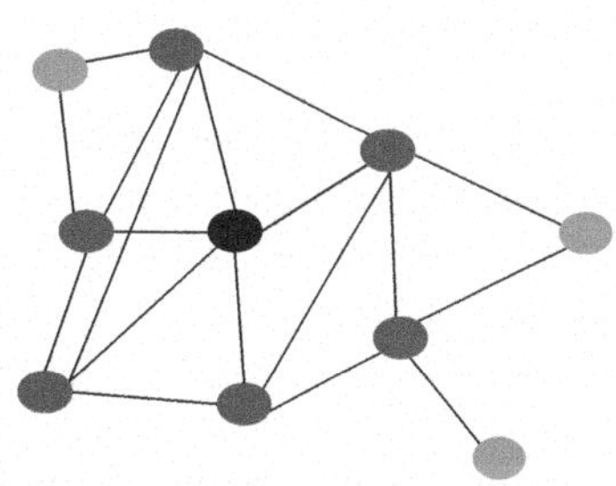

Figure 1.15 Illustration graph for direct neighborhood nodes.

1.7.2 Properties of Graph Neighborhoods

1.7.2.1 *Properties*

1) Most important characteristics such as the node's features, edge's features, and graph's structure are used for learning the insights obtained from the neighboring nodes.
2) Node degree helps to understand a node's influence on its neighbors and also to determine how much information it is gathering from its neighboring nodes. The interaction and influence of a node with its neighbor nodes are high for higher degree nodes and low for lower degree nodes.
3) We can measure how important a node is within a network.
4) Neighboring nodes show similar structural properties that can enhance representation learning.
5) Graph neighborhoods within two graphs are examined to identify similar communities, communication between the communities, and similar patterns.

Understanding the properties of neighborhood nodes is essential for designing efficient GRL models. These properties influence how information propagates, how embeddings are formed, and how well a model performs on graph-based tasks.

1.7.3 Types of Node/Graph Neighborhoods

1.7.3.1 Direct/Local Neighborhood (1-Hop Neighborhood)

Nodes that are directly connected using an edge are direct or local neighbors. They are immediate neighborhood nodes and are also called 1-hop neighborhood nodes. The above figure is an example of a direct neighborhood connection.

These types of nodes are used for identifying close friends in social media (e.g., Facebook, LinkedIn) and help in signifying products, jobs, and friends that can be directly connected in recommendation systems. It is also helpful for identifying fraud easily through direct interaction or connection with people, transactions, and so on. Direct neighbors are used to represent direct protein interactions in biological networks. In healthcare, patients having the same symptoms for a disease can be identified by direct connection and can be used for further analysis of the cause and significance.

1.7.3.2 K-Hop Neighborhood

K-hop neighborhood refers to the number of nodes that are reachable from a given node to more than one edge. "k" refers to the number of edges involved in the connection. The graph given in Fig. 1.16 shows a 2-hop and 3-hop neighborhood where two and three edges are involved in the node's neighborhood, respectively.

These types of nodes help determine how far the news spreads on social media and measure how far the product marketing reaches the people. This type is also

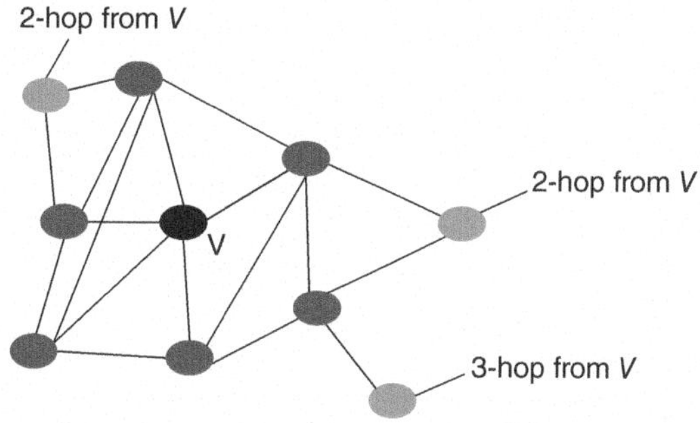

Figure 1.16 K-hop neighborhood example graph.

useful in GRL techniques for node embedding, and in healthcare, we can keep track of the spread of disease globally. We can also analyze the interconnection in telecommunication networks and routing networks.

1.7.3.3 Ego Neighborhood

Ego neighborhood is a subgraph with a central node (ego) and its 1-hop neighborhood nodes (alters) along with edges among them. The equation for the ego neighborhood of a node is

$$Ego(V) - \{N(V) \in E + U \in E'\}$$

where V is the central node (ego), $N(V)$ are the 1-hop neighbor nodes (alters), and U are the remaining nodes in edges E' other than the edges near V.

These types of nodes are used for community detection, anomaly detection by analyzing the subgraph structure, and user profiling.

1.7.3.4 Attention-Based Neighborhoods

In attention-based neighborhoods, nodes assign different importance (weights) to their neighbors during information aggregation. This approach is widely used in GATs to dynamically learn which neighbors contribute more to a node's representation.

In Fig. 1.17, node "c" is the central node, and the neighborhood nodes are assigned weights {$w1$, $w2$, $w3$, $w4$}. In attention-based neighborhood nodes, the most commonly used aggregation function is the attention aggregation function, often implemented using self-attention mechanisms [3]. This function assigns varying attention weights to each neighbor, allowing the model to prioritize more relevant or influential neighbors when aggregating their features.

These types of neighborhood nodes are used for assigning higher importance to the neighboring nodes.

1.7.3.5 Structural Neighborhood (Graphlets and Motifs)

Nodes that are connected in specific patterns are termed as motifs (recurrent subgraphs) or graphlets (small subgraphs).

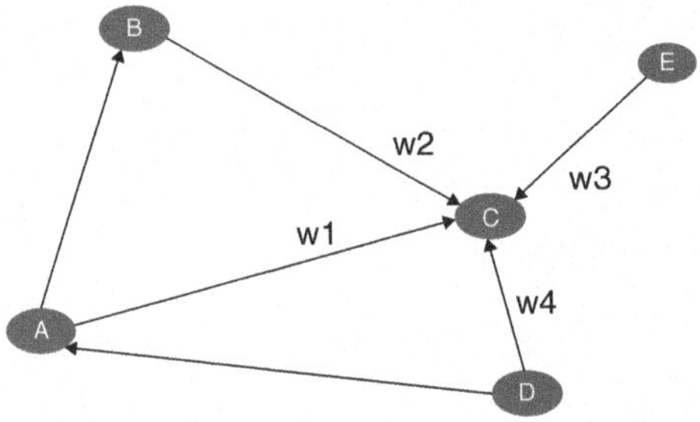

Figure 1.17 Graph used for graph attention networks.

Motifs The motifs help identify meaningful structural patterns in networks. Star motifs, triangle motifs, chain motifs, bipartite motifs, square motifs, and two-star motifs are different types of motifs.

In star motifs, a central node is connected to several other nodes. The other nodes are not connected. In triangle motifs, three nodes are connected one after the other. In chain motifs, nodes are arranged in a linear sequence, each node connected to two others, except for the end nodes. In bipartite motifs, the graph can be divided into two sets of nodes, with all edges connecting nodes from one set to the other and no edges within a set. In two-star motifs, there are two central nodes, each connected to a set of nodes forming two distinct stars. In square motifs, four nodes form a cycle with a diagonal edge connecting two nonadjacent nodes.

Let $G = (V, E)$ be a graph with a set of nodes $\{v1, v2, v3, v4, v5, v6\}$ in V and a set of edges in E (Fig. 1.18). The mathematical representation of all motifs is as follows:

Star motif:

$$\{(v1, v2), (v1, v3), (v1, v4), (v1, v5)\}$$

Triangle motifs:

$$\{(v1, v2), (v2, v3), (v3, v1)\}$$

Chain motifs:

$$\{(v1, v2), (v2, v3)\}$$

Square motifs:

$$\{(v1, v2), (v2, v3), (v3, v4), (v4, v1), (v1, v3)\}$$

Bipartite motifs:

$$\{(v1, v4), (v2, v5), (v3, v6)\}$$

Two-star motifs:

$$\{(v1, v3), (v1, v4), (v2, v5), (v2, v6)\}$$

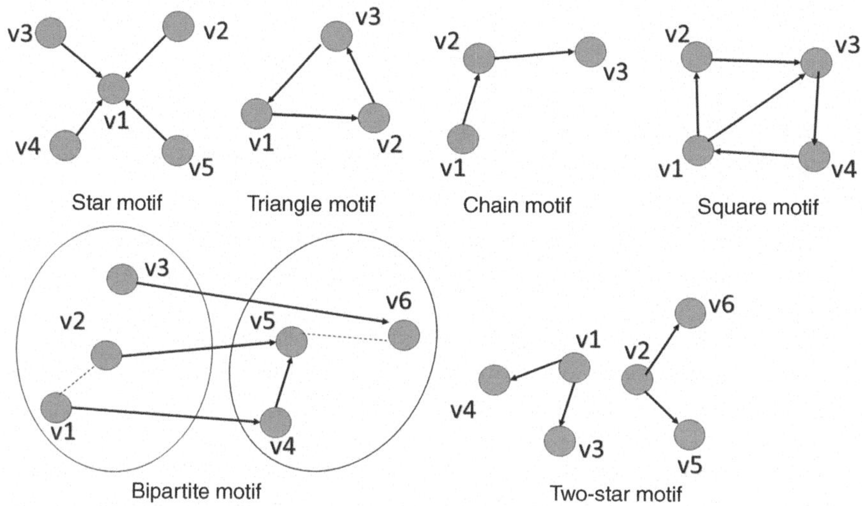

Figure 1.18 Different types of motifs.

1.7.3.6 Graphlets

Graphlets are small, connected, non-isomorphic subgraphs of a larger network that capture diverse topological structures without considering their frequency. A non-isomorphic subgraph has a unique structural arrangement that cannot be transformed into another subgraph through node relabeling within the same or a different graph, ensuring that each graphlet represents a distinct local pattern in the network. Graphlets are used to compare two networks and to find the structural patterns.

Figure 1.19 shows a graph with two-node graphlets with only one edge between the nodes, three-node graphlets in orange color, and four-node graphlets in green color. The number of ith node graphlets in the graph can be calculated using the

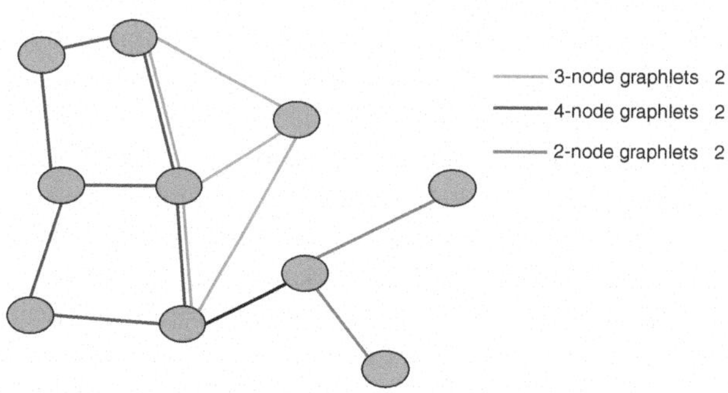

Figure 1.19 Graphlets example.

mathematical formula:

$G_i = \Sigma i(V)$ where $i(V)$ is the count of ith node graphlets.

Importance of neighborhoods in graph theory Neighbor nodes play a crucial role in graph analysis, as they define the local structure and interactions within a network. Their importance includes the following:

1) It determines the flow of information from one node to another node. In social network examples, the users share their interests, ideas, or habits with other users.
2) It can influence the characteristics or features of nearby nodes. In the author citation graph example, one author's paper can influence the information or knowledge in another author's paper.
3) It can be used to perform various machine learning tasks such as node classification, clustering, and link prediction. In healthcare example, the patient nodes that are nearby have similar symptoms, and they can be grouped as affected patients and non-affected patients.
4) It helps understand the structure of the graph and do topology analysis.

Neighbor nodes play a fundamental role in graph analysis, as they shape the structure, connectivity, and functionality of a network. They are crucial in information propagation, where data, influence, or signals spread through neighboring nodes, enabling applications in social networks, telecommunications, and biological systems. The properties of a node's neighbors also determine its centrality and significance within the network, helping identify key influencers, hubs, or bottlenecks in traffic and communication networks. In GRL, neighborhood aggregation is essential for embedding techniques and GNNs, where a node's representation is learned from its neighbors, improving tasks such as node classification, anomaly detection, and clustering.

Also, neighborhood structures assist in community detection, as closely connected nodes tend to form dense subgroups, which is vital for understanding social structures, protein interactions, and financial fraud detection. Link prediction and recommendation systems also heavily rely on neighborhood information, as common neighbors increase the likelihood of future connections—this is widely applied in friend suggestion algorithms, e-commerce recommendations, and citation network analysis. Additionally, neighbor nodes are key in graph traversal algorithms such as Breadth First Search (BFS) and Depth First Search (DFS), which are used in pathfinding, web crawling, and network routing.

Overall, neighborhood nodes are integral to both theoretical and practical graph-based applications, influencing diverse domains such as biology, computer networks, finance, transportation, and artificial intelligence. Their study enables better insights into network behaviors, enhances predictive modeling, and improves decision-making in complex systems.

1.8 Applications of Graph

Graphs are powerful mathematical structures that capture relationships and interactions within complex systems. Nodes and edges of the graph represent data across diverse domains. From social networks to molecular biology, graphs enable the modeling of intricate dependencies that would be difficult to analyze using traditional methods.

Their applications range from optimizing traffic flow in smart cities and predicting molecular properties in drug discovery to detecting fraud in financial transactions and enhancing recommendation systems in e-commerce platforms. Their main purpose is for prediction, classification, detection, and learning. Following are some of the applications of graph.

1.8.1 Traffic Prediction in Transportation

Traffic prediction is a crucial application of GRL in transportation. Road networks can naturally be modeled as graphs, where intersections of roads are represented as nodes and roads as edges. Graph-based methods excel at capturing spatial dependencies in these networks, making them powerful for traffic forecasting.

Traffic prediction involves forecasting traffic conditions, including vehicle volume and travel times, for specific areas or roadways. This task is vital in optimizing transportation systems and easing traffic congestion. For example, estimating vehicle density, speed, or flow at specific road segments for the next few minutes or hours for traffic flow prediction. Graph-based models predict traffic flow by considering both temporal patterns and spatial dependencies.

1.8.2 Pattern Recognition

Graphs are used in pattern recognition extensively due to their ability to model complex relationships between objects, making them useful in various real-world applications. By representing data as graphs, pattern recognition systems can efficiently identify structures, similarities, and anomalies.

In image and video analysis, graphs are used to represent image structures, where pixels, regions, or objects are treated as nodes, and relationships between them as edges. Graph-based feature extraction and classification improve image segmentation, object recognition, and scene understanding. For example, face recognition can be done by extracting similar features. Signature verification systems use graph matching to detect forgery. Graph-based neural networks analyze time-series data in speech signals for pattern classification. For example, virtual assistants (e.g., Siri, Alexa, and Google Assistant) use graph-based representations to recognize and classify speech patterns. Graph-based models detect cancerous patterns in medical imaging, such as MRIs and CT scans. For example, brain network analysis uses graphs to identify neurological disorders like Alzheimer's and epilepsy.

1.8.3 Social Network Analysis

Graphs play a crucial role in social network analysis (SNA) by modeling relationships between nodes such as individuals, groups, and organizations. Their interaction is represented using edges. Facebook and LinkedIn use graphs to identify friends and academicians doing research in a similar area. Twitter uses graphs to identify communities based on shared interests. Instagram, YouTube, and TikTok use graph-based influence analysis to recommend content and identify top influencers. Researchers who have a common interest can be linked together. Customer service platforms such as Amazon use feedback from customers and perform sentiment analysis and opinion mining using graph-based models. Twitter, Instagram, and Facebook can detect fake profiles, spam bots, and fraudulent actions by analyzing unusual network structures.

1.8.4 Application of Graphs in Biology

Graphs are fundamental in biology, visualizing and analyzing complicated relationships across diverse fields. They model food webs and species interactions in ecology, illustrating energy flow and habitat connections. In genomics, graphs depict gene regulatory networks, protein–protein interactions (PPIs), and metabolic pathways. Evolutionary biologists use phylogenetic trees to show species relationships, while neuroscientists map brain connectivity through neural networks. Graphs are also vital in epidemiology for modeling disease spread and contact tracing. Furthermore, they support computational biology in protein folding and bioinformatics algorithms, proving indispensable for comprehending biological systems and processes.

1.8.5 Application of Graphs in Chemistry

Graphs play a vital role in chemistry by modeling and analyzing complex chemical systems. In molecular structure representation, chemical graph theory visualizes atoms as nodes and bonds as edges, aiding in isomer identification and reaction pathway analysis. Reaction networks, including catalytic and metabolic pathways, are represented graphically to understand chemical transformations. In quantum chemistry, graphs depict molecular orbitals and calculate properties such as bond orders. Drug discovery leverages graphs for pharmacophore mapping, Quantitative Structure–Activity Relationship (QSAR) models, and molecular docking. Crystallography and materials science use graphs to model crystal lattices, bonding patterns, and network structures. Chemical informatics employs graph-based methods for database searches and molecular fingerprinting. Spectroscopy utilizes graphs to analyze mass spectrometry fragmentation and Nuclear Magnetic Resonance (NMR) interactions effectively. Polymer chemistry uses graphs to study polymer networks and topologies, while environmental chemistry models pollutant transport and chemical interactions. Theoretical chemistry applies graphs in topology optimization and reaction dynamics, making them indispensable for bridging theoretical and experimental insights in chemistry.

1.9 Case Studies of GRL

In the previous section, we explored various applications of graphs, focusing on how traditional graph algorithms help in areas such as social networks, road navigation, and network security. While these applications rely on well-established techniques such as Dijkstra's algorithm, BFS, and PageRank, they often fall short in capturing the deeper, more complex relationships hidden within large-scale graphs. This is where GRL comes into play, transforming the way we analyze and utilize graph data.

Unlike traditional graph algorithms that operate on discrete structures, GRL enables us to learn low-dimensional vector embeddings for nodes, edges, or entire graphs. These embeddings preserve the structural and feature-based relationships within a graph, allowing us to apply machine learning models for tasks such as classification, clustering, and prediction. This approach has revolutionized various fields by enabling more scalable, efficient, and accurate graph-based applications.

One of the most prominent applications of GRL is in SNA, where platforms such as Facebook and LinkedIn use node embeddings to recommend friends and professional connections based on learned relationships. These methods go beyond simple mutual friends and leverage the entire network structure to suggest meaningful connections. Similarly, in financial fraud detection, GRL models help identify suspicious transactions by analyzing money flow between accounts and detecting anomalous subgraphs that indicate fraudulent behavior.

In the field of bioinformatics and drug discovery, GRL methods have made significant contributions by learning molecular representations. Instead of treating chemical compounds as strings, GRL converts molecules into graphs and learns representations that predict drug effectiveness, toxicity, and interactions. This has led to breakthroughs in AI-driven drug discovery, reducing the time and cost of finding new treatments.

Another important application lies in cybersecurity, where GRL models detect intrusions and anomalies in network traffic by learning network activity patterns.

Unlike traditional rule-based systems, which rely on predefined attack signatures, GRL-based methods can generalize to identify new and evolving threats.

These applications demonstrate the power of GRL in extracting hidden patterns and enabling data-driven predictions that were previously challenging using conventional graph algorithms. As graphs continue to grow in scale and complexity, GRL will play a pivotal role in advancing research and real-world applications across multiple domains.

1.9.1 Case Study in SNA

Social networks, such as Facebook, Twitter, and LinkedIn, consist of massive graphs where users (nodes) are connected by friendships, follows, or interactions (edges). GRL plays a crucial role in analyzing, predicting, and optimizing various aspects of social networks by capturing the hidden structure of user connections.

1.9.1.1 Friend and Connection Recommendations

Traditional recommendation systems use mutual friends or shared interests to suggest new connections. However, GRL-based models learn richer node embeddings that encode a user's entire network position. By comparing these embeddings, platforms such as LinkedIn and Facebook can recommend highly relevant connections even if users don't share direct mutual friends.

For example, a social network is represented as a graph, where nodes (V) represent users; edges (E) represent friendships or follow relationships; node attributes may include user interests, activity level, location, etc.; and edge attributes may include interaction frequency, message count, or strength of connection. The goal is to predict new edges (friendships) that should exist in the network based on graph embeddings. The benefits of GRL-based friend recommendations [4] are capturing indirect relationships beyond mutual friends, handling large-scale networks efficiently by learning compact embeddings, personalizing recommendations based on user behavior, not just structural links, and continuously updating as new connections and interactions occur.

1.9.1.2 Community Detection and Group Formation

Detecting communities in social networks helps platforms suggest groups, events, and discussions that match user interests. GRL models use learned node representations to identify clusters of users with similar engagement patterns. This improves user engagement by fostering more relevant social interactions.

Community detection is an essential problem in SNA, where the goal is to identify clusters of users who share similar interests, behaviors, or interactions. Traditional graph-based methods rely on network modularity and structural patterns, but GRL enhances this by learning rich, low-dimensional representations that capture hidden relationships and dynamic community structures.

Platforms such as Facebook, Twitter, and LinkedIn use community detection to recommend relevant groups, pages, and discussion forums, significantly enhancing user engagement through personalized social interactions. These social networks are modeled as a graph $G = (V, E)$, where nodes (V) are users and edges (E) represent connections (like friendships, follows, or interactions). User profiles provide node features (e.g., age, location, interests), while edge features can include message frequency or relationship duration.

A community is a subset of nodes highly connected internally but sparsely connected externally. Identifying these groups enables better recommendations, targeted advertisements, and network analysis. The benefits of GRL in community detection include capturing nonobvious connections beyond direct friendships. It handles large-scale and dynamic networks efficiently, identifies overlapping communities by allowing users to belong to multiple groups, and enhances personalized recommendations by improving user engagement.

1.9.1.3 Fake Account and Bot Detection

GRL helps in identifying fake accounts, bots, and fraudulent activities by learning network structures. Bots often exhibit unusual connection patterns, and GRL-based models can detect these anomalies by analyzing structural deviations. This enhances platform security and improves trust in social networks.

Fake accounts and bots are a major issue in social networks, affecting platform integrity, misinformation spread, and fraud. Traditional rule-based and heuristic methods struggle with large-scale bot networks due to their dynamic and developing approaches. GRL provides a powerful approach by using network structure, user interactions, and machine learning models to detect fake users more effectively.

For example, platforms such as Twitter, Facebook, and LinkedIn use GNNs, node embeddings, and anomaly detection algorithms to identify and eliminate suspicious accounts, ensuring a safer and more authentic user experience. Fake accounts and bots in social networks typically follow distinct behavioral patterns, which can be analyzed using graph-based techniques. These include automated bot networks where bots create fake engagement by liking, commenting, and retweeting posts. They follow each other in structured patterns, forming dense clusters. Furthermore, bots are used for spamming, political manipulation, and fake news promotion. Fake profiles send spam links, phishing messages, or impersonate real people.

Fake accounts and bots, typically, have low interaction diversity, mainly engaging with other fake accounts. A social network can be represented as a graph $G = (V, E)$ where nodes (V) represent users (real or fake); edges (E) represent interactions (follows, likes, comments, messages); node features include account age, number of posts, and engagement patterns; and edge features include interaction frequency, sentiment, and reciprocity. The goal is to detect fake accounts, and its benefits are capturing hidden bot networks beyond simple rule-based detection by dynamically adapting to new bot behaviors using real-time updates, detecting fake accounts before they become active, and preventing large-scale manipulation. This works efficiently on large social networks (Twitter, Facebook, LinkedIn).

1.9.1.4 Sentiment and Opinion Analysis

By modeling social interactions as a graph, GRL enables sentiment analysis by learning how opinions propagate. This is useful for detecting political polarization, misinformation spread, and public sentiment trends, helping policymakers and organizations respond proactively.

Sentiment and opinion analysis play a crucial role in understanding public perception, analyzing trends, and detecting misinformation across social media, news platforms, and product reviews. Traditional natural language processing techniques use text-based sentiment analysis, but they fail to capture network-driven influences, opinion propagation, and contextual relationships between users.

GRL enhances sentiment analysis by having user interactions, discussion networks, and contextual dependencies to improve the accuracy of sentiment classification. Social networks (e.g., Twitter, Facebook, Reddit), e-commerce platforms (e.g., Amazon, Yelp), and news aggregators benefit significantly from graph-based sentiment analysis. A sentiment network is modeled as a graph $G = (V, E)$ where nodes (V) represent users, posts, or discussions; edges (E) represent interactions (likes, retweets, replies, comments); node attributes include sentiment scores, user credibility, and writing style; and edge attributes include interaction polarity (support vs. disagreement), frequency, and sentiment shift over time. The goal is to do sentiment and opinion analysis. The benefit of GRL in sentiment analysis is to capture sentiment propagation beyond isolated text analysis. It handles large-scale, dynamic discussions in real time, identifies opinion leaders and misinformation spreaders, and enhances personalized recommendations based on sentiment trends.

1.9.2 Case Study in Fraud Detection for Financial Transactions

In financial organizations, there were increasing cases of fraud involving online transactions. Traditional systems were not able to detect obvious fraud, such as large transactions from unusual locations or credit card fraud [5]. However, more subtle and well-organized fraudulent acts were going unnoticed.

To address this, the organizations decided to utilize GRL. They began by viewing all transactions and participants as a network of connected entities. Each person, account, transaction, device, and location was treated as a point (or "node") in the network, and the relationships between them, such as who used which device or which account sent money to whom, were considered as connections (or "edges").

By using GRL, the bank could automatically learn hidden patterns and relationships in this network. It became possible to identify suspicious links, like a single device being used by multiple unrelated accounts or accounts frequently connected to known fraudulent ones.

This graph-based view helped the team detect fraud not by looking at transactions individually, but by understanding how everything is connected. Even if a single transaction looked normal, its links to other suspicious nodes raised red flags.

As a result, the institution significantly improved its ability to spot fraud earlier and more accurately. GRL allowed them to see the bigger picture of how fraud spreads through complex connections.

1.9.3 Case Study in Molecular Biology

Case Study 1.1

Identifying Disease Genes Through PPI Networks Using GRL

Overview

In molecular biology, PPI networks represent the physical and functional interactions between proteins within a cell. These networks are modeled as graphs, where nodes represent proteins and edges denote interactions. Understanding these networks is critical for identifying key proteins (or genes) involved in diseases such as cancer, Alzheimer's, and genetic disorders.

Traditional methods to identify disease genes often depend on direct genetic mutations or expression studies, which may overlook important indirect interactions and network-level patterns. Moreover, the complexity and scale of PPI networks pose challenges for manual analysis or conventional statistical models. Researchers have developed graph-based machine learning models, particularly using GRL techniques such as GCNs and node embedding (e.g., node2vec, DeepWalk), to analyze PPI networks. These methods allow for automatic feature extraction from graph structure, enabling efficient and accurate prediction of potential disease-associated genes.

Workflow

Data Preparation:

The PPI network is constructed from databases such as BioGRID, STRING, or IntAct. Known disease genes are labeled using resources such as Online Mendelian Inheritance in Man (OMIM) or DisGeNET.

(Continued)

Case Study 1.1 (Continued)

Graph Embedding:

Each protein (node) is encoded into a low-dimensional vector based on its topological and relational properties using algorithms such as DeepWalk or GCNs.

Training and Prediction:

A machine learning model (e.g., logistic regression and neural network) is trained on the embedded features to classify proteins as disease-related or not.

Validation:

The model's predictions are validated against known disease genes and experimentally verified pathways.

Results

Studies show that GRL-based models significantly outperform traditional statistical or similarity-based methods. For example, in cancer genomics, GCNs have uncovered previously unknown oncogenes by leveraging indirect interactions that were overlooked in gene expression analysis. In neurobiology, GRL helped identify proteins implicated in neurodegenerative disorders through their network proximity to known disease genes.

Impact

This approach has revolutionized drug target discovery, biomarker identification, and personalized medicine. By uncovering hidden patterns in large-scale biological networks, graph-based models enhance our ability to understand complex disease mechanisms and identify novel therapeutic strategies.

Case Study 1.2

Identifying Disease Genes Through PPI Networks Using ModulePred and Discriminative Network Embedding

Overview

Identifying genes associated with specific diseases is a cornerstone of biomedical research. PPI networks offer an invaluable framework for this challenging task, as they inherently capture the complex web of relationships between proteins within a cell. Increasingly, GRL, particularly through GNNs, has emerged as a powerful technique to model the intricate topologies of these PPI networks, paving the way for the discovery of novel gene–disease associations.

One significant innovation in this space is ModulePred [7], a deep learning framework designed to predict disease–gene associations. As described in studies like those found on BioMed Central and PubMed Central (PMC), ModulePred masterfully integrates diverse biological information, including known disease–gene links, identified protein complexes, and augmented protein interactions. It does this by constructing a heterogeneous module network. Through sophisticated graph augmentation and embedding techniques, ModulePred learns robust representations for each node (protein or gene) within this network. This capability allows it to accurately predict disease–gene associations, with experimental results consistently demonstrating its superiority over traditional methods. This underscores the profound efficacy of leveraging functional modules and graph augmentation in disease gene prediction.

Another noteworthy advancement is the discriminative network embedding (DNE) framework, detailed in a study published in *Science*. DNE employs a self-supervised network embedding approach that excels at capturing both the localized and global topological information present in PPI networks. What makes DNE particularly impactful is its ability to learn robust node embeddings without relying on extensive labeled data. This is a critical advantage in biological research, where comprehensive annotations are often scarce, making DNE highly valuable for enhancing the identification of disease genes even in data-limited scenarios.

These breakthroughs in GRL methodologies highlight the immense potential of leveraging PPI networks for identifying disease genes. By effectively capturing intricate biological interactions and seamlessly integrating diverse data sources, GRL approaches such as ModulePred and DNE are fundamentally reshaping our understanding of disease mechanisms, leading to more accurate and comprehensive insights.

1.10 Conclusion

Graphs serve as a powerful and intuitive way to represent complex relationships and interactions in real-world systems. From the fundamental understanding of graph types—such as directed, undirected, weighted, and hierarchical graphs—to the exploration of connectivity and structure, this chapter has laid the foundation for understanding how data can be structured beyond traditional formats.

GRL has emerged as a transformative approach, enabling machines to learn meaningful representations from graph-structured data. The benefits of GRL such as capturing relational patterns and enabling predictive insights are evident in various domains, including social networks, transportation systems, biology, and financial fraud detection. The case studies presented demonstrate the versatility and real-world impact of GRL in solving complex problems.

As data continues to grow in complexity and interconnectivity, the role of graph theory and representation learning will become increasingly vital. By equipping readers with foundational concepts and practical insights, this chapter sets the stage for deeper exploration into graph-based methods in artificial intelligence and data science.

References

1 R. Kaur, R. Saini, and Sanjivani, "Introduction to graph theory and its types," *J. Emerg. Technol. Innovat. Res. (JETIR)*, vol. 6, no. 4, 2019 ISSN-2349-5162, www.jetir.org.

2 V. T. Hoang, H.-J. Jeon, E.-S. You, Y. Yoon, S. Jung, and O.-J. Lee, "Graph Representation Learning and Its Applications: A Survey," *Sensors*, vol. 23, no. 8, p. 4168, 2023, doi: 10.3390/s23084168.

3 W. L. Hamilton, R. Ying, and J. Leskovec, *Representation Learning on Graphs: Methods and Applications*. IEEE Computer Society Technical Committee on Data Engineering, 2017. https://www-cs.stanford.edu/people/jure/pubs/graphrepresentation-ieee17.pdf.

4 W. Tayyab, "Graph representation learning using AI, ML, methods and applications," *Int. J. Adv. Eng. Technol. Innov*, vol. 1, no. 01, 2021.

5 Yao Zou, Dawei Cheng, Effective high-order graph representation learning for credit card fraud detection, Proc. Thirty-Third Int. Joint Conf. Artificial Intelligence (IJCAI-24), Jeju 03.08.24–09.08.24, pp. 7581–7589, https://www.ijcai.org/proceedings/2024/0839.pdf.

6 J. Gao, J. Wu, and J. Ding, "Heterogeneous Graph Condensation," *IEEE Trans. Knowl. Data Eng*, vol. 36, no. 7, pp. 3126–3138, 2024, doi: 10.1109/TKDE.2024.3362863.

7 X. Jia *et al.*, "A deep learning framework for predicting disease-gene associations with functional modules and graph augmentation," *BMC Bioinformatics*, vol. 25, p. 214, 2024.

2

Fundamental Concepts of Graph Structure

Now that you have a foundational understanding of graphs, graph representation learning (GRL), and graph connectivity from Chapter 1, this chapter takes you into the fundamental building blocks of graph structures.

In this chapter, we explore the essential features that define a graph at both the node and graph levels. At the node level, we examine properties such as degree, centrality measures (degree centrality, betweenness, closeness, eigenvector, PageRank), clustering coefficient, motifs, and egographs. Each of these features provides valuable insights into the role and influence of individual nodes within a graph. We will discuss their definitions, applications, and the advantages and limitations of using them in different graph-based tasks. Beyond individual nodes, we shift our focus to graph-level features that capture the overall structure and complexity of a network. This includes graph density, eccentricity, modularity, graph centralization, Weisfeiler–Lehman (WL) kernel, and graphlets, among others. These features help characterize entire networks, enabling a deeper understanding of their connectivity, efficiency, and structural patterns.

To extract meaningful insights from graphs, we also need a structured way to represent them mathematically. Therefore, this chapter introduces graph representation matrices such as adjacency, Laplacian, and transition matrices. Additionally, we discuss various graph measures, including spectral properties and graph similarity metrics, which are crucial for analyzing network dynamics. This chapter will also cover traditional methods for extracting these features, comparing their strengths and weaknesses. By the end, you will have a comprehensive understanding of how graphs are analyzed at different levels, setting the stage for more advanced topics in GRL.

2.1 Introduction to Graph Structures

A graph structure is a mathematical representation of a set of nodes (vertices) and the edges (connections) between them. Formally, a graph is defined as $G = (V, E)$, where V is the set of vertices and E is the set of edges. Graphs can be directed or undirected, weighted or unweighted, and can exhibit various structural properties that define their complexity and connectivity. Graph structures are fundamental in representing relationships and interactions across various domains, including social networks, biological systems, transportation networks, and knowledge graphs. Their ability to capture both local and global relationships makes them essential for analyzing patterns, connectivity, influence, and structural dependencies in complex systems. By using graph structures, researchers and engineers can model real-world problems more effectively, leading to advancements in fields such as data science, artificial intelligence, and data mining.

2.1.1 Characteristics of Graph Structure

Graphs or networks in machine learning have several key characteristics/features based on the types of nodes, attributes of the nodes, relationships between nodes, patterns of connectivity between the nodes, the importance of the node, and how likely the neighbors of a node are to be connected. Studying the characteristics of graph structures in machine learning offers several benefits that enhance the ability to model complex relationships and extract meaningful patterns from data. Graphs provide a flexible and powerful way to represent structured data, and understanding their characteristics allows machine learning practitioners to design better algorithms, improve performance, and apply models in a wide range of applications. The two types of graph characteristics are node-level and graph-level characteristics, which are discussed in Section 2.2.

Example ***Healthcare Graph for Patient Management and Disease Diagnosis***

Graph structures in healthcare are commonly used to model complex relationships between attributes, such as patients, diseases, treatments, and medical facilities. The key characteristics include the types of nodes (patients and doctors), their attributes, relationships between nodes, patterns of connectivity, node importance, and neighborhood connectivity.

In the graph, patients are represented as nodes; each patient is a unique entity in the graph. Doctors are nodes representing healthcare providers who interact with patients. The attributes of patient nodes include age, gender, medical history, genetic factors, lifestyle data, and current symptoms. The attributes of doctor nodes include specialty, experience, location, and hospital affiliation. The relationship between patient and doctor is represented as patient-to-doctor. The edges represent consultations, referrals, or ongoing treatment relationships.

The patterns of connectivity between nodes are referral networks, where doctors frequently refer patients to other specialists, creating dense subgraphs of doctor-to-doctor connections. The importance of patient nodes is that patients who consult multiple specialists or have complex conditions may serve as key nodes in the graph. On the other hand, the doctors' nodes represent highly specialized doctors who are crucial for connecting with these patients. Likelihood of neighbor connectivity are patient networks, where patients who visit the same doctor or have similar conditions are likely to be interconnected, and doctor referral networks, where doctors who frequently refer to each other (e.g., a general practitioner referring to a cardiologist and vice versa), form tightly connected neighborhoods.

2.2 Node-Level Features

Node-level characteristics refer to the properties and metrics associated with individual nodes within a graph. These characteristics describe the role, influence, and behavior of each node in the overall graph structure. Node-level characteristics provide a foundational understanding of individual elements within a network, revealing how nodes contribute to the overall graph's structure and function. Node-level characteristics include node degree, node centrality, clustering coefficient, eccentricity, PageRank, K-core numbers, structural holes, and node motif participation.

2.2.1 Node Degree

- **Definition:** The node degree [1] of a node in a graph is the number of edges connected to it. For a directed graph, it includes in-degree (number of incoming edges) and out-degree (number of outgoing edges).

Example ***Healthcare Graph***
The healthcare graph in Fig. 2.1 has both the patient and doctor nodes. Patients (Ahmed, Jerry, Sarah, Pettrisa, Giftson, and Seetha) are connected to doctors (Jessie, Jeff) based on the "diagonalized by" relationship, highlighting which doctor diagnosed each patient.

The node degree for the nodes {"jerry," "Sarah," "Giftson," "Ahmed," "Seetha," "Pettrisa"} is 1, as they are directly connected with only one doctor. Doctor node "Jeff" has node degree 4, and "Jessie" node has node degree 2.

Benefits of Finding Node Degree

1) High-degree nodes are often influential or central within a network. In healthcare, doctors with higher degrees are treating more patients, highlighting their importance in patient care.

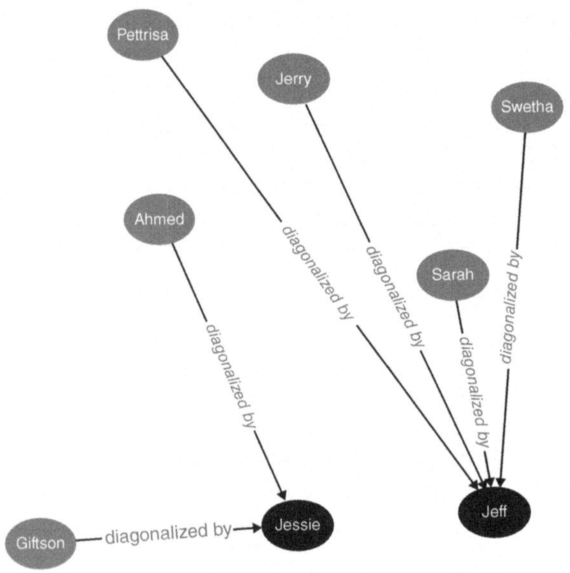

Figure 2.1 Graph representing patient–doctor relationship based on "diagonalized by" factor.

2) Node degree helps in understanding which nodes have high connectivity in assessing how the network might respond to node failures or attacks. Nodes with high degrees are critical points of failure.
3) Node degree plays a role in grouping the nodes by identifying tightly connected groups of nodes.
4) It helps in resource allocation, such as assigning tasks or resources more efficiently. In healthcare, understanding which doctors are highly connected can guide patient distribution to balance workloads.
5) Unusual degree patterns can indicate anomalies or outliers in the data, such as fraud or unusual behavior.

2.2.2 Node Centrality Measures

Node centrality is a fundamental concept in graph theory used to measure a node's importance, influence, or prominence within a network. It is essential for analyzing and understanding graphs/networks. Centrality metrics help determine which nodes are most vital to the structure and functioning of the network based on various criteria, such as connectivity, influence, or position within the graph. It assigns numerical values or rankings to nodes according to their position within the graph/network.

- **Definition:** Centrality measures assess a node's importance or influence within the graph.

2.2.2.1 Importance of Node Centrality

Centrality helps identify the most important nodes in a graph, such as influential people in social graphs, critical proteins in biological graphs, or key routers in communication graphs. By understanding which nodes are most central, organizations can develop strategies to protect or reinforce these nodes, enhancing the overall resilience of the graph. Resources can be allocated more efficiently by prioritizing nodes with high centrality, ensuring maximum impact or coverage. Central nodes are often the most efficient at disseminating information. Identifying them helps enhance communication strategies within graphs. High-centrality nodes are often critical points that, if compromised, can disrupt the entire graph. Understanding these points allows for better protection and contingency planning. Centrality metrics help identify the most influential nodes within communities, aiding in the study of group dynamics and interactions. Nodes with high centrality are more likely to attract new connections. Understanding this helps predict how the graph will evolve. Central nodes often serve as critical waypoints in navigation, optimizing pathfinding algorithms.

2.2.2.2 Types of Node Centrality

The types of node centrality are as follows:

A) Degree centrality
B) Closeness centrality
C) Betweenness centrality
D) Eigenvector centrality

A. Degree Centrality

Definition Degree centrality is the simplest form of centrality and is defined as the number of direct connections a node has. It measures the node's local importance based purely on the number of links (edges) it has to other nodes.

In a directed graph, such as one involving patient and doctor nodes, the degree centrality score can be divided into:

Out-degree

This represents the number of outgoing connections from the node to other nodes. In the case of patient–doctor relationship, out-degree is the number of patients who are consulting a specific doctor.

In-degree

This refers to the number of incoming connections to the node. Similarly, the doctor who has got appointments from many patients.

Let $N_1, N_2, N_3, \ldots, N_n$ be the number of nodes. Let N_n be the node with the highest degree and a degree centrality of 1. The degree centrality of other nodes N_i

can be calculated by

$$\text{deg\_}cen(N_i) = \frac{\text{Number of edges of } N_i}{\text{Number of edges of } N_n}$$

The greater the degree, the more central the node becomes. This is often a useful indicator, as nodes with a high number of connections frequently exhibit high centrality according to other metrics as well. For the example given in Fig. 2.1, the node "jeff" has the highest number of edges associated with it. So, the degree centrality of nodes "jerry," "Seetha," "sarah," "pettrisa" is calculated as

$$\text{deg\_}cen(\text{"jerry"} \mid \text{"Seetha"} \mid \text{"pettrisa"} \mid \text{"sarah"}) = 1/4 = 0.25$$

Applications

- Identifying hubs in social networks (e.g., individuals with many direct friends).
- Recognizing important intersections or routers in transport or communication networks.
- Understanding popularity in social platforms, where nodes with higher degree centrality are typically influencers.

Advantages

- Easy to compute.
- Gives a straightforward indication of the activity or direct influence of a node.

Limitations

- Does not account for the influence or importance of the node's neighbors.
- Only captures local, rather than global, importance.

B. Closeness Centrality While degree centrality measures a node's influence based on its immediate connections, it does not account for the broader structure of the graph. A node with a high degree may still be far from many other nodes, limiting its overall accessibility within the graph.

Closeness centrality addresses this limitation by considering the shortest path distances between a node and all other nodes in the graph. It quantifies how quickly a node can reach others, making it a useful measure of efficiency in communication or information spread. A node with high closeness centrality is well-positioned to access the entire network with minimal steps, making it particularly relevant in applications such as transportation networks, social influence, and information flow.

The formula for closeness centrality is:

$$C(v) = \frac{N-1}{\sum d(v,u)}$$

where $d(v,u)$ represents the shortest path distance between node v and every other node u. Since doctors have direct connections to multiple patients, their centrality values will be higher compared to patients, who can only connect to each other through doctors.

Compared to degree centrality, which only considers direct neighbors, closeness centrality provides a more global perspective on a node's position within the network.

Definition Closeness centrality measures how close a node is to all other nodes in the network. It is based on the average shortest path length from the node to every other node. A node with high closeness centrality can quickly interact with all other nodes in the graph. A higher closeness centrality means a node is more central and can reach others faster.

Measuring node closeness

Example ***Healthcare Graph***

Figure 2.2 shows the healthcare graph with nodes representing patients and doctors as circles, and they are connected as patients to the doctors who diagnosed them with the "diagonalized by" relationship.

For each node, closeness centrality is computed as:

$$C(v) = \frac{N-1}{\sum d(v,u)}$$

The graph shows that connections (edges) represent which doctor diagnosed which patient:

Jessie → {Ahmed, Jerry, Sarah}

Jeff → {Pettrisa, Giftson, Seetha}

This forms a bipartite graph, where doctors are directly connected to patients, but no direct connections exist between patients.

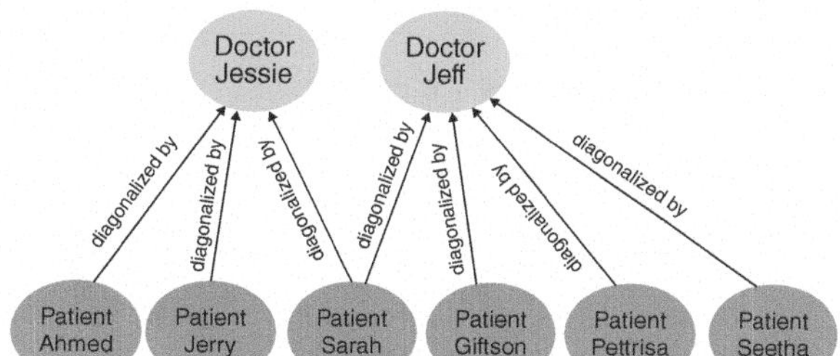

Figure 2.2 Healthcare graph with patient-to-doctor relationship.

Table 2.1 Shortest path distance for healthcare graph.

Node pair	$d(u,v)$
Ahmed–Jessie	1
Jerry–Jessie	1
Sarah–Jessie	1
Pettrisa–Jeff	1
Giftson–Jeff	1
Seetha–Jeff	1
Ahmed–Jerry	2
Ahmed–Sarah	2
Jerry–Sarah	2
Pettrisa–Giftson	2
Pettrisa–Seetha	2
Giftson–Seetha	2
Jessie–Jeff	2
Ahmed–Jeff	3
Jerry–Jeff	3
Sarah–Jeff	3
Pettrisa–Jessie	3
Giftson–Jessie	3
Seetha–Jessie	3

1. Steps to Calculate Shortest Path Distances $d(u,v)$

For each pair of nodes, the shortest path distance is computed and given in Table 2.1.

2. Compute Closeness Centrality for Each Node

Total number of nodes:

$$N = 8 \text{ (2 doctors + 6 patients)}$$

For Doctor Jessie

$$\sum d(\text{Jessie}, v) = 1 + 1 + 1 + 2 + 2 + 2 + 2 = 11$$

$$C(\text{Jessie}) = \frac{8 - 1}{11} \approx 0.636$$

For Doctor Jeff

$$\sum d(\text{Jeff}, v) = 1 + 1 + 1 + 2 + 2 + 2 + 2 = 11$$

$$C(\text{Jeff}) = \frac{8-1}{11} \approx 0.636$$

For Each Patient (Example: Ahmed)

$$\sum d(\text{Ahmed}, v) = 1 + 2 + 2 + 3 + 3 + 3 + 2$$

$$\mathbf{C(Ahmed)} = \frac{8-1}{16} \approx 0.4375$$

Doctors (Jessie and Jeff) have the highest closeness centrality (0.5), meaning they are the most central and connected to the rest of the network.

Patients have lower closeness centrality (0.35) since they are only connected to one doctor.

This confirms that doctors act as central hubs in the network, while patients are on the periphery.

Applications

- Identifying key nodes for fast dissemination of information in social networks.
- Improving routing efficiency in communication or transport networks.
- Understanding which individuals in an organization can quickly reach others.

Advantages

- Indicates how efficiently information or resources can be spread from a node to the rest of the network.
- Captures global network position.

Limitations

- Does not work well for disconnected networks, where some nodes cannot reach others.
- Relies heavily on the accuracy of shortest path calculations.

C. Betweenness Centrality While degree centrality focuses on a node's direct connections and closeness centrality measures how efficiently a node can reach others, neither of these metrics considers a node's role as a bridge between different parts of a network. Some nodes may not have the highest degree or be the closest to all others, but they play a crucial role in controlling the flow of information by connecting distant parts of the graph.

Betweenness centrality captures this idea by measuring how often a node appears on the shortest paths between other nodes. A node with high-betweenness centrality acts as a key intermediary, facilitating communication and influencing

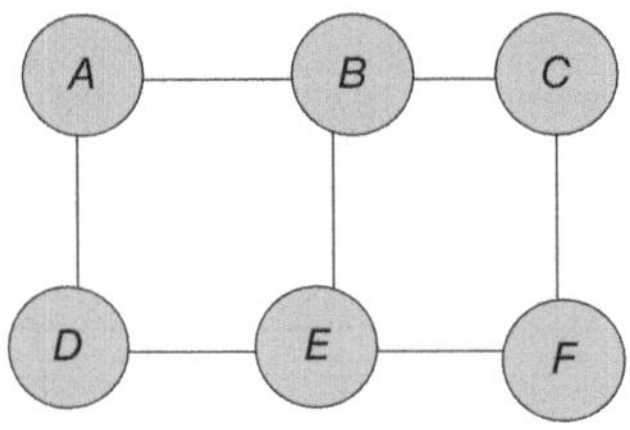

Figure 2.3 Example of betweenness centrality measure.

the spread of information across the network. This measure is useful in identifying influential people in social networks, critical routers in communication systems, or bottlenecks in transportation networks.

Definition Betweenness centrality is a measure of how often a node appears along the shortest paths between other nodes in a graph.

Consider the following graph (Fig. 2.3) with six nodes (A, B, C, D, E, F). Identify the shortest path from A to C, A to F, and D to C.

The shortest path from A to C is: $A \rightarrow B \rightarrow C$

The shortest path from A to F is: $A \rightarrow D \rightarrow E \rightarrow F$

The shortest path from D to C is: $D \rightarrow E \rightarrow B \rightarrow C$

Count the paths through each node. Node B is on the shortest path between A and C, so it has a higher betweenness score. Node E is on multiple shortest paths (A to F, D to C), meaning it has high-betweenness centrality. Nodes like B and E have higher betweenness centrality because they connect different parts of the graph. Removing them would significantly disrupt communication. Nodes like A and C have lower betweenness centrality since they are endpoints and don't act as intermediaries in shortest paths.

Mathematically, betweenness centrality is defined as:

$$B(v) = \sum_{s \neq v \neq t} \frac{\sigma_{st}(v)}{\sigma_{st}}$$

where σ_{st} is the total number of shortest paths between nodes s and t and $\sigma_{\mathrm{st}}(v)$ is the number of those shortest paths that pass through node v.

Example ***Healthcare Graph***

Betweenness centrality measures how often a node lies on the shortest paths between other nodes. Let us take Fig. 2.2 graph example. Doctor Jessie connects Patient Ahmed, Patient Jerry, and Patient Sarah to the rest of the graph. Doctor Jeff connects Patient Giftson, Patient Pettrisa, and Patient Seetha to the graph. There are no direct edges between patients, meaning that any communication between patients from different doctors must go through Doctor Jessie or Doctor Jeff.

Any shortest path between a patient diagnosed by Doctor Jessie and a patient diagnosed by Doctor Jeff must pass through either Doctor Jessie or Doctor Jeff.

Since Doctor Jessie and Doctor Jeff act as bridges between different patient groups, they will have the highest betweenness centrality. Patients have a betweenness centrality of 0 since they are endpoints and do not lie on paths between other nodes.

After computing betweenness centrality, Doctor Jessie and Doctor Jeff have high-betweenness centrality because every shortest path between patients under different doctors must pass through them. Patients have a betweenness centrality of 0 because they are endpoints and do not serve as intermediaries.

Applications Various applications of betweenness centrality are identifying influential people in a network who act as intermediaries between different groups in social networks. This centrality measure is useful in marketing, as high-betweenness individuals can spread information widely. In a corporate network, an employee with high-betweenness centrality might be a key connection between different departments. In transportation and traffic networks, this measure is used to identify critical roads, intersections, or airports that act as major hubs in a transportation system. It is helpful to transfer data and detect router issues. In financial crime investigations, detecting accounts with high betweenness can help uncover money laundering schemes.

Advantages

- Highlights nodes that serve as crucial intermediaries in a network, making it useful for detecting bottlenecks, influential individuals, or critical infrastructure points.
- Helps understand how information, resources, or influence travel through a network by identifying nodes that control the shortest paths.

Disadvantages

1) Requires calculating all shortest paths in a network, making it inefficient for large-scale graphs, especially in real-time applications.
2) Considers global influence in the network and does not account for how well-connected a node is within its immediate neighborhood.
3) Adding or removing nodes can significantly alter betweenness values, making it less stable in dynamic networks.

D. Eigenvector Centrality While degree centrality measures a node's influence based on the number of direct connections, and closeness centrality evaluates how quickly a node can reach others, both measures treat all connections equally. However, in many real-world networks, not all connections are of equal importance. A node connected to highly influential nodes should have more influence than a node connected to less significant ones.

Eigenvector centrality [2] addresses this by assigning higher importance to nodes that are connected to other highly central nodes. It is based on the idea that a node's significance is derived from the significance of its neighbors. This makes it particularly useful in ranking nodes in social networks, citation networks, and web page ranking systems.

Definition Eigenvector centrality is a measure of a node's influence in a network that considers not only the number of connections (degree centrality) but also the importance of the nodes it is connected to. A node connected to highly influential nodes will have a higher eigenvector centrality than one connected to less influential nodes.

- Eigenvector centrality recognizes a node that is connected to highly central nodes as a highly influenced node. In Fig. 2.4, B and E are connected to many other high-importance nodes outside this graph. Even though C and F have similar degree centrality as B and E, their eigenvector centrality will be lower because their connections are to less influential nodes. As a result, B and E will have higher eigenvector centrality.

  Mathematically, eigenvector centrality is defined as:

$$x_v = \frac{1}{\lambda} \sum_{u \in N(v)} x_u$$

where x_v is the centrality of node v, $N(v)$ is the set of neighbors of v, λ is a constant (the largest eigenvalue of the adjacency matrix), and x_u represents the centrality of neighboring nodes.

Steps in calculating eigenvector centrality are as follows:

Step 1:
Construct the adjacency matrix for the graph such that

- $A_{ij} = 1$ if there is an edge between nodes i and j. $A_{ij} = 0$ if there is no edge.

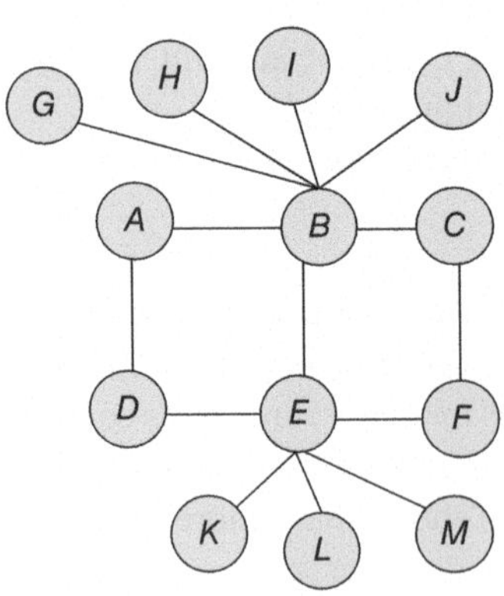

Figure 2.4 Eigenvector centrality measure example.

Step 2:
Compute the eigenvalues and eigenvectors of the adjacency matrix.

Step 3:
Take the eigenvector corresponding to the largest eigenvalue.

Step 4:
Normalize the eigenvector so that its values sum to 1.

Applications Eigenvector centrality is widely used in various fields to measure the influence of nodes in a graph by considering both direct connections and the importance of connected nodes. Some key applications include:

1) Google's PageRank algorithm is based on eigenvector centrality. Websites with links from other high-importance sites get higher rankings. It helps to improve search engine results by ranking pages based on their relevance.
2) It identifies influential people on social media platforms (Twitter, Facebook, LinkedIn) and helps in detecting key influencers and trendsetters in online communities.
3) It measures the impact of research papers by considering citations from influential papers and helps to identify landmark research in scientific fields.
4) It identifies critical proteins or genes in biological networks.
5) It determines important hubs in airline, railway, and road networks and helps optimize traffic flow and improve public transportation systems.

Advantages

1) Unlike degree centrality, which only considers the number of direct connections, eigenvector centrality considers neighboring nodes' importance.
2) Since it focuses on the importance of a node, it can be used for information retrieval based on page ranking.
3) It helps to identify key influencers among the nodes. So, this measure can be used in social networks.
4) This makes it useful for understanding the overall structural importance of nodes.

Limitations

1) Eigenvector centrality works well in fully connected networks but fails when the graph has isolated nodes or multiple disconnected components.
2) Nodes with a high number of connections tend to have higher eigenvector centrality, even if their connections are not strategically important.

2.3 Structural-Level Features

2.3.1 Introduction to Structural-Level Features

After understanding the importance of node-level features in characterizing individual nodes, we now shift our focus to structural-level features [3], which provide insights into the local and global connectivity patterns of a graph. These features help capture the relationships between multiple nodes and reveal essential structural patterns that influence network behavior.

In this section, we will explore key structural properties such as the clustering coefficient, closed triangles, egographs, and motifs. These features are particularly useful in understanding community structures, network resilience, and information flow within a graph. By analyzing them, we can extract meaningful representations that aid in tasks such as node classification, anomaly detection, and graph-based learning.

2.3.1.1 Clustering Coefficient Measure

In real-world networks, nodes tend to form local clusters rather than being randomly connected. For example, in social networks, if two of your friends know each other, then they form a triangle with you. This tendency to form closed groups or tightly connected neighborhoods is captured using the clustering coefficient, which measures the degree to which nodes in a network cluster together.

The clustering coefficient helps in understanding network transitivity, small-world properties, and community formation. It plays a crucial role in social network analysis, biological networks, and recommendation systems, where interconnectedness influences behavior and decision-making. A higher clustering coefficient means the node is in a tightly connected local community. A lower clustering coefficient suggests a more sparse, less connected neighborhood.

Definition The clustering coefficient measures the degree to which nodes in a network tend to cluster together. It quantifies the likelihood that two neighbors of a node are also connected, forming triangles. It is an important metric for analyzing the local connectivity and cohesiveness of a graph. The mathematical representation of the clustering coefficient is

$$C_i = \frac{2T_i}{K_i(K_i - 1)}$$

where C_i is the clustering coefficient of node i, T_i is the number of closed triangles involving node i, and k_i is the degree of node iii (number of neighbors). The denominator represents the maximum possible number of connections among the neighbors of i.

The workflow process starts with the representation of the graph as an adjacency matrix. The next step is to find the neighborhood nodes (nodes that are directly connected) for each node. The set of neighbors for each node is determined if $A(u,v) = 1$, where u is the node and v is the neighbor node. For example, if the adjacency list for node A is $\{B, C, D\}$, then the degree for node A is 3. The next step is to detect a triangle by counting the closed triangles. A node forms a triangle if it has two nodes directly connected to it. Finally, the local clustering coefficient can be computed for each node. The result will be fully clustered if all neighbors are connected, $C_v = 1$ or there is no local clustering if no neighbors are connected, $C_v = 0$.

Example 2.1 Consider a graph with nodes A, B, C, D connected. Node A has three neighbors: B, C, and D. The possible connections among A's neighbors are B and C, C and D, B and D. All three neighbors of A are interconnected, forming a closed triangle. Number of

TA = 3 (closed triangles).

$kA = 3$, so the maximum possible connections among neighbors is 3. Clustering coefficient of A:

$$C_A = \frac{2(3)}{3(3-1)} = \frac{6}{6} = 1$$

This measure helps to find the local connectivity within the graph, identifying tightly knit communities and structural patterns. So, node A has a clustering coefficient of 1, indicating that its neighborhood is fully and tightly connected. The clustering coefficient for the other nodes can also be calculated.

Example 2.2 To find whether node 5 is fully connected in Fig. 2.5, first count the number of neighbors it has. The set of neighbors it has is Node 5 → {2, 4, 6, 8}. Count the closed triangles for node 5 as Node 5: Neighbors → {2, 4, 6, 8}, Possible connections: (2–4, 4–6, 6–8, etc.) → Forms 3 triangles. Calculate the clustering coefficient for each node. This involves the number of triangles and the number of neighbors. In this example, calculate for node 5.

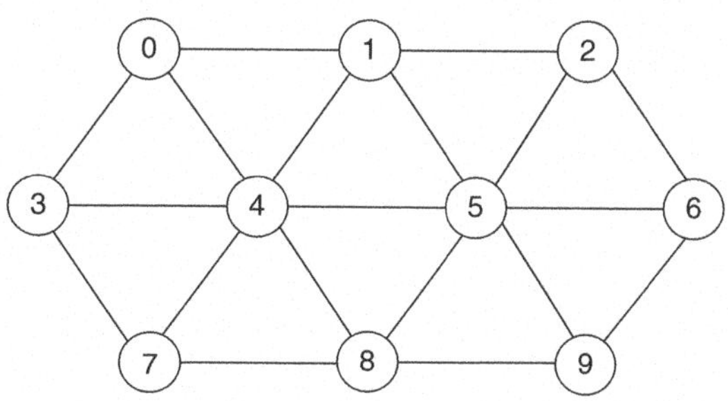

Figure 2.5 Graph for calculating clustering coefficient.

$k_5 = 4$ (Neighbors: $\{2, 4, 6, 8\}$) $T_5 = 3$

- Possible connections $= \frac{4(4-1)}{2} = 6$
- Clustering coefficient $= \frac{2(3)}{4(4-1)} = \frac{6}{12} = 0.5$

2.3.1.2 Closed Triangles

The previous section gives an overview of the clustering coefficient, which measures the formation of local clusters within a graph. This section focuses on closed triangles.

A closed triangle is a small group of three connected nodes in a network, where each node is linked to the other two. It helps us understand how tightly connected a network is.

Closed triangles are important because they show how well a group of nodes sticks together, help in finding communities, and improve network stability. They also play a key role in spreading information and making networks stronger.

A closed triangle in a graph is a set of three nodes that are all connected to each other by edges, forming a fully connected subgraph of size three. Consider a graph with three vertices (A, B, C) such that edges exist between each pair (A, B), (B, C), (C, A). They are closely connected and form a closed triangle. This measure is mostly used in social networks, where we can find closely connected friends.

2.3.1.3 Egographs

In the previous sections, we introduced the concept of clustering coefficient and closed triangles. The clustering coefficient measures the likelihood of a node's neighbors being interconnected, while closed triangles indicate local connectivity patterns. Egographs extend this by explicitly representing the structure surrounding a node, making it easier to analyze its local community and influence. Egographs provide a focused view of local connectivity within a network. In this section, we learn about the egograph with its definition and its usage in the graph network.

Definition An egograph (or ego network) of a node A in a graph G is the subgraph that consists of A, its immediate neighbors, and all edges between these neighbors. It represents the local connectivity around A and helps in understanding how a node is embedded within the network.

Example ***Author Citation Graph***

In the citation graph G_2 given in Fig. 2.6, nodes represent research papers authored by different individuals, and directed edges indicate citation relationships. To construct an egograph, we select a particular node (paper) as the "ego" and consider its immediate neighbors (papers it cites or is cited by), along with the connections among these neighbors.

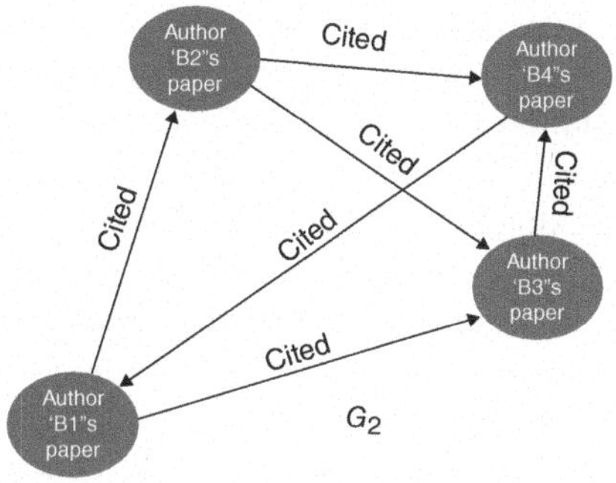

Figure 2.6 Citation graph for egograph.

Example ***Egograph of "Author B1's Paper"***
If we consider "Author B1's Paper" as the ego node:

- Immediate neighbors (directly connected nodes):
  - "Author B2's Paper" (cited by B1)
  - "Author B3's Paper" (cited by B1)
- Connections among neighbors:
  - "Author B2's Paper" cites "Author B3's Paper."

Thus, the egograph of "Author B1's Paper" consists of:

1) Node: "Author B1's Paper" (ego)
2) Neighbors: "Author B2's Paper" and "Author B3's Paper"
3) Edges among neighbors: The citations between these papers.

This egograph representation provides insights into how a particular research paper is embedded in a citation network, highlighting collaborative influences and research impact.

k-Egograph is an egograph that includes nodes up to k-hops (k represents the number of edges in the path) away from the central node. In a social network, a 2-egograph of a person includes their direct friends (1-hop) and friends of friends (2-hop).

Usage and Its Challenges Egographs are widely used in network analysis to understand the local structure around a specific node (ego). They help various domains such as social network analysis to identify influential users in a social media network by analyzing how well their connections interact and to understand personal communities, such as friend groups on Facebook or LinkedIn. It is also used in fraud detection in financial networks for detecting suspicious activities by analyzing connections of a fraudulent entity, and in recommender systems to enhance personalized recommendations by analyzing the immediate connections of a user's interests.

Egographs are crucial for understanding local connectivity in complex networks. Their importance spans multiple domains, including social networks, citation networks, fraud detection, and biological systems. Egographs provide deeper insights into local structures within networks, enabling better decision-making in multiple fields. Their ability to capture and analyze local interactions makes them indispensable for network science, AI, and real-world applications.

Egograph faces scalability issues, handling of frequently updated data, identifying missing or inaccurate data, and difficulty in analyzing and interpreting data. Egographs focus on local structures but may not always reflect the global importance of a node in a network. By addressing these challenges, egographs can serve as a powerful tool for understanding network structures and relationships across various domains.

2.3.1.4 Motifs

The structured-level feature measures we have discussed so far are clustering coefficient, closed triangles, and egographs; we now move to the concept of motifs. Motifs are small, recurring subgraph patterns that appear more frequently in a graph than expected in a random structure. They help in identifying fundamental building blocks of complex graphs. While clustering coefficient and closed triangles focus on local connectivity, motifs go one step further by capturing specific structural patterns that define how nodes interact beyond immediate neighbors.

For example, in a citation network, if three papers frequently cite each other in a loop, this forms a triangle motif. In a centralized network connection, a star motif appears when multiple users are connected to a single network server. These patterns help in recognizing influential structures, understanding graph dynamics, and improving prediction models in various domains. Now, let's understand the concept of motifs and their real-world significance with its types.

2.3.1.5 Definition with Its Types

Motifs are small, recurring subgraph patterns that appear frequently in a network and provide insights into its structural properties. They help in understanding the fundamental building blocks of complex networks and reveal hidden relationships between entities.

There are different types of motifs as shown in Fig. 2.7. The triangle motif is a three-node structure where each node is connected to the other two, forming a closed triangle. A feedforward motif is a three-node directed network pattern where one node influences a second node, which in turn influences a third, while the first node also directly influences the third. This structure is common in information flow, signaling pathways, and hierarchical systems. A star motif is a network structure where a central node is directly connected to multiple peripheral

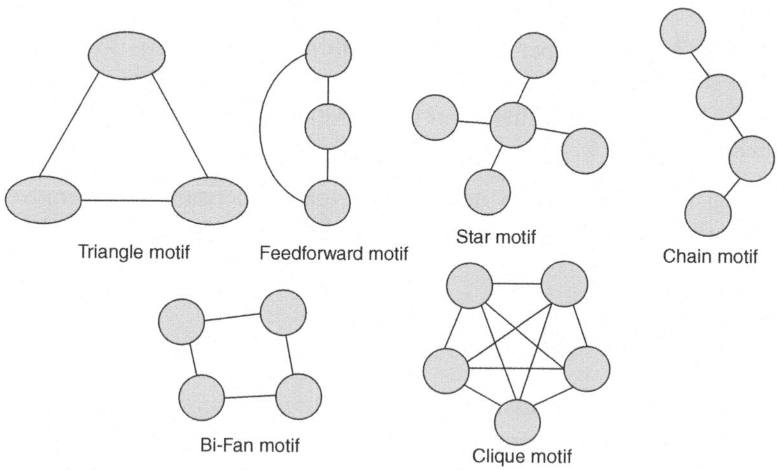

Figure 2.7 Types of motif.

nodes, while the peripheral nodes have no connections among themselves. This pattern commonly appears in social networks, communication systems, and citation networks. A chain motif is a sequential network structure where nodes are connected linearly, with each node linking to the next. This pattern represents information flow, dependency chains, or hierarchical progression in networks. A Bi-Fan motif is a four-node network pattern where two source nodes are connected to two target nodes, forming a bipartite-like structure. A clique motif is a fully connected subgraph where every node is directly linked to every other node within the motif. In network analysis, cliques represent tightly knit communities, such as co-authorship groups in citation networks.

Example ***Author Citation Graph***

In an author citation graph, motifs can help analyze citation behaviors and academic influence. Some common motifs include:

1) Triangle Motif (Closed Triad)
   - Definition: A small cycle where three papers cite each other.
   - Example: Paper A cites Paper B, Paper B cites Paper C, and Paper C cites Paper A. This represents a tightly connected group of related research.
2) Feedforward Motif
   - Definition: A pattern where Paper A cites Paper B, and Paper B cites Paper C, but Paper A also directly cites Paper C.
   - Example: If an author writes a foundational paper, then another builds on it, and a third directly references both, forming a hierarchical citation structure.

3) Star Motif
   - Definition: A single paper is cited by multiple other papers, forming a star-like structure.
   - Example: A highly influential paper that is widely cited by many authors in the field.

By analyzing motifs in citation networks, we can understand collaborative trends, influential research topics, and knowledge flow in academia.

2.4 Graph-Level Features

In the previous section, we discussed the structural-level features that capture the local and global patterns within graphs, focusing on the relationships and arrangements of individual nodes and edges. Now, let's shift our attention to graph-level features, which aim to represent entire graphs as holistic entities.

When working with graph-level features, we are less concerned with individual nodes or edges and more focused on summarizing the graph as a whole. This approach is particularly useful when comparing multiple graphs.

In this section, we'll look into how graph-level features are constructed, the techniques used to extract meaningful information, and why they play a crucial role in tasks that require a comprehensive understanding of the entire graph.

2.4.1 Structural Properties of Graphs

Understanding the structural properties of graphs is fundamental to extracting meaningful insights from complex networks. These properties describe how nodes and edges are organized and interact at a global level, providing a comprehensive view of the graph's architecture. By analyzing structural properties, we can uncover patterns such as community formations, centrality of nodes, and the overall connectivity of the network.

In this section, we'll explore key structural properties, including degree distribution, clustering coefficients, and graph density.

2.4.1.1 Graph Degree and Density

Graph degree and node degree have the same meaning, as they both describe the number of edges connected to a node in a graph. The term "node degree" is more specific, highlighting the degree of an individual node, while "graph degree" can sometimes refer to the distribution of degrees across all nodes in the graph. Analyzing degrees helps identify influential nodes, understand community structures, and detect anomalies in networks. Its main advantage is its straightforward degree measure that is easy to compute and interpret, providing a basic understanding of node connectivity. In a social network example, a user with a high degree has many connections, indicating potential influence.

Graph density refers to the number of edges between every pair of nodes. This measure is used to find how closely the nodes are connected. This must take into consideration whether the graph is directed or undirected, as they yield different results. For an undirected graph with n nodes and m edges, the density is calculated as

$$D = \frac{2m}{n(n-1)}$$

For a directed graph, the density is calculated as

$$D = \frac{m}{n(n-1)}$$

Every node in a graph is linked to every other node if the density is 1, and the graph is said to be fully connected. Otherwise, when the density is 0, the graph is said to be sparse. Finding graph density is important, as it provides an understanding of how the information is spread across the graph. Graph density is useful for efficiently comparing two graphs for similarity in pattern and connectivity. In large graphs, density is often very low, making it less informative for analyzing highly sparse networks.

Example of Graph Density

Let G be a graph with four nodes and five edges, as given in Fig. 2.8.

The maximum possible edges are $\frac{4\,(4-1)}{2} = 6$

Density is $5/6 = 0.83$.

A density of 0.83 suggests a highly connected network, indicating that most possible connections are present.

2.4.1.2 Graph Eccentricity and Modularity

To know which are the nodes that have long and good relationships/connections with other nodes, and which are the nodes that have short and fewer relationships/connections with other nodes, graph eccentricity is used. If a

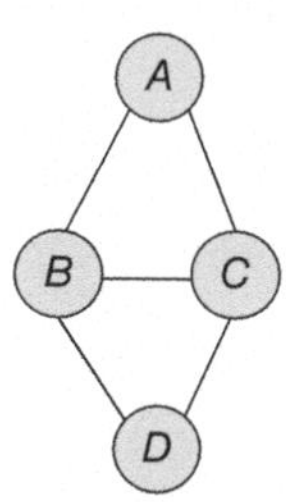

Figure 2.8 Example graph for calculating graph density.

node has a low eccentricity, it means it's relatively close to all other nodes. On the other hand, nodes with high eccentricity can show the distance among the nodes as high. By analyzing eccentricity, we can gain insights into the structure and efficiency of communication within the graph. Eccentricity helps to determine which nodes are central (closer to all other nodes) and which are peripheral (farther from other nodes) within a network. Graph modularity is defined as a measure used to divide the graph into clusters or communities. It basically tells us how well-connected nodes are within a community compared to connections between different communities. High modularity indicates that nodes form tightly knit groups with sparse connections to other groups.

Definition of Graph Eccentricity The graph eccentricity of a node is defined as the maximum shortest path distance from that node to any other node in the graph. In other words, it measures how far a node is from the node that is most distant from it. It is mathematically represented as

$$E(v) = \max d(v, u)$$

where $u \in V$ and V is the set of all nodes in the graph, and $d(v,u)$ is the shortest path distance between nodes v and u.

Example

For the graph given in Fig. 2.9, eccentricity is calculated as follows:

$e(A) = \max\{d(A,B), d(A,C), d(A,D)\} = \max\{1,2,3\} = 3$
$e(B) = \max\{d(B,A), d(B,C), d(B,D) = \max\{1,1,2\} = 2$
$e(C) = \max\{d(C,A), d(C,B), d(C,D) = \max\{2,1,1\} = 2$
$e(D) = \max\{d(D,A), d(D,B), d(D,C) = \max\{3,2,1\} = 3$

Here, nodes B and C are more central (closer to all the other nodes) due to lower eccentricity, while nodes A and D are more peripheral (farther from other nodes).

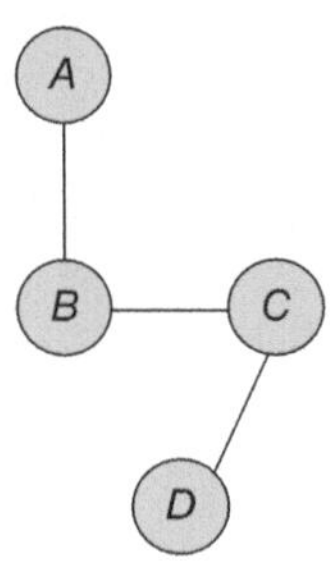

Figure 2.9 Graph for finding eccentricity.

Definition of Graph Modularity Graph modularity is a measure that evaluates the strength of division of a graph into communities or clusters. It compares the actual density of edges within communities to the expected density if edges were distributed randomly. High modularity indicates strong community structure with dense connections within clusters and sparse connections between them.

Modularity M is calculated by using the formula

$$M = \frac{1}{2m} \sum_{i,j} \left[A_{ij} - \frac{k_i k_j}{2m} \right] \delta(c_i, c_j)$$

where A_{ij} represents an adjacency matrix (1 if an edge exists between i and j, 0 otherwise), k_i, k_j are the degrees of nodes i and j, m is the total number of edges, c_i, c_j are the communities to which nodes i and j belong, and $\delta(c_i, c_j) = 1$ if i and j belong to the same community, else 0.

Example

Consider a graph with nodes A, B, C, D split into two clusters: cluster 1—$\{A, B, C\}$ and cluster 2—$\{D\}$ given in Fig. 2.10.

Total edges $m = 4$. Adjacency matrix $A_{i,j}$ is $\begin{bmatrix} 0 & 1 & 1 & 0 \\ 1 & 0 & 1 & 0 \\ 1 & 1 & 0 & 1 \\ 0 & 0 & 1 & 0 \end{bmatrix}$

Degrees for nodes are $k_A = 2, k_B = 2, k_C = 3, k_D = 1$

$A_{ij} = 1$ if there is a direct edge between node i and node j.

$A_{ij} = 0$ if there is no direct edge between node i and node j.

Using this, find the connectivity between nodes.

Node A (row 1):

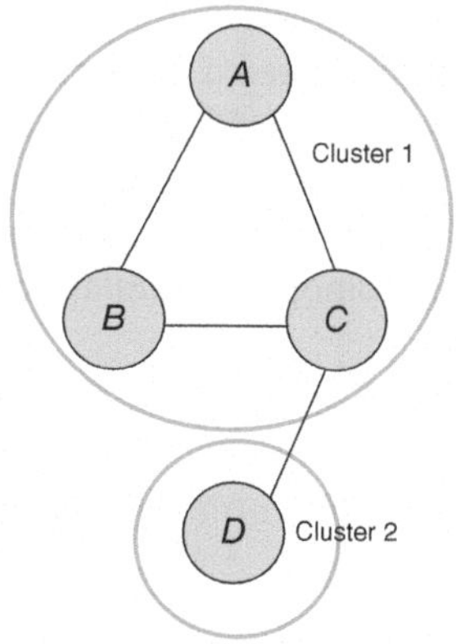

Figure 2.10 Cluster community.

No self-loop: $A_{11} = 0$. Edge to B: $A_{12} = 1$. Edge to C: $A_{13} = 1$. No edge to D: $A_{14} = 0$.

Node B (row 2):

Edge to A: $A_{21} = 1$. No self-loop: $A_{22} = 0$. Edge to C: $A_{23} = 1$. No edge to D: $A_{24} = 0$.

Node C (row 3):

Edge to A: $A_{31} = 1$. Edge to B: $A_{32} = 1$. No self-loop: $A_{33} = 0$. Edge to D: $A_{34} = 1$.

Node D (row 4):

Edge to A: $A_{41} = 0$. Edge to B: $A_{42} = 0$. Edge to C: $A_{43} = 1$. No self-loop: $A_{44} = 0$.

$$\text{Using the modularity formula } M = \frac{1}{2X4}\left[1 - \frac{2X2}{8}\right] + \left[1 - \frac{2X3}{8}\right] + \left[1 - \frac{2X3}{8}\right] + \left[1 - \frac{3X1}{8}\right]$$
$$= \frac{1}{8}\{[1 - 0.5] + [1 - 0.75] + [1 - 0.75] + [1 - 0.375]\}$$
$$= \frac{1}{8}\{0.5 + 0.25 + 0.25 + 0.625\} = 81 \times 1.625 = 0.203$$

A modularity score of 0.203 indicates a moderate community structure, showing that the nodes are more interconnected within their communities than between different communities.

2.5 Graph-Based Representation Techniques

This section gives an overview of different graph-based representation techniques, their strengths, limitations, and practical applications in diverse domains.

2.5.1 Graph Clustering Coefficient

In GRL, the graph clustering coefficient is used to measure the degree to which the nodes are tightly clustered together. The purpose of this measure is to identify the community structures. Closely clustered nodes quickly share their information. High clustering coefficients indicate dense local connections and support models in distinguishing between core and peripheral nodes. A high clustering coefficient often suggests homophily (similar nodes connecting more frequently).

Definition The clustering coefficient of a node v is defined as the ratio of the number of actual connections between its neighbors to the maximum possible connections between them. Formally, it is expressed as:

$$C_v = \frac{2E_v}{K_v(K_v - 1)}$$

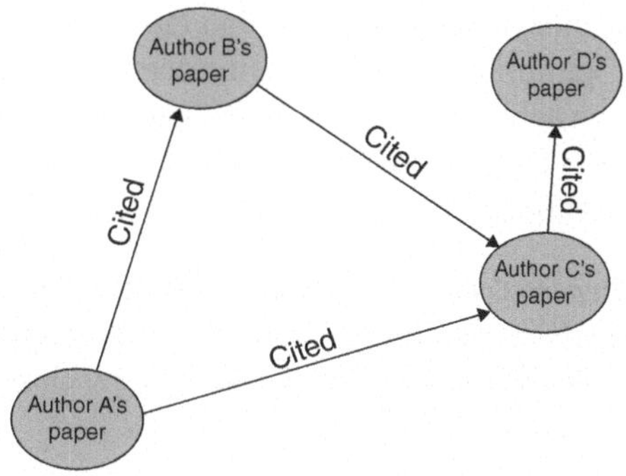

Figure 2.11 Author citation graph example for calculating clustering coefficient.

where E_v represents the number of edges between the neighbors of node v and K_v is the degree of node v (number of neighbors). The average clustering coefficient of the graph is the mean of the clustering coefficients of all nodes.

Example ***Author Citation Graph***

In the author citation graph given in Fig. 2.11, nodes represent authors and edges represent citation relationships between them. Consider a small author citation graph with four authors: A, B, C, and D. The citation details are represented as edges $A \rightarrow B, A \rightarrow C, B \rightarrow C, C \rightarrow D$.

The graph shows that A cites B and C, B cites C, and C cites D.

Calculating the Clustering Coefficient for Author A To calculate the clustering coefficient for author A, we must find the neighbors of A. The neighbors of A are B and C. The possible connections among neighbors are only one possible edge between B and C. Actual connections among neighbors: $B \rightarrow C$ exists.

Using the clustering coefficient formula:

$$C_A = \frac{\text{Number of actual edges between neighbors}}{\text{Maximum possible edges between neighbors}} = \frac{1}{1} = 1$$

A clustering coefficient of 1 for Author A indicates that A's neighbors (B and C) are fully connected, suggesting a tight-knit citation community.

Calculating the Clustering Coefficient for Author C The neighbors of C are A, B, and D.

Maximum possible connections $= \frac{3(3-1)}{2} = 3$ possible edges among neighbors.
Actual connections = No direct edges among A, B, D.

$$C_C = \frac{0}{3} = 0$$

A clustering coefficient of 0 for Author C suggests that C's neighbors do not form a connected community, indicating a more dispersed citation pattern. In this author citation graph, a high clustering coefficient (1 for A) suggests a close-knit community. A low clustering coefficient (0 for C) indicates a broader or less cohesive network. This example illustrates how the clustering coefficient helps identify local citation communities and understand the structural cohesion in the author citation graph.

Steps to Compute Clustering Coefficient Here's a step-by-step algorithm to calculate the local clustering coefficient for a given node in an undirected graph. The local clustering coefficient measures how closely a node's neighbors are connected to each other.

Step 1:
Take the graph as the input. Indicate the target node "v" for which to calculate the clustering coefficient.

Step 2:
Find Neighbors of Node "v".

- Identify the set $N(v)$ of immediate neighbors of v.

Step 3:
Check for Minimum Degree Condition

- If $k_v < 2$, the clustering coefficient $C_v = 0$ (as fewer than two neighbors cannot form a triangle). Terminate if this condition is met.

Step 4:
Count Actual Connections Among Neighbors

- Determine the number of edges E_v that exist among the neighbors of v.
- For each pair of neighbors (i, j) in $N(v)$, check if an edge (i, j) exists.
- Increment E_v for each existing edge.

Step 5:
Calculate Maximum Possible Connections

- Compute the maximum possible number of connections between neighbors:

Step 6:
Compute the Clustering Coefficient

Step 7:
Return C_v as the local clustering coefficient for node v.

2.5.2 Bag of Nodes

In GRL, the bag of nodes (BoN) approach offers a simple yet powerful way to convert graph-structured data into a format that traditional machine learning algorithms can easily handle. Unlike more advanced graph-based techniques that strive to retain both node features and structural information—such as edges and connectivity—the BoN method streamlines the process by concentrating exclusively on the features of individual nodes while ignoring the edges that link them.

The purpose of BoN is to use only the feature information without bothering about the connections or patterns, thereby simplifying the complex graph structure. Handling edge information in large graphs can be computationally demanding. The BoN approach simplifies this process by concentrating solely on node features, thereby reducing memory usage and computational costs. This efficiency makes it an effective choice for managing large-scale graphs.

A key motivation for adopting the BoN approach is its simplicity. Most traditional machine learning algorithms, including support vector machines (SVMs), random forests, and gradient boosting, are built to process fixed-length feature vectors instead of complex graph structures. The BoN method enables us to directly apply these well-established models without modification by converting a graph into a collection of independent feature vectors. It serves as a method for many machine learning models by treating nodes as independent samples. The main advantage of using BoN is that it reduces the computational cost, as it does not consider the edge information.

2.5.2.1 Approach

The BoN method treats a graph as an unordered collection of nodes along with their associated features, completely disregarding the edges and the overall topology of the graph. In this approach, each node is considered an independent data point represented by a feature vector that may include attributes such as node degree, centrality measures, categorical properties, or any other domain-specific information. This approach does not consider the connections among the nodes. In a graph $G = (V,E)$, where V is the set of nodes and E is the set of edges. The BoN approach transforms G into a collection of $\{v_1, v_2, v_3 \ldots, v_n\}$ nodes, with each node v_i represented by a fixed-size feature vector x_i. This method focuses entirely on the feature information rather than on the connection among the nodes.

Figure 2.12 shows the architecture of the BoN and its components. The components include an input graph with nodes and edges. The next component in the process of flow is the node feature extraction process, which involves extracting features for each node (like degree, centrality). A BoN represents a collection of independent feature vectors (without edges). The next component is the traditional machine learning models such as SVM, random forest, or gradient boosting receiving these feature vectors as input. The final component is the output layer, which represents the output for tasks such as classification, prediction, or clustering.

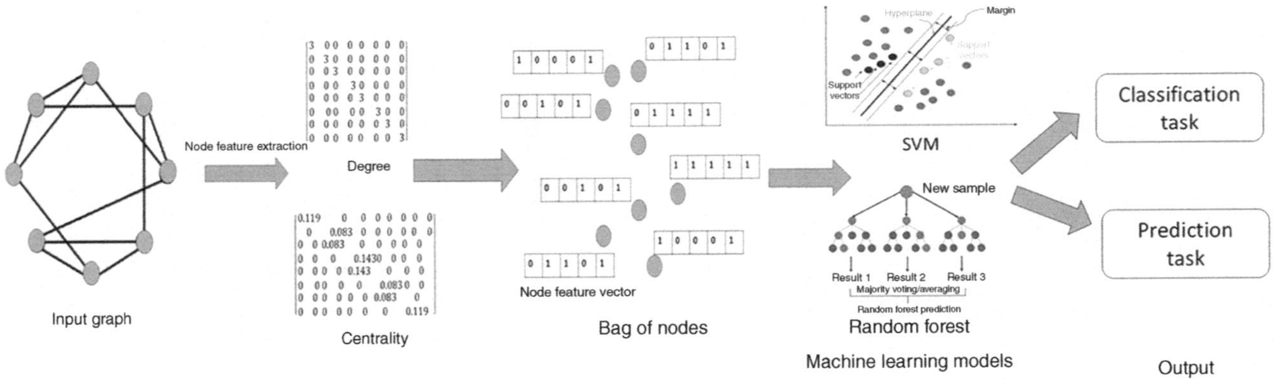

Figure 2.12 Architecture of bag of nodes and its components.

Example ***BoN in Social Network Analysis***

Let us consider a social network graph G where nodes represent users with features such as age, interests, and activity level. Edges represent friendship connections between users. Each user is treated as an independent data point with a feature vector. For example, user A is [25 years, sports, high activity], and user B is [30 years, music, medium activity]. This representation allows us to train a classifier to predict user characteristics (e.g., interests) using standard machine learning techniques.

2.5.3 WL Kernel

Continuing from the BoN approach, which simplifies graph representation by focusing only on node features, we encounter a significant limitation: the loss of structural information, such as how nodes are interconnected. To address this, the WL Kernel offers an effective solution by incorporating both node features and structural patterns into graph representations. This method enhances the expressiveness of graph learning models, enabling them to capture the underlying topology and relationships within the graph without sacrificing efficiency. Unlike the BoN method, the WL Kernel preserves connectivity patterns by using a neighborhood aggregation mechanism. This allows it to distinguish between different graph structures effectively [4].

The primary limitation of the BoN method is that it completely disregards edge information and graph topology. In many applications—such as molecule classification, social network analysis, and fraud detection—the structure of connections is as crucial as the node attributes themselves. The WL Kernel overcomes this by extending node features iteratively based on their neighbors, thereby encoding both local and global structural information. We define WL Kernel as a graph kernel that measures the similarity between graphs by comparing their structural and feature-based information.

2.5.3.1 Working Process of the WL Kernel

The WL Kernel operates by transforming graphs into a series of enriched representations through an iterative node labeling procedure. This process captures both local and global structural information and enables effective comparison of graph similarity. Here's a step-by-step breakdown of how the WL Kernel works:

Step 1: Initial Labeling

Let $G_1 = (V_1, E_1)$ and $G_2 = (V_2, E_2)$ be two graphs, where $v_i \in V_1$ and V_2, $i = 1, 2, 3\ldots, n$ (number of nodes), and E_1 and E_2 are the set of edges. Initial label $\ell_0(v_i)$ is assigned to each node of the two graphs based on its features (e.g., node degree, categorical attributes, or a default label if no features are available).

Step 2: Iterative Label Propagation

Capture structural information by iteratively refining node labels based on their neighbors. For each node v_i, collect the labels of its neighboring nodes. Create a new label by concatenating the current label of v_i with the sorted labels of its neighbors. Compress this concatenated string into a unique new label using a hash function.

$$\ell_{k+1}(v_i) = \text{hash}(l_k(v_i) \parallel \text{sort}(\{l_k(u_j) \mid u_j \in N(v_i)\}))$$

where "i" represents the number of nodes, j represents the number of neighbors for each node v_i, $l_k(v_i)$ represents the label of node v_i at iteration k, $N(v_i)$ represents the set of neighbors of v_i, and $\parallel$ is the concatenation operator.

Step 3: Histogram Generation for Each Iteration

For each graph, generate a label histogram after every iteration. Histograms represent the frequency of each label across the graph.

Step 4: Kernel Computation Using Histogram Matching

Measure graph similarity by comparing label histograms by computing the inner product between histograms of two graphs G_1 and G_2 at each iteration:

$$K(G_1, G_2) = \sum_{k=0}^{h}\sum_{l} H_k^l(G_1) X\, H_k^l(G_2)$$

where h is the number of iterations, and $H_k{}^1(G)$ is the count of nodes with label l at iteration k in graph G.

Step 5: Convergence and Termination

The iteration stops when there is no change in the labels or a fixed number of iterations h is reached.

Let G_1 and G_2 be two graphs with four nodes (A, B, C, D) each. The graph is given in Fig. 2.13.

Step 1: Initial Labeling

All nodes in both graphs have the same initial label. $\ell_0(A) = \ell_0(B) = \ell_0(C) = \ell_0(D) = 1$.

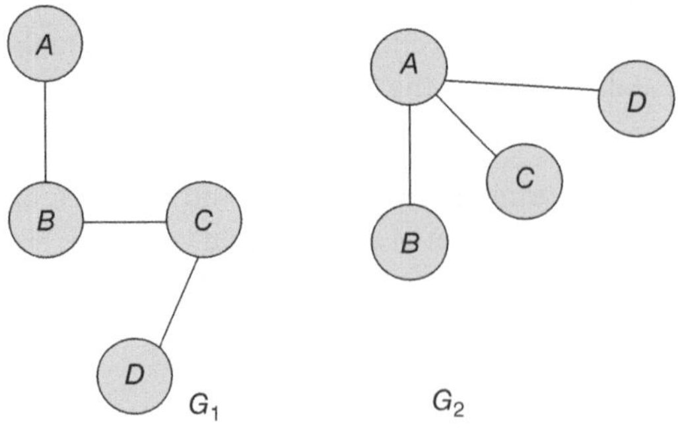

Figure 2.13 Example illustrating working process of the Weisfeiler–Lehman (WL) Kernel.

Step 2: First Iteration (Label Propagation)

For G_1, Node A has Neighbor $\{B\}$, so the hash function is

Concatenation:

$1 \,||\, 1 = 1{-}1 \rightarrow$ New Label: $\ell_1(A) = \text{hash}(1{-}1) = 2$.

Node B has Neighbors $\{A,C\} \rightarrow 1 \,||\, [1,1] = 1{-}1{-}1 \rightarrow \ell_1(B) = \text{hash}(1{-}1{-}1) = 3$.

Node C has Neighbors $\{B,D\} \rightarrow 1 \,||\, [1,1] = 1{-}1{-}1 \rightarrow \ell_1(C) = 3$.

Node D has Neighbor $\{C\} \rightarrow 1 \,||\, 1 = 1{-}1 \rightarrow \ell_1(D) = 2$.

Updated labels for G_1 are A: 2, B: 3, C: 3, D: 2.

For G_2, Node A has Neighbors $\{B,C,D\} \rightarrow 1 \,||\, [1,1,1]{=}1{-}1{-}1{-}1 \rightarrow \ell_1(A) = \text{hash}(1{-}1{-}1{-}1) = 4$.

Nodes B, C, D have A as the only neighbor $1 \,||\, 1 = 1{-}1$

New Label: $\ell_1(B) = \ell_1(C) = \ell_1(D) = 2$.

Updated Labels for G_2 A: 4, B: 2, C: 2, D: 2.

Step 3:

Histogram Generation (histograms represent the frequency of each label across the graph).

G_1 Histogram {2,3}. // nodes A and D have updated labels as 2, and B and C have updated labels as 3.

G_2 Histogram {2,4}. // nodes B, C, and D have updated labels as 2, and node A has an updated label as 4.

Step 4: Kernel Computation (Histogram Matching)

$$K(G_1, G_2) = \sum_{\text{labels}} \min\,(H(G_1), H(G_2))$$

where $H(G_i, \ell)$ = the count of nodes with label ℓ in graph G_i.

Matching Labels: Graph G_1 has two nodes with label 2. Graph G_2 has three nodes with label 2.

- The minimum of these counts is 2.

Label 2:

$\min(2, 3) = 2$.

Label 3:

$\min(2, 0) = 0$ (no such label in G_2).

Label 4:

$\min(0, 1) = 0$ (no such label in G_1).

Kernel Value:

$K(G_1, G_2) = 2 + 0 + 0 = 2$

The kernel value $K(G_1, G_2) = 2$ indicates a limited similarity between G_1 and G_2. The WL Kernel effectively distinguishes the structural differences between the chain and star graphs by refining node labels iteratively. This example highlights how the WL Kernel captures structural information through iterative label propagation and histogram comparison.

2.5.4 Graphlets and Path-Based Methods

In the realm of GRL, extracting meaningful patterns from graph-structured data is essential for understanding complex networks. Graphlets and path-based methods serve as two powerful approaches to capture local and global structures within graphs. While graphlets focus on identifying and counting small, connected subgraphs to characterize local topology, path-based methods emphasize the importance of node sequences and connectivity patterns to capture both local neighborhoods and long-range dependencies. Understanding these techniques not only enhances our ability to interpret graphs effectively but also supports tasks such as node classification, link prediction, and graph similarity assessments.

2.5.4.1 Definition of Graphlets

Graphlets are small, connected, non-isomorphic subgraphs of a fixed size extracted from a larger graph. They serve as building blocks for understanding the local structural patterns within graphs. Typically, graphlets range from two-node to five-node subgraphs, each capturing a distinct aspect of local connectivity.

The idea behind graphlets [5] is to count the frequency of various subgraph patterns and use these counts as features to represent the graph. By analyzing these small, recurring structures, we can derive insights into the graph's topology, such as motifs (frequent subgraphs indicating biological functions in networks) or anomalies in social networks. The purpose is to capture local topology effectively, to differentiate between graphs based on their subgraph compositions, and to serve as a feature set for machine learning tasks on graphs.

2.5.4.2 Different Types of Graphlets

Graphlets are small, connected subgraphs with a fixed number of nodes (typically 2–5 or sometimes up to 6). Each unique way that nodes can connect forms a different graphlet. For instance, with three nodes, you have two graphlets as shown in Fig. 2.14.

- Path (or chain): $A \rightarrow B \rightarrow C$
- Triangle: $A \leftrightarrow B \leftrightarrow C \leftrightarrow A$

By choosing the number of nodes (k), you can decide how many nodes you want in each graphlet (e.g., 3-node, 4-node, or 5-node graphlets). The larger the k, the more unique the graphlets. If two nodes are there, they form one graphlet (i.e., an edge as a unique graphlet). If there are 3 nodes, the number of graphlets is 2, one of which is a path and the other one is a triangle. If the number of nodes is 4, 6 unique graphlets can be formed. They are path, star, cycle, tailed triangle, and clique. If the number of nodes is 5, 21 unique graphlets can be formed.

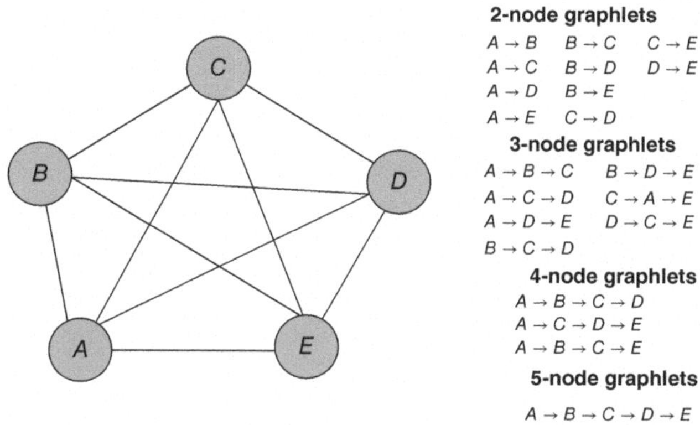

Figure 2.14 Different types of graphlets.

Example

In a social network, a 3-node graphlet might represent a triangle indicating a mutual friendship between three users, while a 2-node graphlet might represent a user connected to two others who are not connected to each other.

2.5.4.3 Path-Based Methods

Definition Path-based methods focus on exploring and analyzing sequences of nodes and edges (or paths) within a graph. These methods leverage path information to encode both local neighborhoods and global connectivity patterns.

In path-based methods, the fundamental idea is to count or encode paths of various lengths between nodes. This approach helps in understanding reachability and proximity between nodes, which is crucial for tasks such as link prediction and recommendation systems. Its purpose is to capture long-range dependencies in graphs and to enhance link prediction by analyzing the presence of paths between node pairs. In a transportation network, a path between two nodes (stations) can indicate a potential route. Analyzing multiple paths helps in identifying bottlenecks or the most efficient routes.

Approach For each node pair in the graph in Fig. 2.15, count the number of possible paths and their length. Create a feature vector for each node based on path counts and lengths. Use these vectors for link prediction (e.g., predicting if an edge might form between A and E) or node classification (e.g., identifying node roles based on connectivity patterns).

1) **Paths of Length 1 (Direct Connections)**
   - $A \rightarrow B, A \rightarrow C, B \rightarrow D, C \rightarrow D, D \rightarrow E$

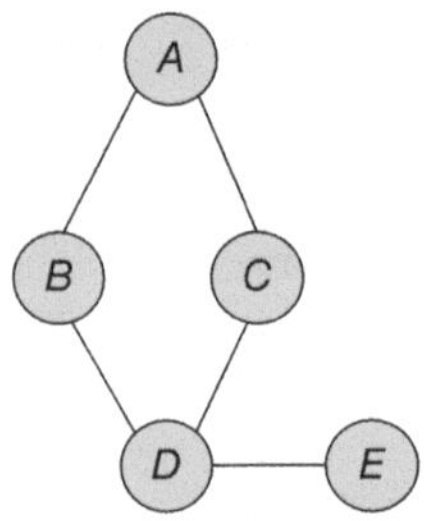

Figure 2.15 Path-based method graph example.

2) **Paths of Length 2**
   - $A \to B \to D$ (connects A to D via B)
   - $A \to C \to D$ (connects A to D via C)
   - $B \to D \to E$ (connects B to E via D)
   - $C \to D \to E$ (connects C to E via D)
3) **Paths of Length 3**
   - $A \to B \to D \to E$ (connects A to E via B and D)
   - $A \to C \to D \to E$ (connects A to E via C and D)

2.6 Graph Representation Matrix

2.6.1 Types of Graph Representation Matrices

In the realm of GRL, matrices play a crucial role in transforming graph-structured data into formats suitable for machine learning algorithms. By capturing different aspects of a graph's structure and relationships, these matrices enable us to efficiently process, analyze, and extract meaningful insights from complex networks.

This section explores four fundamental types of graph representation matrices: the adjacency matrix, incidence matrix, Laplacian matrix, and transition matrix. Each matrix serves a specific purpose. The adjacency matrix highlights direct connections between nodes, making it essential for understanding local neighborhoods. The incidence matrix focuses on node–edge relationships, providing a detailed view of graph topology. The Laplacian matrix is instrumental for spectral methods, offering insights into graph connectivity and smoothness. The transition matrix captures the probability of transitioning between nodes, which is vital for random walk-based approaches.

2.6.1.1 Adjacency Matrix

Definition An adjacency matrix is a square matrix used to represent a graph by capturing the direct connections (or edges) between its nodes. In the context of GRL, it serves as a fundamental tool to encode graph structure in a way that can be processed by machine learning models. The adjacency matrix serves as an input to aggregate information from neighboring nodes. It facilitates message passing by enabling the exchange of information across connected nodes and is used for tasks like node classification and clustering.

For a graph $G = (V,E)$ with $\mathbf{N}$ nodes ($V = \{v_1,v_2, \dots, v_N\}$, the adjacency matrix A is an $N \times N$ matrix defined as:

$$A_{ij} = \begin{cases} 1 & \text{if there is an edge between node } v_i \text{ and } v_j \\ 0 & \text{otherwise} \end{cases}$$

For an undirected graph, the entries in the matrix are 0 if there is no edge between the pair of nodes or 1 if there is an edge. For weighted graphs, A_{ij} can represent the weight of the edge between nodes v_i and v_j instead of just 0 or 1.

Consider a graph with nodes A, B, C, D shown in Fig. 2.16. The adjacency matrix A is

$$A = \begin{bmatrix} 0 & 1 & 1 & 1 \\ 1 & 0 & 0 & 1 \\ 1 & 0 & 0 & 0 \\ 1 & 1 & 0 & 0 \end{bmatrix}$$

Properties of Adjacency Matrix

- **Diagonal Elements:** Typically 0 for simple graphs (no self-loops).
- **Sparsity:** Often sparse for large real-world graphs, making efficient storage important.
- **Symmetry:** Indicates if the graph is undirected.

2.6.1.2 Incidence Matrix

Definition An incidence matrix is a matrix used to represent the relationships between nodes and edges in a graph. Unlike the adjacency matrix, which focuses on connections between pairs of nodes, the incidence matrix captures how nodes are associated with edges. It is particularly useful for understanding and analyzing the topological structure of a graph. The incident matrix facilitates the encoding of edge-based information in graphs, which is crucial for models that need to understand node–edge relationships. It is useful in tasks such as network

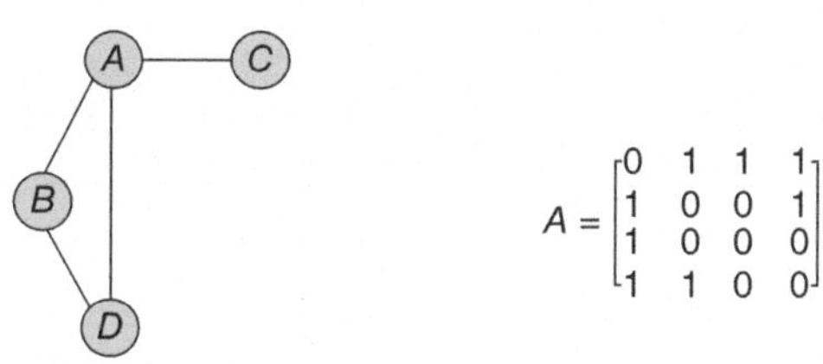

Figure 2.16 Adjacency matrix illustration graph.

flow analysis, spectral clustering, and topological data analysis. It supports edge feature incorporation in graph neural networks (GNNs) by representing edge associations explicitly.

For a graph $G = (V, E)$ with N nodes $V = \{v_1, v_2, \dots, v_N\}$ and M edges $E = \{e_1, e_2, \dots, e_M\}$, the incidence matrix B is an $N \times M$ matrix defined as

$$B_{ij} = \begin{cases} 1 \text{ if node } v_i \text{ is incident to edge } e_j \\ 0 \text{ otherwise} \end{cases}$$

For directed graphs, we can use

$$Bij = \begin{cases} 1 & \text{if node } v_i \text{ is the starting point of edge } e_j \\ -1 & \text{if node } v_i \text{ is the endpoint of edge } e_j \\ 0 & \text{if node } v_i \text{ is not incident to edge } e_j \end{cases}$$

Example

Consider the graph in Fig. 2.17 with nodes A, B, C, D, and the incident matrix B is

$$B = \begin{bmatrix} 1 & 1 & 0 & 0 \\ 1 & 0 & 1 & 0 \\ 0 & 1 & 0 & 1 \\ 0 & 0 & 1 & 1 \end{bmatrix}$$

Properties of Incidence Matrix

- Binary Matrix: Typically consists of 0s and 1s (or −1s for directed graphs).
- Dimension: $N \times MN$, where N is the number of nodes and M is the number of edges.
- Degree Calculation: The sum of entries in a row gives the degree of the corresponding node.

2.6.1.3 Laplacian Matrix

Definition The Laplacian matrix is a matrix representation of a graph that highlights its structural properties, particularly the connectivity and flow of information between nodes. It plays a crucial role in spectral graph theory and is widely used in graph-based machine learning tasks such as community detection and clustering. It helps analyze the flow of information and connectivity within a graph.

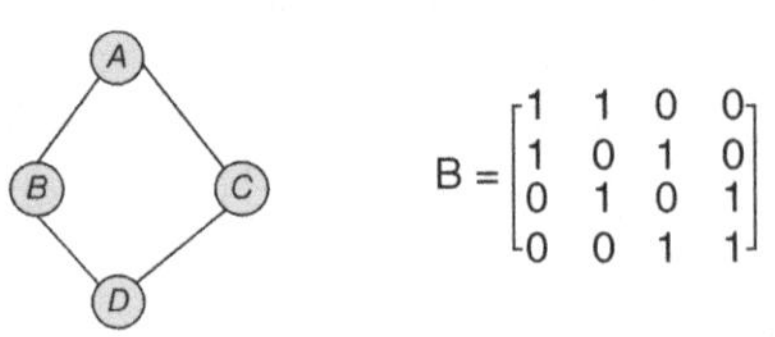

Figure 2.17 Graph for incidence matrix.

Types of Laplacian Matrices

1) Unnormalized Laplacian L
2) Normalized Laplacian L_{norm}

1) Unnormalized Laplacian Matrix

The unnormalized Laplacian matrix L is a matrix representation of a graph that highlights the difference between node degrees and their direct connections.

The unnormalized Laplacian matrix L for a graph $G = (V,E)$ is defined as:

$$L = D - A$$

where D is the degree matrix (a diagonal matrix where D_{ii} is the degree of node I) and A is the adjacency matrix (a matrix representing the connections between nodes).

The formula for degree matrix D is

$$D_{ii} = \sum_j A_{ij}$$

Consider a graph given in Fig. 2.18 with nodes A, B, C, D

$$A = \begin{bmatrix} 0 & 1 & 1 & 0 \\ 1 & 0 & 0 & 1 \\ 1 & 0 & 0 & 1 \\ 0 & 1 & 1 & 0 \end{bmatrix} \qquad D = \begin{bmatrix} 2 & 0 & 0 & 0 \\ 0 & 2 & 0 & 0 \\ 0 & 0 & 2 & 0 \\ 0 & 0 & 0 & 2 \end{bmatrix}$$

Laplacian Matrix $L = D–A$

$$L = \begin{bmatrix} 2 & -1 & -1 & 0 \\ -1 & 2 & 0 & -1 \\ -1 & 0 & 2 & -1 \\ 0 & -1 & -1 & 2 \end{bmatrix}$$

2) Normalized Laplacian Matrix

The normalized Laplacian matrix L_{norm} is a matrix representation of a graph that adjusts for variations in node degrees, making it easier to compare and analyze graphs with different structures. The normalized Laplacian [6] helps

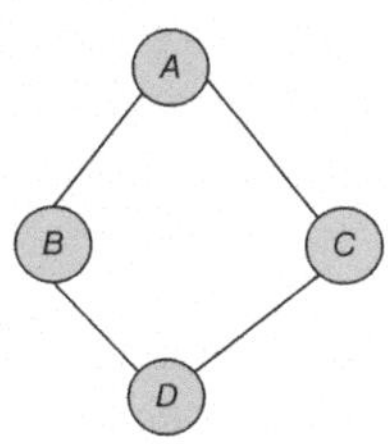

Figure 2.18 Graph for unnormalized Laplacian matrix.

in understanding spectral properties of graphs and is widely used in spectral clustering and graph-based learning tasks.

It is defined as:

$$L_{\text{norm}} = I - D^{\frac{-1}{2}}\, A\, D^{\frac{-1}{2}}$$

where I is the identity matrix, D is the degree matrix (a diagonal matrix with node degrees), A is the adjacency matrix, and $D^{\frac{-1}{2}}$ represents the inverse square root of the degree matrix.

Example

$$D^{\frac{-1}{2}} = \begin{bmatrix} \frac{1}{\sqrt{2}} & 0 & 0 & 0 \\ 0 & \frac{1}{\sqrt{2}} & 0 & 0 \\ 0 & 0 & \frac{1}{\sqrt{2}} & 0 \\ 0 & 0 & 0 & \frac{1}{\sqrt{2}} \end{bmatrix}$$

$$L_{\text{norm}} = I - D^{\frac{-1}{2}}\, A\, D^{\frac{-1}{2}}$$

$$L_{\text{norm}} = \begin{bmatrix} 1 & 0 & 0 & 0 \\ 0 & 1 & 0 & 0 \\ 0 & 0 & 1 & 0 \\ 0 & 0 & 0 & 1 \end{bmatrix} - \begin{bmatrix} \frac{1}{\sqrt{2}} & 0 & 0 & 0 \\ 0 & \frac{1}{\sqrt{2}} & 0 & 0 \\ 0 & 0 & \frac{1}{\sqrt{2}} & 0 \\ 0 & 0 & 0 & \frac{1}{\sqrt{2}} \end{bmatrix} \begin{bmatrix} 0 & 1 & 1 & 0 \\ 1 & 0 & 0 & 1 \\ 1 & 0 & 0 & 1 \\ 0 & 1 & 1 & 0 \end{bmatrix} \begin{bmatrix} \frac{1}{\sqrt{2}} & 0 & 0 & 0 \\ 0 & \frac{1}{\sqrt{2}} & 0 & 0 \\ 0 & 0 & \frac{1}{\sqrt{2}} & 0 \\ 0 & 0 & 0 & \frac{1}{\sqrt{2}} \end{bmatrix}$$

$$L_{\text{norm}} = \begin{bmatrix} 1 & \frac{-1}{2} & \frac{-1}{2} & 0 \\ \frac{-1}{2} & 1 & 0 & \frac{-1}{2} \\ \frac{-1}{2} & 0 & 1 & \frac{-1}{2} \\ 0 & \frac{-1}{2} & \frac{-1}{2} & 1 \end{bmatrix}$$

Properties of Normalized Laplacian

- Useful for graphs with nodes of varying degrees.
- Ensures that the influence of nodes is balanced.
- Widely used in spectral clustering and GNNs.

2.6.1.4 Transition Matrix

In GRL, the transition matrix serves as an effective tool for capturing how information or influence spreads across a network. It defines the probabilities of transitioning between nodes. By encoding the likelihood of movements between nodes, the transition matrix provides insights into the dynamics and connectivity of graphs.

Definition A transition matrix P is a square matrix that represents the probabilities of moving from one node to another within a directed or undirected graph. Each element P_{ij} of the matrix specifies the probability of transitioning from node i to node j. To ensure that P is a stochastic matrix, the sum of each row must be equal to 1. A stochastic matrix is a square matrix used to describe the transitions of a Markov chain. It has the following key properties:

Non-Negative Entries: All elements of a stochastic matrix are non-negative ($P_{ij} \geq 0$ for all i,j).

Row Sum Equals One: The sum of the elements in each row is 1.

The transition matrix P is derived from the adjacency matrix A and the degree matrix D. It is defined as:

$$P = D^{-1} A$$

where A is the adjacency matrix of the graph, $A_{ij} = 1$ if there is an edge from node i to node j, or 0 otherwise; D is the degree matrix, a diagonal matrix where D_{ii} represents the degree (number of edges) of node i; and D^{-1} is the inverse of the degree matrix, used to normalize the adjacency matrix.

This formulation ensures that each row of P sums to 1, making it a row-stochastic matrix.

Consider a simple directed graph with three nodes given in Fig. 2.19.

Adjacency Matrix A:

$$A = \begin{bmatrix} 0 & 1 & 1 \\ 0 & 0 & 1 \\ 1 & 0 & 0 \end{bmatrix}$$

Degree Matrix D:

$$D = \begin{bmatrix} 2 & 0 & 0 \\ 0 & 1 & 0 \\ 0 & 0 & 1 \end{bmatrix}$$

Transition Matrix $P = D^{-1}A$

$$P = \begin{bmatrix} \frac{1}{2} & \frac{1}{2} & 0 \\ 0 & 0 & 1 \\ 1 & 0 & 0 \end{bmatrix}$$

Figure 2.19 Graph used for transition matrix.

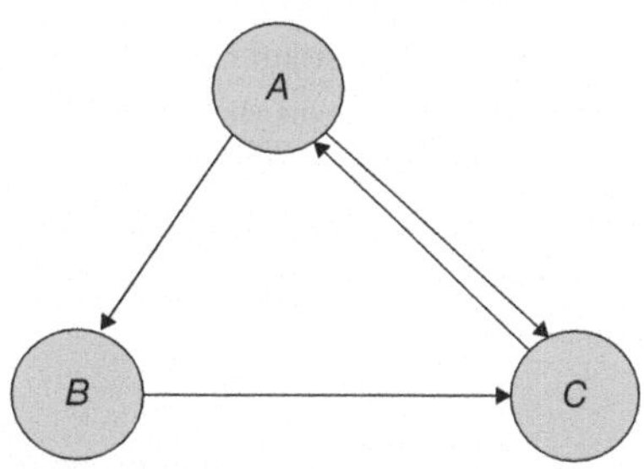

From the above example, we see that from node A, there is a 50% probability of moving to node B and a 50% probability of moving to node C. From node B, the probability of moving to node C is 100%. From node C, the probability of moving to node A is 100%.

2.7 Conclusion

This chapter explored the foundational aspects of graph structures, offering insight into how graphs represent relationships through nodes and edges. Key node-level and structural-level features, such as degree, centrality, clustering coefficients, and motifs, were introduced to illustrate how local and global patterns can be analyzed. At the graph level, properties such as density, modularity, and eccentricity further enrich our understanding of graph behavior. Graph-based representation techniques and matrices such as adjacency, incidence, and Laplacian were discussed to show how graphs can be mathematically encoded. These concepts form the backbone of advanced graph analytics and learning methods, making them essential for any graph-based modeling or data analysis.

References

1 Raul B. Barbosa, Diego Carvalho, Priscila M. V. Lima, Felipe M. G. Franca, A bag of nodes primer on weightless graph classification, ESANN 2021 Proc. Euro. Symp. Artificial Neural Networks, Comput. Intel. Machine Learning. Online event, 6–8 October 2021, i6doc.com publ., ISBN 978287587082-7.

2 K. Khan, "Machine learning methods with node-level features," *Int. J. Multidiscip. Res. (IJFMR)*, vol. 4, no. 6, 2022 www.ijfmr.com.

3 Hejie Cui, Zijie Lu, Pan Li, Carl Yang, On positional and structural node features for graph neural networks on non-attributed graphs, CIKM '22, 2022, Atlanta, GA, USA © 2022 Association for Computing Machinery, ACM.

4 N. Shervashidze, P. Schweitzer, E. J. van Leeuwen, K. Mehlhorn, and K. M. Borgwardt, "Weisfeiler-Lehman Graph Kernels," *J. Mach. Learn. Res*, vol. 12, pp. 2539–2561, 2011.

5 F. Safaei, F. Kashkooei, and S. Fathi, "Graphlets importance ranking in complex networks based on the spectral energy contribution," *Int. J. Comp. Mathematics: Com. Syst. Theory*, vol. 6, no. 1, 2021.

6 M. Rajesh Kannan, N. Kumar, and S. Pragada, "Normalized Laplacians for gain graphs," *Am. J. Combinator. Res.Article*, vol. 1, pp. 20–39, 2022.

3

Overlapping Neighborhood in Graph

In the previous chapter, we examined the fundamental concepts of node-level and graph-level features with their properties. Building on our understanding of graph structures and their fundamental features, this chapter explores the idea of graph neighborhoods, focusing on how nodes interact within local substructures and the significance of neighborhood overlap detection. By analyzing these relationships, we advance deeper understandings into graph connectivity, clustering behavior, and community formation, which are needed for various real-world applications. This chapter begins with the definition and importance of graph neighborhoods in Section 3.1. Section 3.2 explores the properties and similarity measures, followed by methods for detecting neighborhood overlap, and examines some techniques used for detecting neighborhood overlap visualization techniques with challenges in the other sections.

3.1 Definition and Its Importance

Neighborhood overlap in graph representation learning (GRL) measures the similarity between two nodes based on their shared neighbors. Higher neighborhood overlap indicates stronger connectivity, often seen in social networks, citation graphs, and biological networks. Neighborhood overlap is mathematically formulated as

$$\text{Neighborhood overlap} = \frac{\text{Number of common neighbors}}{\text{Total number of unique neighbors, excluding } u \text{ and } v}$$

$$\text{no(G)} = \frac{|N(u) \cap N(v)|}{|N(u) \cup N(v) - \{u, v\}|}$$

where no(G) is the neighborhood overlap between nodes u and v.

Neighborhood overlap in a graph measures the similarity between two nodes based on the proportion of their shared neighbors. It quantifies how strongly two nodes are connected by comparing their common neighbors to their total neighbors. This metric is widely used in link prediction, community detection, and GRL to analyze structural relationships. The main purpose of neighborhood overlap is to determine how nodes are closely connected based on shared neighbors. This will help to estimate the probability of shared neighbors among the nodes. We can also detect unusual nodes, which is an anomaly by indicating low neighborhood overlap [2]. It also supports representation learning and graph embedding by generating important information among the nodes. It helps capture structural relationships, improve node embeddings, and enhance tasks such as link prediction, community detection, and anomaly detection. In the next section, we will discuss the methods for detecting neighborhood overlap.

Consider an author citation graph where nodes represent the author's papers and edges represent citations. If two papers (nodes A and B) cite the same author's papers (nodes D and E), it refers to neighborhood overlap.

In the given graph with $\{A, B, C, D, E, F, G\}$ nodes shown in Fig. 3.1, let node A's neighbors be $\{C, D, E, F\}$ and node B's neighbors be $\{D, E, G\}$, then the common neighbors are $\{D, E\}$, which are considered neighbor nodes that overlap.

$$\text{No(G)} = \frac{2}{5} = 0.4$$

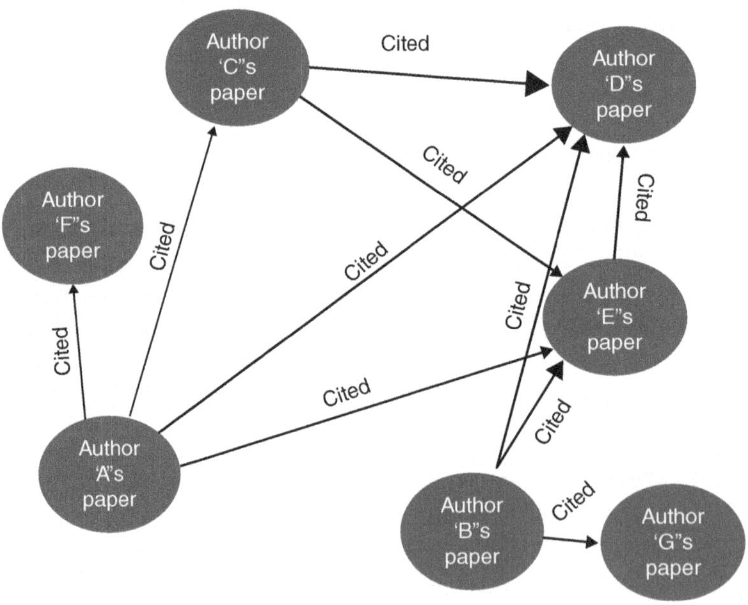

Figure 3.1 Graph for finding common neighborhood.

3.2 Methods for Detecting Neighborhood Overlap

This section deals with the methods for detecting neighborhood overlap. The importance of detecting overlap is to identify the strengths and weaknesses of the connections, measure node similarities, and improve the prediction of future connections and representation learning. There are local and global overlap measures. Local overlap measures are based on the shared neighbors of two directly connected nodes. They focus on capturing small-scale structural patterns within a limited neighborhood. Global overlap measures overlap by considering the connectivity of nodes across the entire graph. They focus on the large-scale connectivity patterns and overall network cohesion. Some of these methods are discussed in detail in the subsections.

3.2.1 Local Overlap Measures

Local overlap measures estimate the similarity between two nodes based on their shared neighbors within a particular area of the graph. These measures help identify strong local connections, detect clusters, and improve link prediction by capturing structural relationships. Their purpose is to understand node-level connection and communication within the graph. Local overlap measures enhance the learning and gaining knowledge of nodes as they deal with the graph locally. This type of measure is efficient and useful for analyzing the nearby and immediate neighbor nodes' behavior, which is applicable for closely connected groups.

3.2.1.1 Jaccard Similarity Measure

Jaccard similarity measure is a technique used to measure the similarity between two nodes based on the ratio of their shared neighbors to their total unique neighbors. The mathematical representation is

$$J(u, v) = \frac{|N(u) \cap N(v)|}{|N(u) \cup N(v)|}$$

where u and v are nodes with $N(u)$ and $N(v)$ as neighboring nodes to each other. The numerator represents the number of common neighbors, and the denominator represents the total number of unique neighbors.

Example ***Author Citation Graph***

Consider the example of an author citation graph where node A paper cited the papers $\{B, C\}$ and node B paper cited papers $\{A, D, E\}$ as shown in Fig. 3.2.

Neighbor nodes for nodes A and B are

$$N(A) = \{B, C\} \text{ and } N(B) = \{A, D, E\}$$

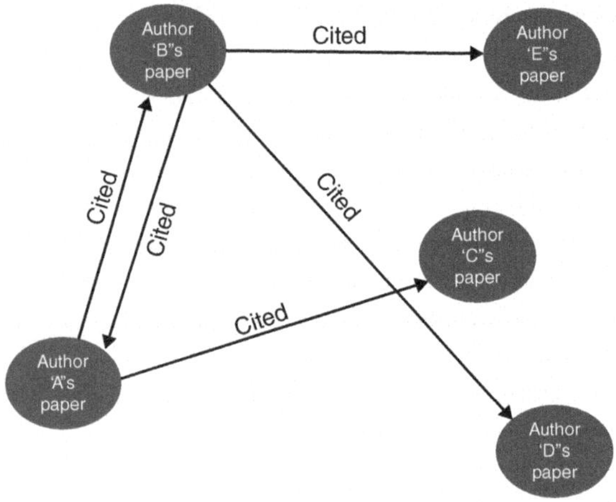

Figure 3.2 Author citation graph for Jaccard similarity measure.

Common neighbors $|N(u) \cap N(v)| = \{B\} = 1$
Total unique neighbors $|N(u) \cup N(v)| = \{A, C, D, E\} = 4$
Jaccard similarity measure can be calculated as

$$J(A, B) = \frac{1}{4} = 0.25$$

From the above, we infer that A and B share 25% neighborhood similarity. A higher Jaccard value indicates that two nodes share a strong structural relationship based on features and structures. A lower Jaccard value indicates weak connectivity, useful in link prediction, clustering, and network analysis.

3.2.1.2 Adamic–Adar Index

The Adamic–Adar (AA) index is a local overlap measure used to quantify the similarity between two nodes in a graph based on their shared neighbors. It improves upon simple neighbor-counting methods by assigning more importance to common neighbors with a lesser number of overall connections (low-degree nodes). The Jaccard similarity treats all common neighbors equally by measuring the ratio of shared to total neighbors, but the AA index assigns higher importance to low-degree common neighbors. The purpose of using this measure is to find the importance of each node for similarity analysis and prediction. It helps in finding stronger relationships among the nodes. The mathematical representation of the AA index is

$$\text{AA}(u, v) = \sum_{x \in N(u) \cap N(v)} \frac{1}{\log(|N(x)|)}$$

where x is the common neighbor of nodes u and v.

Example ***Author Citation Graph***

For the above graph, the neighbor nodes for nodes A and B are

$$N(A) = \{B, C\} \text{ and } N(B) = \{A, D, E\}$$

Common neighbors $|N(u) \cap N(v)| = \{B\} = 1$
Degree of common neighbor B: $|N(B)| = 3$

$$\text{Log}(3) = 1.1$$

$$\text{AA}(A, B) = \sum_{\{B\} \varepsilon N(u) \cap N(v)} \frac{1}{\log(3)} = \frac{1}{1.1} = 0.91$$

3.2.1.3 Resource Allocation Index

The resource allocation (RA) index is a local overlap measure used to find the likelihood of a link forming between two nodes. It follows the principle that common neighbors allocate their influence to connected nodes, with low-degree shared neighbors having a greater impact on the similarity score. Unlike Jaccard similarity, which treats all common neighbors equally, and AA index, which uses a logarithmic scale, RA index directly gives higher weight to low-degree common neighbors. RA index is well-suited for a graph where node connection is inadequate. Jaccard similarity is purely ratio-based (strict neighbor overlap). AA index focuses on reducing the influence of high-degree nodes via logarithm. RA index balances both approaches by giving more weight to low-degree nodes.

The mathematical equation is

$$\text{RA}(u, v) = \sum_{x \varepsilon N(u) \cap N(v)} \frac{1}{|N(x)|}$$

where the inverse of common neighbor ensures that shared neighbors with fewer connections contribute more to the similarity score.

A higher RA value suggests stronger connectivity based on resource-sharing principles.

A lower RA value means that the nodes have few low-degree shared neighbors, making a direct connection less likely.

RA value is useful in sparse graphs, link prediction, and network analysis, where low-degree nodes carry more significance.

Example ***Author Citation Graph***

$$\text{RA}(A, B) = \sum_{\{B\} \varepsilon N(u) \cap N(v)} \frac{1}{3} = \frac{1}{1.1} = 0.33$$

3.2.2 Global Overlap Measures

Global overlap measures evaluate node similarity by examining their connections across the entire graph rather than limiting the scope to immediate neighbors. These measures capture broader structural relationships, detecting long-range dependencies and overall network patterns. They are valuable for identifying community structures, network connectivity, and global influence in larger graphs. Some of the measures are the Katz index, SimRank, PageRank-based similarity, WL kernel, and spectral similarity measures.

3.2.2.1 Katz Index

Katz index is defined as the measure used to find the similarity based on the number of paths between two nodes. In this, the direct or near-connected nodes are given more weightage, as they show more similarity than the indirect or farther-away nodes. This priority enhances the performance of capturing more meaningful information.

The Katz index is highly effective for link prediction, as it considers both direct and indirect paths, capturing global structural information. By assigning higher weights to shorter paths, it balances local and long-range connections, making it more accurate than simple neighbor-based measures. The mathematical representation is

$$\text{K\_sim}(u, v) = \sum_{l=0}^{\infty} d^{l} \cdot |\text{path}_{l}(u, v)\,|$$

where d stands for decay factor, l represents the length of the path, and path represents the number of paths of length l between nodes u and v.

The decay factor reduces the impact of longer paths in the similarity calculation, giving higher importance to shorter connections. The weighting of longer paths in the similarity calculation ensures that shorter paths contribute more, emphasizing that closer nodes are more likely to be similar. A smaller decay factor further diminishes the effect of distant connections, helping the model prioritize local structures over long-range dependencies.

Consider a family relationship graph where nodes represent people and edges represent their relationships. Identify the relationship between people and calculate the Katz index.

In Fig. 3.3, the path of length *1* is the direct path.

Son → Father, Daughter → Father

The indirect path of length 2 shows the relationship of the son/daughter to their grandfather, and the path of length 3 shows the relationship to their great-grandfather.

Son → Father → Father, Daughter → Father → Father

Figure 3.3 Family relationship graph for Katz index.

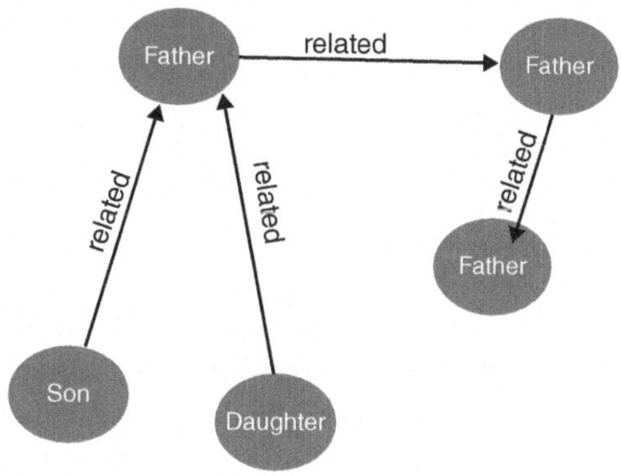

By applying the Katz index formula with decay factor $d = 0.5$ and length as 1,

$$\text{K\_sim(son, father)} = (0.5)^1(1) = 0.5$$

Length up to 2 $\quad \text{K\_sim(son, grandfather)} = (0.5)^1(1) + (0.5)^2(2)$

$$= 0.5 + (0.25)(2) = 1$$

Length up to 3 $\quad \text{K\_sim(son, great} - \text{grandfather)}$

$$= (0.5)^1(1) + (0.5)^2(2) + (0.5)^3(3)$$

$$= 0.5 + (0.25)(2) + 0.125(3) = 1.38$$

Since nodes "son" and "grandfather" have both direct and multiple indirect connections, the Katz index assigns a nonzero similarity score. Shorter paths contribute more, making the score meaningful for predicting potential future links.

The Katz index of 0.5 suggests a moderate but potential connection between nodes. The score of 1 or above 1 gives a stronger connection between nodes. The decay factor reduces the weight of longer paths, ensuring that closer connections have a greater influence on link prediction.

3.2.2.2 SimRank

The Katz index relies on path connectivity, which may not always capture the functional similarity between nodes. So, SimRank measure is used to find overlap. It is a similarity measure based on the principle that two nodes are similar if their neighbors are similar. It recursively computes similarity scores by comparing the neighbors of two nodes rather than direct connections. This measure is useful for link prediction, recommendation systems, and web ranking by capturing structural similarities in a graph. It focuses on similarity based on neighbor relationships, making it useful for identifying nodes with similar roles in a network, even if they are not directly connected. It uses an iterative approach to update similarity scores between node pairs. The formula for calculating the measure is

$$\text{sim\_s}(u, v) = \frac{C}{|N(u)] \cdot |N(v)|} \sum_{x \epsilon N(u), y \epsilon N(v),} \text{sim\_s}(x, y)$$

where sim_s(u,v) is the similarity score between nodes u and v, C is the decay factor (typically between 0 and 1) to reduce the influence of distant neighbors, and $N(u)$ and $N(v)$ are the sets of neighbors of nodes u and v. The summation iterates over all pairs of neighbors x and y of u and v, respectively. This equation captures structural similarity recursively, ensuring that nodes with similar neighborhoods have higher scores. Since SimRank is recursive, the similarity of two nodes depends on the similarity of their neighbors, propagating structural information throughout the graph.

In the graph given in Fig. 3.4, find the similarity between A and C.

- First find the neighbors of A and C.
- Find similarity between neighbors of neighbor A and C.

- Neighbors of A: $\{B, D\} \rightarrow |N(A)| = 2|N(A)| = 2|N(A)| = 2$
- Neighbors of C: $\{B, E\} \rightarrow |N(C)| = 2|N(C)| = 2|N(C)| = 2$

Assume 1 for the nodes that have direct neighbors, otherwise 0. Find the similarity between B (A's neighbor) and its neighbor, and D (A's neighbor) and its neighbor. Also, similarity between D and E is needed since it is the neighbor of C.

- sim_s(B,E) → Measures if B and E are similar (important because A links to B and C links to E).
- sim_s(D,B) → Measures if D and B are similar (A connects to D and C connects to B).
- sim_s(D,E) → Measures if D and E are similar (A connects to D and C connects to E).

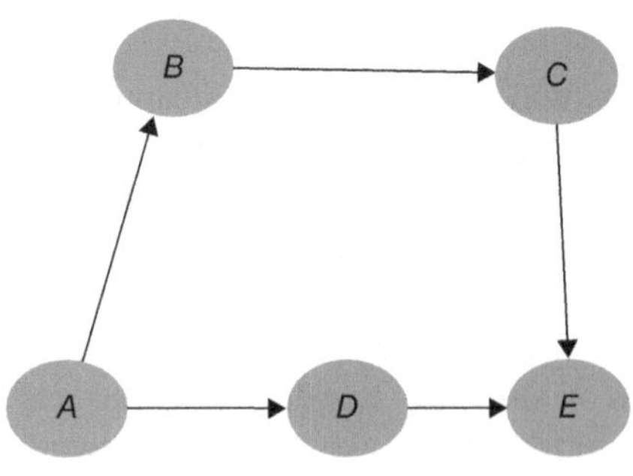

Figure 3.4 Graph for finding similarity.

$$\text{sim\_s}(A, C) = \frac{0.8}{2.2}\text{sim\_s}(B, B) + \text{sim\_s}(B, E)\ \text{sim\_s}(D, B) + \text{sim\_s}(D, E)$$
$$= \frac{0.8}{4}(1 + 0 + 0 + 0.5) = 0.3$$

- The SimRank score of 0.2 indicates a weak similarity between A and C, as they share a common neighbor (B) but are not directly connected. If A and C had more common neighbors, their SimRank score would be higher.

3.2.2.3 PageRank-Based Similarity

PageRank-based similarity measures node similarity [5] by analyzing the importance of nodes based on their connections using a random walk model. It assigns higher similarity scores to nodes that are frequently visited together in the PageRank process. The formula is

$$\text{PR}(u) = \frac{1 - d}{N} \sum_{x \varepsilon N(u), y \varepsilon N(v),} \text{sim\_s}(x, y)$$

3.3 Neighborhood Overlap Visualization Techniques

3.3.1 Venn Diagrams

A Venn diagram is a simple graphical representation used to visualize the overlap or shared elements between two or more sets. In the context of graph neighborhoods, Venn diagrams help illustrate the common neighbors (intersection) between nodes, making it easier to observe the degree of neighborhood overlap. Each circle in the diagram represents a node's neighborhood, and the overlapping area shows the shared nodes or features, providing intuitive insight into local connectivity. It helps in visually analyzing the extent of shared neighbors between two nodes.

3.3.1.1 Neighborhood Overlap Analysis

Venn diagrams are used to visualize overlapping neighborhoods of nodes. This helps researchers understand common relationships or connections between different nodes, especially in tasks such as link prediction and community detection.

3.3.1.2 Subgraph Comparison

When comparing two or more subgraphs (e.g., user clusters in a social network), Venn diagrams can show shared nodes or features, useful in graph alignment and node classification tasks.

3.3.1.3 Feature Distribution Understanding

In attributed graphs, Venn diagrams can highlight common and distinct features across node groups, assisting in feature selection and embedding analysis.

3.3.1.4 Analyzing Multi-Relational or Heterogeneous Graphs

For graphs with multiple types of nodes or edges, Venn diagrams can be used to show shared participation in different relation types, which aids in meta-path analysis and heterogeneous GNN design.

3.3.2 Node-Link Diagrams (Graph Representation)

Node-link diagrams are a type of graphical representation used to visualize graphs, where nodes (or vertices) are shown as dots or circles. Edges (or links) are represented as lines or arrows connecting the nodes. This layout captures the structure of relationships, making it easier to visually understand how entities (nodes) are connected through edges.

3.3.2.1 Usage of Node-Link Diagrams

Understanding Graph Topology Helps visualize the global structure, such as clusters, hubs, and isolated nodes, before applying GNN models.

Analyzing Neighborhood Connectivity Supports identification of 1-hop, k-hop, or ego networks, which are central to message passing in GNNs.

Explaining Model Predictions Used for model interpretability—e.g., to highlight paths or subgraphs a GNN relied on for a prediction (similar to explainable AI).

Visualizing Graph Embeddings Once node embeddings are learned, they can be projected (e.g., using t-SNE or UMAP) and then visualized as a node-link diagram to reveal latent structure or grouping.

Detecting Anomalies or Outliers Outlier nodes often have sparse or unusual links. Node-link diagrams help spot anomalous connections in tasks such as fraud detection or intrusion monitoring.

3.3.3 Heatmaps

Heatmaps are color-coded visual representations used to display intensity, similarity, or importance values across graph components (like nodes or edges). Each cell in a heatmap represents a specific relationship or metric (e.g., similarity score, attention weight [3], or distance) between pairs of nodes or features.

3.3.3.1 Usage of Heatmaps

1) Heatmaps are used to visualize pairwise similarities between nodes.
2) They help in understanding node embedding quality by showing how closely nodes are grouped in the learned vector space.
3) In GATs, heatmaps show attention scores between nodes.
4) They help explain which neighbors had more influence during message aggregation.
5) Heatmaps display Jaccard similarity, AA, or RA scores between nodes.
6) They are useful for detecting overlapping communities [4] or linking prediction tasks.
7) In explainable GRL models, heatmaps highlight the importance of edges or node pairs in making a classification decision (e.g., in GNNExplainer).
8) Heatmaps can reveal sparse or irregular interaction patterns, helping to spot anomalous nodes or edges in graphs such as social or financial networks.

3.3.4 Edge Bundling

Edge bundling is a graph visualization technique used to reduce visual clutter by grouping (or "bundling") edges that share similar paths or directions. Instead of drawing all edges individually, which can result in a chaotic "hairball" visualization, edge bundling consolidates similar edges into smooth, flowing curves.

3.3.4.1 Usage of Edge Bundling

1) In large and dense graphs (e.g., citation networks, social graphs), edge bundling reduces clutter, making node relationships and structures more interpretable.
2) Bundled edges often visually reveal communities or clusters, especially when intra-community connections are tightly bundled and distinct from intercommunity edges.
3) In heterogeneous graphs or multilayer networks, edge bundling helps trace transitions between different types of nodes (e.g., from authors to papers), which is useful in tasks such as knowledge graph traversal.
4) It reduces clutter in large graphs and helps in detecting shared neighborhoods visually.

3.3.5 Graph Embedding and Projection (t-SNE, UMAP)

In GRL, graph embedding transforms nodes, edges, or entire graphs into low-dimensional vector representations while preserving graph structure and properties. To visualize these high-dimensional embeddings, projection techniques such as t-SNE (t-distributed stochastic neighbor embedding) and UMAP (uniform manifold approximation and projection) are used to reduce the vectors to 2D or 3D space.

3.3.5.1 Usage of Graph Embedding and Projection (t-SNE, UMAP)

1) t-SNE and UMAP reveal hidden patterns or natural groupings in node embeddings, helping to identify communities in social, biological, or citation graphs.
2) Outlier nodes or unusual behavior in graph structures become more visible in the projected space, which is useful for fraud detection, intrusion detection, and network forensics.
3) Projection provides a visual means to assess how well an embedding model (e.g., graph convolution networks [GCN], Node2Vec) separates node classes or maintains locality.

3.3.6 Ego Networks (Subgraph Extraction)

An ego network is a local subgraph centered around a specific node (called the "ego"), including the ego node itself and all the nodes it is directly connected to (called "alters"), along with the edges among these alters.

3.3.6.1 Usage of Ego Networks (Subgraph Extraction)

1) Highlights direct and indirect neighbor overlap.
2) Helps in community detection and influence analysis.
3) Helps detect unusual patterns or behaviors around a specific node (e.g., fraudulent behavior in transaction networks).

3.4 Overlapping Neighborhoods in Heterogeneous Graphs

In this section, we introduce the concept of heterogeneous graphs and provide an overview of overlapping neighborhoods. In heterogeneous graphs, where nodes and edges can belong to different types or categories, the concept of overlapping neighborhoods becomes crucial for capturing complex relationships. Unlike homogeneous graphs, where neighborhoods are straightforward, heterogeneous graphs often exhibit nodes that belong to multiple communities or roles simultaneously. This overlap reflects real-world scenarios, such as users in social networks who are part of various groups or proteins in biological networks that interact across different pathways.

Understanding and detecting these overlapping neighborhoods allow us to uncover hidden patterns and multifaceted connections within the graph. By analyzing these overlaps, we can enhance tasks such as community detection, link prediction, and node classification, providing a more nuanced view of the graph's structure and dynamics. In this section, we explore methods for identifying and leveraging overlapping neighborhoods in heterogeneous graphs, along with their challenges and practical applications.

3.4.1 Introduction

A heterogeneous graph is a graph that includes various types of nodes and edges, capturing a wide range of entities and relationships. It is designed to model complex systems such as social networks, biological networks, or knowledge graphs, where different kinds of interactions exist simultaneously. This topic was discussed in Chapter 1.

A heterogeneous graph for a citation graph might include the following nodes: authors (A and B), papers (Paper1 and Paper2), and a journal (journal A). The edges in the graph represent relationships such as "writes," "cites," and "published in." The relationships can include "author writes a paper," "paper is published in a journal," and "paper cites another paper."

In a heterogeneous graph, an overlapping neighborhood refers to the scenario where a node shares common neighbors with multiple other nodes across different types of relationships or node categories. In other words, it captures the intersection of neighborhoods for various node types, highlighting how different entities in the graph can be interconnected through shared connections. This concept is particularly useful for understanding complex interactions in multi-relational networks, such as social networks, biological systems, or knowledge graphs, where nodes can belong to different categories and edges can represent diverse types of relationships.

In the heterogeneous citation graph, we have different types of nodes: authors (A and B), papers (Paper1 and Paper2), and journals (journal A), with edges representing relationships such as "writes," "cites," and "published in." The concept of overlapping neighborhoods in this context refers to situations where a node (like an author or a paper) belongs to multiple communities or groups based on different types of relationships. For example, an Author (A) might write multiple papers that are published in different journals, creating overlapping neighborhoods based on the "writes" and "published in" relationships. If Author A collaborates with different groups of co-authors across these papers, the overlap becomes even more significant. A paper (Paper1) can belong to overlapping neighborhoods if it is cited by other papers across different journals or if it addresses multiple research topics. For instance, if Paper1 is published in journal A but is cited by papers from multiple fields, it highlights an overlap in the research communities. Journals may also show overlaps if they publish papers that are widely cited by other fields, suggesting that they serve as a bridge between different research areas.

Detecting these overlaps can help us identify influential authors, interdisciplinary research areas, or key journals that connect different research communities. This insight is valuable for recommending collaborations, suggesting relevant literature, and understanding the impact of research across different fields.

3.4.2 Methods for Detecting Overlapping Neighborhoods in Heterogeneous Graphs

When it comes to uncovering overlapping neighborhoods in heterogeneous graphs, the challenge lies in effectively capturing the complex interactions between different types of nodes and edges. Unlike homogeneous graphs, where a single type of connection makes the analysis straightforward, heterogeneous graphs require more sophisticated methods to identify overlaps accurately. In this section, I'll walk you through some of the most effective approaches, including meta-path-based techniques that trace indirect relationships and clustering-based methods that group similar nodes based on both structural and attribute similarities.

Detecting overlapping neighborhoods in heterogeneous graphs is important because it helps us find complex connections between different types of nodes and relationships. In these graphs, nodes can represent various things—such as people, products, or proteins—and edges can show different types of relationships between them. By identifying overlapping neighborhoods, we can uncover patterns that might be missed if we only looked at one type of connection at a time. For example, in a social network, this method can help find groups of people who share interests across different platforms. In biological networks, it can show how certain proteins or genes are involved in multiple functions. Understanding these overlaps also makes tasks such as predicting new connections, classifying nodes, and recommending items more accurate and effective.

3.4.2.1 Meta-Path-Based Approaches

The meta-path-based approach offers an effective solution for analyzing heterogeneous graphs—those consisting of various types of nodes and edges that represent different entities and relationships. Traditional methods fail to work in complex graphs. In contrast, the meta-path approach utilizes predefined sequences of node and edge types (referred to as meta-paths) to uncover intricate interactions and meaningful patterns within the graph.

Essentially, a meta-path acts as a blueprint that outlines how different types of nodes can be linked via specific types of edges. For instance, in a citation network, a meta-path such as Author → Paper → Author can indirectly reveal co-authorship relationships. By exploring these paths, we can determine semantic proximity between nodes, which significantly improves the performance of tasks such as link prediction, node classification, and clustering. This method effectively addresses major challenges in heterogeneous graph analysis, including the ability to extract semantic insights beyond mere structural connections and to seamlessly integrate diverse information types. In the sections that follow, we will delve into the principles, techniques, and applications of the meta-path-based approach, emphasizing its role in enhancing our understanding of complex networks.

The meta-path-based approach focuses on understanding relationships in heterogeneous graphs by using predefined paths called meta-paths. A meta-path is a sequence of node types and edge types that describe a specific pattern of connections in the graph. This approach helps in uncovering meaningful patterns that traditional methods might miss, especially in graphs with multiple types of nodes and edges. The step-by-step approach involves identifying sequences of node types and edge types relevant to the analysis. Then count the number of times a meta-path connects different nodes to measure their relationship strength. Use these path counts to compute similarity between nodes for tasks such as link prediction and node classification.

Algorithm: Meta-Path-Based Approach for Similarity Computation in Heterogeneous Graphs

Step 1

Let $G = (V, E, T)$ be the graph with set of nodes V, set of edges E, and set of node and edge types T.

Step 2

Define a meta-path $P = (t_1, r_1, t_2, r_2, \dots, t_k)$, where t_i are node types and r_i are edge types. Two nodes v_i, v_j of the same type $t_1 = t_k$.

Step 3

Construct adjacency matrices for meta-path A_r for each edge type r.

$$A_r(i,j) = \begin{cases} 1 & \text{if there is an edge of type } r \text{ between } v_i \text{ and } v_j \\ 0 & \text{otherwise} \end{cases}$$

Step 4

Compute meta-path-based adjacency matrix

Calculate A_P by multiplying adjacency matrices according to the meta-path P.

$$A_P = A_{r1} \cdot A_{r2} \cdot \cdots \cdot A_{rk}$$

$A_P(i, j)$ indicates the number of meta-path instances between v_i and v_j.

Step 5

Compute similarity score by using either the path count or PathSim for similarity.

a) Path Count Method:

Count the number of meta-path instances between v_i and v_j

$$S(v_i, v_j) = A_P(i,j)$$

b) PathSim (Recommended for Symmetry)

Ensures symmetric similarity for meta-paths

$$S(v_i, v_j) = \frac{2\,X\,A_p(i,j)}{A_p(i,i) + A_p(j,j)}$$

where $A_P(i, i)$ is the meta-path instances starting and ending at v_i. It ensures $S(v_i, v_j) = S(v_j, v_i)$.

Step 6

Output similarity score

Return $S(v_i, v_j)$ for the pair of nodes.

Example ***Author Citation Graph***

Let us take a heterogeneous graph as shown in Fig. 3.5 in a research setting with three types of nodes: Authors (A, B), Papers (1), and Cites (A), and two types of edges: "writes" (Author A writes the Paper 1 and Paper 2, Author B writes Paper 2 and Paper 3) and "published in" (Paper 1 published in Journal A).

One meta-path to be considered is Author A writes Paper 1 and Paper 1 is written by Author B (Author → Paper → Author). This represents a co-authorship relationship. If two authors are connected by this path, they have co-authored a paper.

Figure 3.5 Heterogeneous graph for finding meta-path.

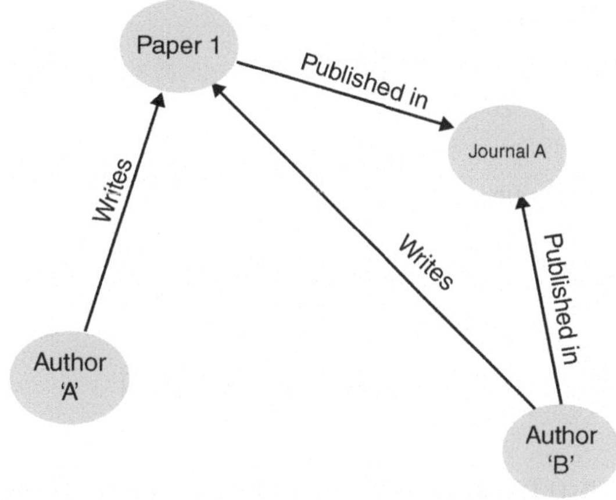

The other meta-path to be considered is Author A writes Paper 1 and Paper 1 is published in Journal A (Author → Paper → Journal). This represents an author's publishing pattern in different journals. This path can help find which journals an author frequently publishes in.

Our goal is to find the similarity score between two authors (A and B) based on the meta-path: (Author→Paper→Author)

Step 1

Define adjacency matrices

a) Author–Paper Matrix A_{writes}: This matrix represents if an author has written a paper.
   Adjacency matrix for Author–Paper (meaning Author writes a paper) meta-path is

$$A_{\text{writes}} = \begin{bmatrix} 1 & 1 & 0 \\ 0 & 1 & 1 \end{bmatrix}$$

   $A_{\text{writes}}(i, j) = 1$ if author A_i wrote paper P_j.

b) Paper–Paper Matrix (the meaning is one paper cites another paper) is

$$A_{\text{cites}} = \begin{bmatrix} 0 & 1 & 0 \\ 0 & 0 & 1 \\ 0 & 0 & 0 \end{bmatrix}$$

$A_{\text{cites}}(i,j) = 1$ if paper P_i cites paper P_j.

Step 2

Compute meta-path-based adjacency matrix A_P

$$A_P = A_{writes} \text{ X } A_{cites} \text{ X } A^T_{\text{writes}}$$

Calculate $A^T{}_{\text{writes}}$

$$A^T{}_{\text{writes}} = \begin{bmatrix} 1 & 0 \\ 1 & 1 \\ 0 & 1 \end{bmatrix}$$

Compute A_{cites} X $A^T{}_{\text{Write}}$

$$\begin{bmatrix} 0 & 1 & 0 \\ 0 & 0 & 1 \\ 0 & 0 & 0 \end{bmatrix} \text{X} \begin{bmatrix} 1 & 0 \\ 1 & 1 \\ 0 & 1 \end{bmatrix} = \begin{bmatrix} 1 & 1 \\ 0 & 1 \\ 0 & 0 \end{bmatrix}$$

$$A_p = \begin{bmatrix} 1 & 1 & 0 \\ 0 & 1 & 1 \end{bmatrix} \text{X} \begin{bmatrix} 1 & 1 \\ 0 & 1 \\ 0 & 0 \end{bmatrix} = \begin{bmatrix} 1 & 2 \\ 0 & 1 \end{bmatrix}$$

$A_P(i,j)$ indicates the number of meta-path instances between A_i and A_j.

$A_P(1,2) = 2$ suggests there are two indirect co-authorship paths between A_1 and A_2.

Step 3

Compute similarity score using PathSim

$$S(A_1, A_2) = \frac{2\,X\;A_p(1,2)}{A_p(1,1) + A_p(2,2)} = \frac{2\,X\,2}{1+1} = \frac{4}{2} = 2$$

The above similarity score of two indicates a significant level of indirect co-authorship between A_1 and A_2 based on the defined meta-path. Higher scores imply stronger relationships.

3.4.2.2 Clustering-Methods

In heterogeneous graphs, where multiple types of nodes and edges exist, detecting overlapping neighborhoods is crucial for understanding complex relationships. Unlike traditional clustering methods that assign each node to a single cluster, overlapping clustering allows nodes to belong to multiple communities, reflecting real-world interactions. Clustering-based methods help group similar nodes while capturing the shared relationships among different node types. Clustering method is needed as the heterogeneous graphs are very complex and the nodes naturally belong to multiple groups.

3.4.2.3 Approach: Clustering for Overlapping Neighborhoods

3.4.2.4 Soft Clustering Methods

Soft clustering methods allow nodes to belong to multiple clusters with different degrees of membership, making them ideal for detecting overlapping neighborhoods in heterogeneous graphs. Unlike hard clustering, where each node is assigned to a single group, soft clustering assigns probabilities or fuzzy memberships to multiple clusters.

3.4.2.5 Fuzzy C-Means

Fuzzy C-means is a soft clustering algorithm that assigns each data point to multiple clusters with different probabilities, rather than placing it into a single cluster. It is particularly useful for detecting overlapping neighborhoods in heterogeneous graphs.

Algorithm Steps

1) **Initialize Cluster Centers**
   - Choose c cluster centers randomly.
   - Define a fuzzy membership matrix U, where each entry u_{ij} represents the degree of membership of node i in cluster j.
2) **Compute Cluster Centers**
   - Update the centroid of each cluster based on the membership values.
     - The new cluster centroid v_j is calculated as: $v_j = \sum u_{ij} m x_i$, where x_i is the feature vector of node i, u_{ij} is the membership value of node i in cluster j, and m is the fuzziness parameter (typically set to 2).
3) **Update Membership Values**
   - The membership matrix is updated using the formula: $u_{ij} = \sum c (d(x_i,v_k)$ $d(x_i,v_j))$, where $d(x_i,v_j)$ is the distance between node i and cluster j.
4) **Check Convergence**
   - If the difference between old and new membership values is below a threshold (ε), the algorithm stops.
   - Otherwise, go back to step 2 and repeat.

Assigns membership scores to nodes based on similarity to cluster centers.

A node has a higher probability of belonging to a cluster if it is closer to the centroid.

Example

An author writing in multiple research domains (e.g., AI and cybersecurity) will have a membership proportion in both clusters.

Overlapping K-Means

Extends traditional K-means by allowing nodes to belong to multiple clusters.

Uses a soft assignment function to distribute nodes based on similarity.

Example

A paper citing both AI and healthcare literature will have a presence in both clusters.

3.5 Case Studies on Neighborhood Overlap Detection in Real-World Scenarios

Below are brief case studies highlighting the application of graph neighborhood across various domains.

3.5.1 Application of Graph Neighborhood in Healthcare

3.5.1.1 Introduction

In recent years, healthcare data has evolved into complex, interconnected structures that go beyond traditional tabular formats. These intricate relationships—among patients, diseases, symptoms, medical procedures, and healthcare providers—can be naturally modeled using graph structures. Within this framework, the concept of a graph neighborhood plays a critical role in uncovering localized interactions and patterns within healthcare networks.

A graph neighborhood refers to the set of nodes directly or indirectly connected to a given node, such as patients linked through similar symptoms, doctors connected via shared patients, or medical facilities interacting through referrals. By analyzing 1-hop, k-hop, ego, or attention-based neighborhoods, healthcare professionals and researchers can detect disease spread patterns in epidemiological networks by observing local patient clusters, identify comorbidity risks by studying the neighborhood of a particular diagnosis node, recommend personalized treatments by identifying similar patient neighborhoods in electronic health records, enhance early diagnosis through symptom similarity neighborhoods, track hospital-acquired infections by analyzing spatial–temporal neighborhoods in hospital ward networks, and detect fraud or anomalous behavior in healthcare insurance networks using structural overlap of suspicious nodes.

For example, in clinical decision support systems, neighborhoods of a patient node can provide insight into similar medical histories, enabling more accurate diagnoses or drug prescriptions. In pandemic modeling, overlapping neighborhood analysis helps identify vulnerable communities or superspreading clusters.

Thus, graph neighborhood modeling offers localized, interpretable insights that are essential for decision-making in modern healthcare systems. It bridges the gap between raw relational data and actionable medical knowledge, enabling more precise, connected, and patient-centered care.

3.5.1.2 Healthcare: Community-Based Anomaly Detection in COVID-19 Spread

Accurate detection of anomalous COVID-19 spread patterns across different districts is vital for effective public health interventions. But there are some challenges in capturing the complex community structures within districts and identifying subtle anomalies that may not be evident through traditional analysis. Francisquini et al. (2022) and the co-authors addressed the challenge of detecting anomalies in the spread of COVID-19 across different districts [1]. Traditional anomaly detection methods often overlook the community structures inherent in such data, potentially missing subtle but significant deviations in disease spread patterns.

Here's a detailed explanation of the solution proposed by Francisquini et al. (2022) in their study on community-based anomaly detection using spectral graph filtering, particularly applied to COVID-19 spread analysis. They introduced SpecF, a novel anomaly detection algorithm that incorporates community structures into the Laplacian matrix. This method enhances the detection of anomalies by considering the underlying community structures, leading to more accurate identification of unusual COVID-19 spread patterns. This approach enhances the detection of anomalies by considering both the attributes of nodes (e.g., COVID-19 case counts) and the community affiliations within the network.

In the methodology, the graph is constructed with each district represented as a node in the graph, and edges are established between nodes if the corresponding districts are within a 5 km radius, with weights inversely proportional to the distance between them. The Louvain method is employed to identify communities within the graph, grouping districts with similar characteristics or interactions. A signal is assigned to each node, representing the weekly variation in COVID-19 cases. This is calculated as the ratio of new cases in the current week to those in the previous week. An extended Laplacian matrix, incorporating community structures, is constructed. A low-pass filter is applied to the graph signals, attenuating high-frequency components that may represent noise or anomalies. The cutoff frequency for the filter is determined based on the number of detected communities.

Finally, anomaly detection is carried out by computing the difference between the original and filtered signals for each node. Nodes exhibiting significant deviations from their community norms are flagged as potential anomalies. Thresholds for anomaly detection are set using statistical measures (mean and standard deviation) within each community. SpecF successfully identified districts with anomalous increases in COVID-19 cases, even when neighboring districts showed declining trends. Approximately 95% of the detected anomalies were characterized by a district's case count deviating significantly from its community's trend. The method also revealed temporal patterns, where anomalies in one district were often preceded by anomalies in neighboring districts in the previous one or two weeks, suggesting potential pathways of virus dissemination.

By integrating community structures, SpecF provides a more nuanced detection of anomalies that might be overlooked by traditional methods. The algorithm effectively identifies both prominent and subtle anomalies without requiring extensive parameter tuning. While demonstrated on COVID-19 data, SpecF's framework is adaptable to various domains where community structures are present.

3.5.2 Case Studies on Social Networks: Overlapping User Communities and Friend Recommendations

The next case study is on social networks focusing on overlapping user communities and friend recommendations. In large social platforms such as Facebook, users participate in multiple communities (e.g., work, family, school). Traditional community detection fails to reflect this overlapping nature, which leads to incomplete network insights, Twitter wants to suggest meaningful "people to follow" recommendations. Relying only on mutual friends misses key latent connections.

Traditional community detection methods in network analysis often partition networks into disjoint groups, assuming each node belongs to a single community. However, in real-world social networks, individuals typically participate in multiple communities simultaneously, such as family, work, and social circles. Recognizing this, Kelley et al. emphasized the need for models that allow for overlapping communities to more accurately reflect the complex structures of social networks. The authors identify several key challenges in detecting overlapping communities. There are many existing methods that lack a rigorous definition of what constitutes an overlapping community, leading to inconsistencies in detection. Previous algorithms often rely on intuitive reasoning rather than empirical evidence to justify the presence of overlapping communities.

Assessing the quality and significance of overlapping communities remains difficult due to the absence of standardized evaluation metrics. To address these challenges, the authors proposed the axiomatic framework with a minimal set of axioms that overlapping communities should satisfy. Each community should form a connected subgraph. Communities should be locally optimal concerning a defined density metric, meaning no addition or removal of a single node can improve the community's density. They also introduced the modified iterative scan algorithm to identify communities that meet the proposed axioms. This involves

- Starting with a seed set of nodes.
- Iteratively adding or removing nodes to optimize the community's density.
- Allowing nodes to be part of multiple communities, facilitating overlap.

Applying their method to a large-scale, real-world communication network, the authors demonstrate that the presence of overlapping communities is not just a theoretical construct but is empirically observable in real networks. Their approach uncovers community structures that traditional disjoint methods fail to detect, highlighting the importance of considering overlap.

Overlapping nodes often play crucial roles in maintaining the structural integrity of multiple communities, underscoring their significance in network dynamics.

3.6 Conclusion

In this chapter, we explored the essential concepts surrounding graph neighborhoods and their overlapping structures, which form the backbone of many graph-based analytical tasks. We began by understanding various types of graph neighborhoods—including direct, k-hop, ego, attention-based, and structural neighborhoods such as graphlets and motifs. Through both local and global similarity measures such as Jaccard, SimRank, and Katz index, we highlighted how neighborhood overlap can be quantitatively assessed.

We also discussed effective visualization techniques such as Venn diagrams, heatmaps, and graph embeddings, which help in interpreting overlap intuitively. In heterogeneous graphs, detecting overlapping neighborhoods becomes even more significant and complex, demanding specialized approaches such as meta-path and clustering-based methods. Real-world case studies, especially in healthcare, demonstrated the practical impact of these concepts in fields such as anomaly detection, disease spread analysis, and community-based interventions. Altogether, the chapter reinforces the importance of neighborhood structures and their overlaps in unlocking deeper insights from graph data across various domains.

References

1 R. Francisquini, A. C. Lorena, and M. C. V. Nascimento, "Community-based anomaly detection using spectral graph filtering," *Appl. Soft Comput.*, vol. 118, March 2022, doi: 10.1016/j.asoc.2022.108489.

2 A. Aytac and E. Kilic, "The common-neighbourhood of a graph," *Boletim da Sociedade Paranaense de Matematica*, vol. 35, no. 1, p. 23, 2015, doi: 10.5269/bspm.v35i1.22464.

3 A. Hassani, S. Walton, J. Li, L. Shen, and H. Shi, "Neighborhood attention transformer," *Comp. Vis. Pattern Recognit.*, doi: 10.1109/CVPR52729.2023.00599.

4 S. Kelley, M. K. Goldberg, K. Mertsalov, M. Magdon-Ismail, and W. Wallace, "Overlapping communities in social networks," *Int. J. Soc. Comput. Cyber-Phys. Syst.*, vol. 1, no. 2, pp. 135–159, 2011, doi: 10.1504/IJSCCPS.2011.044171.

5 C. Tulu and U. Orhan, "PageRank based semantic similarity measure on a graph based Turkish WordNet, International Conference on Computer Science and Engineering (UBMK), IEEE," 2017, doi: 10.1109/UBMK.2017.8093438.

Part II

Core Graph Representation Learning

4

Graph Machine Learning

Traditional machine learning (ML) methods process data in tabular, image, or text formats without explicitly modeling relationships. Algorithms such as decision trees, neural networks, and support vector machines are used to detect patterns, classify data, and make predictions. Feature engineering or statistical methods are used to extract patterns. Connections between data points are inferred rather than directly represented. This type of process can work properly for independent data, but it is not applicable for analyzing complex relationships in networks or social structures.

Also, machine learning with deep learning can handle only structured data and needs a lot of labeled data points to identify the patterns. They fail to learn from interrelated and complex data more effectively. Graph machine learning (GML) overcomes these limitations by using graph structures, allowing models to learn from interconnected data more effectively. In this chapter, we will discuss an overview of GML with its usage, techniques, and case studies.

4.1 Introduction to GML

GML is a field of ML that focuses on evolving techniques and algorithms to process and analyze data represented as graphs [1]. In graphs, data is structured as nodes (entities) and edges (relationships between entities), capturing both the features of individual nodes and the relationships among them. GML uses this relational structure to perform predictive, descriptive, and generative tasks effectively. GML is essential because many real-world problems involve data that is inherently structured as graphs, where relationships between entities play a critical role in understanding and solving complex tasks. Traditional ML models are not designed to handle such interconnected data. GML gives a visual representation for analysis. The core objective of GML is to perform tasks such as node classification, link prediction, graph classification, and clustering that are unique to graph-structured data. GML techniques are preferable for understanding complex systems.

The core concepts needed for GML are graph theory, representation learning methods, and message-passing concepts for finding out the relationships among the data. Techniques such as graph neural networks (GNNs) and graph embeddings are involved in learning data from structured graph data.

4.1.1 Key Features of GML

- **Graph Representation:** A graph uses nodes and edges to represent data with its relationships among other data. This is essential for working on complex structures.
- **Relational Learning:** GML exploits both the features of individual nodes and the structural relationships among them. This enables GML to do relational learning.
- **Adaptability:** It can handle any type of data such as spatial–temporal data types, heterogeneous data types, and dynamic data.

4.1.2 GML vs Traditional ML

Here, we explore how GML differs from traditional ML approaches and why using relationships between data points can lead to more powerful and insightful models, especially in complex, interconnected systems. The comparison is shown in Table 4.1.

While traditional ML is effective for independent data, GML offers a deeper understanding by modeling relationships within the data. This makes GML especially valuable for tasks involving networks, hierarchies, or complex interactions.

Table 4.1 Graph machine learning (GML) vs traditional machine learning.

Traditional Machine Learning	Graph Machine Learning
Data represented as vectors or matrices as tables	Data represented as nodes and edges as graphs
Data are treated independently	Data are interrelated
Learns and gathers information from the features of the data only	Learns and gathers information from the features and structure of the data
Relationship between data points is not handled	Relationship between data points is considered
Techniques are classification, regression, clustering	Techniques are node classification, link prediction, graph classification, community detection
Can handle complex data with huge computation cost	Handles complex data easily and effectively

4.2 Types of Tasks in GML

Various types of learning tasks in GML include supervised and unsupervised tasks. The supervised task is node classification, where the features of the nodes are used to predict the label of the node; the nodes with similar patterns are grouped as similar nodes in the network/graph. This type of task is used to find people with similarity globally, and the node with a different type of label can also be detected. The link prediction task focuses on connecting edges to find the relationship between two nodes directly and among different nodes indirectly. Graph classification can be used to categorize different graphs and is useful in forming a community of similar graphs.

4.2.1 Supervised GML Tasks

Supervised GML involves training a model on labeled graph data, where each node, edge, or entire graph is associated with a label. The model maps inputs to correct outputs based on patterns in the training data. The architecture of the supervised GML model is given in Fig. 4.1.

The supervised GML process starts by getting input from the dataset, images, or text document. The graph is constructed and represented by converting the graph data into numerical representations. The next step is to train the model using a supervised GNN-based model. The produced output might be based on classification or prediction. Some of the evaluation metrics such as accuracy, F1-score (classification), and area under curve-receiver operating characteristic (AUC-ROC) (link prediction) are used to evaluate whether the model works well.

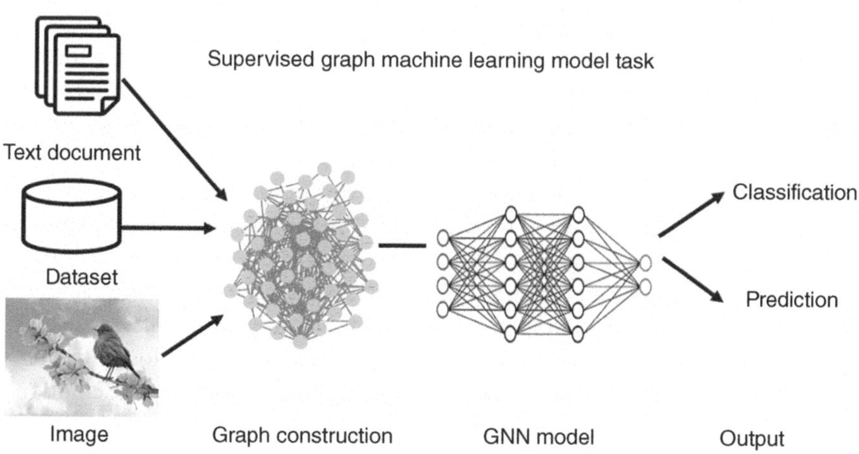

Figure 4.1 Supervised graph machine learning model task.

Example ***Predicting Students' Exam Performance***
Consider a student graph where the students' details are represented in nodes, and the relationship between them, such as students studying in the same course, having similar interests, and the like, are represented in edges. For predicting students' exam performance, we must consider some of the students' attributes such as study hours, previous exam scores, attendance percentage, use of study materials, engagement in the class, and so on. The supervised learning graph has labels "pass" or "fail" as target variables for each student. To predict whether a student will pass (1) or fail (0), we can use GNNs, which learn node embeddings from the graph structure.

Below are the main supervised tasks in GML:

A) Node classification
B) Link prediction
C) Edge classification
D) Graph/subgraph classification

4.2.1.1 Node Classification

Node classification is the fundamental task in supervised GML, where the goal is to assign a category or label to each node in a graph based on its features and the structure of the graph. It allows models to learn from both node attributes and graph structure, making it a powerful tool for tasks that involve interconnected data. By using GNNs, the model can effectively capture relationships between nodes, improving classification accuracy over traditional methods that ignore graph structure. This is particularly useful in applications such as social network analysis, fraud detection, recommendation systems, and biology (e.g., classifying proteins in a molecular network).

Various algorithms are used for the node classification process. They include graph convolution networks (GCN) to aggregate node information from neighbors. They apply a spectral-based method that uses eigenvalues of the graph Laplacian for representation to capture the structural pattern. Also, the message-passing technique is used to update the node information based on its neighbors. GAT algorithm is used to assign different importance weights to neighboring nodes while aggregating features using GCN. Inductive learning is done by another algorithm, GraphSAGE, which samples the neighborhood nodes for generating embeddings. Graph representation learning algorithms are used to represent the graph data in a latent space, and the techniques used for embedding are DeepWalk and Node2Vec. These techniques generate vector representations for nodes.

In supervised node classification, the model is trained on a graph where some nodes already have known labels (training data), and the objective is to predict labels for unclassified nodes (test data). The process involves the following steps:

1) Construct a graph and represent the features.
2) Classify the nodes using models such as GNNs, GCNs, GATs, or GraphSAGE. These models aggregate information from neighboring nodes to learn meaningful node embeddings.
3) Train the model using a supervised learning approach, meaning we have a set of labeled nodes and their corresponding labels.
4) Once the model is trained, it can classify new (unlabeled) nodes.
5) Evaluate the performance using metrics such as accuracy, F1-score, precision, and recall.

Example ***User Classification in a Recommendation System***
In an e-commerce platform (e.g., Amazon, Netflix, Spotify), users interact with various products, movies, or songs. The platform wants to classify the users as users who like the product based on

1) Past interactions (history of liked/disliked products).
2) User attributes (age, preferences, browsing history).
3) Social connections (friends who have interacted with the product).

We can use the graph to represent the users and products as nodes, where each user is the customer on the platform, the product is the item available for recommendation, and their relationships (likes, reviews, or social influence) form edges. User–user edge represents users who are friends or people who have similar tastes. User–product edges represent users who have viewed the product, or liked or rated the product. Product–product edge represents that both products are of similar brand and category, and have similar features. This is illustrated in Fig. 4.2.

The picture in Fig. 4.2 illustrates three types of node classification: user–user friendships in Black, user–product interactions (indicating users who liked a product) in gray, and product–product connections (representing products of the same brand) in gray lines.

Real-World Applications of Node Classification

- **Social Networks:** Identifying fake accounts or categorizing users based on interests.
- **E-Commerce:** Predicting customer preferences based on past purchases.
- **Finance and Fraud Detection:** Detecting fraudulent transactions in banking networks.
- **Healthcare:** Classifying proteins in biological networks for drug discovery.

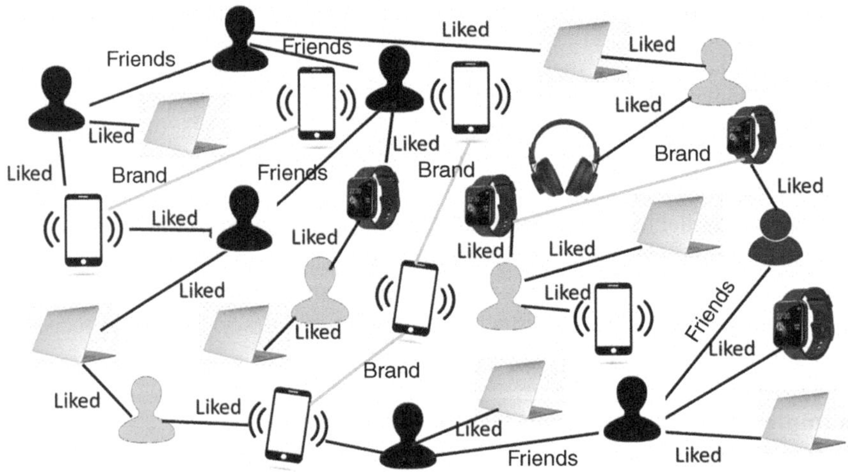

Figure 4.2 Social network.

4.2.1.2 Link Prediction

Link prediction is a fundamental task in supervised GML [2], where the goal is to predict the likelihood of a future or missing connection (edge) between two nodes in a graph. This is widely used in social network expansion, recommendation systems, fraud detection, and biological network analysis. Given a graph with existing relationships, a model learns patterns from the known edges and then predicts whether an edge should exist between two nodes that are currently not connected.

The algorithms used in link prediction are GNNs that use node embedding and edge features to predict missing links. Node embedding is used to convert nodes into a vector representation to find missing links. Autoencoders (GAE/VGAE) are used to encode features into latent representations. Predicting edge existence is done by the GCN algorithm by using similarity measures. The GAT algorithm is also used to assign different importance weights to neighbors while learning node embedding for link prediction.

In supervised learning for link prediction, the model is trained on labeled data where existing edges (connections) are marked as positive examples (1) and nonexistent edges as negative examples (0). The process involves several steps:

1) Represent the data as graph $G = (V,E,X)$, where V is the set of nodes, E is the set of edges, and X is the node and edge features.
2) Represent each pair of nodes using various structural and attribute-based features since ML models require numerical features. For example, in node embedding, each node is transformed into a dense vector representation.

Some similarity metrics such as Jaccard coefficient and AA index are used to estimate the likelihood of a link.

3) Train the ML model by using a binary classification technique where existing edges are represented as 1 and missing or non-existing edges as 0.
4) Predict the probability of connection between nodes after the model is trained.
5) Evaluate the performance using metrics such as accuracy, F1-score, precision, and recall to ensure correct prediction.

Example ***Link Prediction in Recommendation System***
In the same e-commerce platform example (e.g., Amazon, Flipkart), link prediction can be used to recommend products to users based on their interactions, purchases, and preferences. In the graph given in Fig. 4.3.

- User A and User B are friends and have similar characteristics (since in the graph, they are grouped together).
- User A liked mobile phones and laptops.
- User B liked laptop and smartwatch C.
- The nonexistent link between User A and smartwatch node C.

The model predicts that User A will also buy Product (Smartwatch) C based on User B's similar behavior.

Real-World Applications of Link Prediction

- **Social Networks:** Predicting new friendships or professional connections on LinkedIn or Facebook.
- **E-Commerce Recommendation Systems:** Suggesting products to users by predicting future interactions based on browsing and purchase history.

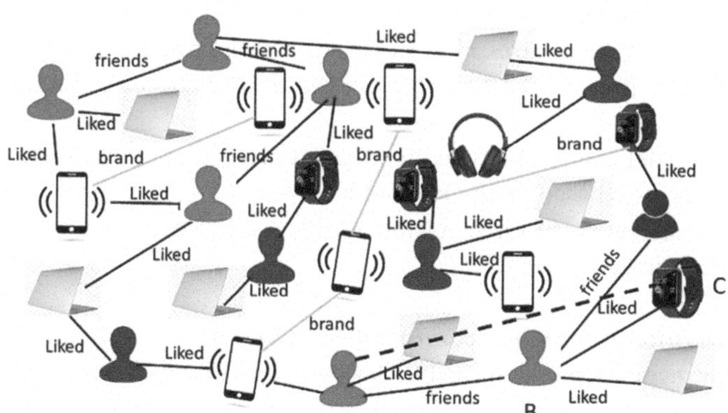

Figure 4.3 Link prediction in recommendation system.

- **Fraud Detection in Financial Networks:** Identifying suspicious relationships between users or transactions in banking networks.
- **Biological Networks:** Predicting protein–protein interactions in drug discovery research.

4.2.1.3 Edge Classification

Edge classification in supervised GML is a critical task where the goal is to predict the type or existence of connections (edges) between nodes in a graph. This technique is widely used in social network analysis, recommendation systems, fraud detection, and biological network modeling applications, where relationships between entities need to be categorized based on existing patterns. Unlike link prediction, which determines whether an edge exists or not, edge classification assigns a specific label to an existing or potential connection.

In supervised learning, the model is trained on a graph dataset where edges are labeled. Each edge has features derived from the two connected nodes and the structural properties of the graph. The model learns to classify new edges based on these patterns. The process involves several steps.

1) It begins with feature extraction, where node features (e.g., user preferences in a recommendation system or molecular properties in a chemical graph) and edge features (e.g., interaction frequency and similarity scores) are gathered. These features are then transformed into numerical representations using node embeddings (e.g., GNNs, Node2Vec) or adjacency matrices. The labeled dataset consists of edges categorized into different types (e.g., "friend" or "colleague" in social networks, "purchase" or "view" in e-commerce).
2) It computes edge embeddings using concatenation, element-wise addition, or the dot product of node embeddings.
3) A ML model, such as a logistic regression classifier, SVM, or deep learning–based GNN, is then trained on this data.
4) During training, the model optimizes a loss function, such as cross-entropy loss for classification tasks, to learn the best way to distinguish between different edge types.
5) Once trained, the model can predict whether a given edge exists or classify it into predefined categories based on the learned patterns.
6) Evaluation metrics such as accuracy, precision, recall, and F1-score are used to assess model performance.

Example ***Edge Classification in a Recommendation System***

In e-commerce recommendation systems, edge classification is used to categorize user–product interactions. Instead of just predicting whether an edge exists (link prediction), edge classification determines the type of interaction (e.g., click, add to cart, purchase, review).

Consider a graph G where users are represented as nodes indicating customers who shop on the platform, and products are also represented as nodes representing items available for purchase. The edge label categories are liked, reviewed, and purchased. Each edge (User → Product) represents a past interaction, and the goal is to predict the edge label for new interactions. Node features and edge features are used in this model. User features can be taken as purchase history, purchase pattern, and demographic details. Product features include brand, category, and price range. Edge features include frequency of past interactions between the user and product, time spent on the product page before making a purchase, and user engagement with similar products. In the figure 4.3, we see that the brand is the label that links the products, specifically mobile phones, and it can be used to classify the edges based on their similarities.

4.2.1.4 Graph/Subgraph Classification

Graph classification is a key task in GML, where each graph is assigned a label instead of assigning a label to each node. This is used for analyzing the entire graph structure, and based on the similar patterns, the graphs are classified. Graphs give meaningful information about the real-world entities. Graph classification helps analyze entire graphs instead of individual nodes. Pooling techniques are essential for transforming node-level embeddings into graph-level features. Instead of analyzing individual nodes, graph classification captures overall graph patterns, making it useful for tasks such as molecular property prediction or fraud detection. The steps in the graph classification process shown in Fig. 4.4 involve

1) Represent graph G=(V,E) where V is the set of nodes and E is the set of edges. Each node and each edge are associated with features/attributes.
2) The structural features are extracted by graph kernels or deep learning–based embedding techniques.
3) For graph-level representation, graph pooling is needed to aggregate node embeddings.

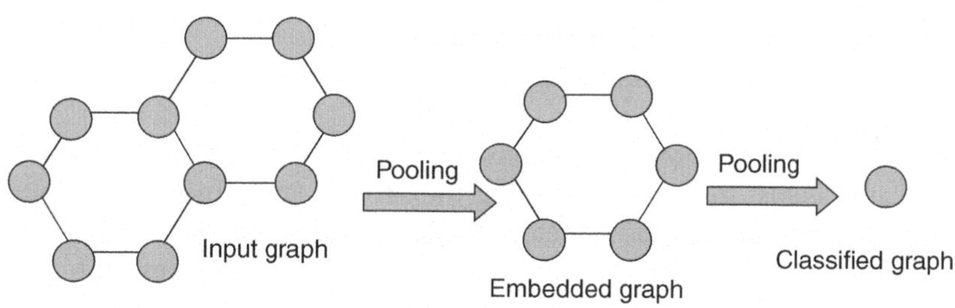

Figure 4.4 Graph classification process.

4) The model is trained by a ML classifier on the embedded graph to predict the graph label.
5) The performance of the prediction model is evaluated by performance metrics.

Example ***Drug Discovery and Toxicity Prediction***
Consider the molecular structure of a chemical compound with nodes representing atoms (such as oxygen, hydrogen, carbon) and edges representing chemical bonds (single, double, or triple). The idea is to predict toxicity based on whether the chemical compound is harmful in its molecular structure. This is useful in the pharmaceutical domain for reducing the risks [4].

Graph classification in GML is a powerful approach to predict molecular properties, such as toxicity, drug efficacy, and biochemical activity. The process involves transforming molecular structures into graphs, applying GNNs, and classifying molecules into categories (e.g., toxic vs nontoxic).

Node feature extraction (such as element type, atomic number) and edge feature extraction (such as bond type, length) are carried out to train the model using GNN.

Once molecules are represented as graphs, the next step is to learn graph embeddings using GNN. Graph embeddings encode molecular structure into vector representations. The most commonly used GNN architectures for drug discovery include GCN, GAT, and message passing neural networks (MPNNs).

Real-World Application of Graph Classification

1) **Healthcare and Bioinformatics**
   In the healthcare system, the medical images, such as magnetic resonance imaging (MRI) or computed tomography (CT) scans, can be converted into graphs where nodes represent regions of interest (e.g., brain regions in an MRI [Magnetic Resonance Imaging] scan) and edges represent spatial or functional connections between these regions. The idea is to classify the graph based on whether the patient has the disease or not.
2) **Fraud Detection in Financial Transactions**
   In financial transactions, a fraudulent transaction using different accounts can occur.
   A fraudster makes multiple transactions across different accounts using stolen credit card details. Instead of analyzing transactions independently, a GNN classifies transaction graphs to detect fraud. A graph is built where nodes represent credit cards, users, merchants, and transactions. Edges represent relationships such as shared devices, frequent transactions, or location-based similarities.

4.2.2 Unsupervised GML Tasks

4.2.2.1 Introduction

In supervised GML, the graph is a labeled graph with nodes and edges being labeled. Even though supervised GML is powerful, it has challenges in obtaining labeled data; large-scale graphs require a huge labeling process, which is not advisable, and the model may face issues with unseen data. To overcome these challenges, unsupervised GML is used, where models learn graph representations without explicit labels.

In unsupervised GML, models extract meaningful representations from graph data without predefined labels. The key tasks include node clustering, where similar nodes are grouped based on connectivity and attributes, graph embedding technique to learn from lower-dimensional representations of graphs, and community detection, which identifies groups of nodes that have dense intra-group connections [3]. Like supervised GML, unsupervised GML uses some techniques such as graph embedding models (DeepWalk, Node2Vec, Graph Autoencoders), self-supervised learning on graphs (contrastive learning, graph infomax), and clustering algorithms on graphs (Louvain method, spectral clustering).

4.2.2.2 Node Clustering

Node clustering is a method to group similar nodes in a graph based on connectivity patterns and features. This helps in community detection, fraud detection, biological network analysis, and recommendation systems. In the graph given in Fig. 4.5, the nodes represent entities (e.g., customers in a social network, proteins in a biological network) and edges represent relationships between nodes (e.g., friendships, interactions, or molecular bonds). The goal is to group similar nodes into clusters based on structural or feature similarities. A clustering algorithm is applied to the graph and grouped into three clusters in the diagram. Clustering algorithms used on graphs are as follows:

1) Spectral clustering
2) Label propagation algorithm (LPA)
3) Louvain algorithm for community detection.

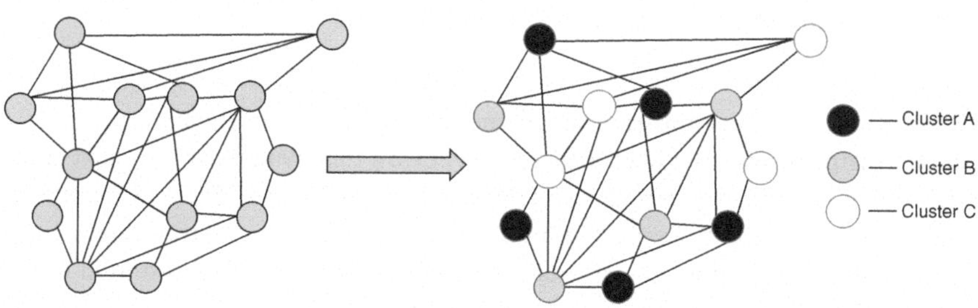

Figure 4.5 Node clustering connecting nodes with similarity.

Graphs that group nodes based on their structural similarity and similar connecting patterns and relationships use three prominent graph clustering algorithms such as spectral clustering, the LPA, and the Louvain method for community detection.

Spectral Clustering Spectral clustering is a powerful technique used to group (or cluster) data points based on their similarities. It is beneficial when the data cannot be grouped into clusters. Instead of working directly with the raw data points, spectral clustering transforms the data into a graph and then applies clustering techniques on this graph. Spectral clustering is efficient in handling complex and nonlinear separable data. The working process is given in a step-by-step procedure. The main objective of using spectral clustering is its usage for any shaped graph, and it can form any complex-shaped clusters. It can easily cluster the nodes, as the nodes are represented in the low-dimensional space. It also works well for small-sized graphs.

Working Process

Step 1: Construct the Similarity Graph Instead of working with raw data points, spectral clustering first constructs a similarity graph. This graph represents the relationships between data points. Each data point is a node in the graph. If two data points are similar, they are connected by an edge. The strength of the connection (weight of the edge) represents the similarity between the points. Techniques such as K-nearest neighbors, fully connected graphs, and epsilon neighborhood graph methods are used. These methods vary in the pattern of connection among the nodes. K-nearest neighbors connect each point to its K-nearest neighbor nodes. A fully connected graph connects every point to every other point with a weight based on similarity. The epsilon neighborhood graph connects points that are within a fixed distance (epsilon) of each other.

Step 2: Compute the Graph Laplacian The graph Laplacian is a matrix representation of a graph that captures its structure and connectivity, defined as $L = D - A$, where D is the degree matrix and A is the adjacency matrix. It is widely used in spectral clustering on graphs.
The Laplacian matrix (L) is then calculated as:

$$L = D - A$$

This matrix helps in capturing the connectivity structure of the graph.

Step 3: Compute Eigenvalues and Eigenvectors Eigenvalues and eigenvectors help in dimensionality reduction, making it easier to identify clusters. Compute the eigenvectors of the Laplacian matrix L. Select the top k eigenvectors, where k is the number of clusters we want. Each data point is now represented by its values in these eigenvectors.

Step 4: Apply K-Means Clustering The next step is to apply the k-means clustering method on the transformed data (from eigenvectors) to group similar points. This step is applied to make the data points more separable.

Example

Consider a simple undirected graph with four nodes and weighted edges given in Fig. 4.6.

Step 1

Construct the adjacency matrix (A), which represents the connections between nodes:

$$A = \begin{bmatrix} 0 & 2 & 3 & 0 \\ 2 & 0 & 0 & 4 \\ 3 & 0 & 0 & 5 \\ 0 & 4 & 5 & 0 \end{bmatrix}$$

Each row and column correspond to a node. Nonzero values indicate edge weights.

Step 2

Compute the degree matrix (D).

The degree matrix (D) is a diagonal matrix, where each entry D_{ii} is the sum of weights in row i.

$$D = \begin{bmatrix} 5 & 0 & 0 & 0 \\ 0 & 6 & 0 & 0 \\ 0 & 0 & 8 & 0 \\ 0 & 0 & 0 & 9 \end{bmatrix}$$

Step 3

Compute the graph Laplacian (L).

$$L = D - A = \begin{bmatrix} 5 & 0 & 0 & 0 \\ 0 & 6 & 0 & 0 \\ 0 & 0 & 8 & 0 \\ 0 & 0 & 0 & 9 \end{bmatrix} - \begin{bmatrix} 0 & 2 & 3 & 0 \\ 2 & 0 & 0 & 4 \\ 3 & 0 & 0 & 5 \\ 0 & 4 & 5 & 0 \end{bmatrix} = \begin{bmatrix} 5 & -2 & -3 & 0 \\ -2 & 6 & 0 & -4 \\ -3 & 0 & 8 & -5 \\ 0 & -4 & -5 & 9 \end{bmatrix}$$

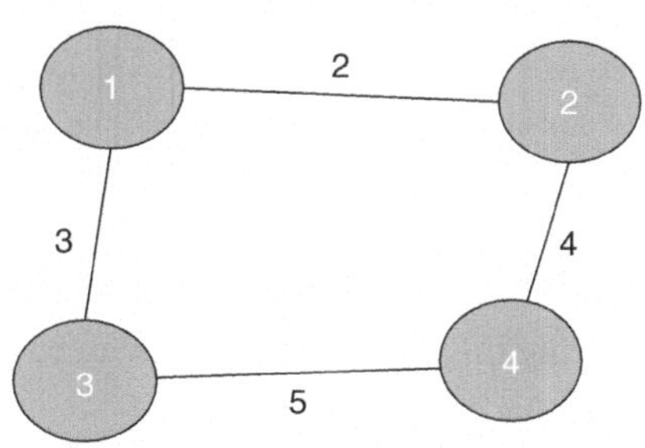

Figure 4.6 Weighted and undirected graph.

Step 4
Compute eigenvalues and eigenvectors.
Step 4.1 Compute the characteristic equation.
Eigenvalues λ satisfy

$$Det(L - \lambda I) = 0$$

Subtract λI from L

$$L - \lambda I = \begin{bmatrix} 5-\lambda & -2 & -3 & 0 \\ -2 & 6-\lambda & 0 & -4 \\ -3 & 0 & 8-\lambda & -5 \\ 0 & -4 & -5 & 9-\lambda \end{bmatrix}$$

Now, compute the determinant. $\begin{vmatrix} 5-\lambda & -2 & -3 & 0 \\ -2 & 6-\lambda & 0 & -4 \\ -3 & 0 & 8-\lambda & -5 \\ 0 & -4 & -5 & 9-\lambda \end{vmatrix} = 0$

Expanding, we get

$$(5-\lambda)\begin{vmatrix} 6-\lambda & 0 & -4 \\ 0 & 8-\lambda & -5 \\ -4 & -5 & 9-\lambda \end{vmatrix} + 2\begin{vmatrix} -2 & 0 & -4 \\ -3 & 8-\lambda & -5 \\ 0 & -5 & 9-\lambda \end{vmatrix}$$

$$+3\begin{vmatrix} -2 & 6-\lambda & -4 \\ -3 & 0 & -5 \\ 0 & -4 & 9-\lambda \end{vmatrix} = 0$$

Solving this determinant, we get eigenvalues as $\lambda_1 = 0$ $\lambda_2 = 2.31$ $\lambda_3 = 9.49$ $\lambda_4 = 16.2$

Step 4.2 Compute eigenvectors.
For each eigenvalue λ *solve*

$$(L - \lambda I)v = 0$$

For $\lambda_1 = 0$

$$\begin{bmatrix} 5 & -2 & -3 & 0 \\ -2 & 6 & 0 & -4 \\ -3 & 0 & 8 & -5 \\ 0 & -4 & -5 & 9 \end{bmatrix} \begin{bmatrix} \begin{bmatrix} v_1 \\ v_2 \\ v_3 \\ v_4 \end{bmatrix} \end{bmatrix} = 0$$

Solving this yields the eigenvector $v_1 = \frac{1}{2}\begin{bmatrix} \begin{bmatrix} 1 \\ 1 \\ 1 \\ 1 \end{bmatrix} \end{bmatrix}$

Similarly, solving for other eigenvalues gives additional eigenvectors. The smallest nonzero eigenvectors (for λ_2 and λ_3) are used as features for k-means clustering.

Step 5

Apply k-means on eigenvectors.

Using k-means clustering, we classify nodes into two clusters:

Cluster 1:

(1, 3)

Cluster 2:

(2, 4)

This partitions the graph based on connectivity.

Advantages of Spectral Clustering

It works well for **non-linearly separable data**.

It can detect complex cluster shapes.

It uses graph-based similarity, making it more flexible than k-means.

Limitations

1) Computationally expensive for large datasets.
2) Requires choosing the right similarity function and number of clusters.

Label Propagation Algorithm Spectral clustering can work with small-sized graphs, while the LPA works with large graphs. LPA can handle millions of nodes efficiently, rather than spectral clustering, which struggles with large graphs. Spectral clustering needs the number of clusters to be specified, while LPA can detect the communities without the predefined cluster count. This leads to the concept of LPA. The LPA is an iterative method that assigns labels to nodes based on the majority label of their neighbors. It operates under the assumption that connected nodes are likely to share the same label, making it particularly useful for large-scale networks due to its simplicity and computational efficiency. Each node in a graph is assigned an initial unique label. Nodes update their labels iteratively by adopting the most frequent label among their neighbors. The process continues until convergence, forming clusters (communities).

Example

Consider a graph with six nodes, A, B, C, D, E, F, connected as shown in Fig. 4.7. Initially, each node is assigned a unique label.

Step 1

Each node updates its label based on the majority label in its neighborhood.

In the LPA, when a node updates its label, it chooses the most frequent (majority) label among its neighbors. However, in cases where there is no clear majority (i.e., all neighbors have different labels or equal occurrences), the node retains its current label temporarily to avoid arbitrary changes.

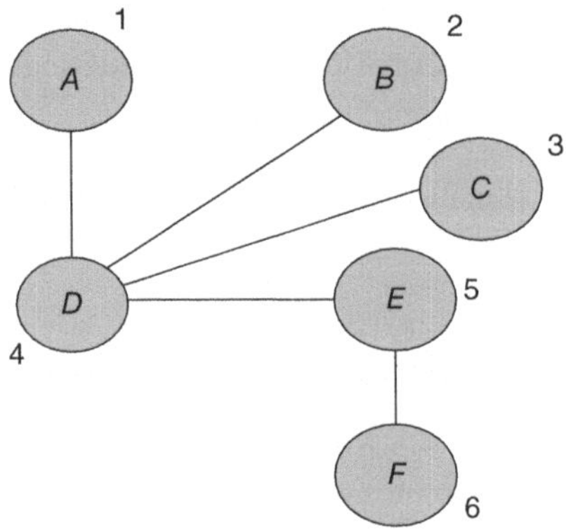

Figure 4.7 Graph illustration for label propagation algorithm.

Node D has neighbors A(1), B(2), C(3), and E(5). Since all labels are unique (no majority), D retains its label (4) for now. Node E has neighbors D(4) and F(6). It keeps 5 for now.

Step 2

Nodes update labels based on their most frequent neighbor labels: Assume that nodes A, B, and C update to label 1 because their neighbors also start adopting 1 (due to an external influence or previous majority updates).

D's neighbors: A(1), B(1), C(1), and E(5).

Majority label: Three neighbors (A, B, C) have label 1, while only one neighbor (E) has label 5.

Since label 1 is the majority, D changes to 1.

Node E: If D becomes 1, and F(6) changes to 1, then E adopts 1.

After iterations, nodes group into communities:

Since there are only two neighbors, and no clear majority (1 and 6 appear equally once), E might keep its current label (5) for now. However, if we assume a tiebreaker favoring the smallest label, then E might update to 1 in the next round when more updates happen.

All node labels are updated to 1, and they are grouped together into one cluster. This is shown in Fig. 4.8.

Process

1) **Initialization:** Assign a unique label to each node in the network.
2) **Propagation:** Iteratively update each node's label to the most frequent label among its neighbors.
3) **Convergence:** Repeat the propagation step until labels no longer change, indicating that communities have been detected.

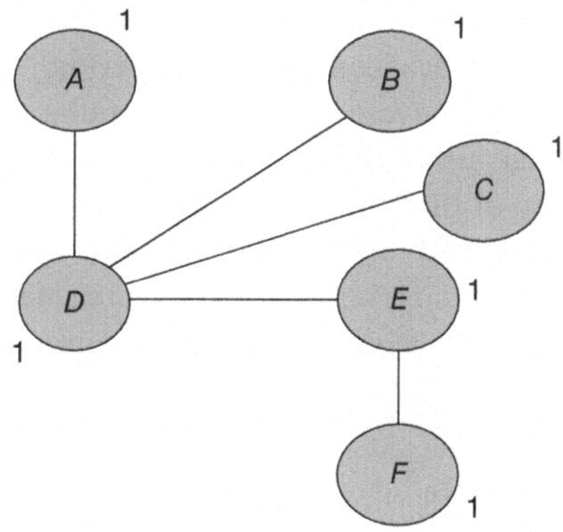

Figure 4.8 Label updated graph illustration for LPA.

Advantages of LPA

- Since LPA uses a simple update rule, it is highly efficient for large-scale graphs and does not require matrix computations.
- It does not require predefined clusters or labeled data, making it useful for unsupervised learning.
- The algorithm quickly detects communities in just a few iterations, even for massive networks.
- The algorithm dynamically determines the number of communities, removing the need to specify cluster numbers in advance.
- LPA is simple to understand and implement, making it accessible for practical use.

Limitations of LPA

- The final clustering result depends on the initial label assignments, leading to different outputs across runs.
- Some labels become dominant too quickly, leading to imbalanced clusters or even a single large cluster (poor resolution).
- In graphs with low connectivity, LPA may fail to propagate labels properly, resulting in inaccurate communities.
- The algorithm does not impose any constraint on community size, leading to uneven cluster sizes.
- Some nodes may continuously flip labels in certain structures, preventing proper convergence.

Louvain Method for Community Detection The challenges of using spectral clustering and LPA are that they are slow and not scalable. They struggle to form a community structure more easily. They provide only a single clustering result and need a predefined cluster count. Unlike spectral clustering and LPA, the Louvain method is faster and scalable. It does not require a predefined cluster count. It forms a hierarchical community clustering.

The Louvain method is a popular algorithm designed to detect communities in large networks by optimizing the modularity measure, which quantifies the density of links inside communities compared to links between communities. It is renowned for its speed and efficiency. Initially, each node is assigned to its own community (i.e., each node is considered as a unique community). Move the nodes to neighboring and aggregate communities into a single node. Continue the process till convergence.

Example

Consider the graph with six nodes as A,B,C,D,E,F, and the number in the edge represents the weightage. This is shown in Fig. 4.9.

Step 1: Initially, each node is considered a community node.

Step 2: First Phase—Modularity Optimization

Nodes are grouped into communities by merging based on edge weights and maximizing modularity.

Nodes A and D have a strong connection (weight 4) → Merged into Community 1.

Nodes B and C have a strong connection (weight 3) → Merged into Community 2.

Nodes E and F have a strong connection (weight 3) → Merged into Community 3 as shown in Fig. 4.10.

Updated Community Structure

Final community detection output is shown in Fig. 4.11.

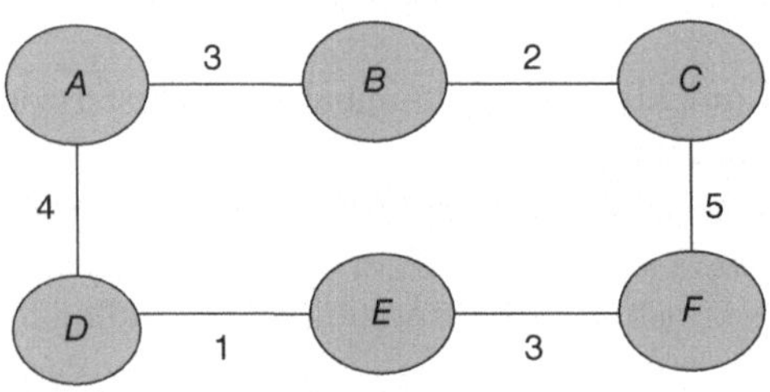

Figure 4.9 Graph sample for community graph.

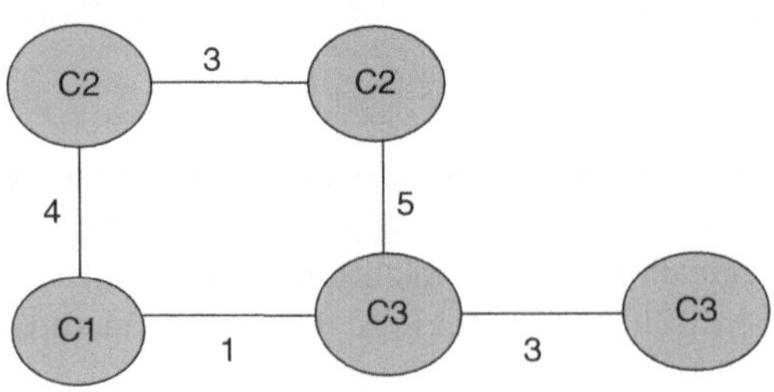

Figure 4.10 Updated community structure.

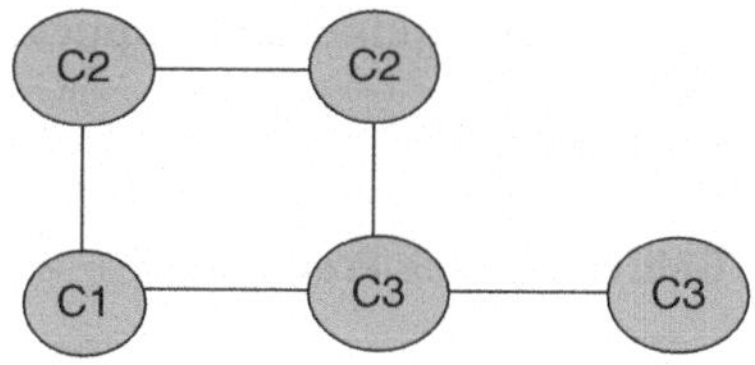

Figure 4.11 Final community detection output.

- Community 1 (C1) → Nodes A, D.
- Community 2 (C2) → Nodes B, C.
- Community 3 (C3) → Nodes E, F.

Process

1) **Initialization:** Assign each node to its own community.
2) **Local Optimization:** For each node, consider moving it to the community of each neighbor and calculate the modularity gain. Move the node to the community that results in the highest modularity gain.
3) **Aggregation:** Once no further modularity gains can be achieved, aggregate nodes belonging to the same community into a single node, creating a new network.
4) **Iteration:** Repeat the local optimization and aggregation steps on the new network until modularity can no longer be increased.

Advantages

- The Louvain method is highly efficient and can handle large-scale networks with millions of nodes.
- Unlike some clustering methods, it does not require the number of clusters (k) to be predefined.
- It provides a multi-level hierarchy of communities, which can be useful for analyzing network structures at different granularities.
- Louvain maximizes modularity effectively, leading to better-quality community structures.
- Produces more stable results compared to algorithms such as label propagation, which can be random and non-deterministic.

Limitations

- The method may merge small but significant communities, missing finer details.
- Different initializations can lead to slightly different results, making it not fully deterministic.
- Since it focuses on modularity optimization, it may struggle with detecting smaller communities in large networks.
- It assumes each node belongs to only one community, making it less effective for networks with overlapping communities.
- While efficient for large networks, it can still be costly for dense graphs.

4.2.3 Case Studies and Applications of GML

Case Study 4.1

GML in Disease Prediction

Article [5] focuses on the application of GML to predict disease using electronic health data. They employed two tasks: link prediction and node classification. The objective is to predict the risk or status of individual patients based on their electronic health records (EHRs). Also, discovering potential disease relationships, such as comorbidities, by analyzing the connections in patient data is carried out using the link prediction task. Fig. 4.12 depicts two graphs such as the patient graph and the disease graph.

Node classification in GML involves predicting the disease status or health risk of individual patients based on their EHRs. Each patient is represented as a node in a graph, with edges connecting them based on medical similarities, such as shared diagnoses, treatments, or demographic characteristics. The dataset is taken from an Australian private health fund that has administrative patient records. As a preprocessing step, the authors use filtering and sampling techniques to create two groups of patients: type 2 diabetes (T2D) and non-T2D patients. The approaches used in this article are extracting useful information about patients from EHR graphs using GNNs; the patient health data is propagated through the graph structure, allowing the model to learn patterns from similar patients, and the supervised and unsupervised methods are used to classify new patient data based on the disease presence or risk factors. The patient data and network structure are used as input to train and test GML models. The goal is to predict chronic diseases (such as T2D) based on a patient's position in the network and their health profile. The key idea is that the node classification helps identify patients at risk for chronic diseases using graph-based patient relationships.

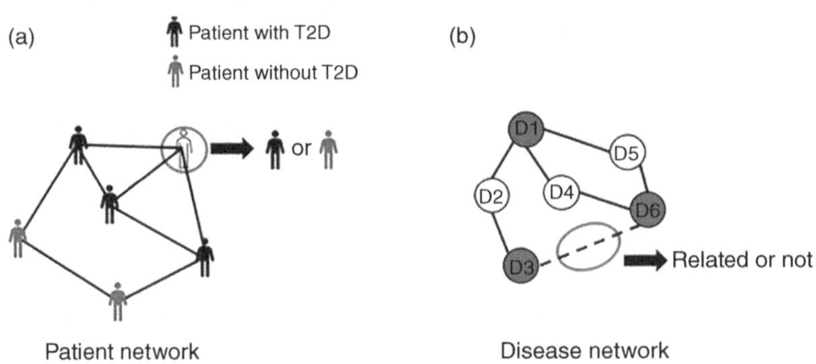

Figure 4.12 Patient–disease network.

The next task applied is link prediction. The task is to identify relationships between diseases. In this article, meta-path–based network analysis is employed to analyze the relationship between diseases. The method applied is to predict whether two diseases are likely to co-occur based on their relationships in the network. This helps predict how diabetes is related to heart disease.

Case Study 4.2

Drug Discovery and Development

Article [6] focuses on drug discovery and development as its case study domain. This involves identifying new therapeutic compounds, refining their properties, and evaluating their efficacy before approval. GML plays a crucial role in modeling intricate biological interactions, predicting drug–target binding, optimizing molecular structures, and discovering potential drug repurposing opportunities. By representing molecules, proteins, and biological systems as graphs, GML improves the accuracy and efficiency of drug discovery, significantly reducing both time and costs in the development process.

The article presents an in-depth review of the application of GML techniques throughout different phases of drug discovery and development. It explores the role of GML in key areas such as target identification, small molecule design, biologics development, and drug repurposing. Fig. 4.13 depicts the various applications of drug disease and development using GML.

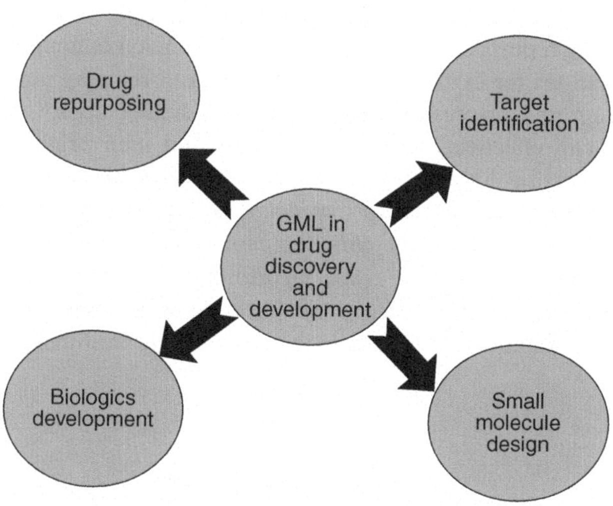

Figure 4.13 GML in drug diseases and development.

- **Target Identification:** The initial phase of drug discovery involves identifying biological molecules, such as proteins, enzymes, or genes, that play a role in a disease. The objective is to pinpoint a drug target whose modulation can influence disease progression, paving the way for effective therapeutic interventions. GML models examine protein–protein interaction networks to identify potential drug targets. The graph is represented with proteins, genes, and small molecules as nodes and protein–protein interactions between them as edges. GML algorithms analyze these complex networks to predict potential drug targets based on connectivity patterns, biological pathways, and disease associations.
- **Small Molecule Design:** Small molecule design plays a vital role in drug discovery, focusing on the development and refinement of low molecular weight compounds that interact with biological targets, such as proteins or enzymes, to regulate their function. These compounds have the potential to serve as drugs by either stimulating or inhibiting the activity of a specific target. Molecular structures are represented as graphs, enabling GML to predict bioactivity and optimize drug-like properties. The atoms are represented in nodes, and chemical bonds between atoms are represented in edges. GML techniques are used to generate novel small molecules with desirable drug-like properties, predict interactions between molecules and biological targets, and optimize molecular structures by modifying chemical bonds.
- **Biologics Development:** Biologics development involves the design and production of large, complex molecules derived from living organisms to treat various diseases. Unlike small molecule drugs, biologics encompass proteins, monoclonal antibodies, cell-based therapies, and vaccines, offering highly precise targeting of specific biological processes. GML assists in modeling complex structures of biologics, such as antibodies, to enhance their effectiveness. The graph consists of proteins, peptides, nucleic acids, or living cells.
- **Drug Repurposing:** Drug repurposing, or drug repositioning, involves finding new therapeutic applications for existing drugs. Rather than developing new medications from the ground up, researchers investigate whether approved or experimental drugs can effectively treat conditions beyond their original intended use. By constructing knowledge graphs from various biomedical data sources, GML identifies existing drugs that could be effective for new therapeutic uses. The graph represents complex biological relationships (e.g., drug–target, protein interactions). GML algorithms identify hidden drug–disease connections by analyzing large biomedical datasets and accelerate screening of repurposable drugs by predicting their effects in different biological systems.

4.3 Conclusion

This chapter deals with the GML, which is an advanced technique for supervised and unsupervised ML. GML is compared with the traditional ML approaches, highlighting some of the key features in GML. GML is categorized into two main tasks such as supervised and unsupervised learning. Supervised tasks include node classification, link prediction, edge prediction, and graph classification, and the unsupervised tasks include node clustering. Node clustering techniques such as spectral clustering, LPAs, and Louvain methods are discussed in this chapter with their advantages and limitations. Finally, the chapter concludes with the case study taken from the articles. It presents real-world case studies, showcasing GML's applications in disease prediction and drug discovery, demonstrating its significance in healthcare and biomedical research.

References

1 Zach Blumenfeld, *Graph machine learning: An overview, 2023, towards data science*. Available: https://towardsdatascience.com/graph-machine-learning-an-overview-c996e53fab90/.

2 Muhan Zhang, Yixin Chen, "Link Prediction Based on Graph Neural Networks", in *32nd Conference on Neural Information Processing Systems (NeurIPS 2018)*, Montréal, Canada.

3 Y. Zhu, Y. Xu, F. Yu, Q. Liu, and S. Wu, "Unsupervised graph representation learning with cluster-aware self-training and refining," *ACM Trans. Intell. Syst. Technol.*, vol. 14, no. 5, Aug. 2023 Art. no. 82.

4 S. Krix *et al.*, "MultiGML: Multimodal graph machine learning for prediction of adverse drug events," *Heliyon*, vol. 9, no. 9, e19441, Sept. 2023.

5 H. Lu and S. Uddin, "Disease prediction using graph machine learning based on electronic health data: a review of approaches and trends," *Healthcare*, vol. 11, no. 7, p. 1031, 2023, doi: 10.3390/healthcare11071031.

6 T. Gaudelet *et al.*, "Utilizing graph machine learning within drug discovery and development," *Bioinformatics*, vol. 22, no. 6, pp. 1–22, Nov. 2021.

5

Graph Sampling

Imagine you are planning to open a new restaurant in your place. You want to know whether the restaurant will succeed in the long run. You want to know people's food preferences, food habits, and favorite dishes. It's impossible to go and ask each person in all the houses. The solution is to pick a few houses, interact with the people, and get their responses. Analyzing their responses gives you a solid idea of what kind of restaurant might succeed in that area. The idea of picking out a few people instead of the entire population is called sampling.

In the same way, in the world of graph data—such as social media networks, healthcare, or biological interaction graphs—it's not possible to analyze the entire network at once as frequently because the size is huge and the graph is too complex. That's where graph sampling comes in. It allows us to take a meaningful subset of the graph and make decisions, train models, or make predictions effectively without the need to use the entire graph data. In this chapter, we'll explore the meaning of graph sampling, why it matters, and how different strategies assist us in navigating through the massive graphs more wisely.

5.1 Introduction

In the current trend of big data environments, real-world graphs—such as social networks, web graphs, recommended systems, secured databases, biological networks, or transportation systems—can have millions or even billions of nodes and edges. Processing these full-scale graphs is not feasible regularly due to space requirements, time, and resource constraints. The key idea behind graph sampling is to enable scalable and efficient analysis by working with smaller, manageable parts of the graph that still reflect the larger structure.

5.1.1 Issues Related to Large and Complex Graphs

In the recent modern and knowledgeable world of real-time applications such as social networks, healthcare, bioinformatics, and recommendation systems, the representation of information using graphs consists of millions or billions of nodes and edges. Handling of graphs faces numerous significant challenges. Understanding and addressing these issues is critical for building effective, scalable, and correct graph-based machine learning systems. Below, we explore the main problems connected with handling large and complex graphs.

- Accessing the nodes and edges is very difficult and computationally expensive.
- The processing time of graphs will exponentially grow with the increase in nodes and edges.
- Large graphs often require enormous memory space to work with the graph.
- Complex and large graphs often have sparse connections and noisy or redundant information, which can delay learning models from collecting meaningful patterns or relationships efficiently.
- Many real-world graphs are based on time limits in nature—there will not be continuous involvement or interactions of the users in the graph. The connections may be cut off, and irregular interactions constantly evolve. Preserving an up-to-date graph representation and learning from its dynamic structure in real time is the main task, particularly for applications such as web security, anomaly detection, or real-time recommendation.
- In the current trend, graphs can be heterogeneous, having multiple types of nodes and edges (e.g., users, items, reviews, transactions). It requires various techniques and methods to model such complex, multi-relational graphs as simple homogeneous graphs, improving algorithmic and architectural complexity.
- Handling of enormous, duplicate, and inappropriate information in a graph is very tedious, and it will also decrease the model's performance.
- A serious compliance problem may arise when dealing with secured, sensitive, and private data.

5.1.2 Definition with Examples

Graph sampling is defined as the process of selecting a representative subset of nodes, edges, or subgraphs from a larger graph to reduce computational complexity while preserving important similar patterns/structures and statistical properties of the original graph.

Consider the example of a citation graph where nodes represent an author's research papers on deep learning and edges represent citations between them. To analyze how deep learning research is progressing in more depth, we need to sample a subgraph containing only papers published in reputed journals or top-tier conferences within particular years. Within that, you apply sampling to trace citation paths and identify influential authors or papers based on sampled citation flows.

In a large-scale social network such as Twitter, nodes represent each user and edges represent the followers; it is not practical to work with the entire graph. We need to apply sampling techniques—start with a few influential users, then iteratively sample their followers and followings to construct a local social neighborhood. This subgraph supports examining influence patterns, detecting communities, or predicting viral tweet propagation.

To analyze patient–drug interactions, a healthcare analyst could sample a graph where nodes represent patients and medications, and edges denote prescriptions. This allows for training models to predict adverse drug interactions or optimize treatment plans by including diverse patient demographics (e.g., age groups, comorbidity profiles) without requiring access to the entire health network's data.

5.1.3 Challenges of Using Sampling

- Sampling a subset of nodes or edges can lead to the loss of important topological properties, such as community structure, centrality, or clustering. This can affect the performance of models relying on the complete graph context.
- In case of uneven data distribution, applying tasks such as classification or link prediction may result in poor model performance.
- While sampling effectively reduces computational load and often preserves local neighborhood structures, it commonly sacrifices global graph properties. This includes long-range dependencies, overall connectivity, and graph diameter, particularly in complex social or biological networks.
- Consequently, smaller samples can struggle to capture the full diversity or dynamic behavior, leading to a potential loss of accuracy, especially in temporal or evolving graphs.
- Although sampling reduces computational load, it often comes at the cost of accuracy. Smaller samples may not fully capture the diversity or dynamics of the original graph, especially in temporal or evolving graphs.
- Developing effective sampling strategies for complex graphs remains a significant research challenge.

5.2 Types of Graph Sampling

To effectively handle huge and difficult graphs, enormous sampling techniques have been introduced. These techniques vary in how they select nodes, edges, or substructures, and are chosen based on the intended task—whether it is node classification, link prediction, or graph embedding. Understanding the different types of graph sampling helps in selecting the most suitable approach for correct and efficient graph analysis. Sampling nodes, edges, and subgraphs is possible. Here, we will discuss the process of all three samplings.

5.2.1 Node Sampling

5.2.1.1 Overview of Node Sampling

Node sampling is a graph sampling technique where a subset of nodes is selected from the original graph, and the corresponding edges among these selected nodes are included to form a smaller subgraph. The goal is to retain a representative portion of the graph while reducing size and complexity.

For illustration, let us take an example of a social network graph where each node is a user and edges represent friendships. In node sampling, randomly select 1,000 users (nodes) from a network of 1 million. You then include all the edges (friendships) among those selected users, forming a smaller graph that can still reveal meaningful patterns such as community structures or influential users.

Mathematical Representation Let $p(v)$ be the probability of selecting node $v \in V$. The sampled subgraph $G' = (V', E')$, where $V' \subseteq V$ such that each node $v \in V$ is included with probability $p(v)$ and $E' = \{(u, v) \in E \mid u \in V', v \in V'\}$—edges are included only if both nodes are included in the selection.

If uniform sampling is used, then

$$p(v) = k / \mid V \mid,$$

where k is the number of nodes to sample.

Graph-Based Example Let $G_1 = (V, E)$ be a graph with $V = \{A, B, C, D, E\}$ as nodes (e.g., people in a social network) and $\{(A, B), (B, C), (C, D), (D, E), (A, E)\}$ as edges (e.g., friendships), as shown in Fig. 5.1. Randomly select or sample a few nodes using the node sampling technique $V' = \{A, B, C\}$, and the induced subgraph will be

- $V' = \{A, B, C\}$
- $E' = \{(A, B), (B, C)\}$—only the edges among the selected nodes are kept.

5.2.1.2 Types of Node Sampling

The exponential growth of data renders working with entire graphs computationally prohibitive and often inefficient for large-scale analysis. Node sampling emerges as a critical and efficient solution, enabling faster and more scalable

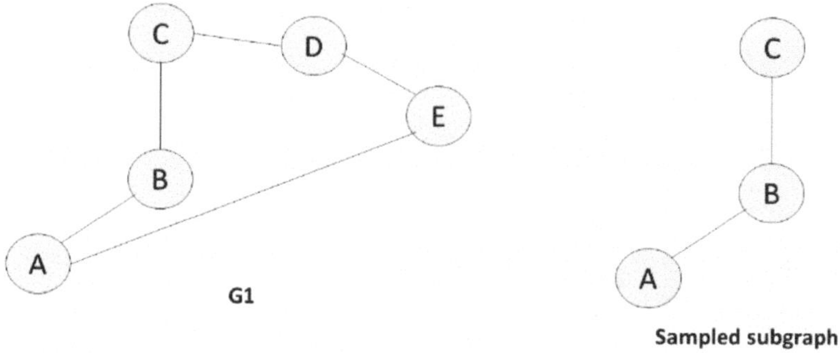

Figure 5.1 Sampling graph example.

learning by judiciously selecting a subset of nodes from the original graph, typically without significant compromise to structural integrity.

However, the efficiency of sampling methods is highly context-dependent; no single sampling technique is universally optimal for every analytical task. This underscores the critical importance of understanding and meticulously studying the diverse types of node sampling strategies. Different approaches are designed to preserve distinct graph properties, such as node degree distribution, community structure, or influence. The deliberate selection of an appropriate sampling technique is paramount for achieving superior model performance, mitigating bias, and ensuring a more accurate representation of the underlying data [1]. The following sections explore various node sampling techniques and their unique advantages. The types of node sampling given in Fig.5.2 are as follows:

A. Uniform Node Sampling Uniform node sampling is one of the simplest and most commonly used graph sampling techniques, where each node in a graph has an equal probability of being selected. This technique is mainly useful when there is no prior knowledge of the graph's structure. It helps reduce the computational burden while retaining the essential statistical properties of the original graph.

Let us consider a graph $G_1 = (V, E)$, where $V = \{A, B, C, D, E, F\}$ are nodes representing users in a social network and E is the set of edges representing friendships. If we apply uniform node sampling and randomly select three nodes—say, $V' = \{A, C, E\}$, we then include all edges between these sampled nodes (e.g., if (A, C) exists in E, it's retained in the subgraph). The resulting induced subgraph contains nodes $\{A, C, E\}$ and the edges that exist between them in the original graph.

Mathematical Formulation Let $G_1 = (V, E)$ be the original graph with $|V| = n$ nodes. In uniform sampling, each node $v \in V$ is selected with equal probability:

$$P(v) = \frac{K}{N}$$

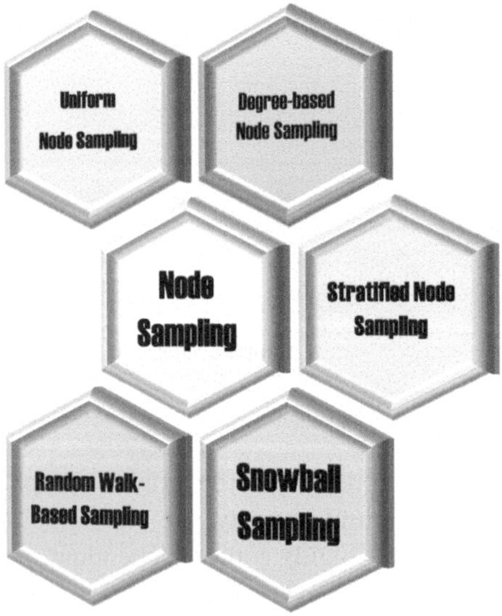

Figure 5.2 Types of node sampling.

where K is the number of nodes to sample and N is the total number of nodes.

The sampled subgraph $G' = (V', E')$, where

$$V' \subseteq V, \text{such that } |V'| = k,$$

$$E' = \{(u, v) \in E \mid u \in V', v \in V'\}$$

Consider the following graph G_1 given in Fig. 5.3 (a) with nodes $(V) = \{A, B, C, D, E, F\}$ and edges $(E) = \{(A, B), (A, C), (B, D), (C, D), (C, E), (D, F), (E, F)\}$.

$$|V| = 6$$

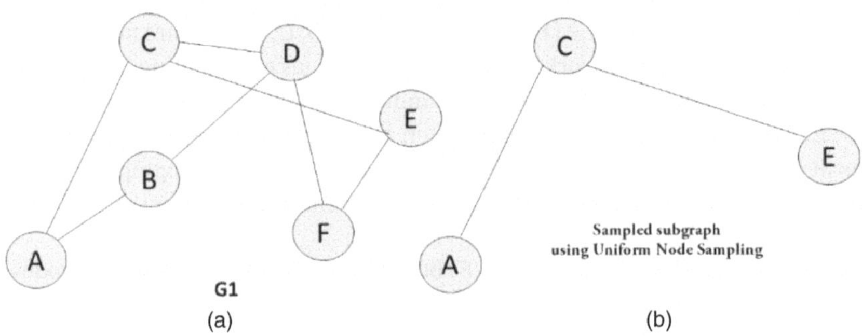

Figure 5.3 (a) Original input graph; (b) sampled subgraph using uniform node sampling.

Let us select three nodes $K = 3$ from the 6-node graph.

$$P(v) = \frac{K}{N} = \frac{3}{6} = 0.5$$

This means each node has a 50% probability of being included in the sampled graph.

Randomly sample any three nodes: Let us select $V' = \{A, C, E\}$.

Now, construct the subgraph $G' = (V', E')$ by including edges where both endpoints are in V'.

From the original edges:

- $(A, B) \rightarrow$ only $A \in V'$ (discard)
- $(A, C) \rightarrow$ both $A, C \in V'$
- $(C, D) \rightarrow$ only $C \in V'$ (discard)
- $(C, E) \rightarrow$ both $C, E \in V'$
- Others: none have both nodes in V'

So, $V' = \{A, C, E\}$ and $E' = \{(A, C), (C, E)\}$ are the final graphs that are shown in Fig. 5.3 (b).

Note

So, the expected inclusion rate is 50%; each individual node does not independently have a 50% chance in a single trial.

Algorithm: Uniform Node Sampling

Input:
Graph $G = (V, E)$, sample size k

Output:
Sampled subgraph $G' = (V', E')$

1) Initialize $V' \leftarrow \emptyset$
2) Randomly select k nodes from V without replacement $\rightarrow V'$
3) Initialize $E' \leftarrow \emptyset$
4) For each edge $(u, v) \in E$:
   If $u \in V'$ and $v \in V'$:
   Add (u, v) to E'
5) Return $G' = (V', E')$

B. Degree-Based Node Sampling Degree-based node sampling is a nonuniform sampling technique where nodes are selected with probabilities proportional to their degrees. This method ensures that highly connected or more influential nodes (often central in the graph structure) are more likely to be sampled, which is particularly useful in applications such as influence analysis, recommendation systems, and social network studies. Unlike uniform sampling, which treats all nodes equally, degree-based sampling biases the sample toward hubs or key connectors, preserving important structural properties of the original graph.

Mathematical Formulation Let $G_1 = (V, E)$ be a graph with node degrees deg(v). The probability of selecting node "v" is

$$P(v) = \frac{\deg(v)}{\sum_{u \in V} \deg(u)} = \frac{\text{Degree of a node}}{\text{Total Degree}}$$

Let K be the number of nodes to sample: the sampled set is $v' \subseteq V$, such that $|V'| = K$ and nodes are selected proportionally to degree.

The resultant subgraph is

$$G' = (V', E') \text{ where } E' = \{(u, v) \in E \mid u \in V', v \in V'\}$$

Let us consider a simple undirected graph $G_1 = (V, E)$ with nodes $V = \{A, B, C, D, E\}$ and edges $E = \{(A, B), (A, C), (B, C), (C, D), (D, E)\}$. This is shown in Fig. 5.4 (a).

Step 1

Now, calculate the degrees of each node:

- $\deg(A) = 2$
- $\deg(B) = 2$
- $\deg(C) = 3$
- $\deg(D) = 2$
- $\deg(E) = 1$

Total degree $= 2 + 2 + 3 + 2 + 1 = 10$

Step 2

Sampling probability of each node (proportional to degree):

$$P(v) = \frac{\text{Degree of a node}}{\text{Total Degree}}$$

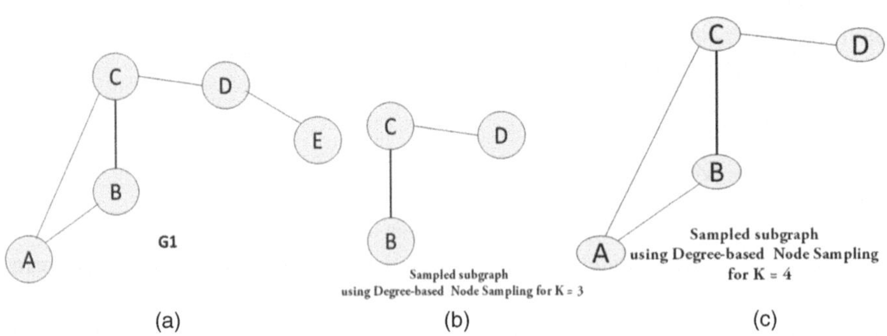

Figure 5.4 (a) Original input graph; (b) sampled subgraph $K = 3$; (c) sampled subgraph $K = 4$ using degree-based node sampling technique.

So,
$P(A) = 2 / 10 = 0.20$
$P(B) = 2 / 10 = 0.20$
$P(C) = 3 / 10 = 0.30$
$P(D) = 2 / 10 = 0.20$
$P(E) = 1 / 10 = 0.10$

Step 3
Let's sample $K = 3$ nodes, based on the above probabilities. Suppose we randomly select: $V' = \{B, C, D\}$.

Step 4
Check for existing edges among the sampled nodes:

- (B, C)
- (C, D)

Thus, the final result is $V' = \{B, C, D\}$ and $E' = \{(B, C), (C, D)\}$, as shown in Fig. 5.4 (b)

For the same graph, let us take the sample count $K = 4$ nodes.

We sample based on the probabilities above. Suppose the result of weighted random sampling is $V' = \{A, B, C, D\}$. Now identify which edges connect the sampled nodes:

Original edges:

- (A, B)
- (A, C)
- (B, C)
- (C, D)
- (D, E) (E is not in V')

Included edges: $(A, B), (A, C), (B, C), (C, D)$
Final Sampled Subgraph $G' = (V', E')$

- Nodes $(V') = \{A, B, C, D\}$
- Edges $(E') = \{(A, B), (A, C), (B, C), (C, D)\}$, as shown in Fig. 5.4 (c)

This subgraph preserves much of the local structure and hubs due to C's high degree.

Algorithm: Degree-Based Node Sampling

Input
Graph $G = (V, E)$, sample size k

Output
Sampled subgraph $G' = (V', E')$

1) For each node v in V:
   Compute degree: deg(v)
2) Compute total degree: D = sum(deg(v) for all v in V)
3) For each node v in V:
   Compute sampling probability $P(v)$ = deg(v) / D
4) Sample k nodes from V using weighted probabilities → V'
5) Initialize $E' \leftarrow \emptyset$
6) For each edge $(u, v) \in E$:
   If $u \in V'$ and $v \in V'$:
   Add (u, v) to E'
7) Return $G' = (V', E')$

C. Stratified Node Sampling Stratified node sampling is a technique used to ensure representative sampling from different subgroups, or "strata," within a graph. Instead of sampling uniformly or by degree, nodes are first grouped based on predefined characteristics such as community, label, node type, or degree class. Then, sampling is performed independently within each group according to a chosen strategy. This approach is especially valuable in graphs where certain strata are underrepresented or where fairness and coverage across all groups are critical, such as in social networks, citation networks, or biological datasets.

Mathematical Formulation Let a graph $G_1 = (V, E)$ be partitioned into disjoint strata:

$$V = V_1 \cup V_2 \cup \cdots \cup V_s$$

where $V_i \cap V_j = \emptyset$ for $i \neq j$ and "S" is the number of strata.

Let K_i be the number of nodes to sample from stratum V_i, such that

$$\sum_{i=1}^{s} K_i = K$$

Sampling within each V_i is performed independently using uniform or weighted sampling.

Let us consider a graph $G_1 = (V, E)$ with nodes representing users and edges representing friendships. The graph is given in Fig. 5.5 (a). Suppose the nodes are divided into two communities based on user interests:

- $V1$ (Community 1) = $\{A, B, C\}$
- $V2$ (Community 2) = $\{D, E, F\}$

Edges: $(A, B), (B, C), (C, D), (D, E), (E, F)$

Suppose we want to sample $K = 4$ nodes, ensuring equal representation from both communities.

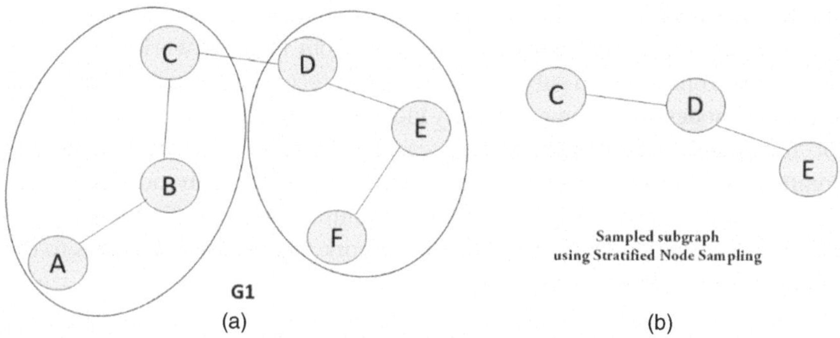

Figure 5.5 (a) Original input graph; (b) sampled subgraph using stratified node sampling technique.

Step 1

Divide the node set: Stratum $S_1 = \{A, B, C\}$ and Stratum $S_2 = \{D, E, F\}$.

Step 2

Use uniform sampling within each stratum, selecting two nodes from each group:

From Stratum $S_1 \rightarrow$ Sample $\{A, C\}$ and from Stratum $S_2 \rightarrow$ Sample $\{D, E\}$

So, $V' = \{A, C, D, E\}$

Step 3

Now extract the subgraph from the sampled nodes.

Edges among them are (C, D) and (D, E).

Final subgraph: $V' = \{A, C, D, E\}$ and $E' = \{(C, D), (D, E)\}$. This is shown in Fig. 5.5 (b).

Algorithm: Stratified Node Sampling

Input:

Graph $G = (V, E)$, strata $V1, V2, \ldots, Vs$, sample sizes $k1, k2, \ldots, ks$

Output:

Sampled subgraph $G' = (V', E')$

1) Initialize $V' \leftarrow \emptyset$
2) For each stratum Vi:
   Sample ki nodes uniformly or by weight $\rightarrow Vi'$
   Add Vi' to V'
3) Initialize $E' \leftarrow \emptyset$
4) For each edge $(u, v) \in E$:
   If $u \in V'$ and $v \in V'$:
   Add (u, v) to E'
5) Return $G' = (V', E')$

D. Snowball Sampling Snowball node sampling is an iterative sampling technique used to explore and extract relevant subgraphs from large networks, especially when starting from a known subset of nodes. The process begins with a seed node (or set of seed nodes) and then recursively includes its neighbors over a fixed number of "hops" or until a sampling limit is reached. This method mimics real-world exploration, such as how information or diseases spread through social or biological networks. It is particularly effective in community detection, influence propagation modeling, and survey-based social network analysis, where access to the full graph is limited or expensive.

Mathematical Formulation Consider the graph $G_1 = (V, E)$ as the original graph, $S_0 \subset V$ as the initial seed set, and S_i as the set of nodes discovered at hop i.

Then,

$$S_{i+1} = S_i \cup \{v \in V \mid \exists u \in S_i \text{ and } (u, v) \in E\}$$

After "h" hops, the final node set is: $V' = S_0 \cup S_1 \cup \cdots \cup S_h$ and $E' = \{(u,v) \in E \mid u \in V', v \in V'\}$. Consider an undirected graph $G_1 = (V, E)$ with nodes $V = \{A, B, C, D, E, F, G\}$ and edges $E = \{(A, B), (A, C), (B, D), (C, E), (D, F), (E, G)\}$. This is given in Fig. 5.6 (a).

Step 1

Using snowball sampling, start from seed node A and go up to two hops.

Hop 0 (seed): Nodes: $\{A\}$

In hop 1, the neighbors of A are B and C. So, the total number of nodes sampled so far is $\{A, B, C\}$.

Hop 2 for node A includes neighbors of B, and C. Neighbors of B is D and the neighbors of C is E. So, the new nodes are D and E. The total number of nodes sampled: $\{A, B, C, D, E\}$.

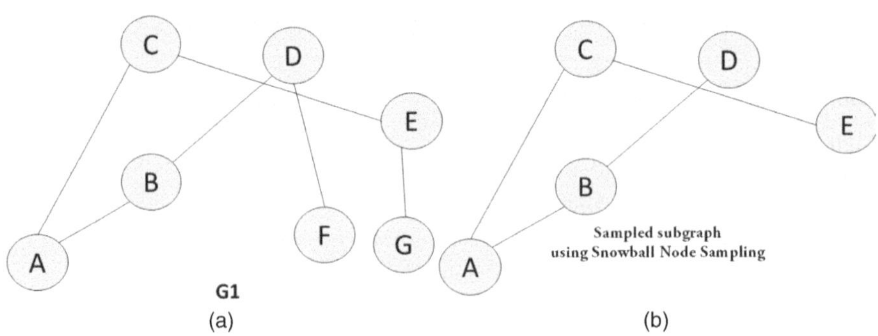

Figure 5.6 (a) Original input graph and (b) sampled subgraph using snowball node sampling.

Step 2

Now, extract edges among the sampled nodes: (A, B), (A, C), (B, D), (C, E).

So, the final subgraph is $V' = \{A, B, C, D, E\}$; $E' = \{(A, B), (A, C), (B, D), (C, E)\}$ as given in Fig. 5.6 (b).

Algorithm: Snowball Node Sampling

Input:

Graph $G = (V, E)$, seed node s, number of hops h.

Output:

Sampled subgraph $G' = (V', E')$

1) Initialize $V' \leftarrow \{s\}$
2) For $i = 1$ to h:
   For each node u in V' at hop i–1:
   Add all neighbors of u to V'
3) Initialize $E' \leftarrow \emptyset$
4) For each edge $(u, v) \in E$:
   If $u \in V'$ and $v \in V'$:
   Add (u, v) to E'
5) Return $G' = (V', E')$

E. Random Walk-Based Sampling Random walk node sampling is a stochastic graph exploration technique where sampling is guided by a simulated "walk" that traverses the graph step by step. Starting from a seed node, the walk selects the next node from the current node's neighbors with a defined probability (usually uniform), continuing for a predefined number of steps or until a certain number of unique nodes is visited. This method tends to favor high-degree nodes, as they are more likely to be encountered, making it well-suited for analyzing large-scale networks such as social graphs, web graphs, and biological networks, where full traversal is computationally expensive. Random walk sampling captures local structure and is widely used in graph embedding (e.g., DeepWalk, Node2Vec).

Mathematical Formulation Let us consider $G_1 = (V, E)$ as the graph. The transition probability from node "u" to neighbor "v" is

$$P(u \rightarrow v) = \frac{1}{\deg(u)} \text{ for } all\, v \in N(u)$$

Let v_0 be the starting node and l be the walk length. Then the walk is: $v_0 \rightarrow v_1 \rightarrow v_2 \rightarrow \cdots \rightarrow v_{l.}$

The final node set: $V' = \{v_i \mid 0 \leq i \leq l\}$.

The edge set E' includes edges between any pairs in V' present in E.

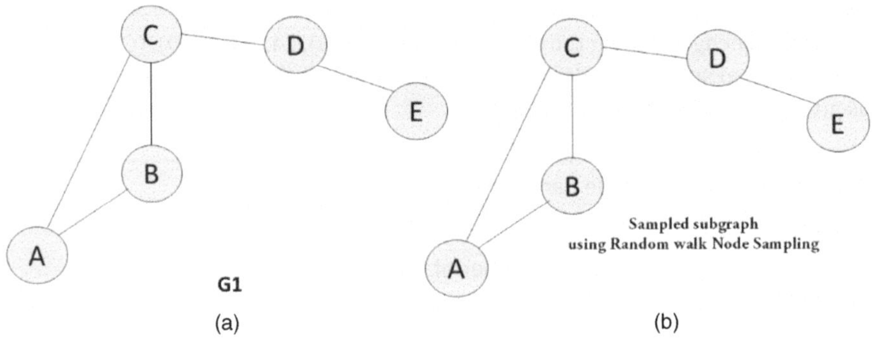

Figure 5.7 (a) Original input graph; (b) sampled subgraph using random walk node sampling.

Consider a simple undirected graph $G_1 = (V, E)$ with nodes $V = \{A, B, C, D, E\}$ and edges $E = \{(A, B), (A, C), (B, C), (C, D), (D, E)\}$. The original input graph G_1 is given in Fig. 5.7 (a).

Sampling Process: Node A is taken as the start node, and the walk length is five steps.

Step-by-step walk (random choices shown for example):

1) Start at $A \rightarrow$ neighbors: $\{B, C\} \rightarrow$ randomly choose B
2) At $B \rightarrow$ neighbors: $\{A, C\} \rightarrow$ choose C
3) At $C \rightarrow$ neighbors: $\{A, B, D\} \rightarrow$ choose D
4) At $D \rightarrow$ neighbors: $\{C, E\} \rightarrow$ choose E
5) At $E \rightarrow$ neighbor: $\{D\} \rightarrow$ return to D

Visited nodes: $\{A, B, C, D, E\}$

Resulting Sampled Subgraph

Nodes visited: $\{A, B, C, D, E\}$

Edges among them: All are present, $V' = \{A, B, C, D, E\}$, $E' = \{(A, B), (A, C), (B, C), (C, D), (D, E)\}$. This is shown in Fig. 5.7 (b).

Algorithm: Random Walk Node Sampling

Input:

Graph $G = (V, E)$, start node $v0$, walk length l

Output:

Sampled subgraph $G' = (V', E')$

1) Initialize $V' \leftarrow \{v0\}$
2) Set current_node $\leftarrow v0$
3) For $i = 1$ to l:

Get neighbors of current_node → N(current_node)
Randomly choose next_node ∈ N(current_node)
Add next_node to V'
Set current_node ← next_node
4) Initialize $E' \leftarrow \emptyset$
5) For each edge $(u, v) \in E$:
If $u \in V'$ and $v \in V'$:
Add (u, v) to E'
6) Return $G' = (V', E')$

5.2.2 Edge Sampling

Imagine you're trying to understand how rumors spread in a social group, but instead of focusing on the people (the nodes), you're more interested in who talks to whom—the connections themselves. Now, rather than selecting people randomly, you decide to randomly pick conversations and trace who is involved. This approach is called edge sampling, and it's a powerful alternative to node sampling, especially when the relationships between entities matter more than the entities themselves.

5.2.2.1 Overview of Edge Sampling

There are several issues in working with node sampling technique alone. Node sampling results in a sparse or disconnected subgraph, as many of the edges between sampled nodes may not exist—especially if those nodes were not neighbors in the original graph. This disrupts structural properties such as clustering, connectivity, and community structure, making it less suitable for tasks that depend on relationship patterns (e.g., link prediction or influence modeling). Additionally, node sampling can diminish high-degree nodes, particularly in scale-free networks, which can bias analytical outcomes. Another key issue is loss of context: sampled nodes may appear in isolation, missing the interactions that define their roles within the network.

Edge sampling is beneficial, as it includes nodes that are actively involved in interactions, which often leads to denser and more connected subgraphs. This enhances the preservation of critical graph properties such as degree distribution, edge clustering, and network flow, which are essential in domains such as transaction networks, social interactions, and communication graphs. Edge sampling also increases the likelihood of including highly influential or active nodes—since such nodes participate in many edges—thus offering a more representative view of network activity. Overall, it supports more accurate modeling of relational patterns, making it especially effective when the primary focus is on interactions rather than isolated entities.

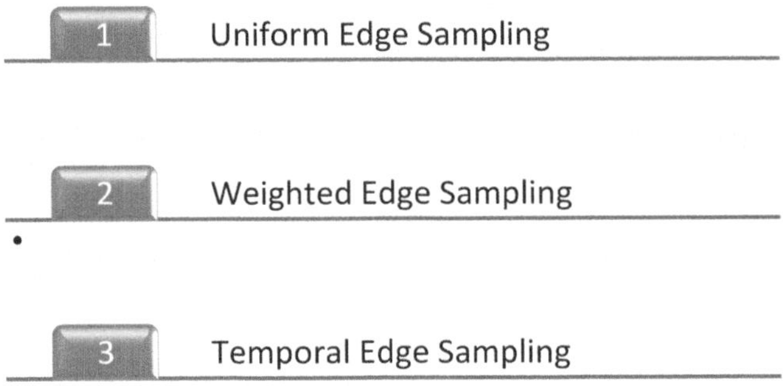

Figure 5.8 Types of edge sampling.

Edge sampling is a technique where a subset of edges (connections) is randomly selected from a graph, and the corresponding nodes connected by these edges are included in the sample. It focuses on the interactions or relationships rather than the entities. Edge sampling is especially useful when studying link-centric phenomena such as communication patterns, co-authorship behavior, or fraud detection based on transactions.

5.2.2.2 Types of Edge Sampling

Edge sampling can be classified into several types based on how the edges are selected, either randomly or based on certain structural properties of the graph. The most common types are shown in Fig. 5.8.

A. Uniform Edge Sampling Uniform edge sampling is a basic and commonly used technique where each edge in the graph is given an equal probability of being selected. Unlike node sampling, which focuses on individual entities, uniform edge sampling emphasizes the relationships between nodes and ensures that the sampled subgraph reflects actual interactions. This approach is particularly useful in scenarios where edge-based analysis is critical, such as communication networks, transaction systems, or citation graphs. One of the main advantages of uniform edge sampling is its simplicity and unbiased nature—it does not require prior knowledge or weighting of edge importance, making it suitable for large-scale graphs with limited metadata.

Mathematical Formulation Let $G = (V, E)$ be a graph with $|E| = m$ edges.

Let K be the number of edges to sample, such that $K < m$.

Then, for uniform edge sampling, each edge $e_i \in E$ has a probability:

$$P(e_i) = \frac{1}{m} \text{ for } all\ i = 1, 2, \ldots, m$$

The sampled edge set $E' \subseteq E$ is chosen such that $E' = \text{RandomSample}(E, K)$

And the corresponding node set V' is $V' = \{u \in V \mid \exists (u, v) \in E'\}$.

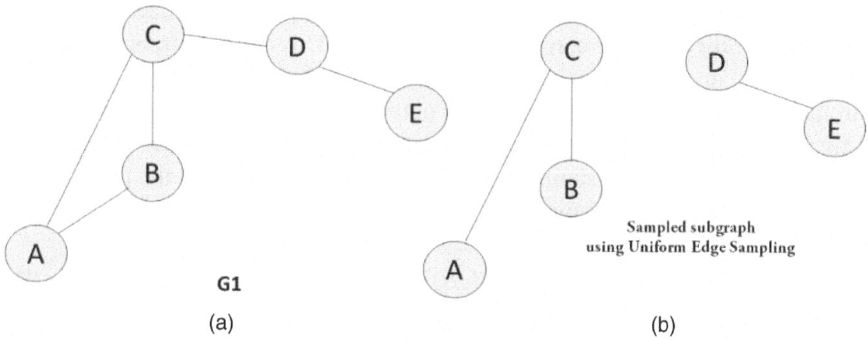

Figure 5.9 (a) Original input graph; (b) sampled subgraph using uniform edge sampling.

Consider an undirected graph $G = (V, E)$ with nodes $V = \{A, B, C, D, E\}$ and edges $E = \{(A, B), (A, C), (B, C), (C, D), (D, E)\}$. This is shown in Fig. 5.9 (a).

There are a total of five edges. Apply uniform edge sampling to sample $K = 3$ edges.

Suppose we randomly select the edges $(A, C), (B, C), (D, E)$.

The nodes involved in these edges are A, B, C, D, E.

The sampled subgraph $G' = (V', E')$ has nodes $V' = \{A, B, C, D, E\}$ and edges $E' = \{(A, C), (B, C), (D, E)\}$. The resulting graph is shown in Fig. 5.9 (b).

Although all original nodes are included, only selected relationships are preserved.

Algorithm: Uniform Edge Sampling

Input:
Graph $G = (V, E)$, number of edges to sample K

Output:
Sampled subgraph $G' = (V', E')$

1) Initialize $E' \leftarrow$ empty set
2) Randomly select K edges from E without replacement $\rightarrow E'$
3) Initialize $V' \leftarrow$ empty set
4) For each $(u, v) \in E'$:
   Add u and v to V'
5) Return $G' = (V', E')$

B. Weighted Edge Sampling Weighted edge sampling is a refined method of graph sampling where each edge is selected based on an assigned weight, reflecting its importance, frequency, or strength. Unlike uniform edge sampling, where all edges are equally likely to be selected, weighted sampling prioritizes edges that are more significant in the context of the graph [2]. This makes it especially useful in real-world applications where interactions vary in importance—for instance, stronger social ties in a communication network or high-volume transactions in a financial network. Weighted edge sampling helps preserve these meaningful patterns, resulting in a sampled subgraph that more accurately reflects the dynamics of the original network.

Mathematical Formulation Let $G_1 = (V, E)$ be a graph with edge weights $w: E \to R^+$. Let the total edge weight be $W = \sum w(e)$.

Each edge $e_i \in E$ is sampled with probability

$$P(e_i) = \frac{w(e_i)}{W}$$

Sampled edge set $E' \subseteq E$ of size K is generated based on these probabilities.

Sampled node set $V' = \{u \in V \mid \exists (u, v) \in E'\}$.

Consider a weighted undirected graph $G_1 = (V, E)$ with nodes $V = \{A, B, C, D\}$ shown in Fig. 5.10 (a).

Take a sample of $K = 2$ edges using weighted probabilities.

Step 1

Compute total weight

$$W = 5 + 3 + 2 + 1 = 11$$

Step 2

Calculate selection probabilities for each edge

$$P(A, B) = \frac{5}{11} \; P(A, C) = \frac{3}{11} \; P(B, C) = \frac{2}{11} \; P(C, D) = \frac{1}{11}$$

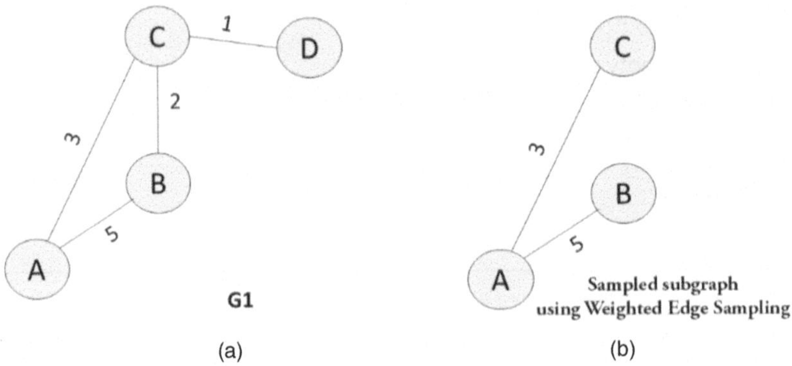

Figure 5.10 (a) Original input graph; (b) sampled subgraph using weighted edge sampling.

Step 3

Randomly select two edges based on the probabilities.

Suppose the selected edges are (A, B) and (A, C), then the resulting subgraph G' includes nodes $V' = \{A, B, C\}$ and edges $E' = \{(A, B), (A, C)\}$, which is shown in Fig. 5.10 (b).

Algorithm: Weighted Edge Sampling

Input:

Graph $G = (V, E)$, edge weight function w, number of edges to sample K

Output:

Sampled subgraph $G' = (V', E')$

1) Compute total weight: $W \leftarrow$ sum of all $w(e)$ for e in E
2) For each edge e in E:
   Compute probability $P(e) = w(e) / W$
3) Initialize $E' \leftarrow$ sample K edges from E with probabilities $P(e)$
4) Initialize $V' \leftarrow$ empty set
5) For each (u, v) in E':
   Add u and v to V'
6) Return $G' = (V', E')$

C. Temporal Edge Sampling Temporal edge sampling is a specialized technique used for dynamic or time-evolving graphs, where edges are associated with timestamps indicating when the interaction occurred. Instead of treating all edges equally, this method samples edges based on their temporal attributes—such as recency, frequency within a time window, or chronological intervals [3]. This approach is crucial in applications where time plays a significant role, such as social networks, communication systems, and transaction logs. By sampling edges that occur within specific time frames, we can better analyze trends, detect patterns, and monitor real-time behaviors, making it a valuable tool for temporal graph learning and stream processing.

Mathematical Formulation Let $G_1 = (V, E, T)$ be a temporal graph where each edge $e_i \in E$ has a timestamp $t_i \in T$.

Define the time window $[t_{\min}, t_{\max}]$.

The temporal edge sample set $E' \subseteq E$ is $E' = \{e_i \in E \mid t_i \in [t_{\min}, t_{\max}]\}$.

The corresponding node set is $V' = \{u \in V \mid \exists (u, v) \in E'\}$.

Consider a temporal undirected graph $G_1 = (V, E, T)$ with nodes $V = \{A, B, C, D\}$, as shown in Fig. 5.11 (a),

Consider edges with timestamps (A, B) at time 1, (A, C) at time 3, (B, C) at time 5, (C, D) at time 8, and (A, D) at time 10.

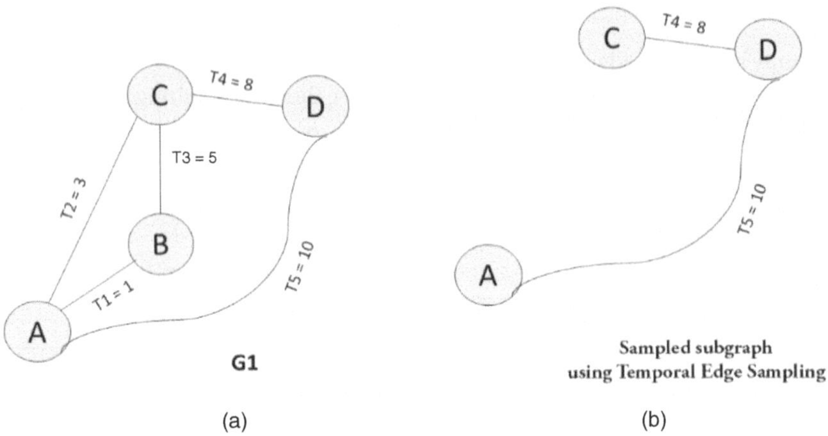

Figure 5.11 (a) Original input graph and (b) sampled subgraph using temporal edge sampling.

Suppose we want to sample edges that occurred within the last five time units (i.e., time window = [6, 10]).

Edges with timestamps ≥6 are selected. So edges (C, D) at time 8 and (A, D) at time 10 are selected. The sampled subgraph G' with nodes $V = \{A, C, D\}$ and edges $E = \{(C, D), (A, D)\}$ is the final result, and the graph is shown in Fig. 5.11 (b).

Algorithm: Temporal Edge Sampling

Input:
Graph $G = (V, E, T)$, time window [t_min, t_max]

Output:
Sampled temporal subgraph $G' = (V', E')$

1) Initialize $E' \leftarrow$ empty set
2) For each edge $e\_i \in E$:
   If $t\_i \in$ [t_min, t_max]:
   Add e_i to E'
3) Initialize $V' \leftarrow$ empty set
4) For each edge (u, v) in E':
   Add u and v to V'
5) Return $G' = (V', E')$

5.2.3 Neighborhood Sampling

Imagine you're trying to understand how information spreads in a school. Instead of interviewing every student (node sampling) or listening to every conversation (edge sampling), you pick one student and explore their group of friends, and then their friends' friends. This way, you start small and expand locally. That's the idea behind neighborhood sampling—you start from a few important points and carefully walk through their surrounding connections to see what the local network looks like.

5.2.3.1 Overview of Neighborhood Sampling

Neighborhood sampling is a method where you select a subset of nodes and their immediate or multi-hop neighbors to form a sampled subgraph. Rather than randomly picking isolated nodes or edges, neighborhood sampling preserves local structure and connectivity, which is crucial for learning tasks such as node classification, link prediction, or community detection.

It maintains local graph structure and context. It efficiently supports mini-batch training in GNNs. It reduces computational load while preserving important relational patterns. While neighborhood sampling is effective for preserving local structure, it comes with several challenges. First, sampling bias can arise, especially if high-degree nodes dominate the neighborhood, leading to skewed learning outcomes. Second, computational overhead increases as the neighborhood size grows exponentially with the number of hops, especially in dense graphs. This can cause memory bottlenecks and slower training times. Third, information redundancy is common—nodes may appear in multiple neighborhoods, leading to duplicated computations. Lastly, neighborhood sampling is often dependent on a starting node, which may limit its generalization ability and coverage if the initial seed nodes are not well-chosen.

5.2.3.2 Types of Neighborhood Sampling

Neighborhood sampling techniques help in selecting relevant subsets of nodes and their surrounding structures to enable scalable graph learning. The key types include k-hop sampling, which collects nodes within a fixed number of hops; fixed-size sampling, which selects a specific number of neighbors per node; and layer-wise sampling, used in GNNs to sample neighbors layer-by-layer. Other methods such as importance-based and random walk sampling prioritize neighbors based on relevance or traversal paths. These approaches balance efficiency and structural preservation in large graphs.

The main types of neighborhood sampling are k-hop, temporal, and random walk techniques.

A. K-Hop Neighborhood Sampling K-hop neighborhood sampling is a technique where the neighborhood of a given node is defined as all nodes that are reachable within k hops (edges). This method captures a broader structural context than immediate (1-hop) neighbors by recursively expanding the neighborhood. It is especially useful in GNNs, where the goal is to learn a node's representation based not only on its direct neighbors but also on more distant nodes. However, one of the key trade-offs is that as k increases, the number of nodes in the neighborhood may grow exponentially, which could lead to scalability issues. Despite this, k-hop sampling remains a fundamental approach to retaining locality and structure in large graphs.

Mathematical Formulation In k-hop neighborhood sampling, the mathematical formulation focuses on capturing all nodes that lie within k steps from a given seed node v in a graph $G = (V, E)$.

Define $N^{(k)}(v)$ as the set of nodes reachable from v within k hops.

$$N^{(k)}(v) = \{u \in V \mid \text{shortest path from } v \text{ to } u \leq k\}$$

The k-hop neighborhood, denoted as $N^{(k)}(v)$, includes every node $u \in V$ such that the shortest path between v and u is less than or equal to k.

The k-hop subgraph $G^{(k)}(v)$ is defined as follows:

$$G^{(k)}(v) = (V^{(k)}(v), E^{(k)}(v))$$

where

- $V^{(k)}(v) = \{v\} \cup N^{(k)}(v)$
- $E^{(k)}(v) = \{(u, w) \in E \mid u, w \in V^{(k)}(v)\}$

$V^{(k)}$ includes the seed node and all its k-hop neighbors, and $E^{(k)}$ includes all edges among them.

Let the graph be $G_1 = (V, E)$ with nodes $V = \{A, B, C, D, E, F\}$ and edges $=$ $E=$ $\{(A, B), (A, C), (B, D), (C, E), (D, F)\}$, as shown in Fig. 5.12 (a).

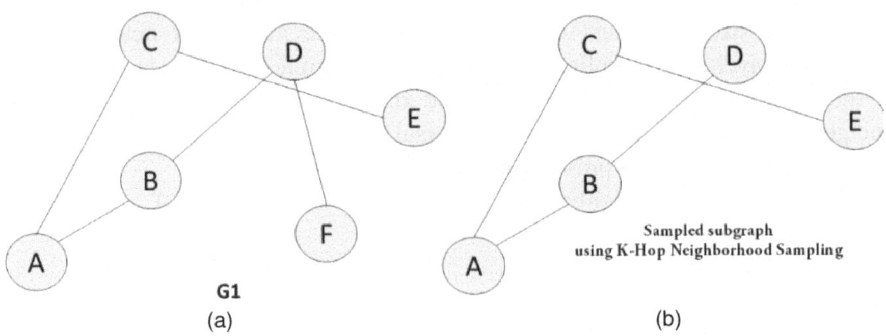

Figure 5.12 (a) Original input graph; (b) sampled subgraph using K-hop neighborhood sampling.

The 2-hop sampling from node A is given as follows:

1-hop neighbors of A is $\{B, C\}$ and 2-hop neighbors are from $B \rightarrow D$ and from $C \rightarrow E$.

So, the 2-hop neighborhood of A:

$$N^{(2)}(A) = \{B, C, D, E\}$$

The resulting sampled subgraph contains nodes: $\{A, B, C, D, E\}$ and relevant edges: $\{(A, B), (A, C), (B, D), (C, E)\}$. This is shown in Fig. 5.12 (b).

Algorithm: K-Hop Neighborhood Sampling

Input:
Graph $G = (V, E)$, seed node v, hop count k

Output:
Subgraph G_k = (V_k, E_k)

1) Initialize V_k ← {v}
2) Initialize frontier ← {v}
3) For $i = 1$ to k:
   Initialize next_frontier ← ∅
   For each node u in frontier:
   For each neighbor w of u:
   If w not in V_k:
   Add w to V_k
   Add w to next_frontier
   frontier ← next_frontier
4) E_k ← all edges $(u, w) \in E$ such that $u, w \in$ V_k
5) Return G_k = (V_k, E_k)

B. Random Walk Neighborhood Sampling Random walk neighborhood sampling is a powerful method for efficiently extracting a node's local context by simulating a random traversal over a graph. Instead of collecting all neighbors within a fixed distance (like k-hop sampling), random walk sampling selects a subset of nodes by walking through the graph probabilistically from a target node. This is particularly useful in large-scale graphs where full neighborhood expansion becomes computationally expensive. It helps preserve important structural and connectivity patterns without traversing the entire graph.

Mathematical Formulation Let $G_1 = (V, E)$ be a graph, and let $v \in V$ be the seed node. Define L as the length of the walk (number of steps), T as the number of walks to perform per seed, and $N^{RW}(v)$ as the random walk neighborhood of v.

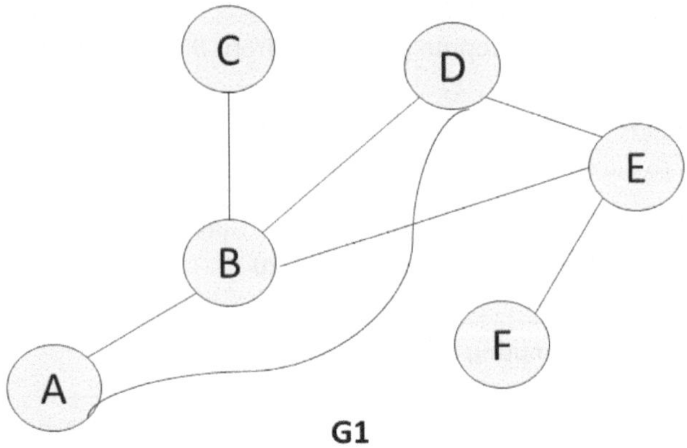

Figure 5.13 Sample graph for random walk neighborhood sampling.

Each walk $W = \{v_0 = v, v_1, \ldots, v_L\}$ is sampled such that:

$$P(v_{i+1} = u \mid v_i = w) = \frac{1}{\deg(W)} \text{ if } (w, u) \in E$$

After T walks, the neighborhood is

$$N^{\text{RW}}(v) = \cup\{v^1(t), v^2(t), \ldots, v^L(t)\}$$

Consider the graph shown in Fig. 5.13.

Suppose we start a random walk from node A, and we want to sample a neighborhood of size 4 using a walk length of 3.

Let's define the steps of one random walk:

1) Start at A.
2) From A, randomly choose between B and D.
3) Suppose B is chosen. From B, next choose between A, C, and E.
4) Suppose E is chosen. From E, choose between B, D, and F.
5) Suppose F is chosen.

The sampled nodes from this walk would be: [A, B, E, F]—forming a local neighborhood.

Algorithm: Random Walk Neighborhood Sampling

Input:
Graph $G = (V, E)$, seed node v, walk length L, number of walks T

Output:
Neighborhood sample $N\_RW(v)$

1) Initialize $N\_RW(v) = \{v\}$

2) Repeat T times:
   a) Set current_node = v
   b) For $i = 1$ to L:
      i) Randomly choose a neighbor $u \in$ Neighbors(current_node)
      ii) Add u to $N\_RW(v)$
      iii) Set current_node = u
3) Return $N\_RW(v)$

C. Layer-wise Neighborhood Sampling Layer-wise neighborhood sampling is a sampling technique commonly used in training deep GNNs, especially when dealing with large graphs. Instead of sampling all neighbors at once, this method samples a fixed number of neighbors separately at each GNN layer, allowing the model to progressively build receptive fields layer-by-layer. This reduces computational overhead and memory usage, making GNNs more scalable while preserving important hierarchical information in the graph structure. It's widely used in methods such as GraphSAGE and FastGCN, allowing GNNs to scale to massive graphs by sampling a fixed-size local neighborhood at each layer.

Mathematical Formulation Let $G = (V, E)$ be the input graph with L number of GNN layers and S_l sampling size at layer l and $N^{(l)}(v)$ sampled neighbors of node v at layer l.

The sampling is defined recursively:

$$N^{(L)}(v) = \{v\}, N^{(l)}(v) = \cup u \in N^{(l+1)}(v) \text{ Sample(Sl, Neighbors}(u))$$

where Sample(S, Neighbors(u)) randomly selects S neighbors of u.

Consider this simple graph given in Fig. 5.13.

To compute the embedding for node A using a 2-layer GNN, take sample 2 neighbors at each layer:

- Layer 1: For node A, randomly sample 2 neighbors → $\{B, D\}$.
- Layer 2: For B and D, sample 2 neighbors each:
  - B → randomly pick $\{A, E\}$
  - D → randomly pick $\{A, E\}$

So, the sampled nodes are: A (target), B, D (1-hop), A, E (from B), A, E (from D). Redundant nodes are merged, and the final sampled subgraph is: $\{A, B, D, E\}$.

This localized subgraph will be used for aggregation during training.

Algorithm: Layer-wise Neighborhood Sampling

Input:

Graph $G = (V, E)$, seed node v, number of layers L, neighbors per layer [S_1, S_2, …, S_L]

Output:

Layer-wise sampled subgraph nodes for node v

1) Initialize $N[L] = \{v\}$ // seed node at final layer
2) For $l = L - 1$ down to 0:
   a) $N[l] = \{\}$
   b) For each node u in $N[l + 1]$:
      i) Sample S_l neighbors from Neighbors(u)
      ii) Add sampled neighbors to $N[l]$
3) Return the union of all $N[0], N[1], \ldots, N[L]$

5.2.4 Subgraph Sampling

Subgraph sampling is an essential technique used in graph machine learning to reduce the size of a large graph while preserving its structural properties. Instead of sampling nodes or edges independently, this method extracts a smaller connected subgraph that maintains the relationships and topological features of the original graph. The goal is to provide the GNN with a representative view of the entire graph, enabling efficient training on massive networks such as social, biological, or financial graphs. Subgraph sampling is particularly effective in capturing both local and global structural patterns, making it ideal for tasks such as node classification, link prediction, or graph classification.

Mathematical Formulation

Let $G_1 = (V, E)$ be the original graph and $G' = (V', E')$ be the sampled subgraph. $|V'| = k$ where $k < |V|$. Seed(v) is the initial seed node.

Subgraph sampling involves

$$V' = \text{Expand}(v, h) \text{ or } \text{V}' = \text{SampleSubgraph}(G, k)$$

where

Expand(v, h) samples nodes within h hops from seed v.

SampleSubgraph can also be defined by random walks or Metropolis–Hastings sampling.

$$E' = \{(u, w) \in E \mid u, w \in V'\}$$

Consider the graph given in Fig. 5.13.

To extract a subgraph of four nodes, start by selecting a seed node, say B, and expand its neighbors up to a fixed number of hops or use random walks. Start at B. The 1-hop neighbors of B are A, C, E. Select B, A, E, and randomly one more (say, D). The resulting subgraph contains nodes $\{A, B, D, E\}$ and edges $\{(A, B), (A, D), (B, E), (D, E)\}$, forming a smaller connected graph that preserves local structure.

5.3 Case Studies

5.3.1 Case Study: Sampling Patient Networks for Disease Prediction

Modern healthcare analytics grappling with electronic health records (EHRs) face a significant challenge: EHRs generate immense graphs where nodes represent patients and edges signify clinical similarities such as shared diagnoses, medications, or procedures. Analyzing these vast patient graphs for tasks such as disease progression prediction or early diagnosis is often computationally overwhelming and impractical. To overcome this, researchers are increasingly turning to graph sampling techniques, particularly subgraph and neighborhood sampling. These methods are crucial for extracting manageable yet representative portions of the graph, ensuring that vital medical relationships are preserved. For example, a study predicting diabetes might construct a graph connecting patients based on similar blood glucose patterns and comorbidities, then apply sampling to make the analysis feasible.

The system selected local patient groups centered on individuals at risk using k-hop neighborhood sampling, capturing their clinical framework without the necessity of the entire dataset. This approach preserved critical temporal and relational information and allowed GNNs to train effectively on smaller, yet informative, subgraphs. Results showed significant improvement in prediction accuracy and training time. Moreover, random walk sampling was used to simulate patient journeys through different clinical states, mimicking transitions between diagnoses or treatment stages. These sampled subgraphs provided insight into disease trajectories and treatment outcomes across populations. This case illustrates how graph sampling not only makes large healthcare graphs tractable but also enhances the interpretability and scalability of predictive models in sensitive and high-stakes environments such as clinical decision support systems.

5.3.2 Case Study: Sampling in Learning Management System

In modern education, especially within online learning environments such as Massive Open Online Courses (MOOCs), Learning Management Systems (LMS), and intelligent tutoring platforms, the sheer volume of student-generated data naturally forms large-scale graphs. These "educational graphs" map complex relationships: nodes might represent students, courses, concepts, activities, or assessments, while edges capture interactions such as course enrollments, peer collaborations, learning sequences, or concept dependencies. As these graphs grow, involving millions of students and countless resources, analyzing them in their entirety quickly becomes computationally unfeasible. Consequently, graph sampling emerges as an indispensable tool, enabling the extraction of manageable, meaningful subgraphs essential for downstream analysis and machine learning.

For example, consider a platform like Coursera or edX. Suppose researchers want to understand how student engagement with video content relates to course completion. Using neighborhood sampling, they can focus on students who have interacted with certain course modules and examine how their peer interactions or concept mastery influences dropout risk. Stratified node sampling can be applied to ensure equal representation across high-performing, average, and at-risk students, allowing for balanced training of predictive models. Additionally, random walk sampling can simulate a student's pathway through various learning modules or knowledge concepts—mimicking the way learners naturally explore content. This approach helps in building knowledge tracing models or prerequisite learning graphs, which predict what concept a student should learn next.

From a computational perspective, layer-wise neighborhood sampling helps train GNNs for education without loading the entire graph into memory. For instance, if a platform aims to recommend personalized learning resources, sampling allows the model to consider only relevant peer behaviors or concept clusters, vastly improving efficiency and scalability.

In real-world applications, such graph sampling has been used to

- Identify significant learners in peer forums who help others.
- Cluster learners based on their learning patterns for differentiated instruction.
- Detect bottlenecks in learning pathways using sampled concept graphs.

Ultimately, graph sampling enables adaptive, data-driven education systems that are scalable, personalized, and responsive to learners' needs—making it a key component of modern educational data mining and learning analytics.

5.3.3 Case Study: Community-Based Sampling for Efficient Social Network Analysis

Social networks, such as Facebook and Twitter, encompass vast and intricate graphs comprising millions or even billions of nodes (users) and edges (connections). Analyzing these massive networks in their entirety is computationally intensive and often impractical. To address this challenge, researchers have explored graph sampling techniques that aim to extract representative subgraphs, preserving essential properties of the original network while significantly reducing computational overhead [4].

The primary goal is to develop a sampling method that maintains critical graph properties, particularly community structures, enabling accurate and efficient analysis without processing the entire network.

Methodology

In the study "Graph Property Preservation under Community-Based Sampling" by Gao et al. [5], the authors propose a heuristic approach that leverages known community structures within social networks to guide the sampling process. The key steps include the following:

1) **Community Identification**
   Utilize existing community detection algorithms or use known community labels to partition the original graph into distinct communities.
2) **Stratified Sampling Within Communities**
   Apply stratified sampling techniques within each identified community to select nodes and edges. This ensures that the sampled subgraph retains the internal structure and characteristics of each community.
3) **Sample Aggregation**
   Combine the sampled nodes and edges from all communities to construct the final representative subgraph.

Results

The community-based sampling approach demonstrated superior performance in preserving key graph properties compared to traditional random node or edge sampling methods. Specifically,

- **Community Structure Preservation**
  The sampled subgraphs maintained the modularity and internal connectivity of the original communities, enabling accurate community detection and analysis.
- **Degree Distribution Maintenance**
  The degree distribution within the sampled subgraphs closely mirrored that of the original graph, ensuring that node centrality measures remained consistent.
- **Computational Efficiency**
  By focusing on representative subsets of the graph, the approach significantly reduced computational requirements for various graph algorithms, facilitating faster analysis without substantial loss of accuracy.

Community-based sampling offers a practical and effective solution for analyzing large-scale social networks. By leveraging inherent community structures, this method ensures that essential properties of the network are preserved in the sampled subgraph, enabling efficient and accurate analysis. This approach is particularly beneficial for tasks such as community detection, influence analysis, and information diffusion studies in expansive social networks.

5.4 Conclusion

Graph sampling serves as a powerful strategy to manage and analyze large-scale, complex networks efficiently. By exploring various types of sampling—such as node, edge, neighborhood, and subgraph sampling—this chapter highlights their unique advantages and suitable applications. Through case studies in healthcare, education (LMS), and social networks, we demonstrated how sampling not only reduces computational burden but also preserves key structural and functional properties, enabling insightful, scalable analysis across diverse real-world domains.

References

1 A. Sevilla, A. Mozo, and A. F. Anta, "Node sampling using random centrifugal walks," *J. Comput. Sci*, vol. 11, pp. 34–45, 2015.

2 C. M. Le, "Edge sampling using local network information," *J. Machine Learn. Res.*, vol. 22, pp. 1–29, 2021.

3 N. Ahmed, J. Neville, and R. R. Kompella, *Network Sampling via Edge-based Node Selection with Graph Induction*. West Lafayette, IN: Purdue University, 2011.

4 T. Wang, C. Yang, Z. Zhang, T. Xu, L. Jin, and H. Pan, "Understanding graph sampling algorithms for social network analysis, 2011 31st Int. Conf. Distrib. Comp. Syst. Workshops, Minneapolis, MN, USA,", pp. 123–128, ISBN:978-1-4577-0384-3, 2011, doi: 10.1109/ICDCSW.2011.34.

5 R. Gao, P. Hu, and W. C. Lau, "Graph property preservation under community-based sampling, 2015 IEEE Global Commun. Conf. (GLOBECOM), E-ISBN:978-1-4799-5952-5,", doi: 10.1109/GLOCOM.2015.7417471.

6

Graph Pooling

6.1 Introduction to Graph Pooling

In the previous chapter, we explored the foundations of deep learning on graphs, focusing on how graph neural networks (GNNs) and graph convolutional networks (GCNs) are designed to learn from graph-structured data. We discussed the key components of GNNs, such as message passing, graph convolutions, and node/graph embeddings, which enable these models to extract meaningful representations from complex relational data.

While these techniques are powerful, they come with challenges, especially when dealing with large or dense graphs. As the size of the graph grows, learning meaningful representations becomes computationally expensive, and the network might struggle to capture high-level global features effectively. Graph pooling plays a crucial role in solving these challenges.

6.1.1 What Is Graph Pooling?

Graph pooling (Fig. 6.1) is a method applied in GNNs to simplify a graph by decreasing its size while maintaining crucial structural and feature-related information. Just as pooling layers in convolutional neural networks (CNNs) shrink the spatial dimensions of images, graph pooling reduces the number of nodes and edges in a graph, allowing the model to concentrate on more abstract, high-level representations.

6.1.2 Why Is Graph Pooling Important?

Graph pooling plays a crucial role in GNNs by simplifying large, complex graphs into smaller, more meaningful representations while retaining essential structural and feature-based information. Without pooling, GNNs would face challenges in scalability, computational efficiency, and generalization, particularly when

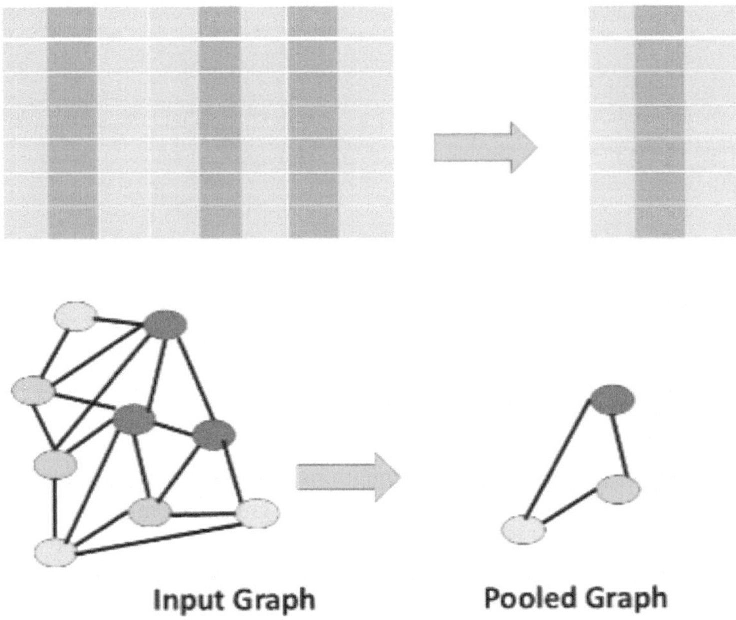

Figure 6.1 Example of pooled graph.

handling graphs of varying sizes [1]. By enabling dimensionality reduction, pooling reduces computational overhead and enhances model performance by prioritizing the most relevant nodes and substructures.

In fields such as molecular property prediction, social network analysis, and image classification, pooling helps uncover hierarchical relationships, detect key patterns, and improve classification accuracy. Whether applying sum, mean, max, or attention-based pooling, these techniques ensure that graph-based models learn compact yet informative representations, making them more efficient, adaptable, and scalable for real-world applications.

- Pooling reduces the computational cost of processing large graphs by creating smaller, more manageable representations.
- Pooling helps GNNs [4] move beyond local neighborhoods to capture global graph structures, making them suitable for graph-level tasks such as classification and regression.
- By progressively reducing the graph size, pooling enables the creation of hierarchical representations, which are critical for understanding multi-scale graph features.
- By reducing graph size, pooling acts as a regularizer, preventing the model from overfitting to fine-grained details.

6.2 Types of Graph Pooling

When working with large graphs, you often need a way to reduce their size while keeping the most important information intact. That's where graph pooling comes in. There are three main types of graph pooling, each with its approach.

6.2.1 Flat Pooling

- **Definition and Characteristics.**

Flat pooling is a graph pooling technique where all the nodes in a graph are aggregated into a single fixed-size representation, without considering any hierarchical relationships. Since flat pooling directly compresses the entire graph into a single feature vector, it is most commonly used for graph-level classification tasks where we are interested in the overall properties of the graph rather than individual node relationships. The following are its key characteristics:

- Flat pooling compresses all node features into a single feature vector.
- Uses sum, mean, or max pooling to aggregate information across the graph.
- Does not preserve hierarchical structures or local subgraph details.
- Flat pooling produces a fixed-size output regardless of the number of nodes or edges.
- Makes it easier to feed graph data into fully connected neural networks for classification.
- Fast and scalable, since it performs a one-step aggregation instead of multiple iterations.
- Requires fewer parameters, making it suitable for large-scale datasets.
- Works well for problems where the overall properties of the graph are more important than individual node interactions.
- Commonly used in graph classification, anomaly detection, and regression tasks.

Figure 6.2 shows that the information (feature values) of all the nodes (A,B,C,D,E) of the graph is aggregated into a single vector representation.

Example ***Flat Pooling in Molecular Graph Classification***

Consider a molecular graph G, which consists of atoms (nodes) and chemical bonds (edges). The node features are atomic properties (e.g., atomic number, valency). We need to classify a molecule as toxic (molecules that can cause disease) or non-toxic based on atomic features.

Assume we have a simple molecular graph with three atoms (carbon [C], oxygen ([O], and hydrogen [H]), each with a three-dimensional feature vector representing atomic properties such as electronegativity, valency, and atomic

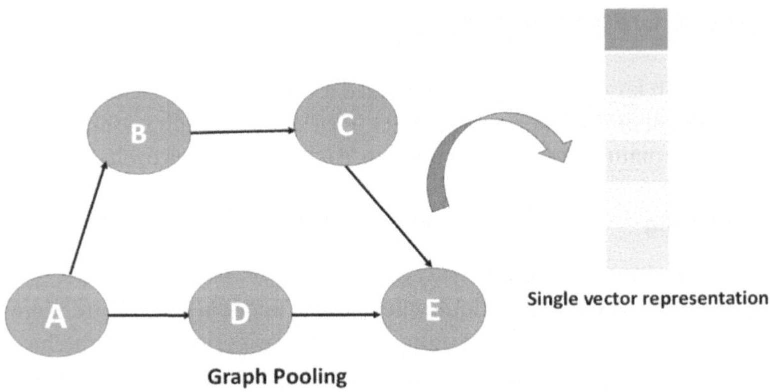

Figure 6.2 Single vector representation of pooled graph.

weight. Edges are represented as a single chemical bond:

$$h1 = [1.0, 2.0, 3.0], \qquad h2 = [0.5, 1.5, 2.5], \qquad h3 = [2.0, 3.0, 1.0]$$

Let us see how global pooling types work.

6.2.1.1 Methods of Flat Pooling

There are several ways to perform flat pooling, each with its own method of aggregating node features. Here, we will explain in detail four key types of flat pooling methods.

Each method has its advantages, depending on whether you want to preserve overall magnitude, balance, or dominant features in your pooled graph representation [7]. The right choice depends on the task and dataset.

A. Sum Pooling Sum pooling is the simplest and most intuitive way to aggregate node information. It sums up all feature vectors across all nodes, producing a single fixed-size vector that represents the entire graph. The mathematical representation of sum pooling for a graph G with N nodes is

$$h_G = \sum_{i=1}^{N} h_i$$

where h_G is the final pooled graph representation, h_i is the feature vector of node i, and N is the number of nodes in the graph.

Example

Applying sum pooling for the same molecular example in the graph given in Fig. 6.3:

$$h_G = h_1 + h_2 + h_3$$

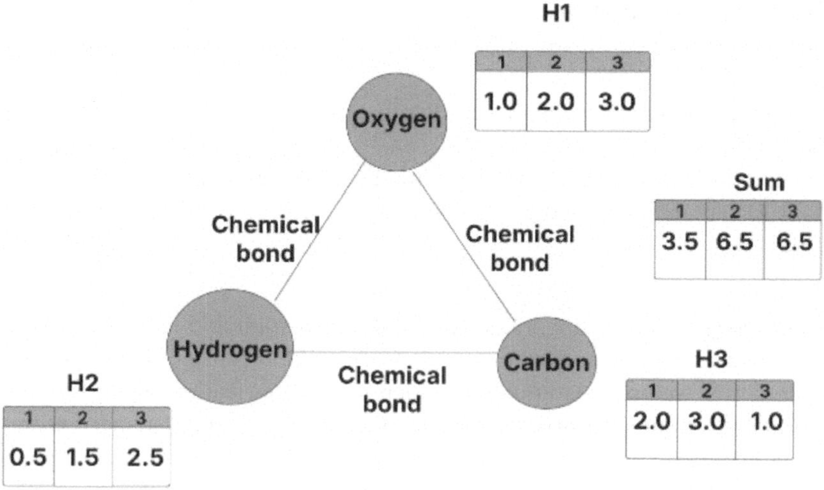

Figure 6.3 Chemical bond example for sum pooling.

$$h_G = [1.0 + 0.5 + 2.0, 2.0 + 1.5 + 3.0, 3.0 + 2.5 + 1.0]$$

$$h_G = [3.5, 6.5, 6.5]$$

The output $h_G = [3.5, 6.5, 6.5]$ from sum pooling represents the total aggregated feature values of all nodes in the graph. Since sum pooling adds up all node features, larger graphs will have higher values, making this method suitable for tasks where the overall magnitude of features matters, such as predicting molecular properties or total transaction volume in financial networks. However, it does not normalize for graph size, which may introduce biases when comparing graphs of different sizes.

Advantages of Sum Pooling

- Retains the overall feature magnitude, making it suitable for tasks where the total contribution of all nodes matters, such as molecular energy prediction or financial transaction aggregation.
- Computationally efficient and easy to implement, as it only requires summing all node features without additional learning parameters.
- Well-suited for graph-level tasks, including classification, regression, and anomaly detection, where the global properties of the graph determine the outcome.
- Robust for large graphs, as it ensures that all nodes contribute to the final representation without bias toward smaller substructures.
- Effective for weighted graphs, where the total sum of node features carries significant meaning, such as in supply chain networks or disease spread modeling.

Disadvantages of Sum Pooling

- It aggregates all node features but does not preserve relationships between nodes.
- Larger graphs tend to have higher feature magnitudes, which can create bias in predictions.
- It treats all nodes equally, even if some are more influential than others.
- It fails to capture substructures or community-based relationships within the graph.

B. Mean Pooling Sum pooling loses structural information and is biased toward larger graphs, as it simply adds up node features without considering graph size. To address this, we use mean pooling, which normalizes feature aggregation by averaging node values, ensuring a scale-independent and more balanced representation for graphs of different sizes. Mean pooling is particularly useful when analyzing graphs with varying node counts, such as documents of different lengths or social networks of different community sizes.

Instead of summing all node features, mean pooling takes the average across all nodes, giving a balanced representation of the graph. The mathematical representation of mean pooling is given as

$$h_G = \frac{1}{N} \sum_{i=1}^{N} h_i$$

where h_G is the final pooled graph representation, h_i is the feature vector of node i, and N is the number of nodes in the graph.

Example

Using the same molecular graph example with three atoms:

$$h_G = \frac{1}{3}\,[3.5, 6.5, 6.5]$$

$$h_G = [1.17, 2.17, 2.17]$$

The output $h_G = [1.17, 2.17, 2.17]$ from mean pooling, given in Fig. 6.4, represents the average feature values across all nodes in the graph. Since mean pooling normalizes the number of nodes, it provides a scale-independent representation, making it suitable for comparing graphs of different sizes. This ensures balanced feature aggregation, making it useful for tasks such as document classification, user behavior analysis, and molecular property prediction without being biased toward larger graphs.

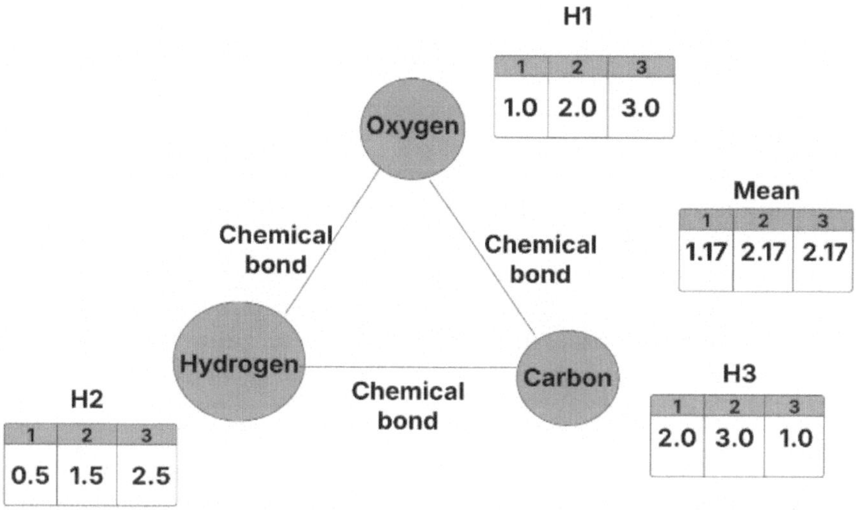

Figure 6.4 Example for mean pooling.

Advantages of Mean Pooling

- Unlike sum pooling, mean pooling ensures that graphs of different sizes produce comparable feature representations by averaging node features instead of summing them. This is particularly useful for tasks such as social network analysis and document classification, where graphs may have varying numbers of nodes.
- Mean pooling effectively captures the overall structure and distribution of node features, making it suitable for graph classification, regression, and anomaly detection.
- Since each node's feature values are averaged, no single node dominates the final representation. This makes mean pooling ideal for applications such as disease spread modeling or customer segmentation, where collective behavior matters more than individual entities.
- Large graphs with more nodes do not artificially inflate feature values, ensuring fair comparisons between graphs of different sizes. This is particularly beneficial in biochemical applications, where molecules of different sizes need to be evaluated on the same scale.
- Mean pooling is simple to compute and does not require additional learnable parameters, making it an efficient choice for large-scale graph processing.
- Since mean pooling normalizes the graph representation, models trained with it are less likely to overfit to variations in graph size and structure.

Disadvantages of Mean Pooling

- Since mean pooling gives equal weight to all nodes, it fails to highlight influential or highly connected nodes. In social networks, for instance, key influencers should have a stronger impact than inactive users, which mean pooling does not capture.
- Mean pooling does not preserve community structures or subgraph patterns, making it less suitable for tasks such as fraud detection, recommendation systems, or hierarchical classification.
- If a small number of nodes have extreme feature values, mean pooling may skew the overall representation, reducing its robustness in graphs with noisy data.
- In cases where some nodes have significantly different distributions from the majority (e.g., network hubs vs isolated nodes), mean pooling blends all values, potentially leading to loss of key differentiating information.

C. Max Pooling Mean pooling treats all nodes equally, ignoring the importance of highly influential nodes, and fails to capture dominant features, making it less effective for graphs with highly skewed structures. To address this, we use max pooling, which selects the most significant feature values across nodes, ensuring that the strongest signals in the graph are preserved for better classification and anomaly detection.

Max pooling selects the highest value for each feature across all nodes, emphasizing the most significant node characteristics. Mathematical representation of max pooling for each feature j is given as

$$h_G^j = \max{}_{i=1}^{N} h_i^j$$

where h_G^j is the jth dimension of the final pooled graph representation, h_i^j is the jth feature of the ith node, and N is the number of nodes in the graph.

Example

Using the same molecular graph example:

$$h_G = [\max(1.0, 0.5, 2.0), \max(2.0, 1.5, 3.0), \max(3.0, 2.5, 1.0)]$$

$$h_G = [2.0, 3.0, 3.0]$$

The output $h_G = [2.0,3.0,3.0]$ from max pooling, given in Fig. 6.5, represents the strongest feature values across all nodes in the graph. Since max pooling selects the highest value for each feature dimension, it highlights the most dominant characteristics of the graph while ignoring weaker signals. This makes it useful for tasks such as anomaly detection, fraud detection, and identifying key influencers in social networks. However, it may lose global context and be sensitive to noise or outliers in the data.

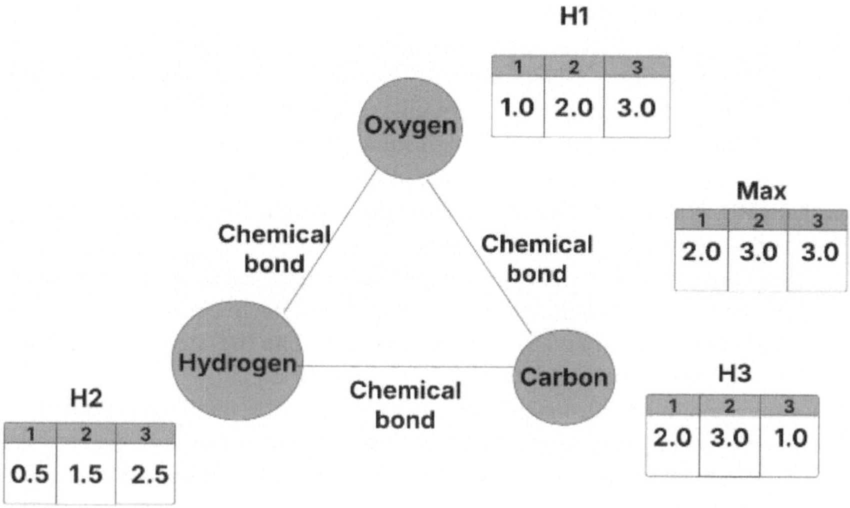

Figure 6.5 Example for max pooling.

Advantages of Max Pooling

- Unlike sum and mean pooling, which blend all node features, max pooling selects the most dominant values from each feature dimension. This ensures that key structural and attribute-based patterns are retained, making it ideal for anomaly detection, fraud detection, and critical feature identification.
- Max pooling ensures that the most informative or extreme values contribute to the final graph representation. This is useful in biomedical applications, where the presence of a specific molecular substructure determines drug effectiveness.
- In cases where some nodes are significantly more important than others (e.g., high-degree hubs in social networks or highly active fraud accounts in transaction graphs), max pooling preserves the most relevant information, reducing the impact of less important nodes.
- Since max pooling picks only the highest feature values, it does not suffer from size-related biases similar to sum pooling. This makes it particularly effective for graphs with variable numbers of nodes, such as user interaction networks in recommendation systems.
- Since max pooling focuses on the most extreme node attributes, it is effective in detecting unusual patterns, such as fake accounts in social networks or defective materials in industrial applications.
- Like mean and sum pooling, max pooling requires no trainable parameters, making it fast and scalable for large datasets.

Disadvantages of Max Pooling

- Since max pooling only retains the highest values, it discards less dominant but still useful information, which might be critical in tasks that require a holistic understanding of the graph (e.g., hierarchical document classification).
- If a single node has an abnormally high value, it will dominate the pooled representation, potentially leading to misleading results in noisy datasets. This is problematic in real-world financial networks, where a single extreme transaction might not represent the overall trend.
- Max pooling only picks the highest values, meaning it does not capture the overall distribution of node features. This makes it less effective in scenarios where the collective behavior of nodes is more important than the strongest individual features (e.g., community detection in social networks).
- Since max pooling only considers the strongest features, it fails to capture relationships between weaker but correlated nodes, making it less suitable for tasks that require context-aware learning, such as sentiment analysis or text-based graph classification.

D. Attention Pooling Sum pooling is biased toward larger graphs, mean pooling treats all nodes equally and loses key features, and max pooling ignores subtle but important information while being sensitive to outliers. To address these limitations, we use attention pooling, which dynamically learns the importance of each node, ensuring that the most relevant features contribute meaningfully to the final graph representation.

Unlike the previous methods, attention pooling assigns learnable importance weights to each node before pooling, ensuring that more relevant nodes contribute more to the final representation. The mathematical representation of attention pooling is

$$h_G = \sum_{i=1}^{N} \alpha_i h_i$$

where α_i is the attention score for node i, learned through a neural network, and h_i is the feature vector of node i. The sum of all attention scores is normalized by

$$\sum_{i=1}^{N} \alpha_i = 1.$$

Example

Suppose we assign the following attention scores to our molecular graph given in Fig. 6.6:

$$\alpha_1 = 0.6, \alpha_2 = 0.3, \alpha_3 = 0.1$$

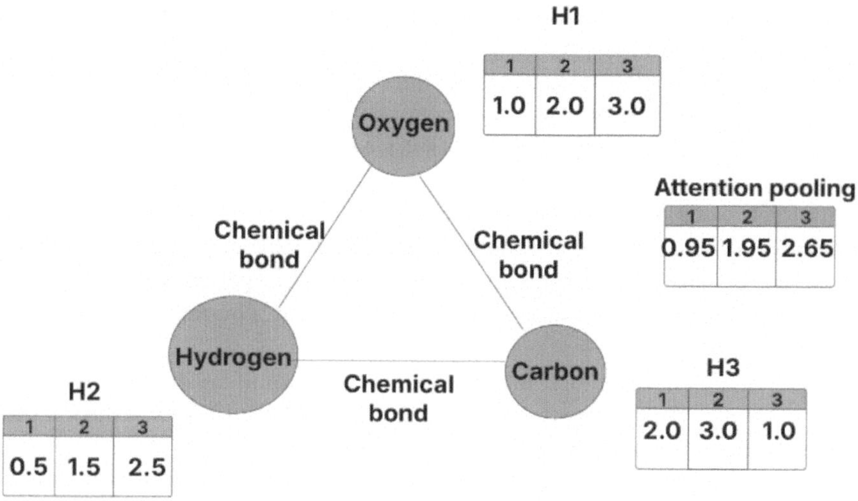

Figure 6.6 Example for attention pooling.

Then, the pooled feature vector is computed as

$$h_G = (0.6 \times h1) + (0.3 \times h2) + (0.1 \times h3)$$

$$h_G = (0.6 \times [1.0, 2.0, 3.0]) + (0.3 \times [0.5, 1.5, 2.5]) + (0.1 \times [2.0, 3.0, 1.0])$$

$$h_G = [0.6 + 0.15 + 0.2, 1.2 + 0.45 + 0.3, 1.8 + 0.75 + 0.1]$$

$$h_G = [0.95, 1.95, 2.65]$$

The output $h_G = [0.95, 1.95, 2.65]$ from attention pooling represents a weighted aggregation of node features, where more important nodes contribute more to the final representation. Unlike sum, mean, or max pooling, attention pooling learns node significance dynamically, ensuring that highly relevant features are emphasized while reducing the influence of less important nodes. This makes it ideal for social network analysis, recommendation systems, and fraud detection, where certain nodes (e.g., influencers or key fraudsters) play a crucial role.

Advantages of Attention Pooling

- Unlike sum, mean, and max pooling, which treat all nodes equally or rely on fixed rules, attention pooling learns which nodes are most important for a given task. This makes it useful in social networks, recommendation systems, and fraud detection, where key nodes have a stronger influence than others.
- Instead of simply selecting the largest values (such as max pooling) or averaging everything (such as mean pooling), attention pooling identifies and preserves

subtle but meaningful features, improving accuracy in sentiment analysis, NLP, and financial risk modeling.
- Since attention pooling adapts to the graph structure, it avoids biases introduced by sum pooling (which favors larger graphs) and mean pooling (which normalizes all nodes equally). This makes it ideal for heterogeneous graphs with varying sizes.
- Attention weights can be analyzed to explain why certain nodes were given more importance, making the model more interpretable in applications such as medical diagnosis (e.g., identifying key biomarkers in a patient's genetic graph) or recommendation systems (e.g., understanding why a particular product was recommended).
- Unlike max pooling, which may be dominated by outliers, attention pooling smoothly distributes importance across multiple relevant nodes, reducing the impact of random noise in the graph.
- In applications where the graph structure evolves over time, such as real-time fraud detection, news trend analysis, and traffic flow prediction, attention pooling adapts by recalculating node importance based on the latest data.
- Attention pooling can be used alongside mean or max pooling to create hybrid models that balance global context and local importance, leading to better graph learning performance.

Disadvantages of Attention Pooling
- Unlike sum, mean, and max pooling, which are simple aggregation operations, attention pooling requires learning attention scores through additional neural network layers, increasing computational cost, especially for large-scale graphs.
- Since attention pooling introduces trainable parameters, it needs a larger dataset to generalize well. For small datasets, simpler pooling methods such as mean or max pooling might perform just as well or even better.
- Because attention pooling dynamically learns node importance, it can overfit to patterns in the training set, making it less generalizable to unseen data. Regularization techniques or dropout strategies are often required to counteract this.
- While attention weights provide some level of interpretability, in deep multi-layer models, it may still be difficult to fully explain why certain nodes were weighted more heavily than others, especially in highly interconnected graphs.
- If a graph has uniformly distributed information across nodes, attention pooling may not offer significant benefits over simpler methods such as mean pooling. In such cases, the additional computational cost of attention pooling may not be justified.

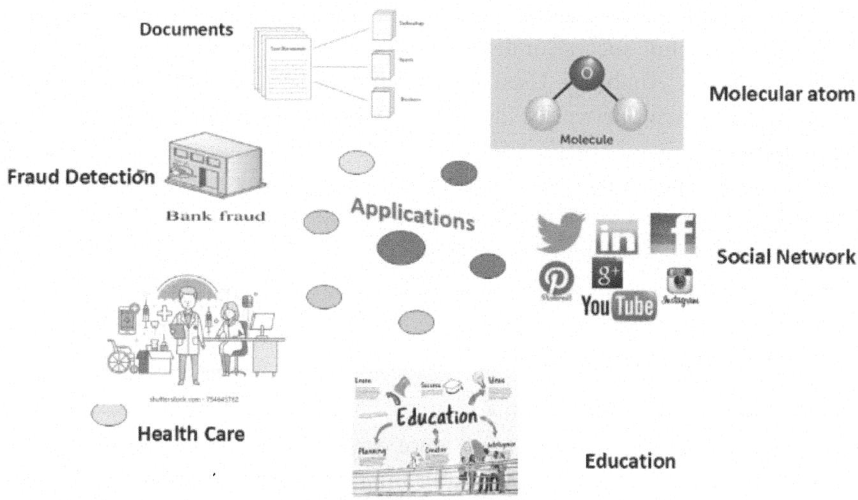

Figure 6.7 Applications of flat pooling.

6.2.1.2 Applications of Flat Pooling in Graph-Level Tasks

Flat pooling is widely used in graph-level tasks, where the focus is on the entire graph rather than individual nodes or edges. By aggregating node features into a single fixed-size representation, flat pooling enables efficient classification, regression, and anomaly detection in various domains. Various applications are depicted in Fig. 6.7.

- Molecular Property Prediction—In drug discovery and chemistry, flat pooling helps classify molecules based on their structural properties, such as toxicity, solubility, or reactivity.
- Document Classification—In text analysis, documents can be represented as word graphs, and flat pooling helps classify texts into categories such as spam detection, sentiment analysis, or topic modeling.
- Financial Fraud Detection—Aggregating transaction networks to detect fraudulent activities at the account or organization level rather than focusing on individual transactions.
- Health Risk Assessment—Flat pooling is used in healthcare for inpatient risk assessment. Electronic health records can be modeled as graphs, where flat pooling enables early disease detection and personalized treatment recommendations.
- Student Performance Prediction—Flat pooling is used in education technology and learning analytics to analyze student interactions, academic performance, and knowledge graphs. By representing students as nodes in a learning network,

flat pooling aggregates features such as test scores, attendance, and engagement to predict academic success or dropout risks.
- Social Network Analysis—Used for community-level classification, such as detecting fake news networks, identifying political groups, or analyzing online discussions.
- By simplifying graph representations, flat pooling makes graph-based learning models scalable and efficient, especially for tasks requiring global graph-level insights rather than localized node details.

6.2.2 Hierarchical Pooling

- **Definition and Characteristics**

Sometimes, you don't just want to collapse everything into one vector; instead, you want to merge nodes step by step, forming a coarser version of the graph at each stage. Methods such as Graclus pooling, differentiable pooling (DiffPool), and top-K pooling group similar nodes together, helping to preserve structural information. This is useful when graphs have hierarchical relationships, such as community detection in social networks.

Hierarchical pooling is a graph pooling technique that reduces the size of a graph step by step, creating a multi-level representation while preserving important structural and feature-based information. Unlike flat pooling, which aggregates all nodes at once, hierarchical pooling creates a coarser graph at each step, preserving hierarchical relationships. This makes it highly effective for tasks such as community detection, molecular structure analysis, and social network clustering, where understanding multi-level patterns within the graph is crucial. The following are its key characteristics:

- Unlike flat pooling, hierarchical pooling merges nodes or subgraphs iteratively, producing a coarser graph representation at each stage while preserving key structural information [2].
- Captures nested relationships within the graph, making it ideal for tasks such as community detection, hierarchical text classification, and molecular analysis.
- Dynamically determines which nodes or clusters to merge, ensuring that important structural components are preserved at every pooling step.
- By gradually reducing graph complexity, it optimizes memory usage and processing time while retaining essential features, making it suitable for large-scale graphs.
- Works effectively with both structured and unstructured graphs, including social networks, citation graphs, molecular structures, and three-dimensional point cloud data.

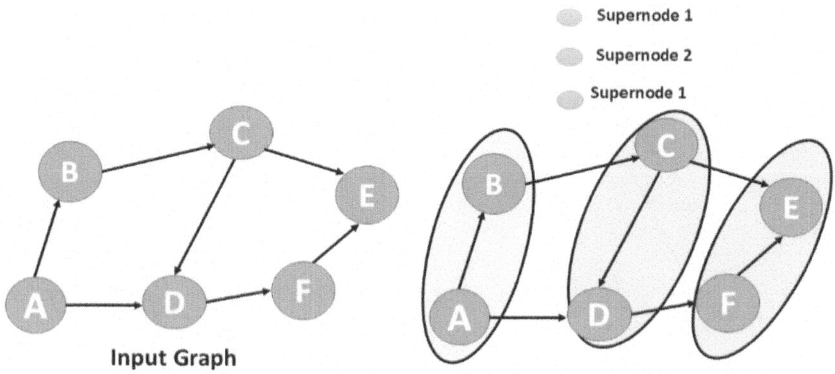

Figure 6.8 Social network illustration in first pooling step (merging nodes).

- Unlike flat pooling, hierarchical pooling retains intermediate graph representations, allowing models to learn both fine-grained and high-level structures, improving classification and clustering performance.

Example ***Social Network***

To illustrate hierarchical pooling, consider a social network graph where nodes (A, B, C, D, E, F) represent users and edges represent connections (friendships or interactions). Each node has a feature vector (e.g., PostFrequency, LikesReceived). The illustration is given in Fig. 6.8.

- First Pooling Step (Merging Nodes)

Similar or closely connected nodes are merged into supernodes based on graph structure or learned embeddings (e.g., {A, B}, {C, D}, {E, F}). Feature vectors are aggregated using sum, mean, or weighted pooling.

- Second Pooling Step (Further Reduction)

Supernodes are merged again as shown in Fig. 6.9, forming an even coarser representation of the graph. The final pooled representation contains fewer nodes while preserving the overall network structure.

- Final Representation

The graph is reduced to a compact form with key structural information retained. This can be used for classification, clustering, or anomaly detection.

6.2.2.1 Types of Hierarchical Pooling

Hierarchical pooling reduces graph size incrementally, preserving its structural integrity and key features at each step. Unlike flat pooling, which aggregates all

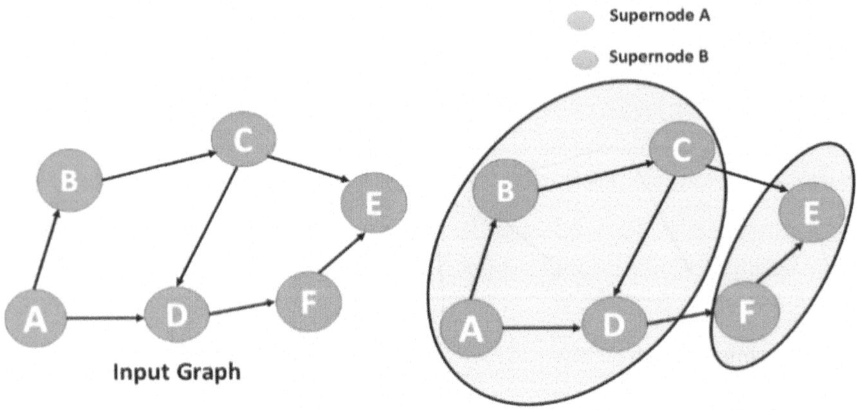

Figure 6.9 Social network illustration in second pooling step.

nodes at once, hierarchical pooling progressively merges nodes or clusters, capturing both local and global graph patterns. Depending on how nodes are selected for pooling, it can be classified into learnable pooling (e.g., DiffPool), structural pooling (e.g., Graclus pooling), and score-based pooling (e.g., top-K pooling, self-attention graph pooling [SAGPool]). Each method offers unique advantages, whether through predefined rules, trainable parameters, or importance-based selection, making them highly effective for tasks such as community detection, molecular structure analysis, and large-scale graph classification.

6.2.2.2 Common Techniques

A. Top-K Pooling Top-K pooling is a score-based hierarchical pooling technique in GNNs that selects the most important nodes while reducing the graph size. Unlike other hierarchical pooling methods such as DiffPool (in the next section), which merge nodes, top-K pooling ranks nodes based on a learned importance score and retains only the top K% of nodes, discarding the rest.

This approach enhances feature selection, reduces computational overhead, and improves model efficiency, all while preserving the most critical structural and feature-based information within the graph.

Top-K pooling follows a three-step process:

1) **Score Computation**

   Assign a learnable score S_i to each node i based on its feature importance. The score is computed as

$$S = Xw$$

   where $X \in R^{N \times d}$ is the node feature matrix (with N nodes and d features).

$w \in R^{d \times 1}$ is a learnable weight vector.
$S \in R^{N \times 1}$ is the importance score vector for all nodes.
Each node's score S_i determines its relevance in the graph.

2) **Node Selection**
After computing the scores, nodes are ranked in descending order based on their scores. We keep only the top $K\%$ nodes:

$$V' = \{v_i \in V \mid s_i \text{ is in the top K\%}\}$$

where
V' is the selected subset of important nodes and K is the retention ratio (e.g., if $K = 0.5$, we keep 50% of the highest-scoring nodes).
Graph Reduction
Construct a new pooled graph using the selected nodes while updating edges and features.

3) **Feature and Edge Update**
The feature matrix X' is updated to include only the retained nodes. The adjacency matrix A' is updated by keeping edges between the selected nodes. The new graph preserves the overall structure but removes less important nodes. The final pooled representation is

$$X' = PX,\ A' = PAP^T$$

where P is a selection matrix that picks the top $K\%$ nodes.
Figure 6.10 shows that out of nine nodes in the original input graph, only six nodes are pooled, and the remaining nodes are removed from the graph.

General Example of Top-K Pooling

Social Network Analysis (Influencer Detection)

In social networks, identifying key influencers is crucial for targeted marketing, trend analysis, and information diffusion modeling. Top-K pooling provides a systematic way to filter out less influential users while retaining the most active and important ones.

Imagine a social network graph where nodes represent users and edges represent interactions (follows, likes, comments). Each node has features such as engagement rate, post frequency, and follower count.

The goal is to identify the top influencers by filtering out low-engagement users using top-K pooling.

Step 1: Compute Scores

Each user i is given a score based on their engagement:

$$S_i = \text{Engagement Rate} \times w_1 + \text{Post Frequency} \times w_2 + \text{Follower Count} \times w_3$$

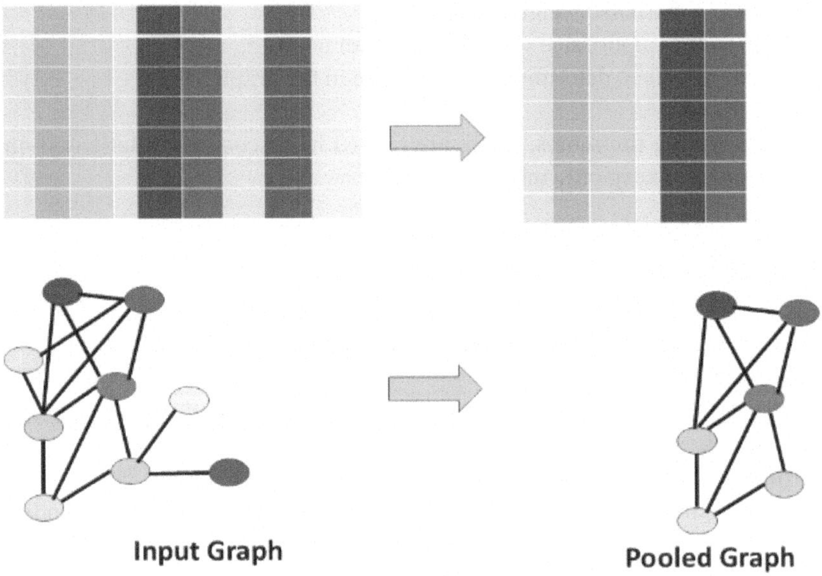

Figure 6.10 Pooling using top-K pooling technique.

where

Engagement Rate = Number of interactions (likes, shares, comments) per post.
Post Frequency = How often the user posts new content.
Follower Count = Total number of followers.
w_1, w_2, w_3 = Learnable weights to adjust the importance of each metric.

Example *Calculation*

From Table 6.1, it is clear that each user is now assigned a numerical score reflecting their influence in the network.

Step 2: Keep the Top-K Users (Highest Scores)

If $K = 50\%$ and there are ten users, we keep only five users with the highest scores.

Sorting the scores in descending order:

Users D and E are removed from the network as given in Table 6.2, leaving only the most influential users A, B, and C.

Step 3: Reduce the Graph

After removing the least important users, the graph structure is compressed, keeping only the most influential users and their connections.

Table 6.1 Score calculation for each user.

User (Node)	Engagement Rate	Post Frequency	Follower Count	Score Calculation
A	0.9	10	1,000	$(0.9 \times 0.5) + (10 \times 0.3) + (1{,}000 \times 0.2) = 200.45$
B	0.7	5	300	$(0.7 \times 0.5) + (5 \times 0.3) + (300 \times 0.2) = 60.35$
C	0.4	8	500	$(0.4 \times 0.5) + (8 \times 0.3) + (500 \times 0.2) = 100.2$
D	0.3	3	200	$(0.3 \times 0.5) + (3 \times 0.3) + (200 \times 0.2) = 40.15$
E	0.2	1	100	$(0.2 \times 0.5) + (1 \times 0.3) + (100 \times 0.2) = 20.1$

Table 6.2 Influence score for each user in top-K pooling technique.

User (Node)	Influence Score	Retained?
A	200.45	Yes
C	100.2	Yes
B	60.35	Yes
D	40.15	No
E	20.1	No

- Graph Adjustments:
  - Nodes removed: Less active users (D, E) are discarded.
  - Edges updated: Links between remaining users are retained or reweighted.
  - New graph structure: A smaller, more focused network with high-engagement users.

Figure 6.11 shows that the original graph is reduced to a smaller graph, more focused on the network with high-engagement users.

Top-K pooling can be used to filter out inactive users by keeping only highly influential users while removing low-impact participants.

Advantages and Disadvantages Table 6.3 lists out the advantages and disadvantages of top-K pooling technique.

B. DiffPool (Differentiable Pooling) While global pooling methods such as sum, mean, and max pooling offer a way to aggregate entire graph representations, they often ignore hierarchical structures and local subgraph information. To overcome these limitations, DiffPool provides a more advanced approach by learning hierarchical cluster assignments in an end-to-end manner.

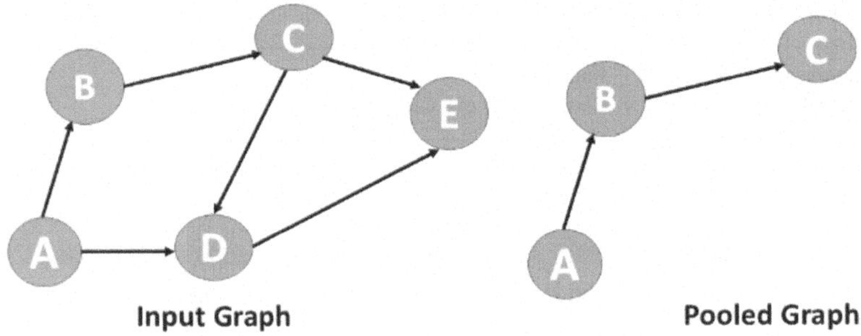

Figure 6.11 Final reduced pooled graph using top-K pooling.

Table 6.3 Advantages and disadvantages of top-K pooling technique.

Advantages	**Disadvantages**
Retains only the most important nodes, improving efficiency.	Choosing K requires careful tuning.
Reduces computational complexity for large graphs.	May remove useful low-score nodes, causing information loss.
Maintains key graph relationships while reducing redundancy.	Sensitive to noisy importance scores.
Works well for heterogeneous graphs across domains.	Requires additional learnable parameters.
Enhances generalization and prevents overfitting.	Can distort graph structure if edges are not updated properly.

DiffPool is a learnable hierarchical pooling method that groups nodes into clusters at each pooling layer, allowing the model to form a coarser representation of the graph while preserving its structural relationships. Unlike traditional pooling methods, which apply fixed aggregation rules, DiffPool learns the optimal clustering of nodes dynamically, making it more flexible and effective for complex graph-based tasks.

By using soft clustering assignments, DiffPool enables gradual and trainable graph reduction, making it particularly useful for applications such as social network analysis, protein interaction modeling, and graph classification. This approach ensures that both local substructures and global graph representations are maintained, leading to better performance in deep GNNs.

Traditional pooling methods such as sum, mean, max, and top-K treat nodes independently, ignoring the hierarchical relationships and multi-scale structures present in graphs. They either aggregate all nodes at once or remove less important

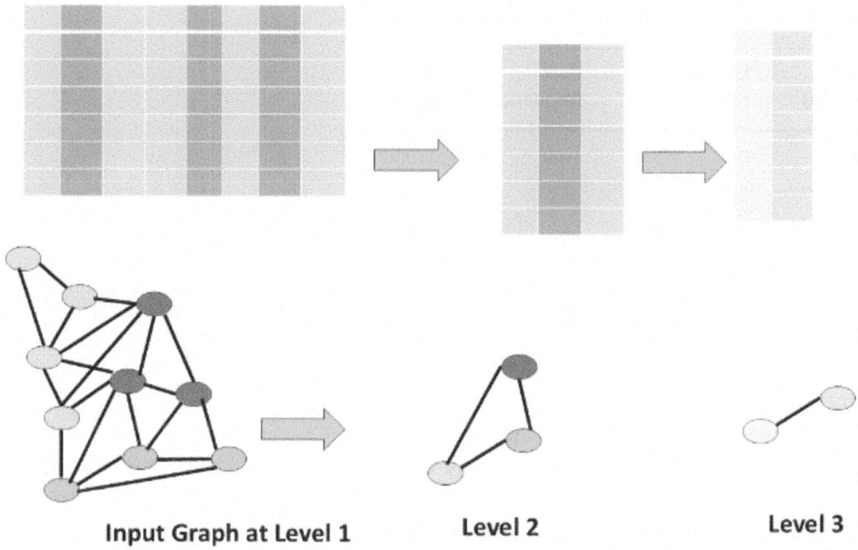

Figure 6.12 Hierarchical graph structure pooled at various levels.

ones, failing to capture higher-level subgraph patterns and long-range dependencies essential for hierarchical learning.

Figure 6.12 shows the hierarchical graph structure pooled at various levels.

The Working Process of DiffPool

- Key Concept: Learnable clustering mechanism where nodes are grouped dynamically.
- Mathematical Formulation:
  - Assignment Matrix $S \in R^{NXk}$, where each node is softly assigned to a cluster.
  - New Node Representations: $X' = S^T X$
  - Updated Adjacency Matrix: $A' = S^T AS$
  - Explanation of how differentiable clustering helps train GNNs end-to-end.
- Visualization of DiffPool Process (graphs being reduced at each pooling stage).

General Example of DiffPool Social Network Analysis (Influencer Detection) Consider a social network where nodes represent users (e.g., Twitter, Instagram users) and edges represent interactions (e.g., follows, likes, comments). Each user has a feature vector representing their engagement level (e.g., post frequency, follower count, engagement rate). The goal is to detect influencer groups (communities of highly engaged users) using DiffPool, rather than just ranking individual users as in top-K pooling.

Table 6.4 Feature vector of each node (A, B, C, D, E).

User (node)	Engagement rate	Post frequency	Follower count
A	0.9	10	1,000
B	0.7	5	300
C	0.4	8	500
D	0.3	3	200
E	0.2	1	100

Step 1:

Node Embeddings and Graph Representation

Each user i is represented by a feature vector (engagement rate, post frequency, follower count).

Node Feature for each node is given in Table 6.4.

Using a GNN, we transform these feature vectors into node embeddings

$$h_i = \text{GNN}(X, A)$$

where X is the feature matrix containing all users' features, A is the adjacency matrix (connections between users), and h_i is the new learned node embedding for each user.

Step 2:

Assign Nodes to Clusters (Influencer Groups)

Instead of selecting top users individually (like in top-K pooling), DiffPool clusters users into communities of similar engagement patterns.

Each user i is softly assigned to a cluster j based on a learned assignment matrix S:

$$S = \text{softmax}(\text{GNN}_{\text{assign}}(X, A)).$$

Softmax ensures assignments are probabilistic rather than hard clustering.

Cluster Assignments:

From Table 6.5, we see that the users A and B belong to Influencer Group 1 (High-Engagement Users). Users C, D, and E belong to Influencer Group 2 (Low-Engagement Users).

Step 3:

Pool the Graph (Create a Higher-Level Representation)

Now that we have grouped similar users, we compress the graph by merging nodes within the same cluster:

$$H' = S^T H$$

Table 6.5 Influencer table for user nodes.

User (Node)	Influencer Group 1 (Community A)	Influencer Group 2 (Community B)
A	0.9	0.1
B	0.8	0.2
C	0.1	0.9
D	0.2	0.8
E	0.05	0.95

$$A' = S^T AS$$

where H' is the new pooled node feature matrix and A' is the new adjacency matrix for the clustered graph. The final result is the graph contains individual users with direct interactions before pooling and after pooling; the graph now contains influencer groups (communities), with edges representing interactions between groups rather than individuals.

Advantages of DiffPool Over Traditional Pooling

DiffPool addresses the limitations of traditional pooling methods by learning hierarchical representations dynamically, rather than applying fixed rules for node aggregation [3]. Below are its key advantages over methods such as sum, mean, max, and top-K pooling:

- Traditional pooling techniques consider graphs as flat structures, losing multi-scale hierarchical information in many real-world graphs. However, DiffPool groups nodes into clusters at each pooling layer, forming a hierarchical representation of the graph. Instead of a single-step compression, DiffPool iteratively coarsens the graph, preserving its multi-level structure.
- Traditional pooling follows predefined rules (e.g., sum pooling always adds node features, max pooling always picks the highest value). Graphs vary across applications, and different graphs may require different ways of grouping nodes. DiffPool learns cluster assignments dynamically by computing an assignment matrix during training. It allows the model to determine which nodes belong together, instead of relying on hard-coded rules.
- Traditional pooling methods (sum, mean, max) lose graph connectivity because they collapse all nodes into a single vector or remove nodes without considering how they affect the structure. Losing connectivity makes it harder to capture long-range dependencies and relationships. Instead of removing nodes arbitrarily, DiffPool assigns nodes to clusters while preserving connectivity between them. The pooled graph maintains a coarsened version of the original adjacency matrix, ensuring that the graph topology is not lost.

- Traditional pooling methods do not scale well to large, structured graphs because they fail to capture hierarchical dependencies. Expressive graph representations are critical in domains such as bioinformatics, financial networks, and recommendation systems. By creating a hierarchical, coarse-grained version of the graph, DiffPool reduces computational complexity while retaining expressive power. It allows models to learn high-level graph structures, making them more interpretable and scalable for large graphs.

Disadvantages of DiffPool DiffPool requires additional parameters for cluster assignment learning. It is not always efficient for very large graphs. It needs tuning for different datasets.

C. SAGPool (Self-Attention Graph Pooling)

Introduction Top-K pooling and DiffPool have limitations that lead us to explore SAGPool. Top-K pooling relies on predefined ranking scores, which may discard globally important nodes due to its fixed selection approach. DiffPool, while effective in learning hierarchical structures, introduces high computational costs and lacks interpretability due to its reliance on learned soft clustering.

To address these issues, SAGPool [6] integrates self-attention mechanisms, dynamically selecting important nodes while maintaining both local and global graph structures.

Definition and Characteristics SAGPool is a hierarchical graph pooling method that utilizes a self-attention mechanism to determine node importance dynamically. Unlike traditional pooling methods that rely on predefined ranking scores or clustering, SAGPool learns which nodes to retain based on their significance in the graph. Its key characteristics includes

- SAGPool uses a self-attention mechanism to evaluate node importance.
- SAGPool preserves key structural patterns by using learned attention scores.
- It compresses the graph in multiple stages, allowing for hierarchical feature extraction and effective representation learning.
- Since attention scores drive node selection, it offers clear insights into which nodes influence the graph's representation.

Advantages and Disadvantages of SAGPool SAGPool uses self-attention to dynamically select important nodes based on relevance, ensuring context-aware pooling. Unlike top-K pooling, which may remove key nodes, SAGPool retains essential graph structures using learned attention scores. It reduces graph complexity step by step, capturing both local and global patterns for better feature extraction. Since attention scores determine which nodes are retained, it provides transparency in decision-making. Some of the disadvantages are: Though more efficient than DiffPool, self-attention mechanisms still require additional computations compared to simpler pooling methods. Despite using attention scores, it may still discard crucial nodes if they receive lower importance scores. The model's performance depends on carefully tuning attention mechanisms and pooling ratios. If the attention mechanism learns to focus too narrowly on specific features, the model may fail to generalize well to unseen graphs.

D. MinCutPool (Minimum Cut Pooling)

Introduction There are limitations of traditional graph pooling methods such as top-K pooling, DiffPool, and SAGPool. They are top-K pooling selects nodes based on individual scores, often discarding important structural information and breaking graph connectivity. DiffPool uses learned clustering but is computationally expensive and may lead to over-smoothing, where node representations become too similar. SAGPool uses self-attention for adaptive node selection but can still lose fine-grained local structures since it does not explicitly optimize for graph cuts. These limitations lead to poor hierarchical representations and inefficiencies in handling large, complex graphs. So, this topic explores the minimum cut pooling (MinCutPool) technique in detail.

MinCutPool is a differentiable graph pooling method that learns to cluster nodes into supernodes while preserving the graph's structural properties.

Definition and Characteristics MinCutPool aims to partition the graph into clusters (supernodes) by learning a cluster assignment matrix that minimizes edge connections between clusters and maximizes connections within clusters. It uses a spectral objective inspired by the MinCut problem in graph theory, promoting densely connected node clusters.

The main components are the assignment matrix, which learns how each of the N nodes maps to k clusters (super nodes); MinCut loss, which encourages fewer edges between clusters (inter-cluster) and more within clusters (intra-cluster); and orthogonality constraint, which ensures clusters are distinct and non-overlapping.

Its characteristics are that MinCutPool is a differentiable graph pooling method that learns to group nodes into clusters (super nodes) while preserving the structural integrity of the graph. It uses a spectral objective to ensure strong intra-cluster connections and minimize inter-cluster edges. Additionally, it enforces orthogonality constraints to maintain distinct and non-overlapping clusters.

Advantages and Disadvantages of MinCutPool MinCutPool maintains strong intra-cluster connections and is fully end-to-end trainable with backpropagation. It captures hierarchical information in the graph. However, it requires matrix multiplications and loss computations, may struggle with very large graphs (due

Table 6.6 Comparison Between flat pooling and hierarchical pooling.

Flat Pooling	Hierarchical Pooling
Applies pooling in a single step across the graph.	Applies pooling progressively in multiple stages or levels.
Reduces the graph to a fixed size directly.	Gradually reduces the graph size while preserving hierarchical information.
Simple.	More complex.
May lose structural hierarchy or multi-scale patterns.	Preserves hierarchical and multi-scale features better.
Suitable for summarization tasks.	Suitable for hierarchical relationship tasks.
Examples are sum, mean, max pooling.	Examples are top-K pooling, DiffPool, MinCutPool.

to spectral computation), number of clusters and regularization weights impact performance, and balancing MinCut loss and orthogonality regularization is tricky.

6.2.3 Comparison Between Flat Pooling and Hierarchical Pooling

Flat pooling and hierarchical pooling differ as detailed in Table 6.6.

6.3 Case Study on Graph Pooling

6.3.1 ContrastPool for Brain Network Classification

Classifying brain disorders using functional MRI (fMRI)-based brain networks is challenging due to noisy signals, variability across individuals, and the complex structure of brain connectivity. Existing GNN models often fail to capture the subtle and meaningful differences between patient and control groups. Therefore, there is a need for a graph pooling method that can highlight important brain regions and learn discriminative patterns across subjects, while also providing interpretable results.

ContrastPool [5] is an advanced graph pooling method designed to enhance the classification of brain networks derived from resting-state fMRI data. It introduces a contrastive dual-attention (CDA) mechanism that emphasizes both region-specific and subject-specific features, addressing the unique challenges posed by fMRI data in GNNs. There are three main components of ContrastPool. First, CDA block. In this, weights are assigned to each region of interest (ROI) to identify the most representative brain regions pertinent to a specific condition, such as Alzheimer's disease. This mechanism helps in mitigating noise inherent in fMRI data by focusing on critical ROIs. Then, after evaluation, it assigns weights to individual subjects within a group, emphasizing those that are most indicative of the group's characteristics. This approach aids in aligning different subjects and reduces the impact of outliers. The second component is contrast graph generation, where the attention-weighted features are aggregated from different groups (e.g., patients vs controls). ContrastPool constructs a contrast graph that captures the discriminative patterns between these groups. This graph serves as a guide for subsequent pooling operations. Finally, hierarchical graph pooling utilizes the contrast graph. ContrastPool performs hierarchical pooling, coarsening the brain network graph by grouping similar nodes (ROIs) based on learned assignments. This process results in a condensed representation that retains essential structural and functional information.

ContrastPool was evaluated on five resting-state fMRI brain network datasets, encompassing conditions such as Parkinson's disease, Alzheimer's disease, and autism spectrum disorder. Across all datasets, ContrastPool outperformed 21 baseline models, including traditional machine learning methods and other GNN-based approaches. The patterns identified by ContrastPool align with established neuroscience findings, enhancing the model's explainability and providing insights into disease-specific brain region interactions.

6.4 Conclusion

This chapter explored a focused and insightful search of graph pooling, a critical component in allowing deep learning techniques to achieve graph-level tasks by reducing graph complexity while preserving important structural information. It began with an introduction to what graph pooling is—a process analogous to pooling in CNNs, where local regions are summarized to achieve lower-dimensional representations. The chapter also made it clear why graph pooling is important: it improves model scalability, reduces overfitting, and helps in capturing hierarchical structures within graphs, especially in large-scale or graph-level prediction tasks.

The chapter then categorized pooling methods into two major types: flat pooling and hierarchical pooling. Flat pooling methods, including sum, mean, max, and attention pooling, operate on the entire graph at once to generate global representations. These techniques are computationally simple yet effective, especially for tasks such as graph classification, where a single fixed-size vector is required. The discussion also emphasized how flat pooling is widely used in molecular property prediction, text classification, and social network summarization. The transition to hierarchical pooling introduced a more advanced family of methods that reduce the graph in stages, allowing models to capture multi-level structures akin to how image pyramids work in CNNs. Techniques such as top-K pooling, DiffPool, SAG-Pool, and MinCutPool were explored, each offering different strategies for selecting and aggregating important nodes. These methods bring in differentiability, attention mechanisms, and spectral insights to form meaningful subgraph hierarchies, making them powerful tools in domains such as brain network analysis, large-scale recommendation systems, and protein interaction modeling.

Additionally, the chapter presented a comparative analysis between flat and hierarchical pooling, helping to clarify when and why one might be preferred over the other. Flat pooling offers simplicity and speed, while hierarchical pooling captures depth and structure, at the cost of additional complexity. The chapter concluded with a case study that illustrated how pooling techniques are applied in practice, reinforcing theoretical concepts through real-world implementation. This practical perspective bridged the gap between theory and application, enhancing understanding of how pooling modules are integrated into full GNN pipelines.

References

1 Zhi-Peng Li, et al., Graph pooling for graph-level representation learning: A survey, *Artif. Intell. Rev. Book (Springer)*, Volume 58, article number 45, (2025).

2 H. Van Pham, D. H. Thanh, and P. Moore, "Hierarchical pooling in graph neural networks to enhance classification performance in large datasets," *Sensors*, vol. 21, no. 18, p. 6070, 2021, doi: 10.3390/s21186070.

3 Rex Ying, Jiaxuan You, Christopher Morris, Xiang Ren, William L. Hamilton, Jure Leskovec, "Hierarchical graph representation learning with differentiable pooling," 32nd Conf. Neural Informat. Process. Syst. (NeurIPS2018), Montréal, Canada, 2018.

4 C. Liu *et al.*, "Graph pooling for graph neural networks: Progress, challenges, and opportunities," Proc. Thirty-Second Int. Joint Conf. AI (IJCAI-23), Macao, China, California," pp. 6712–6722.

5 X. Jiaxing *et al.*, "Contrastive graph pooling for explainable classification of brain networks," *IEEE Trans. Med. Imag*, vol. 43, no. 9, pp. 3292–3305, September, 2024, doi: 10.1109/TMI.2024.3392988.

6 J. Lee, I. Lee, and J. Kang, "Self-attention graph pooling," *Int. Conf. Machine Learn. (ICML 2019), PMLR*, vol. 97, pp. 3734–3743, 2019.

7 Van Thuy Hoang, O-Joun Lee, *Pre-training graph neural networks on molecules by using subgraph-conditioned graph information bottleneck*, Association for the Advancement of Artificial Intelligence (www.aaai.org), 2025.

7

Graph Neural Networks and Deep Representation Learning

7.1 Foundation of Deep Representation Learning on Graphs

Deep learning has revolutionized fields such as computer vision and natural language processing in recent years by leveraging structured data such as images and text. However, many real-world systems such as social networks, biological molecules, and knowledge graphs are best represented as graphs, where entities (nodes) are interconnected by relationships (edges). Unlike regular grid-based data, graphs exhibit complex, non-Euclidean structures, making them a challenging yet powerful domain for deep learning.

Traditional neural networks struggle to process graphs due to their irregular structure and varying node connectivity. This has led to the development of graph neural networks (GNNs), which generalize deep learning to graph-based data by learning node embeddings, capturing dependencies, and enabling tasks such as node classification, link prediction, and graph generation. In this chapter, we will explore the fundamentals of graphs and their mathematical representation, challenges, importance, approaches, and applications with a case study. By the end of this chapter, you will have a solid understanding of how deep learning can extract meaningful insights from complex graph structures, paving the way for innovations in multiple domains.

7.1.1 Basic Concept

Deep learning is a subset of machine learning that uses neural networks with multiple layers to model complex patterns in data. It's a machine learning technology that learns features and tasks directly from data. It receives raw data as input, and the input runs through a neural network, which has hidden layers to extract features using mathematical transformations (e.g., weights, biases, and activation functions). The produced outcome is the final prediction. For example, to recognize a person's face, convolutional layers extract spatial features such as edges, textures, and shapes. The extracted features are compared with a known database of face embeddings (for verification) or classified into predefined categories (for identification). It uses a loss function to ensure embeddings of the same person are closer together and embeddings of different persons are farther apart.

Deep learning is more prevalent as big data requires huge volumes of data and improves hardware architecture as it can handle huge volumes of data and has the computational power that the algorithms require. It automatically extracts features without human intervention. It excels in processing unstructured data such as images, audio, and text.

7.1.2 Challenges and Importance of Deep Learning on Graphs

Before using deep learning on graphs, we need to consider the challenges we faced. Traditional deep learning models such as CNNs and recurrent neural networks (RNNs) work great on structured data—images, sequences, and grids. Graphs aren't regular like grids. Unlike images, where pixels are neatly arranged in rows and columns, graphs have irregular structures. Nodes can have varying numbers of neighbors, making it hard to apply standard neural network techniques. In traditional models, inputs have a fixed shape (e.g., a 28×28 image). But graphs? They grow and shrink dynamically. The other challenge that arises is in capturing long-range dependencies on distant nodes. Many graphs change over time. So, traditional approaches fail to adapt to these changes. To overcome these challenges, deep learning booms into usage in graphs.

Graphs capture relational data, with entities (nodes) and their interactions (edges) forming the foundation of many real-world systems. Deep learning on graphs is necessary for extracting valuable insights and making accurate predictions from these intricate structures, offering greater flexibility, scalability, and performance compared to traditional methods. Graphs are found across diverse domains such as social networks, e-commerce, cybersecurity, and healthcare. These applications demand advanced models that can handle complex, non-Euclidean data structures effectively. Deep learning solves the challenges of capturing unstructured data, large-scale, dynamic, or heterogeneous graphs by learning feature-based information directly from the data [1].

Graphs deal with non-Euclidean data such as social network data, molecular structure, knowledge graphs, and transportation systems, where they do not follow a regular grid pattern. Deep learning is effective in handling Euclidean data. So, a specialized technique known as graph deep learning is needed to model irregular structures.

Deep learning models create graph embeddings that encode node, edge, and graph-level information. These embeddings are useful for tasks such as

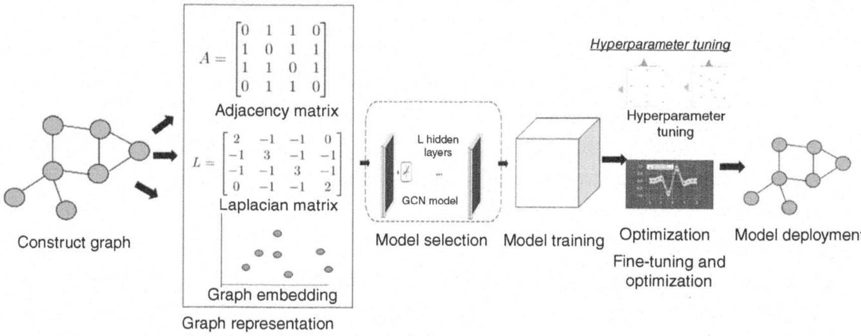

Figure 7.1 Step-by-step process of deep learning on graph.

classification, prediction, and clustering. In social network examples, embeddings can predict user behavior, group memberships, or potential friendships. It uses GNN to handle large-scale dynamic graphs. In a transportation network, dynamic GNNs can predict real-time traffic patterns and optimize routes. It can also process data from heterogeneous graphs and multi-relational graphs by finding complex relationships.

7.1.3 Approach of Deep Learning in Graph

In the deep learning step-by-step process for graphs, as shown in Fig. 7.1, the focus is on preparing graph data (nodes, edges, features), selecting suitable models (GNNs, graph attention networks [GATs], etc.), training the model effectively, and evaluating it with appropriate metrics. Fine-tuning and optimization follow to improve performance, and deployment is the final stage, ensuring the model is ready for real-world applications.

7.1.3.1 Step-by-Step Process

1) **Construct Graph**
   - Select the dataset based on the domain and represent the data as a graph with nodes (entities) and edges (relationships). Each node and edge may have associated features.
2) **Graph Representation**
   - Preprocess the graph by feature scaling. Represent the graph as an adjacency matrix that captures the connections between nodes and a Laplacian matrix that helps in defining the graph structure and is important for certain graph convolution operations and graph embedding techniques (e.g., node2vec, DeepWalk) to convert nodes and edges into dense vectors that are suitable for deep learning.

3) **Model Selection**
   - The next step is to decide on the type of deep learning model based on the task, such as node classification (graph convolutional networks (GCNs)), graph classification, or link prediction (graph autoencoders), and to determine the number of layers, the type of aggregation function (e.g., sum, mean, or max pooling for GCNs), and activation functions (e.g., ReLU or sigmoid).
4) **Model Training**
   - Choose an appropriate loss function depending on the task. Cross-entropy loss can be used for classification tasks (e.g., node or graph classification), mean squared error for regression tasks or when predicting continuous values, and binary cross-entropy loss for binary classification tasks. While training the model, its weights can be updated using optimization algorithms like Adam. Before deployment, evaluate the model by choosing the appropriate evaluation metrics.
5) **Fine-tuning and Optimization**
   - Fine-tune the model using hyperparameters like learning rate, batch size, number of layers, and hidden units to improve model performance and apply optimization techniques. Regularization techniques can be applied to avoid overfitting.
6) **Model Deployment**
   - Deploy the model for real-time or batch inference, such as predicting new links in a graph, classifying nodes, or detecting anomalies. The process can be repeated for continuous learning, monitoring, and improvement.

The approach of deep learning for graphs involves graph representation learning, choosing appropriate GNN architectures, applying model-specific strategies for different tasks, and handling the unique challenges of graph-structured data. With increasing applications in various fields, deep learning on graphs is an essential approach for processing complex, relational data and achieving state-of-the-art performance.

7.1.4 Characteristics and Benefits of Deep Learning on Graphs

Deep learning on graphs combines the power of graph theory and neural networks, enabling advances in analyzing and predicting from relational, non-Euclidean data. Its characteristics, such as the ability to handle complex dependencies and scalability, along with its benefits such as domain adaptability and improved predictions, make it indispensable for modern machine learning applications.

7.2 Introduction to GNNs

Traditional methods for graph analysis include spectral methods, which use eigenvectors of the graph Laplacian for tasks such as clustering and partitioning, and heuristic algorithms such as PageRank for ranking nodes or Dijkstra's algorithm for finding shortest paths. These methods rely on fixed mathematical formulations. However, GNNs are a data-driven method.

A GNN is a specialized deep learning architecture designed to process and analyze data represented as graphs. It enables the relationships and connections between entities (nodes) and their interactions (edges) to learn meaningful representations of individual nodes, edges, or entire graphs. The primary goal is to perform graph representation learning by automatically learning node embeddings, edge embeddings, or graph-level embeddings and other learning [2]. GNN differs from traditional methods in the following ways:

- **Learning Representations:** GNNs automatically learn task-specific node, edge, or graph embeddings, whereas traditional methods rely on predefined features.
- **Dynamic Graphs:** GNNs can adapt to dynamic or temporal graphs, while traditional methods often require recomputation for every graph update.
- **Task-Related Process:** GNN provides a flexible framework for multiple graph-related tasks, including node-level (classification), edge-level (link prediction), and graph-level (classification or regression) tasks, within a single architecture. However, traditional methods are often designed for specific tasks, such as PageRank for ranking nodes or spectral clustering for partitioning graphs.
- **Scalability:** GNNs scale efficiently to large graphs using sparse matrix operations or sampling techniques, whereas traditional methods struggle with computational overhead on massive graphs.
- **Incorporation of Features:** GNNs seamlessly integrate node and edge attributes with graph topology, while traditional methods primarily rely on graph structure alone.
- **Handling Data:** GNNs handle irregular, non-Euclidean structures such as graphs naturally, unlike traditional machine learning methods that work on Euclidean data (e.g., grids or sequences). GNNs can handle heterogeneous graphs with different types of nodes, edges, and weights. Traditional methods struggle with heterogeneous or weighted graphs, requiring custom algorithms for each case.

7.2.1 GNN Architecture Overview

The first GNN architecture used a RNN to perform message passing and updating of node representations until convergence. The core idea was to model the dependencies between nodes and their neighbors in a graph.

Let $G = (V, E)$, where V is the set of vertices/nodes and E is the set of edges. Each vertex/node $v \in V$ has an initial feature vector x_v, and each edge $e_{uv} \in E$ has associated features a_{uv}. Each vertex/node v maintains a state vector h_v, which encodes its representation. Initial state $h_v{}^{(0)}$ is either a zero vector or derived from x_v. Then, message passing is done in a way that the nodes communicate with their neighbors by sending and receiving messages. Messages are computed using a function f_{msg} that takes as input the state of the sender node, the recipient node, and (optionally) the edge features.

$$m_{uv} = f_{\text{msg}}(h_u, h_v, a_{uv})$$

Each node updates its state based on the messages received from its neighbors using a state update function f_{update}.

$$h_{v(t+1)} = f_{\text{update}}\left(h_v^{(t)}, \{m_{uv} \mid u \in N(v)\}\right)$$

$$h_{v(t+1)} = \sigma\left(W_1^* x_v + W_2 \cdot u \in N(v) \sum f_{\text{msg}}\left(h_u^{(t)}, h_v^{(t)}, a_{uv}\right)\right)$$

σ: Nonlinear activation function (e.g., tanh or ReLU).

$N(v)$: the set of neighbors of node v.

W_1, W_2: Learnable parameters of the update functions.

The update function is parameterized using an RNN, enabling iterative updates. The process is repeated until the state vectors h_v converge to a fixed point. This fixed point ensures that the representations capture global graph properties. After convergence, an output function f_{out} maps the final node states h_v to the desired task-specific outputs (e.g., node classification or graph-level prediction) [1].

$$y_v = f_{\text{out}}(h_v)$$

- y_v: Output prediction for node v.

7.2.1.1 Algorithm Steps

1) **Initialization:**
   - Initialize the state vector $h_v{}^{(0)}$ for all nodes.
2) **Iterative Message Passing:**
   - For each time step t:
   - Compute messages m_{uv} for all edges.
   - Aggregate messages from neighbors for each node.
   - Update the state of each node using the aggregated messages.

3) **Convergence Check:**
   - Repeat the above step until the states h_v converge or a fixed number of iterations is reached.
4) **Output Computation:**
   - Use the converged node states h_v for downstream tasks (e.g., predicting labels or graph properties).

7.2.2 Message Passing in GNNs

Message passing is a core process in GNNs that enables nodes to communicate with their neighbors and update their representations based on the information received. This mechanism allows GNNs to capture dependencies within graph-structured data and generate meaningful node embeddings for various tasks [3].

Example ***Predicting a Person's Influence in a Social Network***
Imagine you're looking at a social network where people are connected through friendships. Now, you want to figure out how influential someone is based on how active their friends are. The more active their friends are, the more likely they are to be influential too. Consider a graph with nodes (A, B, C, D) and edges as connections among the friends. The node features activity levels (how often they post).

Graph Structure:

A (3)
/ \
B(5) C(2)
\ /
D (4)
(Numbers in parentheses represent activity levels.)

Step-by-Step Message Passing:

1) Each node gathers information from its neighbors.
   - Node A receives activity info from B and $C \rightarrow (5, 2)$
   - Node D receives activity info from B and $C \rightarrow (5, 2)$
2) Aggregation of messages (taking the average in this case).
   - A's new activity score $= (5 + 2)/2 = 3.5(5 + 2)/2 = 3.5(5 + 2)/2 = 3.5$
   - D's new activity score $= (5 + 2)/2 = 3.5(5 + 2)/2 = 3.5(5 + 2)/2 = 3.5$
3) Node representations are updated.
   - A and D now have refined scores based on their friends' activity.

After multiple iterations, we can predict the most influential users based on updated scores.

7.2.3 Case Study on GNNs

Case Study 7.1

Enhancing Credit Card Fraud Detection with CaT-GNN

Traditional fraud detection systems often struggle to identify complex and evolving fraudulent patterns in credit card transactions [4], especially when fraudsters adapt their behaviors to evade detection. Researchers introduced the causal temporal GNN (CaT-GNN), a novel approach that integrates causal inference with temporal graph structures. This model comprises two main components. The first component is Causal-Inspector, which utilizes attention mechanisms to identify causal relationships within transaction data without introducing additional parameters, and the second component is Causal-Intervener, which applies a causal mix-up strategy to enhance the model's robustness by focusing on environment nodes. By decomposing the fraud detection problem into discovery and intervention phases, CaT-GNN effectively captures inherent correlations in transaction data, leading to improved detection of fraudulent activities.

The proposed CaT-GNN model introduces a causal temporal GNN that integrates causal inference with temporal graph learning. This methodology is designed to detect credit card fraud more effectively by modeling complex dependencies and adapting to evolving fraudulent behaviors. The input data includes credit card transaction logs, including user IDs, transaction timestamps, merchant IDs, transaction amounts, and labels (fraud or not). Each transaction is a node. Edges are created based on predefined relationships (e.g., shared user ID, same merchant, or temporal proximity). The temporal aspect is incorporated to maintain the sequence of transactions.

The CaT-GNN methodology combines temporal modeling, GNNs, and causal inference to build a fraud detection system that is robust, interpretable, and effective. By distinguishing between correlation and causation, CaT-GNN significantly reduces false positives and adapts better to evolving fraud patterns than traditional methods.

Evaluations on multiple datasets are done both on private financial data and on public benchmarks, demonstrating that CaT-GNN outperforms existing state-of-the-art methods in credit card fraud detection. The integration of causal reasoning with GNNs enhances the model's ability to detect complex fraud patterns.

Case Study 7.2

GNNs for Drug–Drug Interaction Prediction in Healthcare

Predicting interactions between different drugs is critical in healthcare to prevent adverse side effects. Traditional methods rely heavily on clinical trials and pharmacological databases, which are expensive and time-consuming. A data-driven, predictive approach is required to assess potential drug–drug interactions (DDIs) before clinical deployment. Some of the issues are that drug properties and interactions are complex and multi-relational; drug molecules can be naturally represented as graphs (atoms as nodes, chemical bonds as edges), but incorporating relational knowledge between drugs (e.g., side effects, similarities) is non-trivial; and existing models often fail to link both molecular structures and interaction graphs jointly.

Researchers used GNNs to model DDIs by constructing a heterogeneous graph where nodes represent drugs; edges represent known interactions, similarities, and side effects; and the molecular structures of drugs are represented using subgraphs. A GNN model—heterogeneous GCN—was trained to learn embeddings that capture both structural (molecular) and relational (interaction) features. The model aggregates information across neighboring drugs and learns rich representations that are then used to predict the probability of interaction between drug pairs.

The GNN-based model outperformed traditional machine learning baselines such as SVMs and random forests in predicting DDIs. It reduced false positives and revealed previously unknown but clinically validated interactions. This approach contributed to the development of safer drug prescriptions and personalized medicine.

7.3 Fundamentals of GCNs

7.3.1 Core Concepts and Motivation for GCNs

- Deep learning algorithms such as CNNs are designed to operate on data with a fixed grid-like structure, such as images with pixels arranged in rows and columns. They operate on Euclidean data and are not applicable to handling non-Euclidean data. They rely on spatial locality. CNNs [5] cannot explicitly model the relationships or interactions between entities, as they process data in fixed grids without explicit connections between elements. As shown in

Fig. 7.3(a), CNN kernels operate on fixed-size neighborhoods (e.g., 3x3 filters in images) and assume uniform connectivity. This approach is ineffective for graphs, where nodes can have varying numbers of neighbors. CNNs process data densely (e.g., all pixels in an image), which leads to inefficiency when dealing with sparse data like graphs, where only a small subset of nodes are connected. CNNs are used for tasks such as image classification or object detection, where the focus is on localized regions. They lack mechanisms to model entire graph structures for tasks such as graph classification or regression.

GCNs effectively address the limitations of CNNs by generalizing convolution to irregular graph structures by aggregating information from a node's neighbors, by incorporating a message-passing system or neighborhood aggregation. The different graph structures of GCN and CNN are shown in Fig. 7.2. GCN dynamically aggregates information from variable-sized neighborhoods by using aggregation functions (e.g., sum, mean, max) that are invariant to the number and order of neighbors. By stacking multiple GCN layers, the model captures both local and global information in the graph.

The graph in Fig. 7.3(b) illustrates how convolution operates in GNNs, focusing on the local neighborhood of each node in the graph. The arrows show the aggregation process of features from neighboring nodes to the central node.

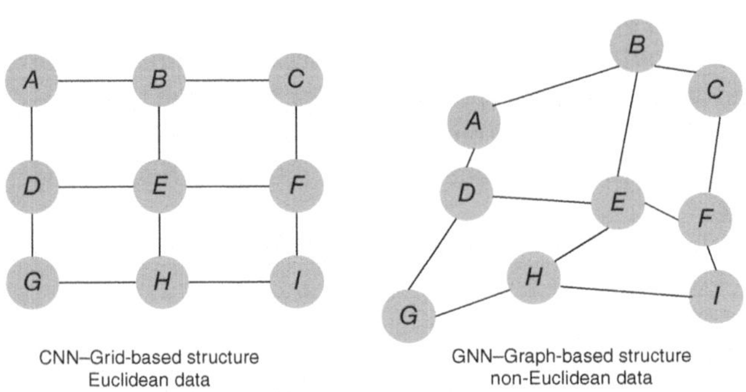

Figure 7.2 CNN and GCN of deep learning model.

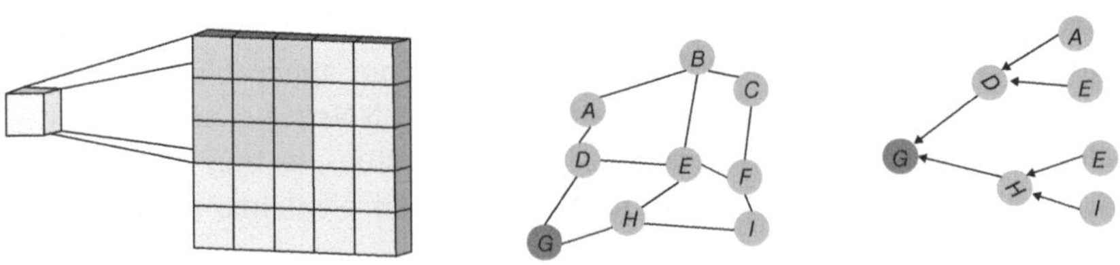

Figure 7.3 (a) CNN uses pooling layer; (b) GNN uses neighborhood information.

GNNs extend traditional neural network methods to effectively process data represented in graph structures. It operates on graph-structured data by propagating and aggregating information through nodes and edges to learn meaningful representations for various tasks.

7.3.2 Workflow Process of GCN

GNNs are powerful models designed to handle graph-structured data by propagating and aggregating information through nodes and edges to learn meaningful representations for tasks. The workflow process of GNNs can be divided into distinct stages, each contributing to how the model learns from the graph data [4]. Below is a step-by-step explanation:

1) **Graph Representation**
   Let $G = (V, E)$ be a graph.
   where V: set of nodes (vertices), E: set of edges, representing relationships or interactions between nodes, X: node features, and A: adjacency matrix, encoding the connectivity between nodes (binary or weighted).
2) **Node Initialization**
   Each node is initialized with its feature vector x_v, where x_v represents the feature vector of node v. This is shown in Fig. 7.4. If edge features are considered, they are represented as e_{uv} for the edge between nodes u and v. The activation unit is initialized as $h_v^{(0)} = x_v$.
3) **Neighborhood Aggregation (Message Passing)**
   The core of GNNs lies in the iterative message passing or neighborhood aggregation process, which occurs over multiple layers. During each message-passing iteration in a GNN, the hidden embedding $h_v^{(k)}$ of each node is updated based on the information aggregated from its graph neighborhood N(v). Each GNN layer performs the following steps:

Step 3.1: Message Generation

Each node v generates a "message" based on its features and its neighbors' features. The message can be calculated using a function Message (h_u, h_v, e_{uv}), where

Figure 7.4 Graph representation with feature vector.

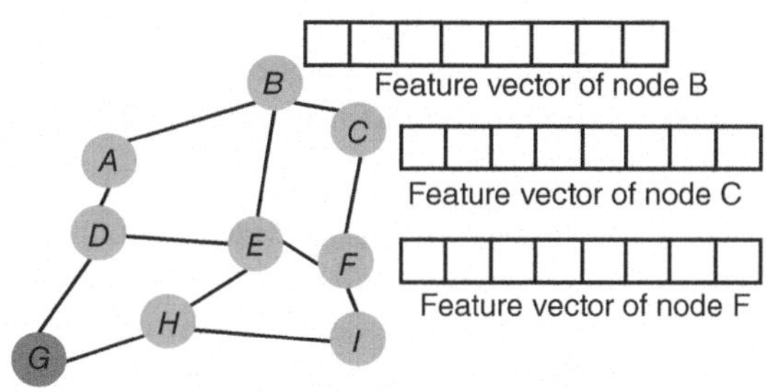

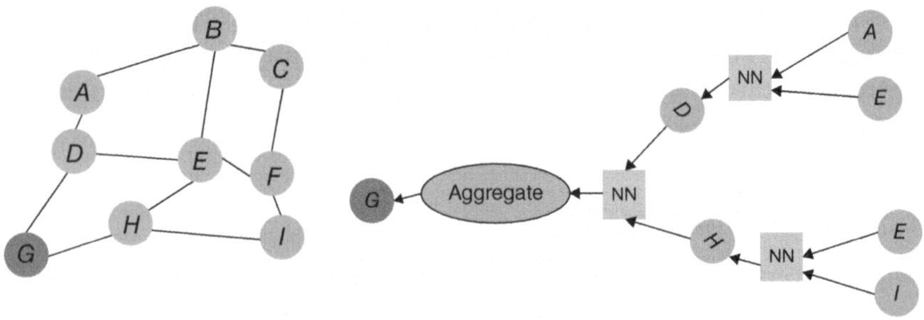

Figure 7.5 Graph representing message aggregation.

h_u and h_v are the features of the neighboring node u and the target node v, and e_{uv} is the edge feature.

Step 3.2: Message Aggregation

Each node aggregates the messages from its neighbors. Aggregation functions (e.g., sum, mean, max). Mathematically,

$$h_v^{\text{agg}} = \text{Aggregate}(\{\text{Message}(h_u, h_v, e_{uv}) \,:\, u \in N(v)\}),$$

where $N(v)$ represents the set of neighbors of v.

Figure 7.5 depicts a graph on the left with interconnected nodes and an equivalent simplified graph representation on the right after applying an aggregation function. In a GNN, the aggregation function is crucial for capturing the local neighborhood's information for each node, enabling the model to learn meaningful representations.

For the highlighted node G, the aggregation function combines information from its directly connected neighbors (D, H, I in this example). The process works as follows: during the message-passing step, each of the neighboring nodes generates "messages" based on their current features. These messages are then aggregated using a predefined aggregation function such as summation, mean, or maximum. For instance,

- **Summation** adds the feature vectors of D, H, and I, creating a combined representation.
- **Mean** takes the average of the feature vectors from these nodes, normalizing the contribution of each neighbor.
- **Max** selects the highest feature value across neighbors, focusing on the most significant signals.

Once the aggregated information is obtained, it is combined with the feature vector of node G to update its representation using a learnable function, such as a neural network. This process allows the node to incorporate information about its local neighborhood while maintaining its unique properties.

The simplified graph on the right illustrates how the aggregation reduces the complexity of the node interactions by summarizing neighborhood features, effectively capturing higher-level graph structure and relationships. This makes GNNs powerful for tasks such as node classification, link prediction, and graph classification.

Step 3.3: Node Update

The aggregated messages are combined with the current node state to produce the updated representation for the node. This step ensures that the new feature representation incorporates both the node's local features and information from its neighbors. This is often achieved using a neural function such as a multi-layer perceptron (MLP):

$$h_v^{(\ell+1)} = \text{Update}\left(h_v^{(\ell)}, h_v^{\text{agg}}\right).$$

- ${h_v}^{(\ell)}$: Node feature vector at layer ℓ.
- ${h_v}^{(\ell+1)}$: Updated feature vector for the next layer.

The process ensures that each node's representation becomes increasingly aware of its local and global context.

4) **Stacking Multiple GNN Layers**
   Multiple GNN layers are stacked to enable information propagation across larger neighborhoods. After L layers, the representation of each node $h_v(L)$ incorporates information from all nodes within L-hops in the graph.

- For shallow tasks like node classification, fewer layers may be sufficient.
- For tasks requiring global context, such as graph classification, deeper GNNs or pooling layers are used.

5) **Pooling (Optional)**
   For graph-level tasks, the representations of all nodes in the graph are pooled into a single graph representation. Common pooling methods include

- **Global Pooling:** Aggregate node features (e.g., summing, averaging, or taking the maximum over all nodes).
- **Hierarchical Pooling:** Summarize substructures within the graph (e.g., DiffPool) to create a multi-resolution graph representation.

6) **Output and Prediction**
   After the final GNN layer or pooling operation, the learned representations are passed to a task-specific prediction layer. This step depends on the application:

- **Node Classification:** Apply a softmax or classification layer to each node's representation *hv*(*L*)*h*_*v*^{(*L*)}*hv*(*L*).

- **Edge Prediction:** Use the features of two nodes (and possibly edge features) to predict the existence or type of an edge.
- **Graph Classification:** Use the pooled graph representation hGh_GhG for classification or regression tasks.

7) **Loss Function and Training**
   The model is trained using a loss function appropriate for the task:

- **Node Classification:** Cross-entropy loss for labeled nodes.
- **Graph Classification:** Cross-entropy or regression loss for the graph-level label.
- **Link Prediction:** Binary cross-entropy for predicting the existence of an edge.

Gradients are computed using backpropagation, and the model parameters (e.g., weights in aggregation functions, MLP layers) are updated using an optimizer like Adam.

8) **Inference**
   During inference, the trained GNN generates predictions for unseen nodes, edges, or graphs. For inductive tasks, the model generalizes to new graphs or nodes without retraining.

7.4 Types of GNNs

7.4.1 Graph RNN

Alright, let's take real-world research. If you're working with dynamic graphs—think social networks, traffic systems, or financial transactions—there are some limits of GCNs. GCNs work well for static graphs, where relationships don't change. But in real-world scenarios, graphs are constantly evolving—new connections form, old ones break, and node attributes change. In a fraud detection system, new fraudulent accounts appear over time. A static GCN won't adapt to these evolving patterns.

It assumes that the graph structure doesn't change, which is a problem if you're dealing with evolving networks such as social interactions, traffic patterns, or knowledge graphs. You need something that can handle temporal changes.

GCN processes information in a fixed number of layers, meaning it struggles with long-range dependencies. If a node needs info from a distant node, GCN might fail to capture it effectively. In a citation network, a research paper might be influenced by work published years ago. GCNs might fail to capture this deep historical dependency. If your data has a time component, such as stock prices or user activity logs, GCN doesn't naturally model the sequence. It processes everything at once, losing the continuity of changes over time. In a traffic prediction system, road congestion changes every few minutes. You can't just retrain a GCN from scratch every time—graph RNNs (GRNNs) handle this better by processing time steps sequentially. That's where GRNN comes in. It combines graph structures with RNNs to capture temporal dependencies while still leveraging the connectivity of graphs. This means it can track changes over time, remember long-term influences, adapt to evolving relationships, adapt to dynamic graphs, capture long-term dependencies, and efficiently handle real-time updates.

7.4.1.1 Definition with Illustration

A GRNN is a deep learning model that combines graph structures with sequential processing using RNNs. It is designed to handle dynamic and evolving graphs where node and edge relationships change over time.

Example ***Social Network Evolution***

Imagine a social media platform where users interact, follow each other, and their interests change over time. Let $G = (V,E)$ be the graph with A, B, C, D as users and edge (friendship) between A and B, B and C, and C and D. Let the node features be user interests, engagement scores, etc. as shown in Fig. 7.6. We can model this as a dynamic graph. At time step $t = 1$. At time step $t = 2$, an additional node E is added with edges from D to E. This addition of a new user is dynamically done.

Graph Representation for GRNN

GRNN [6] processes a graph convolution layer (GCN/GAT) to capture social structure at each time step. It uses a recurrent layer (gated recurrent units [GRUs])/long–short-term memory [LSTM]) to learn temporal changes (e.g., adding a new user "E"). It has a prediction layer to predict future interactions, user churn, or interest evolution. Some of the areas where we can use social network graphs are friend recommendations to predict who will connect next,

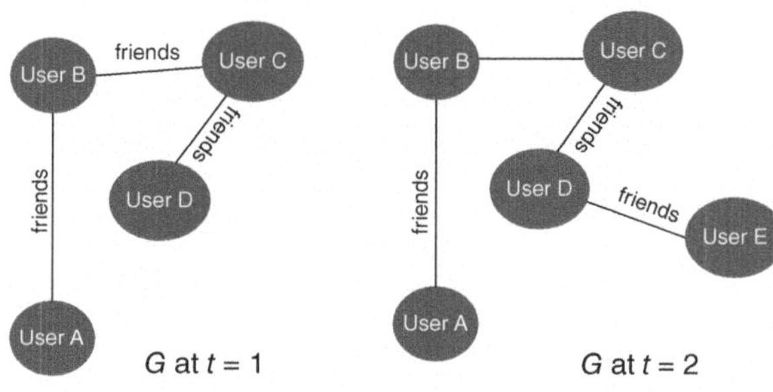

Figure 7.6 Dynamic graph representation of social network.

content personalization to adapt content based on changing interests, and fake account detection to identify bots based on evolving behavior. GRNN is ideal for graphs that change over time.

7.4.1.2 Working Process of GRNN

The working process of GRNN is shown using a flowchart. The flowchart in Fig. 7.7 shows that the graph is represented using an adjacency matrix or edge lists. The GCN captures spatial relationships between nodes. The next step is to process dynamic graph snapshots sequentially using RNNs (LSTMs, GRUs). GRNN maintains hidden states, allowing it to learn patterns over time. The final process is to use the prediction layer to generate outputs such as node classification, link prediction, or forecasting.

7.4.1.3 GRNN Architecture

A GRNN is designed to model dynamic, time-evolving graphs by combining the strengths of GNNs and RNNs. Unlike traditional GCNs that only work with static graphs, GRNN introduces temporal memory to process sequences of evolving graph structures effectively.

Key Components of GRNN Architecture

1) **Graph Representation Layer**
   - Represents the input graph as nodes (V), edges (E), and features (X).
   - Uses adjacency matrices or edge lists to define graph structure.
   - Handles both static and time-varying graphs.

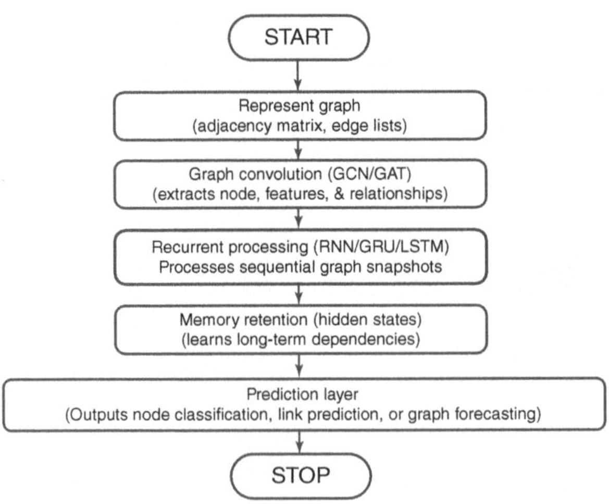

Figure 7.7 Working process of GRNN.

2) **Graph Feature Extraction (Graph Convolution Layer)**
   - Uses GCN or GAT to extract node embeddings.
   - Aggregates neighborhood information for each node.
   - Captures local structural dependencies in the graph.
3) **Recurrent Layer (Temporal Processing)**
   - Uses RNNs such as GRUs or LSTMs to capture temporal dependencies.
   - Maintains hidden states over time to track evolving graph structures.
   - Allows the model to remember past information and adapt to future changes.
4) **Prediction Layer (Output Layer)**
   - Applies a fully connected (FC) layer or softmax activation for classification, regression, or forecasting.
   - Outputs results such as node classification, link prediction, or graph-level tasks.

The architecture of GRNN in Fig. 7.8 consists of several key layers. First, the graph representation layer encodes the input graph structure using an adjacency matrix or edge list, defining node relationships. This layer ensures that the model captures the connectivity and structural changes over time. Next, the GCN or GAT) is applied to extract meaningful node representations by aggregating information from neighboring nodes. This step enables the model to learn localized graph features efficiently.

Once the spatial features are extracted, the recurrent processing layer (using LSTM, GRU, or RNNs) handles the temporal dynamics of the graph. Unlike traditional GCNs that treat graphs as static, this layer processes graph snapshots sequentially, allowing the model to track how nodes, edges, and features evolve

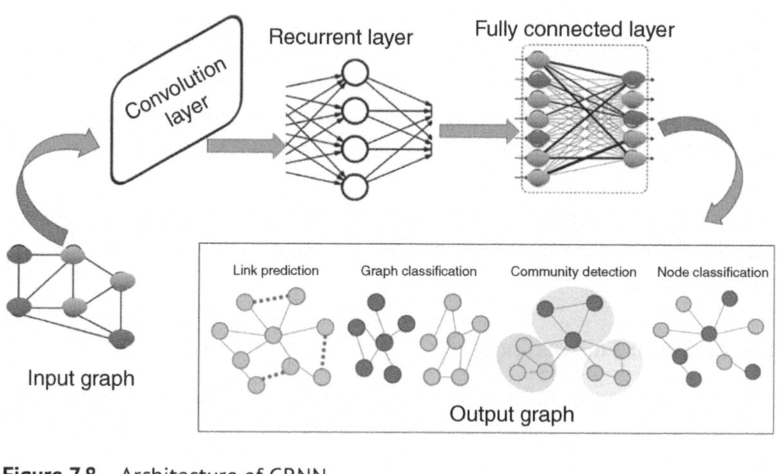

Figure 7.8 Architecture of GRNN.

over time. The recurrent mechanism stores hidden states that help in maintaining long-term dependencies and historical information from previous graph states.

Following the recurrent updates, the prediction layer generates outputs for tasks such as node classification, link prediction, or graph forecasting. This is typically achieved through a FC layer followed by an activation function such as softmax for classification or regression for time-series forecasting.

Overall, GRNN enables a more effective representation of real-world graphs that change over time, such as social networks, traffic flow systems, financial transactions, and biological networks. By integrating graph convolutions for spatial information and recurrent units for temporal learning, GRNN becomes a powerful model for learning from dynamic and evolving graph data.

7.4.1.4 Applications of GRNN

Case Study 7.3

Traffic Forecasting Using GRNN—Modeling Road Networks with Changing Congestion

Traffic congestion poses a significant challenge in urban areas, affecting travel time, fuel efficiency, and environmental pollution. Conventional traffic prediction methods, such as historical averaging and statistical regression, often struggle to accurately capture the intricate spatial and temporal dependencies within real-world road networks. To overcome these limitations, researchers and engineers have adopted GRNNs for real-time traffic forecasting, as they efficiently model both the spatial structure of road networks and the dynamic evolution of traffic conditions over time.

The goal of this case study is to predict future traffic congestion levels based on historical and real-time traffic data. The road network is represented as a dynamic graph with intersecting roads as nodes and adjacent streets being connected as edges. Node features are real-time traffic speed, volume, and congestion levels, and edge features can be road distance, lane capacity, or accident reports.

The challenge is that traffic patterns change dynamically due to factors such as weather, accidents, and rush hours, making it necessary to use a model that can adapt over time.

Why GRNN for Traffic Forecasting?

1) Spatial Dependency Modeling—Traffic conditions on one road segment influence nearby roads. GRNN leverages GCNs to capture these spatial relationships.

2) Temporal Dependency Learning—Traffic flow changes over time (e.g., morning rush hours vs. late-night traffic). GRNN uses RNNs, LSTMs, or GRUs to model these temporal dependencies.
3) Real-Time Adaptation—Unlike static models, GRNN can update predictions dynamically as new traffic data arrives, making it highly effective for real-time applications.

GRNN Architecture for Traffic Forecasting

The GRNN model processes traffic data in several key stages:

1) **Graph Representation Layer—**The road network is converted into a graph where nodes (road segments) and edges (connections) are structured using an adjacency matrix or edge list.
2) **Graph Convolution Layer (GCN/GAT)—**Extracts spatial traffic patterns by aggregating information from neighboring road segments.
3) **Recurrent Processing Layer (LSTM/GRU)—**Captures temporal variations by processing sequential traffic snapshots over time.
4) **Prediction Layer—**Outputs future traffic speed, congestion probability, or travel time using a FC layer with regression or classification functions.

7.4.2 Graph Attention Networks

GCN works well for many graph-based tasks, but it has serious limitations when dealing with complex real-world graphs. The limitations of GCN make researchers shift from GCN and GRNN to GAT in real-time research. GCN treats all neighbors equally, which is unrealistic in real-world scenarios where some connections are more important than others. Fixed aggregation means GCN struggles when different nodes contribute differently to the target node. GCN requires a full adjacency matrix, making it costly for large-scale graphs. In the social networks example, not all friends influence you the same way. Some are more important (close friends vs. acquaintances), and GCN fails to distinguish their influence properly.

GRNN improves GCN by adding temporal memory (using RNNs such as LSTM/GRU), but it has its own set of drawbacks. Like GCN, GRNN does not differentiate which neighbors contribute more at each time step. GRNN processes each graph snapshot sequentially, which is inefficient for real-time applications. In the traffic forecasting example, GRNN learns congestion patterns over time but treats all road connections equally. In reality, some roads influence congestion more than others.

To fix these issues, another variant of GNN occurs, which is GAT.

7.4.2.1 Definition With Illustration

A GAT is an advanced type of GNN that introduces an attention mechanism to improve how nodes aggregate information from their neighbors. Unlike traditional GCNs, which treat all neighboring nodes equally, GAT assigns different importance (weights) to different neighbors, allowing the model to focus on the most relevant connections.

GAT uses an attention mechanism to assign higher weights to important neighbors, solving the issue of equal weighting in GCN and GRNN. Unlike GRNN, which processes graphs sequentially, GAT can learn node dependencies in parallel, making it faster for large-scale dynamic graphs. GAT is widely used in social networks, traffic forecasting, and bioinformatics for more adaptive and efficient graph learning.

Example ***Social Network Influence Prediction***

Let's say we are analyzing a social media network where we want to identify key influencers based on user interactions. In a GAT, each user is represented as a node and connections (friendships, interactions, follows) are represented as edges.

The graph given in Fig. 7.9 is represented as G with nodes (users) Sam, David, Laurel, Johny, Jeff, Ben, and edges (connections) as friendships or interactions between users and node features such as activity level, post engagement, likes, and retweets.

GAT Approach (Adaptive Attention Weights) GAT learns attention scores to determine which neighbors are more important.

Step 1: Compute Attention Scores for David's Neighbors

GAT assigns attention weights based on David's interactions (Table 7.1).

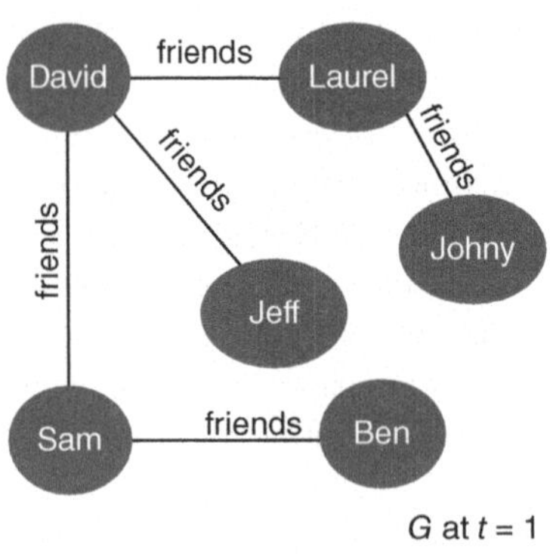

Figure 7.9 Social network example for GAT approach.

Table 7.1 GAT assigns attention weights based on David's interactions.

Neighbor	Interaction Frequency	Attention Weight (α)
Sam	50 messages/week	0.7
Jeff	20 messages/week	0.2
Laurel	5 messages/week	0.1

Step 2: Aggregate Neighbor Information
David's final representation is updated based on the weighted sum:

$$h'_{\text{David}} = \alpha_{Sam}\, h_{Sam} + \alpha_{\text{Jeff}}\, h_{\text{Jeff}} + \alpha_{\text{Laurel}}\, h_{\text{Laurel}}$$

Since Sam has the highest weight (0.7), his influence on David is greater than that of Jeff and Laurel.

Graph Representation After GAT Processing Now, David's new embedding prioritizes Sam's influence (Fig. 7.10), making the model more accurate in predicting his future activity or influence in the network.

(*David's updated representation emphasizes Sam's influence more than the others.) Based on this, we can update as new interactions happen.

Key Features of GAT

- Attention-Based Aggregation—Gives higher weight to important neighbors.
- Parallel Processing—Unlike GRNN, GAT can process graphs in parallel, making it efficient.
- Handles Complex Graphs—Works well on heterogeneous graphs where nodes/edges have different relationships.

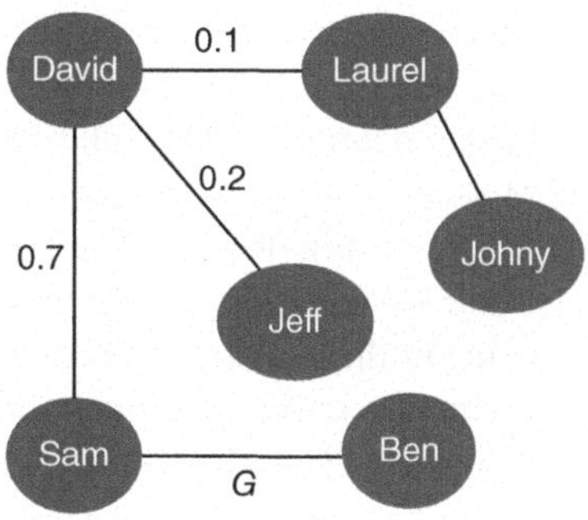

Figure 7.10 Influential graph.

7.4.2.2 Working Process of GAT

GAT improves traditional GNNs by integrating a self-attention mechanism, enabling nodes to dynamically assign varying importance to their neighbors during message passing. The process begins with graph representation, where the input graph is structured using nodes (V), edges (E), and feature vectors that define each node's characteristics. GAT then calculates attention scores for each node's neighbors through a learnable attention function, ensuring that more significant connections receive higher weights. These scores are normalized using the softmax function, balancing influence across neighbors. Once attention weights are determined, message passing and aggregation occur, where nodes update their embeddings by incorporating information from neighboring nodes based on the computed attention coefficients. To enhance stability and expressive power, multi-head attention is employed, allowing multiple attention mechanisms to process the graph in parallel. Finally, the refined node embeddings are fed into an output layer for tasks such as node classification, link prediction, or graph-level analysis. This adaptive learning approach makes GAT highly effective for complex and evolving graph-based applications, including social network analysis, traffic prediction, and fraud detection.

7.4.2.3 Architecture of GAT

GAT improves traditional GNNs by introducing an attention mechanism that allows nodes to learn the importance of their neighbors dynamically. Unlike GCNs, which aggregate information from all neighboring nodes equally, GAT assigns different weights to different neighbors, ensuring that more influential nodes contribute more to the learning process.

Key Components of GAT Architecture The GAT architecture consists of multiple layers, as shown in Fig. 7.11, each designed to efficiently process graph-structured data. The core components are

1) Graph Representation Layer—Encodes the input graph as a set of nodes and edges, where each node has a feature vector representing its characteristics.
2) Self-Attention Mechanism—Computes attention scores for each node's neighbors to determine their relative importance.
3) Message Passing & Aggregation—Updates node embeddings based on the weighted sum of their neighbors' information.
4) Multi-Head Attention—Enhances model stability and representation power by using multiple parallel attention mechanisms.
5) Prediction Layer—Outputs node embeddings for node classification, link prediction, or clustering tasks.

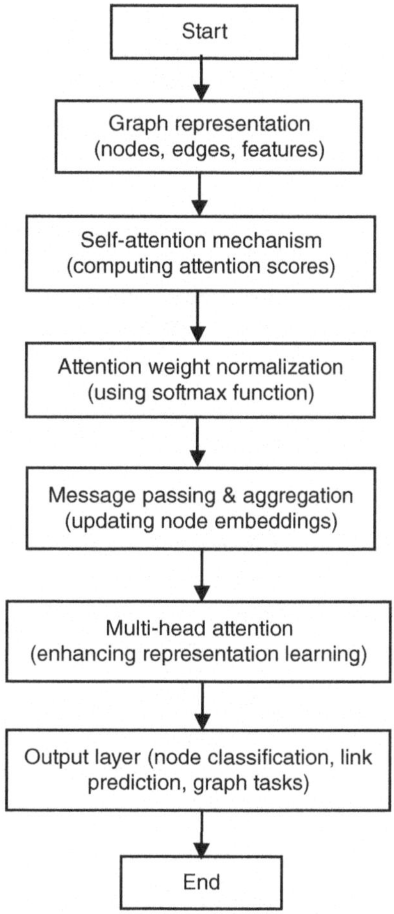

Figure 7.11 GAT architecture.

1) **Graph Representation—Encoding the Graph Structure**

The initial step in GAT involves structuring the input graph into a well-defined format. A graph $G(V, E)$ comprises a collection of nodes (V) and edges (E) that establish connections between them. Each node $v \in V$ is associated with a feature vector that encapsulates its unique properties, such as user profiles in social networks, road characteristics in traffic systems, or molecular attributes in bioinformatics. The relationships between nodes are captured through an adjacency matrix or edge list, specifying how nodes are interconnected within the graph.

2) **Self-Attention Mechanism—Learning the Importance of Neighbors**

Rather than assigning equal importance to all neighboring nodes, as done in GCN, GAT employs a self-attention mechanism to assess the influence of each neighbor individually. For a given node, the model calculates an attention score for each of its neighbors based on their feature representations. Mathematically, the attention score between two nodes i and j is determined as follows:

$$e_{ij} = \text{LeakyReLU}(a^T \cdot [Wh_i \,||\, Wh_j])$$

where

- h_i, h_j are the feature vectors of nodes i and j.
- W is a learnable weight matrix that transforms node features.
- || represents concatenation.
- a^T is a learnable attention vector.
- LeakyReLU is an activation function that introduces non-linearity.

These attention scores ($e\_\{ij\}$) determine how much influence each neighbor has on the central node.

3) **Attention Weight Calculation—Normalizing Scores Across Neighbors**

Once attention scores are computed for all neighbors, they are normalized using the softmax function to ensure they sum to 1. This converts raw scores into attention coefficients:

$$\alpha_{ij} = \frac{\exp(e_{ij})}{\sum_{k \in N(i)} \exp(e_{ik})}$$

where α_{ij} is final attention weight assigned to neighbor j when updating node i.

The sum of all weights for a node's neighbors equals 1, ensuring a proper distribution of influence.

4) **Message Passing and Aggregation—Updating Node Representations**

After computing attention weights, each node updates its representation by aggregating information from its neighbors:

$$h_i' = \sigma\left(\sum_{j \epsilon N(i)} \alpha_{ij} W h_j\right)$$

where

- h_i—updated feature vector for node i.
- σ—an activation function (e.g., ReLU).
- The sum ensures that neighbors contribute based on their computed importance (α_{ij}).

This process prioritizes influential neighbors, allowing them to have a greater impact on the final node embedding, thereby enhancing the quality of the learned representations.

5) **Multi-Head Attention—Improving Stability and Expressiveness**

   To enhance model robustness, GAT [2] employs multi-head attention, where multiple independent attention mechanisms simultaneously capture different aspects of the graph structure. The outputs from these attention heads are processed as follows:

- **Concatenated** → When applied in hidden layers to preserve diverse feature representations.
- **Averaged** → When used in the final layer to create a stable and unified node representation.

The resulting node embeddings are then fed into an output layer for various tasks such as node classification, link prediction, or graph clustering.

6) **Output Layer (Prediction Stage)**

   The final node embeddings are passed to an output layer, which varies based on the task:

- Node Classification → Uses softmax activation to classify each node into categories.
- Link Prediction → Predicts whether an edge exists between two nodes.
- Graph-Level Tasks → Summarizes entire graphs for applications such as molecular property prediction.

7.4.2.4 Application of GAT

Case Study 7.4

Drug Discovery—Identifying Crucial Molecular Bonds in Drug Interactions

Drug discovery is a complex process that involves understanding how molecules interact with biological targets, such as proteins or enzymes. Traditional computational methods, such as molecular docking and statistical models, often fail to accurately capture the intricate relationships between molecular bonds and their biological interactions. GAT have emerged as a powerful tool in drug discovery by modeling molecular structures as graphs, allowing researchers to identify critical molecular bonds that influence drug activity.

The effectiveness of a drug depends on how well its molecular structure interacts with a biological target. The challenge is to

- Identify which molecular bonds are most influential in drug interactions.
- Predict how different molecules will bind to a target protein.
- Improve drug design by prioritizing key functional groups in molecular structures.

(Continued)

Case Study 7.4 (Continued)

Traditional GCNs treat all chemical bonds equally, which may lead to suboptimal predictions. In contrast, GAT dynamically assigns importance to different molecular bonds, allowing for a more precise understanding of which bonds contribute most to drug efficacy.

Graph Representation of Molecular Structures

In this case study, we represent molecules as graphs (Fig. 7.12), where nodes (V) represent atoms (e.g., carbon, oxygen, nitrogen), edges (E) represent chemical bonds (e.g., single, double, aromatic bonds), node features are atomic properties (e.g., electronegativity, valence electrons), and edge features are bond types (e.g., covalent, hydrogen, ionic).

The molecule is converted into a graph format, where each atom is a node and bonds are edges. The graph is represented using an adjacency matrix to encode molecular connectivity. Instead of treating all molecular bonds equally, GAT assigns higher attention scores to bonds that play a significant role in drug–target interactions. The attention scores are normalized using the softmax function, ensuring that important molecular bonds receive higher attention weights while less significant bonds contribute minimally. Information is aggregated from neighboring atoms, with more attention given to strongly influential bonds (e.g., hydrogen bonds critical for drug binding). Multiple attention heads process the molecule in parallel to capture different interaction patterns. The final molecular representation is passed through an output layer to predict drug binding affinity to a protein, toxicity levels based on molecular structure, and potential drug interactions to avoid side effects.

Advantages of Using GAT in Drug Discovery

- Identifies Key Molecular Bonds Dynamically—GAT prioritizes the most crucial interactions.
- Improves Drug–Target Affinity Predictions—Helps pharmaceutical companies design better drug candidates.
- Speeds Up Drug Discovery—Reduces reliance on traditional trial-and-error methods.
- Applicable to Various Drug Classes—Can be used for antibiotics, antivirals, and cancer treatments.

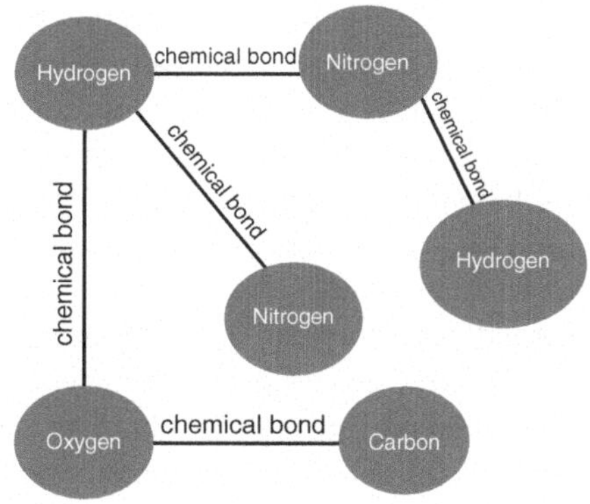

Figure 7.12 Graph representation of molecular structures.

7.5 Applications of Deep Learning on Graphs

In this modern era, rapid change in data leads to fast updates in the information and knowledge. To adapt to this changing environment, deep learning on graphs is used. Using GNNs, we can analyze user behavior, recommend products, detect fraud, predict traffic, and even help discover new drugs. It's all about understanding how things are connected and how those connections evolve.

Deep learning on graphs has revolutionized how we model and understand complex, interconnected systems across multiple domains. In social network analysis and community detection, GNNs are leveraged to capture user behavior, relationships, and influence dynamics. By modeling social media users as nodes and their interactions as edges, GNNs can uncover hidden communities, predict influential users, and detect coordinated behavior, providing deeper insights into how information spreads across networks.

In recommendation systems, GNNs enable collaborative filtering by treating users and items as nodes in a bipartite graph. This allows the model to learn not just direct user–item interactions but also indirect relationships through neighbors, improving personalization. Case studies from platforms such as Pinterest and Alibaba demonstrate how graph-based deep learning dramatically improves recommendation accuracy and diversity by considering multi-hop user behavior patterns. In biology and chemistry, graph-based deep learning is vital for drug discovery and molecular property prediction. Molecules are naturally represented as graphs with atoms as nodes and bonds as edges. GNNs can learn representations of these molecular graphs to predict properties such as solubility, toxicity, or binding affinity, expediting the drug development process. Moreover, protein–protein interaction networks use graph models to study how proteins function together, aiding in disease understanding and therapeutic targeting.

In the field of cybersecurity and fraud detection, GNNs are employed for network anomaly detection and intrusion detection. By modeling user accounts, transactions, or communication flows as graphs, deep learning models can detect unusual patterns that indicate fraudulent activity or malicious behavior. For instance, sudden bursts of communication between normally unrelated nodes might signal a botnet attack, while unusual transaction patterns in financial graphs can indicate money laundering.

Finally, in traffic prediction and urban planning, graph-based models treat road networks as graphs with intersections as nodes and roads as edges. Deep learning methods can forecast traffic congestion by analyzing historical and real-time vehicle flow, enabling more efficient routing and infrastructure development. These models also help city planners optimize public transportation and manage urban mobility based on spatiotemporal graph patterns, improving the quality of urban life.

7.6 Conclusion

This chapter provided a complete investigation of how deep learning techniques are altered to work with graph-structured data—a powerful yet intrinsically complex data form found in countless real-world applications. Beginning with an introduction to deep learning on graphs, the chapter set the stage by explaining why traditional deep learning models fall short in capturing the intricate relationships and non-Euclidean structures of graphs. It then continued into the basic concepts of graph representation, highlighting how nodes, edges, and their attributes are encoded for deep learning purposes, while also addressing the unique challenges of graph data such as irregularity, sparsity, and scalability.

The chapter then transitioned to the approach and benefits of deep learning on graphs, emphasizing how these models harness the power of relational data to outperform traditional methods in tasks such as node classification, clustering, and recommendation. A solid foundation was laid with an explanation of GCNs—the cornerstone of many graph-based learning systems. The workflow and core motivations behind GCNs illustrated how they extend convolution operations to graph domains, enabling effective information aggregation from node neighborhoods. Moving into advanced topics, the chapter covered dynamic GNNs, which adapt to temporal changes in graph structure.

References

1 S. Georgousis, M. P. Kenning, and X. Xie, "Graph deep learning: State of the art and challenges," *IEEE Xplore*, vol. 9, pp. 22106–22140, January, 2021, doi: 10.1109/ACCESS.2021.3055280.

2 P. Velič ković, G. Cucurull, A. Casanova, A. Romero, P. Liú, and Y. Bengio, "Graph attention networks,", vol. arXiv:1710.10903, 2017.

3 Z. Wu, S. Pan, F. Chen, G. Long, C. Zhang, and P. S. Yu, "A comprehensive survey on graph neural networks," *IEEE Trans. Neural Netw. Learn. Sys.*, vol. 32, no. 1, pp. 4–24, 2021. https://ieeexplore.ieee.org/document/9046288.

4 M. A. S. Sejan, M. H. Rahman, M. A. Aziz, J.-I. Baik, Y.-H. You, and H.-K. Song, "Graph convolutional network design for node classification accuracy improvement," *Mathematics*, vol. 11, no. 17, p. 3680, 2023, doi: 10.3390/math11173680.

5 M. Defferrard, X. Bresson, and P. Vandergheynst, "Convolutional neural networks on graphs with fast localized spectral filtering," in *Proc. 30th Int. Conf. Neural Informat. Process. Syst.*, Red Hook, NY, USA, January 2016, pp. 3844–3852.

6 F. Noman, C.-M. Ting, H. Kang, R. C.-W. Phan, and H. Ombao, "Graph autoencoders for embedding learning in brain networks and major depressive disorder identification," *IEEE J. Biomed. Health Informat*, vol. 28, no. 3, pp. 1644–1655, 2024, doi: 10.1109/JBHI.2024.3351177.

8

Advanced Graph Neural Networks

In the previous chapter, we introduced the concept of deep representation learning in graphs and the basics of graph neural networks (GNNs. Some basic models of GNN, such as graph convolution networks (GCNs, graph recurrent neural networks (GRNNs, and graph attention networks (GATs, were explored in the previous chapter and demonstrated their ability to capture the architecture. There are challenges in addressing the models that involve complex higher-order relationships.

In this chapter, advanced GNN architectures were discussed to address these challenges. These models extend the representational power of standard GNNs by incorporating temporal data and heterogeneous data among the nodes in the graph.

8.1 Spatiotemporal GNNs

Recent research demonstrates that spatiotemporal GNNs (ST-GNNs) effectively capture both spatial and temporal dependencies, significantly enhancing performance in applications such as traffic forecasting. Additionally, studies highlight the need for explainability in ST-GNNs to improve their transparency and reliability in critical real-world scenarios.

GCN is great for learning from graph structures [4], but it has a major limitation—it only captures spatial relationships (connections between nodes) and completely ignores time. Imagine predicting traffic congestion in a city. GCN can model road networks well, but it can't track how traffic changes over time. It treats all snapshots independently, which is unrealistic. GRNN improves GCN by adding temporal memory using recurrent neural networks (RNNs) (long-short-term memory [LSTM]/gated recurrent unit [GRU]), allowing it to handle time-evolving graphs. However, GRNN has two key issues. One is that the GRNN focuses on time-series changes but doesn't model spatial relationships well (it doesn't capture graph structures like GCN does). The second issue is that GRNN processes one time step at a time, making it inefficient for large real-time datasets. In weather forecasting, GRNN tracks past weather patterns but struggles to model spatial dependencies (e.g., how air pressure in one region affects another). GAT improves GCN by using attention mechanisms to prioritize important connections in the graph. However, GAT has two major drawbacks. The first one is that GAT only assigns importance to node relationships in a single snapshot, but it doesn't track how node importance changes over time. The second drawback is that computing attention scores for every connection at every time step is extremely expensive for large dynamic graphs. In human activity recognition, GAT helps in identifying important joint movements in a pose graph, but fails to track movement progression over time (like a dance sequence).

8.1.1 Definition With Illustration

A ST-GNN is a deep learning model designed to analyze dynamic graph-structured data by incorporating both spatial dependencies (connections between nodes) and temporal dependencies (changes over time). Unlike traditional GNNs, which focus solely on spatial relationships (e.g., GCN), or RNNs, which handle only temporal sequences (e.g., GRNN), ST-GNN effectively integrates both aspects. This capability makes it particularly powerful for real-time applications such as traffic prediction, financial market analysis, and human activity recognition, where evolving patterns play a crucial role.

8.1.1.1 Key Features of ST-GNN

- Spatial Learning—Uses graph convolution (GCN/GAT) to capture relationships between nodes.
- Temporal Learning—Uses LSTM, GRU, or transformer to track changes over time.
- Feature Fusion—Combines spatial and temporal information for better predictions.

Example ***Traffic Prediction***

Imagine a city's road network, where each node represents a traffic sensor, and edges represent roads connecting different locations. A graph can be represented over time with nodes (A, B, C, D) as traffic sensors, edges as roads connecting locations, and node features such as traffic speed, congestion level, and ST-GNN tracks how congestion spreads over time.

8.1.2 Working Process of ST-GNN

ST-GNNs are specialized for handling dynamic graphs, where both spatial relationships (connections between nodes) and temporal dependencies (changes over time) are essential. Unlike traditional GNNs such as GCN, GRNN, and GAT, which focus on either spatial or temporal aspects separately, ST-GNNs seamlessly integrate both, making them highly effective for real-time applications such as traffic prediction, human activity recognition, and financial forecasting.

The system receives a spatiotemporal graph, where nodes (V) represent entities (e.g., traffic sensors, stock prices, joints in motion tracking), edges (E) define relationships (e.g., road connections, correlations between stock prices), and node features (X) contain time-dependent attributes (e.g., traffic speed, stock trends). This is represented using a series of adjacency matrices to capture graph structure at different time steps. A GCN, or GAT, is applied to capture spatial relationships at each time step. A RNN such as LSTM, GRU, or transformer is used to capture how node states change over time. The spatial and temporal features are combined to create enriched node embeddings that reflect both space and time. The final node embeddings are passed through a fully connected (FC) layer for the target task:

- Traffic Prediction—Predicting future congestion levels.
- Human Activity Recognition—Identifying movement patterns.
- Financial Forecasting—Predicting stock trends.

8.1.3 Architecture of ST-GNNs

ST-GNNs [3] are specialized for handling dynamic graph-structured data by simultaneously capturing spatial dependencies (connections between nodes) and temporal dependencies (changes over time). Unlike traditional GCNs, which focus solely on spatial relationships, or RNNs and GRNNs, which model only temporal sequences, ST-GNNs seamlessly integrate both. This dual capability makes them highly effective for real-time applications such as traffic forecasting, human activity recognition, and financial market prediction, where both structural relationships and time-based patterns are crucial.

To achieve this, ST-GNNs incorporate graph convolutions (GCN/GAT) for spatial learning and temporal sequence models (LSTM, GRU, transformers) for temporal learning, ensuring a holistic understanding of evolving graph structures.

8.1.3.1 Key Components of ST-GNN Architecture

The ST-GNN architecture consists of multiple layers that systematically process spatial–temporal data. The core components are (Fig. 8.1) as follows:

1) Graph representation layer encodes the graph structure over different time steps.

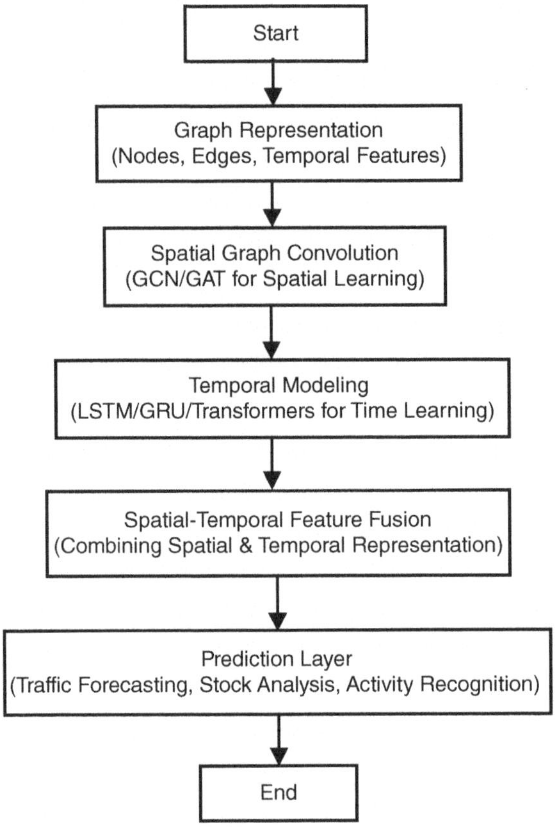

Figure 8.1 Flowchart of spatiotemporal graph neural networks.

2) Spatial graph convolution layer captures spatial relationships using GCN or GAT.
3) Temporal modeling layer captures temporal dependencies using LSTM, GRU, or transformers.
4) Spatial–temporal feature fusion layer merges spatial and temporal features for richer embeddings.
5) Prediction layer outputs results for traffic forecasting, event detection, or anomaly detection.

1) **Graph Representation (Input Layer)**
   - This layer consists of a graph $G = (V, E)$, where V represents a set of nodes and E represents a set of edges. The node features represent time-dependent attributes such as speed, volume, and stock prices. The graph is represented using an adjacency matrix or edge list to capture connectivity at different time steps.

2) **Spatial Graph Convolution Layer (Capturing Spatial Dependencies)**
   - A GCN, or GAT, is applied at each time step to capture spatial relationships between nodes. Each node aggregates information from its neighbors based on edge weights.
3) **Temporal Modeling Layer (Capturing Temporal Dependencies)**
   - Since graphs evolve over time, ST-GNN incorporates time-series models such as LSTMs to capture long-term dependencies in sequential data, GRUs to efficiently model short-term dependencies, and transformers that use attention mechanisms to learn global temporal relationships.
4) **Spatiotemporal Feature Fusion Layer**
   - After spatial and temporal learning, these features are merged into a unified representation. The fusion techniques used are concatenation for merging spatial and temporal embeddings and attention mechanisms to dynamically weight spatial vs temporal importance.
5) **Prediction Layer (Output Layer)**
   - The final embeddings are passed through a FC layer for prediction, detection, or forecasting future trends.

8.1.4 Application of ST-GNNs

8.1.4.1 Case Study on COVID-19 Spread Prediction Using ST-GNN

During the COVID-19 pandemic, accurately predicting how the virus spreads across different regions over time was crucial for public health planning, resource allocation, and lockdown strategies. Traditional forecasting models struggled to capture both spatial interactions (how infections spread between locations) and temporal trends (how cases change over time). ST-GNNs provided a more advanced solution by modeling the disease spread as a spatial–temporal graph, capturing mobility patterns, healthcare infrastructure, and government policies. The application areas where ST-CNNs can be used are to track how infections spread over time by considering mobility patterns between locations and finally improve prediction accuracy for pandemic response.

The spread of infection can be represented as a spatial–temporal graph where cities, districts, or countries are taken as nodes and connections based on human mobility, travel routes, or shared borders are the edges. The attributes of a node are the number of infections, hospital capacity, and lockdown measures. The temporal changes are the infection rates evolving over time.

How ST-GNN Works?

- Graph Representation: A network is formed where regions are nodes, and connections are based on population movement.

- Spatial Learning: The virus spreads through physical movement and interactions between locations, which ST-GNN models using graph convolutions (GCN/GAT). A GCN captures how the virus spreads between connected regions.
- Temporal Learning: Infection trends fluctuate over time due to lockdowns, vaccinations, and policy changes, which ST-GNN learns using LSTMs, GRUs, or transformers. An LSTM or a transformer models how infection rates change over time.
- Spatial–Temporal Fusion: ST-GNN can incorporate real-time mobility data, case reports, and environmental factors, improving predictive accuracy. Both spatial and temporal features are combined for accurate predictions.
- Prediction: The model forecasts future infection hotspots, helping authorities implement timely interventions.
- Optimizing Resource Allocation: The model ensures efficient distribution of medical supplies, ICU beds, and vaccines based on predicted needs.
- Adapting to Policy Changes: ST-GNN dynamically adjusts predictions based on government interventions, such as travel bans or mass vaccinations.

This approach helped researchers and governments predict COVID-19 waves, optimize healthcare resource allocation, and implement better containment strategies.

The latest research on the application of ST-GNNs on COVID-19 data is forecasting case surges for predicting new waves of infections based on historical data and mobility trends, healthcare system readiness to ensure hospitals are prepared for increasing patient loads, evaluating whether restrictions successfully slow down virus transmission, and identifying areas with higher risk populations for priority vaccination.

8.2 Dynamic GNNs

Traditional GNNs assume the graph is static—meaning once the structure (nodes and edges) is given, it doesn't change during learning. But most of the real-world graphs are dynamic. In contrast, many real-world graphs change over time, such as in social media, where people join/leave and follow/unfollow. So, dynamic GNNs are designed to learn from graphs that evolve over time—both in structure and node/edge features.

Dynamic GNNs are GNNs designed to handle graphs that evolve over time, such as social networks where users join/leave and relationships change, financial networks with evolving transaction flows, and citation networks with newly published papers. Unlike static GNNs, dynamic GNNs model how the structure (edges, nodes) and features of a graph change over time, learning from temporal dependencies.

8.2.1 Work Process of Dynamic GNNs

Dynamic GNNs process evolving graphs by capturing both spatial (graph structure) and temporal (time-evolving) information. There are two main types:

1) **Discrete-Time Dynamic GNNs**
   - Time is divided into snapshots (e.g., one graph per day/month).
   - A GNN processes each snapshot, and temporal models such as RNNs or LSTMs handle time evolution.
2) **Continuous-Time Dynamic GNNs**
   - Events (e.g., edge creation) happen at any timestamp.
   - Models such as temporal point processes or graph attention track changes at each event.
     - Learning from evolving graph structures
     - Temporal message-passing frameworks

Step-by-Step Workflow Assume you're working with a dynamic graph where both the structure and features change over time (snapshot-based or event-based), and you want to predict future behavior such as link formation or node classification.

Figure 8.2 shows the entire process of the dynamic GNN. The workflow of a dynamic GNN begins with the construction of a dynamic graph in the first step, which captures the evolution of nodes and edges over time. The input dynamic graph $G(t)$ can either be represented as a sequence of discrete-time snapshots $\{G_1, G_2, \dots, G_T\}$, or a set of timestamped events. Each snapshot or event records

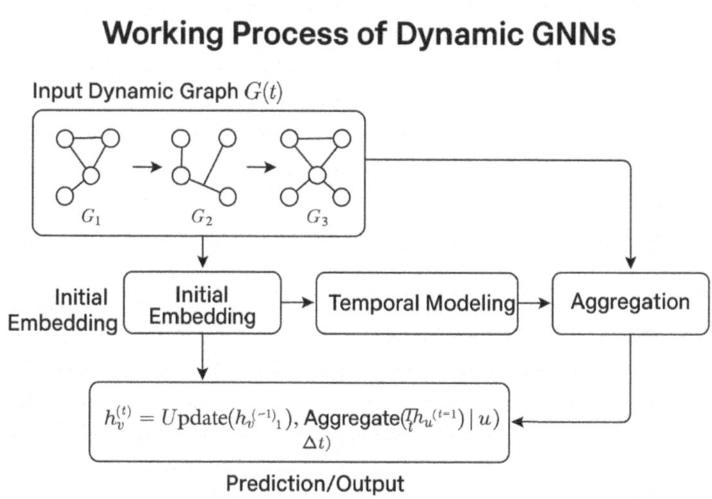

Figure 8.2 Workflow process of dynamic GNN.

the state of the graph, including which nodes are present, which edges connect them, and what features (e.g., age, interests, or transaction amounts) they carry at that point in time. In the next step, the model proceeds to initialize node and edge features, usually as dense vectors (embeddings). Assign initial features or embeddings to nodes: $h_v{}^0$. If the graph contains explicit features (e.g., user profile data), these are embedded directly. If not, nodes may be assigned learned embeddings. These initial representations serve as the foundation for temporal learning.

The next step in the model involves temporal modeling of graph structure and features. In the snapshot-based approach, a GNN (like GCN, GAT) is applied independently to each time snapshot to generate node embeddings at that time step. Then, a temporal model (such as a RNN or a temporal attention mechanism) is used to process the sequence of node embeddings across time, allowing the model to capture the evolution of each node's state. In the event-based approach, instead of processing full graphs, the model updates node embeddings whenever an event occurs (e.g., a new connection between users), using timestamp-aware mechanisms such as time encodings or continuous-time functions (such as Ordinary Differential Equation (ODE) solvers or decay functions). This allows the model to continuously evolve embeddings without needing fixed intervals.

- Snapshot-based: Apply a GNN at each time step t and use RNNs or temporal attention to capture dynamics across time.
- Event-based: Update node embeddings when events occur using time-encoding functions or ODEs.

Following temporal modeling, the message passing and aggregation step takes place. For each node, the model gathers information from its neighbors (defined either in a snapshot or per event), aggregates these messages (using sum, mean, attention, etc.), and updates the node's embedding. This process may include time-decay weighting or temporal attention to give more importance to recent interactions. The updated embedding reflects not only the node's immediate neighborhood but also its temporal evolution.

At each time step or event, update node embeddings via message passing:

$$h_v{}^{(t)} = \text{Update}\left(h_v{}^{(t-1)}, \text{Aggregate}\left(\left\{h_u{}^{(t-1)} \mid u \in N(v)\right\}\right), \Delta t\right)$$

Once updated node embeddings are available, the model uses them for prediction tasks in the final step. For example, it may compute the similarity between two node embeddings to predict whether a link will form between them in the future (link prediction), classify a node into categories (node classification), or identify anomalous behavior over time (anomaly detection). These predictions can be trained using supervised labels or self-supervised tasks (e.g., predicting next interaction time). Finally, during training, the model uses loss functions tailored to the task (e.g., binary cross-entropy for link prediction, cross-entropy for classification) and optimizes using backpropagation. Because the model must learn both structural and temporal patterns, training typically involves carefully managing temporal dependencies and graph sparsity, which may require mini-batching techniques such as neighborhood sampling or event batching for scalability.

8.2.2 Example: Dynamic Graph—Social Interaction

In this example, we consider a social interaction dynamic graph that evolves over three days, where each day is represented as a snapshot of the graph. These snapshots capture changes in node interactions over time, such as new connections forming or existing ones disappearing. The input to the model is a sequence of these graph snapshots for Days 1 to 3, as shown in Fig. 8.3. The prediction predicts whether Steve and Jeff will interact on Day 4.

Initially, node embeddings are assigned to each individual—Steve, Jeff, Jess, and Tina. On Day 1, the graph shows that Steve interacts with both Jeff and Jess, prompting the GNN to update their embeddings based on these interactions. On Day 2, the structure of the graph changes with new edges forming, causing the model to again update the embeddings using information from the new neighbors. On Day 3, Steve and Jeff reconnect, and this recurring interaction is captured by the model, helping it learn the temporal pattern in their relationship. Using the learned history of interactions encoded in the node embeddings, the model then predicts whether Steve and Jeff are likely to interact again on Day 4.

8.2.2.1 Dynamic GNN Process

1) Input: Sequence of graphs for Days 1–3.
2) Node Embeddings: Initialized for Alice, Bob, Charlie, Dana.
3) Day 1 GNN: Alice interacts with Bob and Charlie → embeddings updated.
4) Day 2 GNN: New edges → embeddings updated again based on new neighbors.

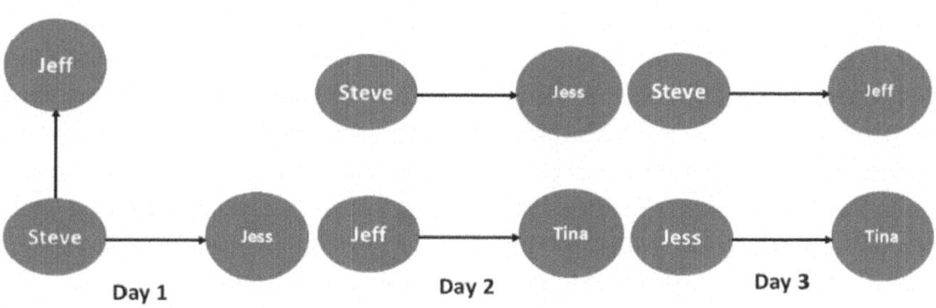

Figure 8.3 Graph snapshot of social interaction dynamic graph.

5) Day 3 GNN: Reconnection of Alice and Bob is captured → model learns pattern.
6) Prediction: Given the embedding history, predict whether Alice and Bob will interact on Day 4.

8.2.3 Dynamic GNN Models

8.2.3.1 Temporal GAT

Imagine you're using a social media app where you interact with different friends at different times—liking a photo in the morning, replying to a message at noon, and commenting on a post in the evening. The timing of each interaction matters: recent interactions might say more about your current interests than older ones. To recommend who you might interact with next, the system must understand who you interacted with and when. This is where temporal GAT (TGAT) comes in. It is a neural model that learns from both the structure of your connections and the timing of your interactions, using attention and time encoding to create dynamic, time-aware node representations.

Architecture The TGAT is a neural architecture specifically designed to model dynamic graphs where interactions between nodes occur at irregular time intervals. TGAT extends the attention mechanism from static GATs to handle temporal dynamics by incorporating time encoding into its attention computation. This allows it to generate node embeddings that evolve over time and depend not only on structure but also on the timing of interactions.

TGAT operates on event-based dynamic graphs, where interactions (edges) between nodes are timestamped. The architecture introduces two main innovations: time encoding and temporal attention. First, each interaction is augmented with a time-encoding vector, which captures the relative time difference between the current time and the time of past interactions. These time encodings are learned using sinusoidal position encodings, similar to those used in transformers, allowing the model to recognize temporal patterns [5]. Next, TGAT uses a multi-head attention mechanism to aggregate information from temporal neighbors—nodes that interacted with the target node in the past. However, unlike standard GAT, the attention weights in TGAT are computed using both the node features and their associated time encodings, allowing the model to attend more strongly to recent or contextually relevant interactions. Once the temporal attention scores are computed, TGAT aggregates messages from the temporal neighborhood and updates the node embedding. This process is repeated for each interaction or prediction task, allowing TGAT to generate dynamic embeddings that capture the historical context and temporal structure of node behavior.

8.2.3.2 Dynamic GCN

Imagine you're a student attending classes throughout the week. On Monday, you sit with Steve and discuss homework; on Wednesday, you work on a group project with Jeff and Jess; and on Friday, you join a study session with Tina. Each day, your interactions change—sometimes with the same people, sometimes new ones—and your academic network evolves over time.

To understand your learning patterns or predict who you might interact with next, we need a model that captures how your connections change across days and how those changes affect your role in the network. This is where the Dynamic GCN (DyGCN) comes in.

DyGCN [6] is a dynamic GNN that processes a sequence of graph snapshots over time using GCN layers at each time step and then uses a temporal model (such as an RNN) to capture how node representations evolve. It learns both spatial (structural) and temporal patterns from dynamic graphs.

Architecture DyGCN is a neural architecture designed to learn from temporal sequences of graph snapshots, where the structure and/or features of the graph evolve over time. Unlike static GCNs that operate on a single graph, DyGCN extends this capability to dynamic graphs by combining graph convolutional layers with temporal sequence models such as RNNs. The goal is to capture both spatial dependencies (relationships between nodes within each snapshot) and temporal dynamics (how those relationships change across time). DyGCN architecture is shown in Fig. 8.4.

The architecture begins by representing the dynamic graph as a sequence of static snapshots: $\{G_1, G_2, \dots, G_T\}$, each corresponding to a different time step. For each snapshot G_t, a GCN layer is applied to learn structural information by aggregating features from neighboring nodes. This generates a sequence of node embeddings $\{H_1, H_2, \dots, H_T\}$, where each H_t represents the graph's structural state at time t. To model temporal evolution, DyGCN passes these node embeddings through a recurrent layer—typically a GRU or LSTM. This temporal model processes the embeddings over time for each node, learning how their states evolve. The output of the RNN provides temporally aware embeddings that incorporate both the graph structure at each time and the progression of changes across time steps.

Finally, these embeddings can be used for tasks such as dynamic node classification, link prediction, or anomaly detection, depending on the application. DyGCN is especially effective in settings where patterns emerge over time, such as social networks, traffic systems, or communication graphs.

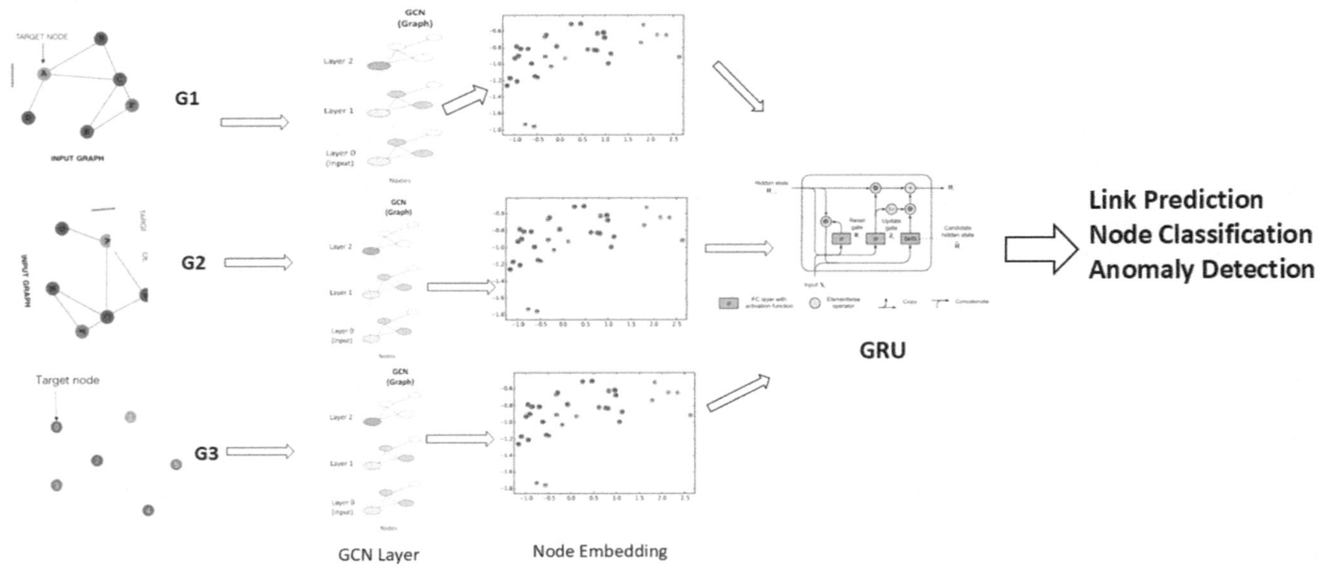

Figure 8.4 DyGCN architecture.

8.3 Hypergraph Neural Networks

Imagine an institution where students participate in multiple group projects. In one project, Steve, Jeff, and Jess are working together on an artificial intelligence assignment. In another, Jeff, Tina, and Reema collaborate on an Internet of Things (IoT) project. Unlike traditional pairwise friendships or messages (which can be modeled as edges between two people in a simple graph), each project connects multiple students at once—forming a many-to-many relationship. This situation cannot be accurately modeled using regular graphs, which only capture pairwise relationships. Instead, we need a structure that can model group-based relationships, where a single connection (like a project group) involves multiple nodes at the same time. This is where a hypergraph neural network (HGNN) comes in. An HGNN is a neural network designed to learn from hypergraphs, where a hyperedge can connect more than two nodes. HGNNs generalize traditional GNNs by capturing higher-order relationships and group-level interactions among nodes, making them ideal for complex relational data that goes beyond simple pairwise connections.

8.3.1 Architecture of HGNN

The architecture of an HGNN is composed of three main components: the node feature matrix, the hyperedge incidence matrix, and a hypergraph convolutional layer. The node feature matrix contains the attributes of all nodes (e.g., each student's profile or skills). The hyperedge incidence matrix defines the relationship between nodes and hyperedges—it tells us which nodes participate in which group (e.g., which students are in which project team). The hypergraph convolutional layer is the core of HGNN. Unlike standard GNNs that aggregate messages from adjacent nodes, HGNN performs a two-step message-passing process. First, node features are aggregated into their associated hyperedges. This step summarizes the group as a whole. Second, the aggregated hyperedge representations are propagated back to all the nodes connected by that hyperedge. This two-way process ensures that each node receives information not just from its direct neighbors but from all members of any group it belongs to.

Formally, this can be written as

$$H^{(l+1)} = \sigma\left(D_v{}^{-1/2}H^{(l)}D_e{}^{-1}H^{(l)T}D_v{}^{-1/2}XW^{(l)}\right)$$

where

- $H^{(l)}$ is the feature matrix at layer l.
- D_v and D_e are the degree matrices of nodes and hyperedges.
- X is the incidence matrix of the hypergraph.
- $W^{(l)}$ is the learnable weight matrix.
- σ is an activation function.

8.3.2 Working Process of HGNN

The working process of HGNN begins by inputting the node features and hypergraph structure (incidence matrix). Each node sends its features to the hyperedges it belongs to, where features from multiple nodes are aggregated—typically using mean or attention-based methods. Then, these combined group features are sent back to all connected nodes, effectively enabling a node to learn from the collective context of its group memberships. This process is repeated across multiple layers, allowing information to flow across increasingly complex combinations of nodes and hyperedges. The final node representations can be used for downstream tasks such as node classification (e.g., predicting a student's project role), hyperedge prediction (e.g., recommending new teams), or clustering. This architecture is especially useful in applications such as recommendation systems (where users co-rate items), scientific collaboration networks (multiple authors on a paper), or multi-party transactions (many users participating in a transaction), where higher-order relationships are crucial.

8.4 Unsupervised Deep Learning Models

8.4.1 Graph Autoencoder

A graph autoencoder (GAE) is an unsupervised deep learning model designed to extract useful information from the node features and adjacency matrix of the input graph and learn from the low-dimensional embedding of graph nodes by encoding into latent space. It then reconstructs the original graph from the encoded embedding using a decoder while preserving the structure and relationships within the graph. Unlike traditional autoencoders, which work on structured data such as images or text, GAEs operate directly on graph-structured data. This process helps in understanding complex graph structures and enables various deeper tasks. GAE's purpose is to capture both node attributes and connectivity patterns and to apply them in various deep learning tasks.

8.4.1.1 Key Components of GAE

The key components of GAE are the input graph with its adjacency matrix and node feature matrix; the encoder, which outputs latent embedding; and the decoder, which reconstructs the original graph, loss function, and output graph.

8.4.1.2 GAE—Workflow With Its Architecture

The key steps involved in the GAE workflow are as follows:

The process of the GAE workflow starts with real-world graph data. Two matrices are created: the adjacency matrix, which contains the details of connections between nodes, and the feature matrix, which contains the attributes of nodes. The node features are normalized to ensure consistency in the data. The next step is to use an encoder neural network to transform the data in high-dimensional representation into a latent space representation [2]. In this type of convolutional neural network, graph convolution layers are used to update each node's representation by applying graph convolution, allowing it to learn from its neighbors and their features while capturing the local graph structure. Then feature aggregation is applied to aggregate the information from neighboring nodes. The dimensional reduction method is applied to transform node representations into a lower-dimensional latent space for efficient processing.

The encoder produces the latent representation of each node, capturing the essential information about the graph structure and node attributes. This process is called feature extraction. This latent representation (Z) is given as input to the decoder for the reconstruction of the graph. It uses the latent representation to reconstruct the original graph structure by predicting the adjacency matrix or node features. The reconstructed graph is compared with the original graph by using a LOSS function such as mean squared error to measure the quality of the reconstruction. During the training process, adjust the weights of the encoder and decoder layers using backpropagation to minimize the reconstruction loss, optimizing the model to learn the best representation of the graph.

8.4.1.3 GAE Algorithm

Step 1:

Input process

- Consider the graph $G = (V,E)$, where V represents the set of nodes (vertices), E represents the set of edges (connections between nodes), X is the node feature matrix containing attributes for each node, and A is the adjacency matrix, representing the connections between nodes.

Step 2:

Encoder process

- The encoder takes node features (X) and the adjacency matrix (A) as input. Each node gathers information from its neighbors.
- A GCN is used to aggregate and transform information. An aggregate function is used to aggregate the features from the neighborhood nodes. The graph convolution operation updates node embeddings iteratively. The mathematical expression is

$$H^{(\ell+1)} = \sigma(\dot{\mathrm{D}}^{-1/2}\tilde{\mathrm{A}}\dot{\mathrm{D}}^{-1/2}H^{(\ell)}\,W^{(\ell)})$$

where $\mathrm{H}^{(\ell)}$ = Node feature matrix at layer ℓ.

- $\tilde{A} = A + I$ Adjacency matrix with self-loops added.
- D = Degree matrix of $\tilde{A}$.
- $W^{(\ell)}$ = Trainable weight matrix.
- σ = Activation function (Rectified Linear Unit (ReLU) is common).
- The encoding process generates a latent representation (Z) of nodes, where

$$Z = GCN(X, A)$$

Step 3:
Decoder Process
- Computes similarity between node embeddings.
- The decoder uses the inner product of the latent vectors to reconstruct the original graph

$$\tilde{A} = (ZZ^T)$$

where σ is an activation function (such as sigmoid) that outputs a probability score for each possible edge.
Step 4:
Reconstruction Loss Process
- The model is trained by minimizing the difference between the original adjacency matrix (A) and the reconstructed matrix ($\hat{A}$).
- The most common loss function is binary cross-entropy loss for link prediction:

$$L = \sum_{ij} A_{ij} \log(\tilde{A}_{ij}) + (1 - A_{ij})\log(1 - \tilde{A}_{ij})$$

Example ***Graph Autoencoder in an Author Citation Graph***
Consider an author citation graph where nodes represent authors and edges represent citations between them. Given an incomplete graph, we want to predict missing citations (i.e., which authors are likely to cite each other in the future) using a GAE. Node features are publication count, research topics, h-index, etc., and the adjacency matrix is the matrix that represents existing citation links ($A_{ij} = 1$ if author i cites author j). This is given in Fig. 8.5.

Encoder: Learning Author Embeddings The encoder (–GCN) learns a low-dimensional representation Z for each author. These embeddings capture research similarities, common collaborators, and citation patterns. Fig. 8.6 shows how author nodes are transformed into vector embeddings.

Decoder: Predicting Missing Citations This step predicts new citations between researchers with similar work.

Loss Function: Training the Model The model learns to minimize the difference between actual and predicted citations.

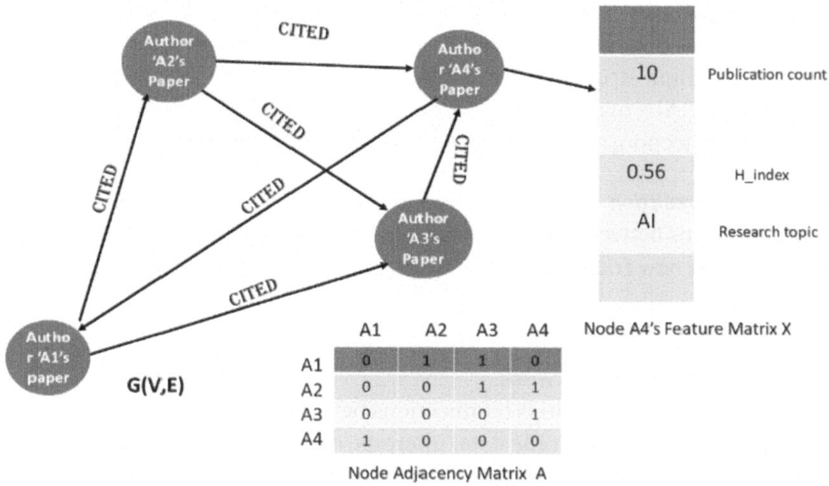

Figure 8.5 Node feature matrix and adjacency matrix for author citation graph.

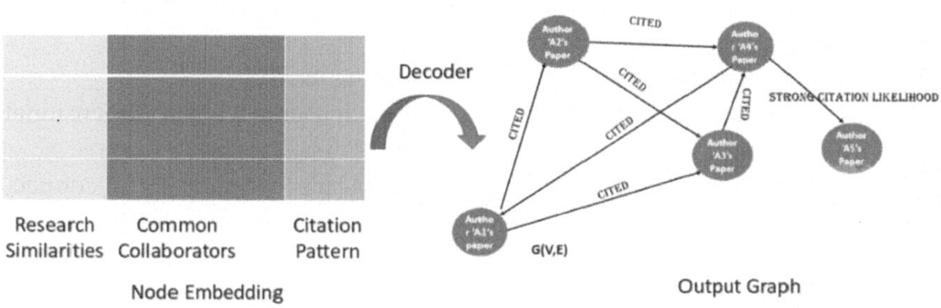

Figure 8.6 Encoder: Learning author embedding.

Output: Predicted Future Citations The model outputs a ranked list of potential citations. High Â_ij scores indicate strong citation likelihood between authors. This is shown in Fig. 8.2.

With this approach, GAE helps predict future citations and enhances research collaboration.

8.4.1.4 Applications of GAE

Imagine you're working with complex graph data—social networks, citation networks, or even molecular structures. You want to uncover hidden patterns, predict missing connections, or cluster similar entities. That's exactly where GAEs come in.

GAEs help you learn meaningful representations of nodes without needing labeled data. In social networks, they can predict new friendships. In citation networks, they suggest likely references for research papers. In bioinformatics, they help discover potential drug interactions by analyzing molecular graphs.

By encoding graph structures into a lower-dimensional space and then reconstructing them, GAEs make it easier for you to perform tasks such as link prediction, anomaly detection, and node classification—all without explicit supervision.

A. GAE in Link Prediction Link prediction aims to identify missing or potential future connections between nodes in a graph. For example, in a social network, a GAE can suggest new friends by predicting likely connections between users.

Input:

Social Network Graph

- Nodes (V): Users in the network.
- Edges (E): Existing friendships (connections between users).
- Node Features (X): User profile data, interests, or activity logs.
- Adjacency Matrix (A): Represents existing relationships between users.

Encoder: GCN

- The encoder processes the graph structure and node features to embed each user into a latent space.
- Uses GCNs to aggregate features from neighboring users.
- Produces Z (node embeddings) that represent each user in a lower-dimensional space.

This step learns meaningful user representations based on their social connections.

Decoder: Predicting Missing Links

- The decoder reconstructs the adjacency matrix Â, estimating the probability of a connection between any two users.
- Uses the inner product of node embeddings to calculate potential links.

This step predicts which users are likely to become friends.

Loss Function: Training the Model

- The model is trained to minimize the difference between the actual adjacency matrix (A) and the predicted one (Â).
- Uses binary cross-entropy loss to improve link prediction accuracy.

This ensures the model learns to correctly predict missing or future links.

Output: Suggested Friendships

- Once trained, the model outputs a ranked list of potential friendships based on link probabilities.
- Users with high Â_*ij* scores are recommended as friends.

The model now suggests new friends based on learned graph patterns!

Other Applications

- **Node Clustering:** Identify groups of similar nodes without explicit labels.
- **Anomaly Detection:** Detect unusual nodes or edges in fraud detection and cybersecurity.
- **Recommendation Systems:** Suggest new connections or products based on learned graph embeddings.

8.4.1.5 Advantages and Limitations of GAE

Traditional methods use graphs as flat data, which may be exposed to loss of information. However, GAE learns both local and global node relationships using GNNs. Traditional models require labeled data for supervised training, which is costly and time-consuming. Whereas GAE learns node embeddings without needing labels, making it great for real-world, unlabeled graphs. Manual feature engineering is needed while using the traditional method, which is inefficient. GAE generates low-dimensional, information-rich embeddings that preserve node relationships. Handling a huge volume of data is expensive with traditional methods, whereas GAE uses graph convolution operations that scale better with large datasets.

Limitations of GAE

- Can struggle with dynamic graphs that change over time.
- Scalability issues with large-scale graphs.
- Lossy reconstruction in complex graphs with high connectivity.

8.4.2 Variational Autoencoder

When working with graphs, you don't always want a fixed embedding for each node, like in a GAE. Instead, you need something more flexible, something that captures uncertainty and allows for better generalization. That's why we go for a new variant of GAE–variational autoencoder (VAE).

Unlike GAE, which directly learns node embeddings, VAE learns a probability distribution over these embeddings. Instead of mapping each node to a single point in latent space, VAE assigns it a range of possible values, ensuring the model doesn't overfit to the training data. This is particularly useful when dealing with noisy, incomplete, or evolving graphs. Another major advantage of VAE is its ability to generate new data. Since it learns a structured latent space, you can sample from this space to create new nodes, predict missing links, or even generate entirely new graphs. This is why VAE is widely used in areas like drug discovery, recommendation systems, and anomaly detection.

While GAEs effectively learn node embeddings in an unsupervised manner, they have a major limitation: GAEs are deterministic and lack uncertainty modeling. This means GAEs encode each node into a fixed representation, which can lead to overfitting and poor generalization in real-world applications. If you need a simple representation learning model, GAE is fine. If you need robust, generalizable, and uncertainty-aware embeddings, VAE is the better choice. If you're working with noisy, sparse, or evolving graphs, VAE performs better due to its probabilistic nature.

A VAE is an unsupervised deep learning model that extends traditional autoencoders by introducing probabilistic modeling. Unlike standard autoencoders that learn a single deterministic encoding for input data, VAEs learn a distribution over possible representations [3].

This allows VAEs to generate new data samples by sampling from this learned distribution, making them highly useful for tasks such as data generation, denoising, anomaly detection, and representation learning.

8.4.2.1 Variational Graph Autoencoder—Workflow With Its Architecture

Workflow of Variational Graph Autoencoder The key step involved in VAE workflow is representing the graph in a low-dimensional latent space. The GCN layer in the encoder encodes node features into two outputs namely the mean vector μ and standard deviation (log variance) log σ. For each node, sample a latent vector z using a sampling technique. Then the decoder reconstructs the graph and outputs the original graph.

Figure 8.7 shows the input graph is passed into the GCN layer to be represented in the latent space. Then the decoder takes the matrix, and, using the inner product, it converts the graph into the original graph and outputs the adjacency matrix.

Algorithm: Variational Graph Autoencoder

Input:

Adjacency matrix A, node features X

Output:

Reconstructed $\hat{A}$, latent representations Z

1) Encode: Use GCN to compute:
   $-\mu = \text{GCN}_{\mu}(X,A)$
   $-\log \sigma = \text{GCN}_{\sigma}(X,A)$
2) Reparameterize: Sample $z_i = \mu_i + \sigma_i \odot \in$, where $\in \sim N(0,I)$
3) Decode: Compute $\hat{A}_{ij} = \sigma(z_i{}^{T} z_j)$
4) Loss Function: Optimize:
   $L = Eq(Z|X,A)[\log p(A|Z)] - KL(q(Z|X,A)||p(Z))$
5) Backpropagation: Update model parameters using gradients of the total loss.

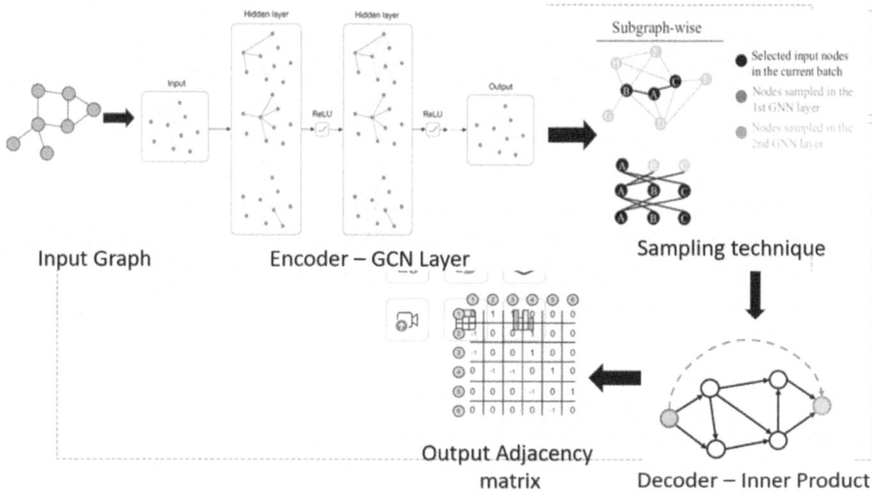

Figure 8.7 Workflow of VGAE.

8.4.2.2 Advantages and Limitations of VGAE

Variational graph autoencoder (VGAE) performs well in the link prediction task, even with sparse data, and helps in capturing uncertainty. VGAE can combine graph topology with node attributes for richer representations. However, VGAE is expensive computationally for large-scale graphs. Also, it requires careful tuning of latent space dimensions and regularization. Reconstruction via inner product may limit modeling complex edge patterns.

8.5 Conclusion

This chapter provided a complete investigation of how deep learning techniques are altered to work with graph-structured data—a powerful yet intrinsically complex data form found in countless real-world applications. A major focus of the chapter was on unsupervised deep learning models, particularly the GAE and the VGAE. These models were discussed in terms of their architectures, algorithms, workflows, and real-world applications, such as link prediction and graph generation. Their advantages—like unsupervised learning ability and scalability—as well as their limitations, including over-smoothing and difficulty in modeling uncertainty, were critically analyzed to give a balanced understanding.

The chapter then transitioned to the approach and benefits of deep learning on graphs, emphasizing how these models harness the power of relational data to outperform traditional methods in tasks such as node classification, clustering, and recommendation. A solid foundation was laid with an explanation of GCNs—the cornerstone of many graph-based learning systems. The workflow and core motivations behind GCNs illustrated how they extend convolution operations to graph domains, enabling effective information aggregation from node neighborhoods. Moving into advanced topics, the chapter covered dynamic GNNs, which adapt to temporal changes in graph structure. Models such as TGAT and DyGCN were introduced to show how dynamic patterns and time-aware relationships can be captured. These models are particularly relevant for domains such as social media, fraud detection, and traffic forecasting. The chapter also included HGNNs, which generalize traditional GNNs to model group-based (many-to-many) interactions, useful in biological networks, collaborative filtering, and beyond.

Finally, the chapter concluded with an in-depth look at the applications of deep learning on graphs, spanning across domains such as social network analysis, recommendation systems, biology and chemistry, cybersecurity, and urban mobility. These case studies not only demonstrated the versatility of graph-based learning but also showcased its impact in solving complex, real-world problems where entities are deeply interconnected.

References

1 Stavros Georgousis, Michael P. Kenning, Xianghua Xie, Graph deep learning: State of the art and challenges, *IEEE Xplore*, 9, pp. 22106 – 22140, January 2021, E-ISSN: 2169-3536, DOI: 10.1109/ACCESS.2021.3055280.

2 F. Noman, C.-M. Ting, H. Kang, R. C.-W. Phan, and H. Ombao, "Graph autoencoders for embedding learning in brain networks and major depressive disorder identification," *IEEE J. Biomed. Health Inform*, vol. 28, no. 3, pp. 1644–1655, 2024, doi: 10.1109/JBHI.2024.3351177.

3 R. Wei and A. Mahmood, "Recent advances in variational autoencoders with representation learning for biomedical informatics: A survey," *IEEEAccess*, vol. 9, pp. 4939–4956, 2020, doi: 10.1109/ACCESS.2020.3048309.

4 M. A. S. Sejan, M. H. Rahman, M. A. Aziz, J.-I. Baik, Y.-H. You, and H.-K. Song, "Graph convolutional network design for node classification accuracy improvement," *Mathematics*, vol. 11, no. 17, p. 3680, 2023, doi: 10.3390/math11173680.

5 Y. Jia, M. Jun Wang, R. Hosseini, W. Shou, W. Peng, and C. Mao, "Temporal graph attention network for building thermal load prediction," *Energ. Buildings*, vol. 21, 2024, doi: 10.1016/j.enbuild.2023.113507.

6 Y. Wang and Q. Ren, "Dynamic graph convolutional network for long short-term traffic flow prediction, 2022 IEEE Symp. Comp. Commun. (ISCC), Rhodes, Greece,", June 2022, doi: 10.1109/ISCC55528.2022.9912866.

Part III

Advanced Analysis and Techniques

9

Graph Alignment and Matching

9.1 Introduction to Graph Alignment and Matching

In the previous chapter, we explored graph pooling, a key process for simplifying complex graph structures by reducing their size while preserving critical information. Pooling techniques enable efficient representation and analysis of graphs, making them particularly useful for handling significant or highly detailed graphs. These methods set the stage for understanding how graphs can be aligned and matched effectively, even when their structures are complex or noisy.

Based on this, this chapter focuses on graph alignment and matching, a vital area of graph analysis where the goal is to identify correspondences between nodes, edges, or subgraphs in two or more graphs. While graph pooling provides a means to simplify graph representations, graph alignment and matching take the next step by comparing and integrating these representations to find meaningful relationships.

This chapter delves into the mathematical foundations, algorithms, and practical applications of graph alignment and matching. It covers techniques for matching nodes, aligning entire graphs or subgraphs, and utilizing embeddings to enhance the matching process. Additionally, it explores real-world scenarios where graph alignment is crucial, such as network analysis, biological pathway alignment, and knowledge graph integration.

9.2 Definition and Purpose of Graph Alignment and Matching

Graph alignment refers to the process of finding the communication/association between the nodes and edges of two or more graphs to identify similarities, differences, patterns, or structural relationships.

Graph matching is the process of determining a mapping or correspondence between the nodes (and sometimes edges) of two graphs, often optimizing a similarity or cost function [1].

9.2.1 Purpose

Comparative Analysis: Enables the comparison of two graphs to identify similarities or differences, such as in evolutionary studies or comparing social media networks.

Data Integration: Aligns graphs from different domains or sources, such as combining protein interaction networks from different organisms or integrating disparate data sources.

Pattern Recognition: Identifies recurring substructures or motifs within graphs, crucial in fields such as cheminformatics or image analysis.

Optimization and Search: Supports optimization problems by finding relationships that maximize or minimize a given objective function, e.g., matching networks to minimize communication costs.

Anomaly Detection: Identifies deviations in the mapping process that may signify anomalies, fraud, or system irregularities.

9.3 Example for Graph Matching and Alignment

Consider a Graph A with nodes $\{A, B, C\}$ and edges from A to B and from B to C, and Graph B with nodes $\{X, Y, Z\}$ with edges from X to Y and from Y to Z, as shown in Fig. 9.1.

9.3.1 Matching

In the above graph, a matching between the nodes of Graph A and Graph B based on their structure was made.

- Nodes $A \leftrightarrow X$, $B \leftrightarrow Y$, and $C \leftrightarrow Z$.
- Edges $(A\text{-}B) \leftrightarrow (X\text{-}Y)$ and $(B\text{-}C) \leftrightarrow (Y\text{-}Z)$.

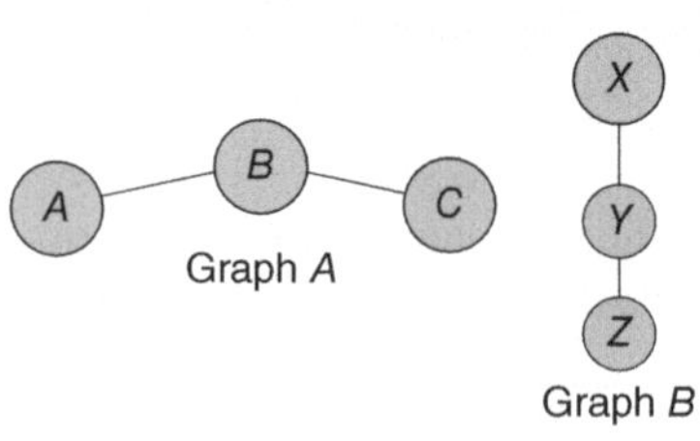

Figure 9.1 Graph example for graph alignment and matching.

This example shows exact graph matching since the structures of Graph A and Graph B are identical.

9.3.2 Example of Graph Alignment

Consider Graph A with nodes $\{A, B, C, D\}$ and edges $\{(A\text{-}B), (B\text{-}C), (C\text{-}D)\}$, and Graph B with nodes $\{X, Y, Z\}$ and edges $\{(X\text{-}Y), (Y\text{-}Z)\}$.

9.3.3 Alignment

- **Objective:** Align the graphs to find the best association.
- **Result**
  - Nodes $A \leftrightarrow X$, $B \leftrightarrow Y$, and $C \leftrightarrow Z$ (node D in Graph A has no match in Graph B).
  - Edges $(A\text{-}B) \leftrightarrow$ (X-Y) and $(B\text{-}C) \leftrightarrow (Y\text{-}Z)$.

9.4 Types of Graph Alignment and Matching

We recognize that graph alignment and matching are fundamental tasks in graph representation learning (GRL), allowing us to compare, integrate, and analyze multiple graphs while maintaining their structural integrity. These techniques play a crucial role in various applications, including bioinformatics, social networks, recommendation systems, fraud detection, and knowledge graph integration, enabling us to extract meaningful insights from complex graph structures.

In recent years of research, a widely used technique in GRL is neighborhood aggregation, where information from surrounding nodes is incorporated into a target node's representation. These refined representations are then compared to determine similarities. More sophisticated methods integrate information from corresponding nodes in a different graph, allowing for deeper structural understanding and enhanced alignment. Some of the variant methods are discussed in this chapter.

9.4.1 Exact Graph Matching (Graph Isomorphism)

In exact matching, two graphs are considered identical if there is a one-to-one mapping between their nodes and edges while preserving structure. This is used in graph isomorphism detection, where the goal is to determine whether two graphs are structurally identical [2].

Given two graphs $G_1 = (V_1, E_1)$ and $G_2 = (V_2, E_2)$, an isomorphism is a bijection $f : V1 \rightarrow V2$ such that $(u, v) \in E_1 \iff (f(u), f(v)) \in E_2$.

Example 9.1 ***Author Citation Graph***
Consider two graphs, G_1 and G_2, each containing nodes with authors' papers $\{A_1, A_2, A_3, A_4\}$ and $\{B_1, B_2, B_3, B_4\}$, respectively. Edges represent direct citations between authors (e.g., $A_1 \rightarrow A_2$ means Author A_1's Paper cites the Paper of Author A_2). Our objective is to determine whether these author citation graphs are structurally identical using exact graph matching (graph isomorphism).

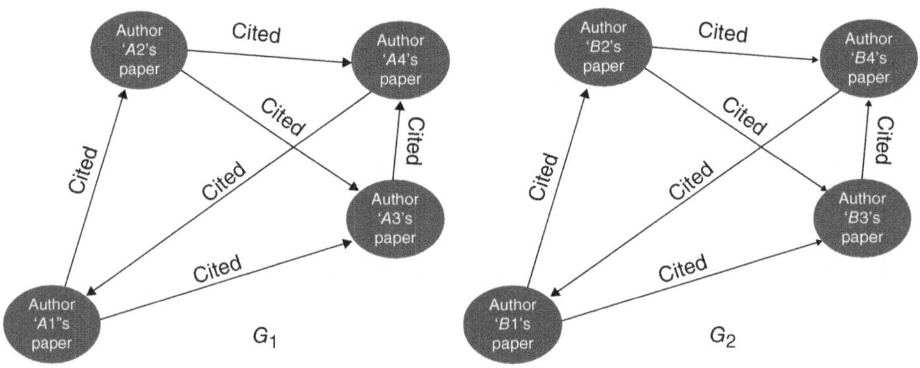

Figure 9.2 Author citation graph for isomorphic graphs.

Since the nodes and edges remain the same under this mapping, G_1 and G_2 are isomorphic as shown in Fig. 9.2, meaning they represent the same author citation structure despite different labels. The bijection function for nodes and edges is represented as

Nodes

$f(A_1) \rightarrow B_1, f(A_2) \rightarrow B_2, f(A_3) \rightarrow B_3, f(A_4) \rightarrow B_4.$

Edges

$(A_1, A_2) \rightarrow (f(A_1), f(A_2))$ $(A_1, A_3) \rightarrow (f(A_1), f(A_3))$, $(A_2, A_4) \rightarrow (f(A_2), f(A_4))$, $(A_3, A_4) \rightarrow (f(A_3), f(A_4))$

Exact graph matching is used in various domains such as natural language processing (NLP), computer vision, social network analysis, bioinformatics, and cybersecurity. In NLP, words are represented in nodes, and the nodes are connected by edges based on the grammatical relationship. Matching is done to find the identical sentences. It helps in finding redundant entries in databases, query matching in search engines, and doing plagiarism-checking. It is a powerful tool for structural consistency, duplication verification, and pattern recognition.

9.4.2 Inexact/Fuzzy Matching

Exact graph matching is suitable for identifying identical structures. An inexact matching method is used to identify missing and noisy data, and variations in data. It looks for similarity in data rather than identical data. It works for finding approximate matches in text search and spell checking. Let us take an example to find very similar sounding words or rhyming words. Consider a graph G with words {BELL, SELL, WELL, TELL, DOG} as nodes and a one-edit difference as a relationship between the words in nodes. This is given in Fig. 9.3.

Find the nodes with a one-edit difference between pairs of nodes using similarity scores. The nodes with one-edit difference are considered closer and neighbor nodes, and other nodes are farther away. In the above figure, the words TELL, WELL, and SELL are considered neighbor nodes for node BELL and the DOG node as a farther node.

9.4.3 Global Alignment: Aligning Entire Graphs

Global alignment is the process of aligning two or more graphs that capture structural relationships between graphs. The main goal is to identify each component (nodes, edges, structure) of one graph that matches another graph. Each graph is composed of nodes (representing entities) and edges (representing relationships). Traverse both graphs, comparing the nodes and edges based on the features/structures. Matching can be done by defining some matching criteria between graphs. A similarity score is used to find out how well two graphs are aligned with each other.

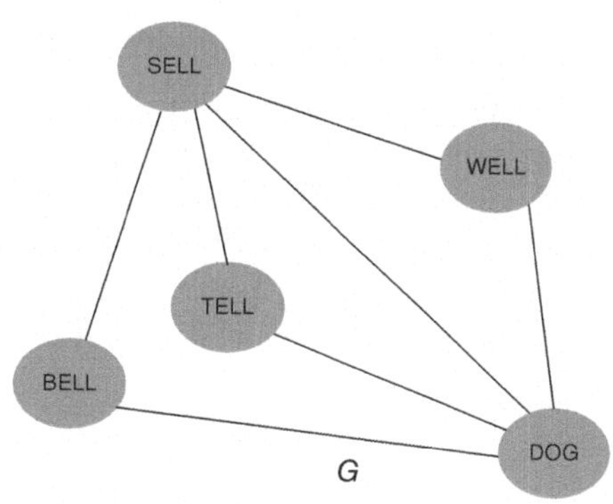

Figure 9.3 Inexact matching graph example.

Example 9.2 ***Author Citation Graph***
Consider the example of the author citation graphs G_1 and G_2 with $\{A_1, A_2, A_3, A_4\}$ and $\{B_1, B_2, B_3, B_4\}$ as authors' nodes and citation relationships among nodes, respectively, as given in Fig. 9.4. The aim is to align two citation graphs from different sources, representing scholarly papers and their citation relationships.

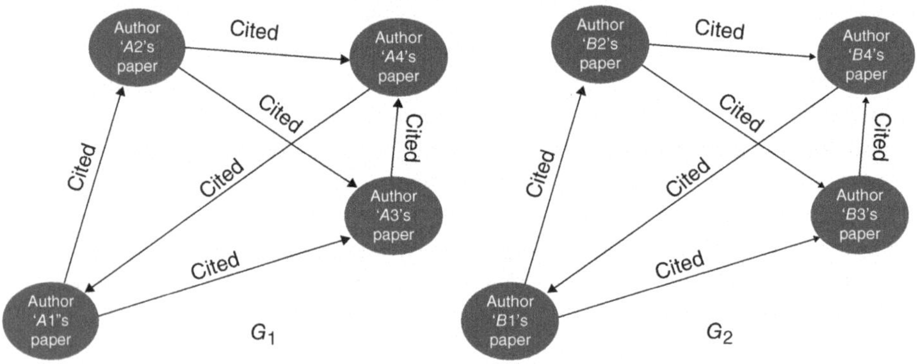

Figure 9.4 Global alignment example using author citation graph.

Authors/Papers in Graph G_1 and Graph G_2 should be aligned if they have similar citation structures (same number of in/out citations, similar type of publication). Node alignment A_1 is aligned with B_1, A_2 is aligned with B_2, A_3 is aligned with B_3, and A_4 is aligned with B_4. Similarly, edge alignment shows that $A_1 \rightarrow A_2$ is aligned with $B_1 \rightarrow B_2$, $A_2 \rightarrow A_3$ is aligned with $B_2 \rightarrow B_3$, and $A_3 \rightarrow A_4$ is aligned with $B_3 \rightarrow B_4$. From the global graph alignment process, the authors in both graphs can be grouped and considered as authors having similar patterns of publishing. This type of graph alignment is useful for analyzing how research from one domain influences another domain by aligning their citation patterns.

9.4.4 Local Alignment: Aligning Specific Substructures

Local alignment is defined as the process of matching subgraphs within a graph, rather than aligning entire graphs globally. The goal is to identify and match smaller, similar regions or components of two graphs, allowing for a more localized comparison. This approach is typically used when we are interested in understanding specific parts of graphs, such as specific subgraphs of entities or relationships, rather than aligning the whole graph structure.

Working Process of Local Alignment in GRL

1) Identify Subgraphs:
   - In this step, specific subgraphs or localized structures are identified in the graphs. A subgraph is typically a part of the graph that includes a set of nodes and edges that are locally connected.
   - These subgraphs may represent local patterns, such as communities, clusters, or specific relationships, such as a group of interconnected nodes that form a functional unit (e.g., a team in a social network or a cluster of related papers in a citation network).
2) Define Matching Criteria for Subgraphs:
   - The alignment of subgraphs is based on a defined set of matching criteria. These criteria can include node features, edge types, or structural similarity.
   - Common criteria involve:
     - Node degree: Matching nodes with similar numbers of connections.
     - Edge types: Ensuring that edges in the subgraph correspond to similar relationships.
     - Subgraph structure: Comparing the local structure of subgraphs, ensuring that they share a similar pattern of connectivity.

9.5 Mathematical Approaches for Graph Alignment and Matching

9.5.1 Graph Embedding + Distance Minimization

Graph embedding + distance minimization is a technique where nodes from different graphs are mapped into a shared vector space using GRL. Once embedded, nodes are aligned by minimizing the distance (e.g., Euclidean or cosine) between their embeddings. The objective of using this technique is for efficient comparison between graphs, enabling node matching across graphs with different sizes or topologies, and it is essential for applications such as knowledge graph fusion and fraud detection.

It is represented as mathematical formulation.

Consider graphs G_1 and G_2, assume the nodes are embedded into Z_1 and Z_2 such that

- $Z_1 \in R^{\mathrm{n}_1 \times d}$ = embeddings of nodes in G_1
- $Z_2 \in R^{\mathrm{n}_2 \times d}$ = embeddings of nodes in G_2

Define the cost matrix:

$$C_{ij} = \| z_1^{(i)} - z_2^{(j)} \|_2$$

Take the minimum value of the summation of C_i, which refers to the total cost or similarity score obtained by adding the values of all individual cost elements C_i across matched node pairs. It represents the overall alignment quality between two graphs in graph matching tasks.

Example 9.3 Consider graphs G_1 and G_2 with nodes {A, B, C} and {1, 2, 3}, respectively. This is given in Fig. 9.5.

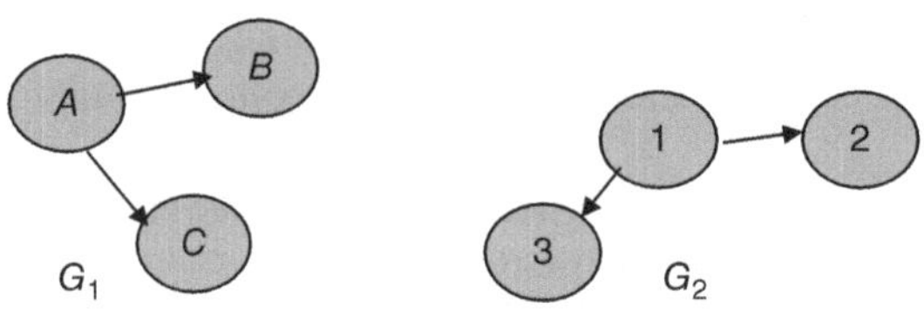

Figure 9.5 Graph to illustrate graph embedding.

Each node is connected in the same structure:
A-B, *A-C* and 1-2, 1-3.

Step 1: Graph Embedding

Assume a graph neural network (GNN) or handcrafted embedding (embedding can be done using an adjacency matrix) gives these vector representations (Table 9.1).

Table 9.1 Embedding values for each node.

Node	Embedding
A	[0.8, 0.2]
B	[0.7, 0.1]
C	[0.2, 0.9]
1	[0.81, 0.21]
2	[0.69, 0.12]
3	[0.19, 0.88]

Step 2: Distance Minimization (Using Euclidean Distance)

We compute distances between all pairs (A–1, A–2, A–3, etc.) and find the best match with minimum total distance.

The Euclidean distance between two points $x = (x_1, x_2, \ldots, x_n)$ and $y = (y_1, y_2, \ldots, y_n)$ in n-dimensional space is given by

$$\text{Distance} = \sqrt{(x_1 - y_1)^2 + (x_2 - y_2)^2 + \ldots + (x_n - y_n)^2}$$

Let $x = (0.8, 0.2), y = (0.81, 0.21)$

$$\text{Distance} = \sqrt{(0.8 - 0.81)^2 + (0.2 - 0.21)^2}$$

$$= 0.0001 + 0.0001 = 0.0002 \approx 0.014$$

Let $x = (0.7, 0.1)$ and $y = (0.69, 0.12)$

$$\text{Distance} = \sqrt{(0.7 - 0.69)^2 + (0.1 - 0.12)^2}$$

$$\approx 0.022$$

Let $x = (0.2, 0.9)$ and $y = (0.19, 0.88)$

$$\text{Distance} = \sqrt{(0.2 - 0.19)^2 + (0.9 - 0.88)^2}$$

$$\approx 0.022$$

After calculating the distance between all combinations of pairs, take the minimum distance. They are the best matching pairs

Best matching:

- $A \leftrightarrow 1$ (very close)
- $B \leftrightarrow 2$
- $C \leftrightarrow 3$

Nodes A–B–C in Graph 1 are aligned with nodes 1–2–3 in Graph 2 based on their embedding similarity.

Graph embedding + distance minimization helps us match similar nodes across two graphs efficiently using learned vector representations, even when node names or orders differ.

9.5.2 Gromov–Wasserstein Distance

The Gromov–Wasserstein (GW) distance is a mathematical metric used to compare two graphs or networks with different sizes, node sets, and structures, even when there's no direct node-to-node correspondence. It measures how well the relational structure (e.g., pairwise distances) of one graph matches that of another [3]. This technique allows graph comparison without needing aligned nodes. It captures structural similarity rather than just feature similarity. Traditional methods (like Euclidean or cosine distance) fail when graphs have different node identities or shapes. GW distance offers a way to align graphs based on structure, not just node labels or features.

Example 9.4 Consider graphs G_1 and G_2 with nodes {1, 2, 3} and {A, B, C}, respectively, as shown in Fig. 9.6.

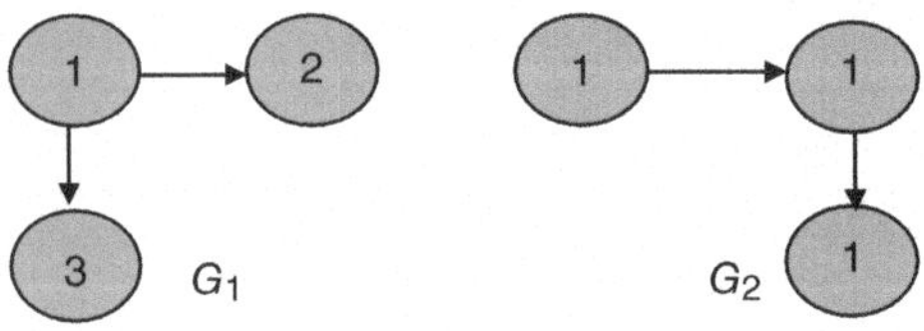

Figure 9.6 "Y"-shaped graphs for finding Gromov–Wasserstein distance.

Both graphs are shaped like a "Y".

Even if node labels differ ($1 \neq a$), the GW distance can tell us that they are structurally similar.

GW distance helps compare graphs by shape and structure, not just labels or features—making it essential in advanced graph matching, especially for unlabeled or cross-domain graphs.

9.5.3 Contrastive Learning for Graph Matching

Contrastive learning for graph matching is a self-supervised technique where a model learns to distinguish between similar (positive) graph pairs and dissimilar (negative) graph pairs. The core idea is to pull together embeddings of matching node pairs and push apart non-matching ones using contrastive loss. It works well when labeled data for graph alignment is limited or unavailable. It enhances the model's ability to generalize across different graph structures.

Example 9.5 Let G_1 and G_2 (same structure, different labels) be two graphs with nodes {user1, user2, user3} and {PersonA, PersonB, PersonC}, respectively. This is given in Fig. 9.7.

- Positive pairs: (User1 ↔ PersonA), (User2 ↔ PersonB)
- Negative pairs: (User1 ↔ PersonC), etc.

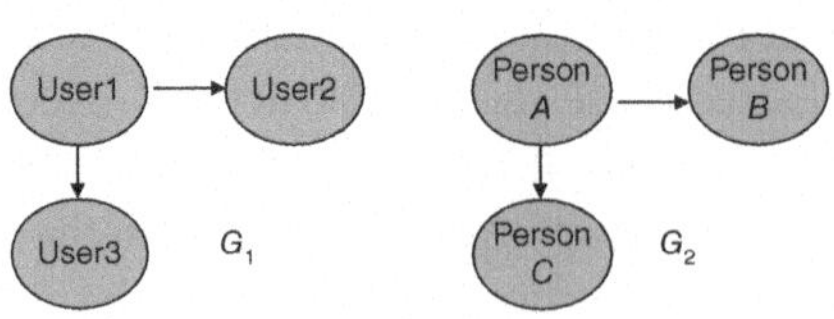

Figure 9.7 Contrastive learning for graph matching.

In training:

- The model learns to embed User1 and PersonA closely.
- It pushes apart embeddings of mismatched pairs like (User1, PersonC).

Contrastive learning for graph matching helps models learn which nodes should be matched based on structure and context, even without direct supervision. It's especially useful in noisy, cross-domain, or large-scale graph matching problems.

9.5.4 Deep Graph Matching Networks

Deep graph matching networks (DGMC) are neural models designed to perform end-to-end graph matching using deep learning. DGMC combines GNNs with differentiable matching modules to learn both node embeddings and correspondences between two graphs. DGMC handles noisy, large, or unlabeled graphs. It learns both local features and global structural patterns. It outperforms traditional handcrafted matching algorithms (e.g., the Hungarian algorithm) in real-world datasets.

DGMC = GNN-based feature learning + iterative node alignment + structure-aware matching.

Example 9.6 Suppose we want to match two graphs representing molecular structures (Fig. 9.8):

Figure 9.8 Graph matching in molecular structure.

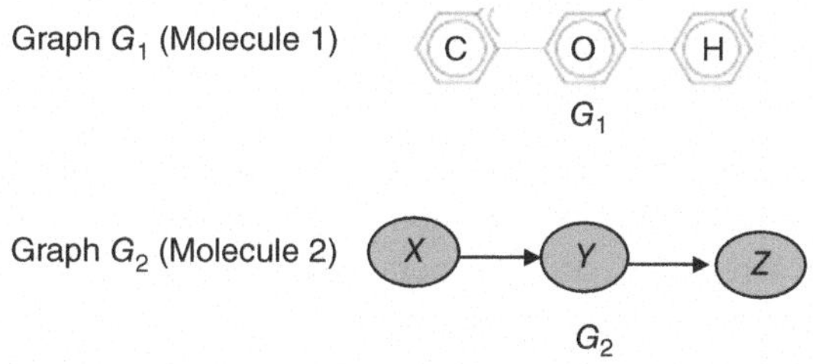

DGMC uses a GNN to learn embeddings for each atom (node) [4]. It uses a graph matching module to align nodes: C ↔ X, O ↔ Y, H ↔ Z. Unlike manual rules, DGMC learns these mappings from data, even if atom names or orders are different.

DGMC provides a powerful, deep learning–based solution for matching graphs in complex, noisy, or unstructured environments. It uses GNNs and differentiable alignment to automate and optimize graph matching, making it essential for domains such as computer vision, chemistry, and social network analysis.

9.6 Case Studies on Graph Alignment and Matching

9.6.1 Graph Alignment and Matching in Healthcare

Healthcare data is often distributed across multiple hospitals, with each hospital maintaining its own electronic health records. To enable cross-institutional analysis, such as identifying similar patient groups or disease progression patterns, graph alignment and graph matching techniques are crucial.

Each hospital has a patient similarity graph, where nodes = patients and edges = similarity based on symptoms, diagnoses, or treatments. Due to privacy and differing data formats, node identities do not match between graphs. The goal is to align patient graphs from Hospital A and Hospital B to identify common disease progression patterns and similar patient cohorts for drug response studies.

9.6.1.1 Method: GW Graph Matching

Apply GW distance to align patient graphs based on structure, not node labels. Use contrastive learning to pre-train patient node embeddings using local medical features (e.g., diagnosis codes, lab tests). Then match graphs from Hospital A and Hospital B by minimizing structural differences between them.

9.6.2 Benefits

- Identifies functionally equivalent patients across hospitals.
- Enables federated learning without sharing raw data.
- Improves generalizability of clinical models (e.g., disease classifiers).
- Detects under-reported comorbidities by comparing graph neighborhoods.

Graph alignment in healthcare allows for meaningful integration of patient data across institutions, without requiring direct patient ID matching. It enhances clinical research, supports personalized medicine, and strengthens cross-hospital analytics while preserving privacy.

9.6.3 Matching Users Across Facebook and Twitter Accounts in Social Networks

People often use different usernames and profile information across social platforms such as Facebook and Twitter. To build a unified user identity, platforms or researchers may need to match user profiles across networks. This challenge can be solved by using graph matching. Each social network can be represented as a graph with users being represented by nodes and edges representing friendships, interactions, likes, and follows.

Graph alignment helps to match nodes (users) from Facebook to those in Twitter by comparing structural similarity, not just based on names or profile text, but also based on how users connect and interact with others.

The procedure is to build user interaction graphs for Facebook and Twitter. Using any one of the embedding techniques, user embedding is to be done. Then, in the latent dimensional space, use contrastive learning or GW distance to find structurally similar users across graphs. DGMC can also be used to learn both local (who they interact with) and global (community structure) patterns. Identify the matches from users in Facebook to a person in Twitter based on similarity in interaction patterns and neighborhood structure.

Example 9.7 Consider Facebook graph with Users A, B, C, D and Twitter graph with Users X, Y, Z, and W. Assume that User A on Facebook often interacts with Users B, C, and D. User X on Twitter frequently retweets or mentions Users Y, Z, and W, who have similar profiles to B, C, and D. Using graph alignment, a match is inferred between User A and User X despite different usernames or no shared content.

Other benefits of using this technique are useful for advertisers, recommendation systems, or academic studies to identify bot networks or duplicated accounts across platforms. Additionally, it can suggest Twitter content to Facebook users based on similar behaviors. Graph alignment and matching provide a powerful framework to map users across social platforms such as Facebook and Twitter by leveraging network structure rather than relying solely on profile or content data. This enables more accurate identity resolution, enhances user experience, and supports intelligent cross-platform services.

9.7 Conclusion

The foundational and advanced concepts of graph alignment and matching, a key area in GRL that enables meaningful comparison and integration of graph-structured data, were discussed in this chapter. Beginning with a clear definition and purpose, we emphasized that the goal of graph alignment is to discover correspondences between nodes or substructures in different graphs, a necessity in domains where entities differ in label, size, or structure.

Through practical examples and classification into types—including exact, inexact, global, and local matching—we saw how different scenarios call for tailored matching strategies. For instance, exact matching is applicable in rigid structure comparison, while fuzzy or local alignment supports real-world problems with partial overlap and noise.

The chapter further deals with mathematical approaches: graph embedding + distance minimization allows comparison via vector spaces; GW distance supports matching graphs with different node sets; contrastive learning enables self-supervised matching through similarity learning; and DGMC leverages neural architectures for end-to-end structural alignment.

Finally, the healthcare case study illustrated the real-world impact of these techniques, showing how graph alignment helps uncover cross-institutional disease patterns, supports federated learning, and enhances clinical insights without breaching privacy.

In summary, graph alignment and matching serve as powerful tools to bridge diverse, complex, and distributed graph data, unlocking new opportunities for analysis and discovery across domains such as healthcare, biology, and social networks.

References

1 Junchi Yan, Shuang Yang, and Edwin Hancock, Learning for graph matching and related combinatorial optimization problems, in *Proceedings of the Twenty-Ninth International Joint Conference on Artificial Intelligence (IJCAI-20)*, January 7–15, 2021, Yokohama, Japan, pp.4988–4996, https://doi.org/10.24963/ijcai.2020/694.

2 K. Riesen, X. Jiang, and H. Bunke, "Exact and inexact graph matching: methodology and applications, In book:," in *Managing and Mining Graph Data*. Springer Nature, pp. 217–247, doi: 10.1007/978-1-4419-6045-0_7.

3 D. H. Nguyen and K. Tsuda, "On a linear fused Gromov-Wasserstein distance for graph structured data," *Pattern Recognition*, vol. 138, 109351, 2023.

4 H. Liu, T. Wang, Y. Li, C. Lang, Y. Jin, and H. Ling, "Joint graph learning and matching for semantic feature correspondence," *Pattern Recognition*, vol. 134, 109059, 2023.

10

Neighborhood Reconstruction Methods

10.1 Introduction

The previous chapters covered the foundational aspects of graph structure, focusing on node-level and graph-level feature extraction methods, as well as the interactions and relationships between graph neighborhoods. As we have discussed on the data-driven information from the nodes within the graph, we must focus on the quality of information in each node and how long node relationships are extended. Also, as the graph grows, the neighborhood information may change. We need to update the neighborhood relationships by reconstructing the neighborhood nodes. This approach will serve as a bridge between raw graph data and more robust, expressive representations suitable for learning.

Neighborhood reconstruction is crucial in uncovering hidden relationships among nodes, addressing incomplete or missing data, and enabling its application in various machine learning (ML) tasks. This chapter explores neighborhood reconstruction methods, emphasizing their ability to connect the fine-grained details of individual node interactions with the broader structural patterns that characterize the entire graph.

10.1.1 Introduction to Neighborhood Reconstruction in Graphs

In any graph, a node's immediate neighborhood that is directly connected captures rich information about its relationships and role within the graph. Neighborhood reconstruction involves approximating or recovering these local structures to enable more effective analysis and inference.

Neighborhood reconstruction [1] in graphs refers to the process of understanding, recovering, or utilizing the structure and relationships of a graph based on the information contained in its local neighborhoods. Neighborhood reconstruction involves leveraging these local neighborhoods to deduce the graph's global or structural properties or perform tasks such as node classification, link prediction, or graph generation.

The main purpose of neighborhood reconstruction is listed as follows:

1) To reconstruct missing edges, nodes, or attributes in a graph by inferring plausible connections based on local patterns.
2) To transform raw graph data into structured inputs for tasks such as node classification, link prediction, and graph embedding.
3) To understand local–global relationships by uncovering how local interactions influence overall graph behavior.

Neighborhood reconstruction is guided by several core principles that ensure its effectiveness in graph-based learning and analysis. The first principle is to capture patterns of relationship among the neighboring nodes. The second principle is to preserve the graph topology. The third principle is to impute the missing information of a specific node, its neighbor nodes, and edges. The fourth principle is to aggregate neighborhood information.

10.1.2 Benefits of Neighborhood Reconstruction in Graphs

1) **Uncovering Hidden Relationships:**
   - Reconstruction reveals implicit or latent connections between nodes, enriching the graph's structure and enabling deeper insights.
2) **Addressing Data Incompleteness:**
   - Many real-world graphs, such as social networks or biological networks, are often incomplete. Neighborhood reconstruction helps fill gaps by predicting plausible relationships.
3) **Improved Graph Representations:**
   - By incorporating neighborhood information, reconstruction methods enhance node embeddings and graph-level features, leading to better performance in tasks such as classification and clustering.
4) **Scalable Analysis:**
   - Focusing on local neighborhoods rather than the entire graph reduces computational complexity, making it feasible to work with large-scale graphs.
5) **Support for Machine Learning Tasks:**
   - Neighborhood reconstruction underpins a variety of tasks, including
     - o Node Classification: Predicting properties of individual nodes using neighborhood context.
     - o Link Prediction: Inferring missing or future edges between nodes.
     - o Community Detection: Identifying groups of closely connected nodes.

6) **Enhanced Interpretability:**
   - By reconstructing neighborhoods, these methods provide insights into how local structures influence overall graph behavior, making models more explainable.
7) **Cross-Domain Applications:**
   - From social network analysis to recommendation systems and bioinformatics, neighborhood reconstruction finds applications in diverse fields, showcasing its versatility and value.

10.1.3 Importance of Reconstructing Graph Structures

Reconstructing graph structures is important to dig deep into the understanding of the relationships and dependencies among the nodes. It is also vital in various fields, as it provides insights into relationships and interactions within complex systems. Just like machine learning models, which need preprocessing techniques, graphs also often suffer from missing, noisy, or incomplete information. This may include absent connections between nodes, incorrect edge weights, or partial knowledge about node attributes. Such imperfections can significantly degrade the performance of machine learning models that rely on graph data.

A complex graph may contain unknown, missing, incomplete, or inappropriate information about the nodes and the relationships between nodes. Also, identifying communities and hidden patterns is needed for various domains such as node classification, fraud detection, and social networks. So, it is important to reconstruct the graph structure.

10.2 Neighborhood Reconstruction Techniques

The following are general techniques or computational tools used to perform reconstruction:

- **Matrix Factorization:** For adjacency matrix reconstruction.
- **Embedding Models:** Node2Vec, DeepWalk, or graph neural networks (GNN)-based embeddings reconstruct neighborhoods in a low-dimensional space.
- **Similarity Measures:** Cosine similarity, Jaccard index, or other measures can estimate the likelihood of neighborhood connections.

10.2.1 Matrix Factorization

Matrix factorization is a mathematical technique that decomposes a large matrix into a product of smaller matrices to uncover hidden structure or patterns in data.

In the context of graphs, the matrix often represents relationships between nodes, such as the adjacency matrix (which indicates connections) [2].

It is used for dimensionality reduction to reduce the huge graph with a large matrix, to reveal hidden features, and to reconstruct the missing links or unknown connections in the graph.

10.2.1.1 Mathematical Definition

Let A be the original matrix, and X, Y be the matrices in the latent space (lower-dimensional matrices). Factorization is the method to find matrices X and Y such that

$$A \approx XY^T$$

Example 10.1 Consider a simple undirected graph with three nodes given in Fig. 10.1.

The adjacency matrix (A) is

$$A = \begin{matrix} 0 & 1 & 0 \\ 1 & 0 & 1 \\ 0 & 1 & 0 \end{matrix}$$

Factorize $A = XY^T$, where X and Y are 3×2 matrices (embedding dimension = 2).

We'll use a simple approach like singular value decomposition or basic trial values to illustrate.

$$\text{Assume } X = \begin{bmatrix} 1 & 0 \\ 0 & 1 \\ 1 & 1 \end{bmatrix} \qquad Y^T = \begin{bmatrix} 0 & 1 & 1 \\ 1 & 1 & 0 \end{bmatrix}$$

Now compute XY^T

$$XY^T = \begin{bmatrix} 1 & 0 \\ 0 & 1 \\ 1 & 1 \end{bmatrix} \begin{bmatrix} 0 & 1 & 1 \\ 1 & 1 & 0 \end{bmatrix} = \begin{bmatrix} 0 & 1 & 1 \\ 1 & 1 & 0 \\ 1 & 2 & 1 \end{bmatrix}$$

Figure 10.1 Simple undirected graph for matrix factorization.

From this, we conclude that this matrix reflects node relationships. The original edge $A(1,2) = 1$ is reflected in $XY^T(1,2) = 1$. Similarly, $XY^T(3,1) = 1$ shows the hidden connection, which suggests a potential link since there is no edge between (3,1) in the original matrix A. $XY^T(3,2) = 2$ reflects stronger connectivity/relationship/similarity, as the value is 2.

10.2.1.2 Application

Matrix factorization can be used in link prediction; based on the criteria if $XY^T(i,j)$ > threshold, we can predict an edge (i,j). It is also applicable in node embedding, where each row in X or Y is a node vector. Other applications include collaborative filtering, matrix factorization in recommendation systems, graph clustering, graph reconstruction, and anomaly/fraud detection.

10.2.1.3 Advantages and Disadvantages

The advantages and disadvantages of matrix factorization is given in Table 10.1.

10.2.1.4 Approaches in Matrix Factorization

Nonnegative Matrix Factorization Nonnegative matrix factorization (NMF) is an effective technique for dimensionality reduction in linear algebra and multivariate analysis. It works by breaking down a nonnegative data matrix into two (or more) smaller matrices, each also constrained to have only nonnegative values. This nonnegativity constraint is key to NMF's strength—it promotes the discovery of interpretable, parts-based representations of data, since the absence of negative values prevents the cancellation of components, making the results more intuitive and meaningful.

Assume a large dataset represented as a matrix V. Each row might correspond to an observation, and each column might represent a feature. NMF

Table 10.1 Advantages and disadvantages of matrix factorization.

Advantages	Disadvantages
Scalable to large, sparse graphs	Linear assumption—may not capture complex, nonlinear interactions
Unsupervised—doesn't require labeled data	Not always interpretable—latent factors are abstract
Captures latent relationships (hidden node similarities)	Sensitive to noise—performance may degrade with noisy or incomplete graphs
Compact embeddings for downstream tasks	Static—doesn't model dynamic changes in graphs over time

aims to approximate this original matrix V by the product of two much smaller nonnegative matrices, W and H.

Mathematically, this can be expressed as

$$V \approx W \times H$$

where

- V is the original $m \times n$ nonnegative data matrix (e.g., m documents, n words).
- W is an $m \times k$ nonnegative "basis" or "feature" matrix.
- H is a $k \times n$ nonnegative "coefficient" or "encoding" matrix.
- k is the chosen "rank" or number of latent features and is typically much smaller than both m and n ($k \ll \min(m,n)$). This reduction in dimensionality is key to NMF's utility.

Deep Asymmetric NMF The authors in the article [1] titled "Deep Asymmetric Nonnegative Matrix Factorization for Graph Clustering" introduced a novel matrix factorization approach tailored for graph data. The proposed method, deep asymmetric NMF (DAsNMF), extends traditional NMF by incorporating asymmetry to effectively handle both undirected and directed graphs. By using deep learning techniques, DAsNMF captures hierarchical and complex structures within graph data, enhancing clustering performance. This approach demonstrates improved results in graph clustering tasks compared to existing methods.

This work introduces a novel approach to graph clustering specifically designed to overcome the limitations of traditional methods when applied to directed graphs. Standard NMF techniques often fail to fully capture the crucial directional information inherent in such networks. To address this, the authors propose the DAsNMF model. This innovative framework integrates hierarchical graph clustering with graph summarization techniques, enabling a better understanding of directed relationships.

The DAsNMF model is engineered to handle both undirected and, critically, directed graphs. It achieves this by decomposing the input graph into multiple layers, systematically extracting node representations from low-level local features to high-level global structures. This hierarchical decomposition allows DAsNMF to capture both granular local patterns and overarching global structural information. Furthermore, the model incorporates asymmetric cosine and PageRank-based similarities to meticulously preserve the graph's directional properties throughout the clustering process. The entire learning process is framed as a unified optimization problem, where representation learning and clustering components are jointly trained. Extensive experiments by the authors demonstrate DAsNMF's superior effectiveness in accurately clustering directed graphs, consistently outperforming existing methods across various benchmarks.

This advancement holds significant implications for applications involving complex networks where directionality is paramount, such as social networks, citation networks, and intricate biological systems. By adeptly capturing the directional relationships between nodes, DAsNMF provides a more profound understanding of the underlying structures within these networks. This contribution not only resolves key limitations of previous NMF-based clustering approaches but also paves new paths for future research and practical applications in graph analysis.

10.2.2 Embedding Models

Embedding models are techniques used to convert graph elements (nodes, edges, subgraphs) into low-dimensional continuous vector representations. These embeddings capture structural and relational information from the graph, making it easier for downstream machine learning tasks such as node classification, link prediction, and clustering.

10.2.2.1 Mathematical Definition

In graph embedding, the goal is to map each node $v \in V$ in a graph $G = (V, E)$ into a low-dimensional vector space such that

$$f : V \to R^d$$

where V is the set of nodes, $d \ll |V|$ is the embedding dimension, and $f(v) = z_v \in R^d$ is the embedding of node v.

They are used for complex and sparse graphs where the dimensions are huge; most traditional ML models use vector inputs and do not use graphs. Also, embeddings make computation efficient and make the models more scalable and faster.

Example 10.2 Consider a graph G with nodes $\{A, B, C, D\}$ given in Fig. 10.2.

Steps:

- Random walks from each node (e.g., walk: $A \to B \to C$)
- Use skip-gram model to predict context nodes from the walk (similar to Word2Vec)
- Learn embeddings:
  - $A \to [0.12, -0.45, 0.88]$
  - $B \to [-0.20, 0.34, -0.11]$
  - $C \to [0.55, 0.21, -0.05]$

These embeddings preserve similarity: B and C may be closer in space, showing structural similarity.

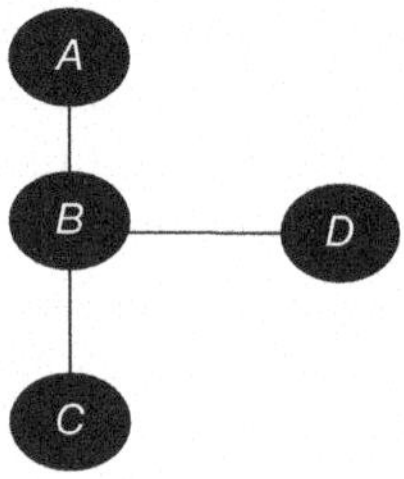

Figure 10.2 Example for graph embedding.

10.2.2.2 Popular Embedding Models

DeepWalk DeepWalk is a graph embedding technique that learns a latent representation (low-dimensional representation) of nodes in a graph. It uses random walks (randomly selecting a neighbor from the starting node), and the skip-gram model from natural language processing. The skip-gram model uses a word and predicts the surrounding similar context words. Likewise, DeepWalk uses nodes as words and relationships as connecting words in a sentence.

In the current scenario, the graphs are complex with a huge volume of data/information. It also has high-dimensional, unstructured, non-grid-based structures. These types of graphs are not comfortable to use for ML models. DeepWalk helps in mapping the high-dimensional data in the nodes to lower-dimensional data. They are represented as dense vectors. The DeepWalk embeddings method focuses on capturing a node's local neighborhood, its role in the graph, and even community membership. Nodes that are structurally similar or have similar "neighborhoods" in the graph will have similar embeddings. Now these graphs can be used for ML tasks [3].

Working Process DeepWalk uses two main steps, namely, random walk generation and Word2Vec training. A "random walk" starts at a node and randomly moves to one of its neighbors, then from that neighbor to one of its neighbors, and so on, for a specified number of steps. The main goal is to generate the nodes that are frequently occurring in the random walk. These generated nodes are treated like "sentences" in natural language.

The next step is Word2Vec (skip-gram) training. The generated sequence of nodes is given as input to the skip-gram model. This model will predict the context of similar neighboring nodes. By training this model, it learns a low-dimensional vector representation (embedding) for each node such that nodes appearing in similar contexts (i.e., frequently co-occurring in random walks) have similar vector embeddings.

Example 10.3 ***DeepWalk on Author Citation Graph***

In the author citation graph, assume that the random walk is applied and the sequence of nodes are generated.

Random walk from Author1: Author1 → Author3 → Author2 → Author3 → Author1

- Walk from Author3: Author3 → Author4 → Author3 → Author1 → Author5

  Using these sequences, train skip-gram to learn embeddings such as
  vec(Author1) ≈ vec(Author5)
  vec(Author3) ≈ vec(Author4)
  Author1 is not directly connected with Author5, and Author3 is not directly connected with Author4. Even though they are not connected directly, by a 1-hop, they have similar structural roles and co-occurrence patterns.

Node2Vec Node2Vec refines DeepWalk by introducing biased random walks that can intelligently balance between breadth-first search (BFS)-like local exploration and depth-first search (DFS)-like global exploration. It achieves this by adjusting two key parameters during the walk: p controls the likelihood of immediately revisiting the previous node and q dictates whether the walk explores widely (BFS-like, high q) or delves deeply (DFS-like, low q). Like DeepWalk, these tailored walks are then fed into a skip-gram model to generate node embeddings that better capture diverse structural contexts.

Example 10.4 ***Author Co-authorship Network***
Consider a network where nodes represent individual authors and edges connect two authors if they have co-authored at least one paper together. This is typically an *undirected* graph. The goal is to learn embeddings for each author so that authors working in similar subfields or having similar collaborative patterns have similar embeddings. For example, consider that Author1 is highly popular in doing research. He co-authors with everyone in his network. Author2 is a bridge between two distinct research communities. He co-authors with a few people in his primary field, and also with a few people in an *entirely different field*, but his immediate neighbors are not highly interconnected themselves. Node2Vec embeds both authors together based on the structural similarity.

Large-Scale Information Network Embedding LINE (large-scale information network embedding) is an embedding technique designed to efficiently generate low-dimensional node embeddings for huge networks by directly capturing both immediate (first-order) and neighborhood-based (second-order) node proximities. Unlike random walk approaches, LINE optimizes these relationships directly, accommodating directed or undirected weighted graphs. It achieves high scalability on massive datasets through edge sampling and asynchronous stochastic gradient descent (SGD), producing rich embeddings that combine local and higher-order structural information. LINE has been widely used in social networks, citation graphs, and web graphs, where preserving fine-grained relationships at scale is essential. The goal is to learn low-dimensional embeddings that preserve the first-order and second-order proximities in a graph.

- **First-Order Proximity:** Direct connections between nodes (i.e., observed edges).
- **Second-Order Proximity:** Similarity between neighborhood structures (shared neighbors).
- **Loss Function:** Two separate loss terms to capture both proximities, optimized using SGD with negative sampling.

Example 10.5 ***Author Citation Graph***
Consider a citation graph where nodes are research papers and directed edges indicate one paper citing another paper. LINE would analyze this network to create embeddings for each paper. For first-order proximity, if Paper A directly cites Paper *B*, they would be pushed closer together in the embedding space, especially if that citation is heavily weighted (e.g., if Paper *A* is a survey paper heavily relying on Paper *B*). For second-order proximity, even if Paper *C* doesn't cite Paper *D*, but both Paper *C* and Paper *D* frequently cite many of the same foundational papers (their neighbors are similar). LINE would learn to place Paper *C* and Paper *D* close together in the embedding space. This suggests that they likely belong to the same research subfield or address similar problems. By optimizing for both these proximities simultaneously across the vast network, LINE can efficiently generate rich, low-dimensional vectors for millions of papers, allowing for tasks such as identifying related papers, predicting future citation links, or clustering papers into emerging research topics, even when direct connections are sparse.

Graph Neural Networks (GNNs) GNNs learn embeddings by aggregating information from neighbors (e.g., GraphSAGE, graph attention network [GAT]). The goal is to learn node embeddings by aggregating information from neighbors in a layered (message-passing) manner. GraphSAGE aggregates using mean, long–short-term memory, or pooling functions; GAT uses attention mechanisms to weigh neighbors differently.

GNNs are powerful models that learn meaningful representations (embeddings) for nodes, edges, or entire graphs by leveraging their inherent structure and features. Their core mechanism is iterative message passing or neighborhood aggregation: each node refines its embedding by gathering and processing information from its immediate neighbors. Starting with an input graph $G = (V, E)$, where nodes $v \in V$ have initial features $h_v{}^0$, each GNN layer l updates a node's embedding $h_v{}^{(l)}$ by aggregating features from its neighbors $N(v)$ (e.g., using sum or mean). This aggregated message then passes through a neural network to form the updated embedding. Stacking multiple layers allows nodes to incorporate information from multi-hop neighborhoods. The resulting embeddings are then used for various tasks such as node classification, link prediction, or clustering. While variants such as graph convolutional networks (GCN), GAT, and GraphSAGE differ in their specific aggregation methods; they all aim to generate rich, structure-aware representations.

10.2.2.3 Applications

An embedded model is used in link prediction to reconstruct missing or future edges based on the proximity in the embedding space. In anomaly or fraud detection, an embedded model is used to flag as suspicious the nodes with embeddings that deviate from normal neighborhood patterns. In community detection, nodes with similar embeddings tend to belong to the same community, allowing identification of hidden structures. In knowledge graph completion, embeddings are learnt to infer missing relationships or facts based on structural similarities. In node classification in noisy graphs, even with corrupted or incomplete links, embedding models preserve latent similarity, improving classification accuracy.

10.2.2.4 Advantages and Disadvantages

The advantages and disadvantages of Embedding models are given in Table 10.2.

10.2.3 Similarity Measures

Similarity measures play a key role in estimating how likely two nodes are to be connected, especially in the absence of complete edge information. These measures compare nodes based on their features, neighbors, or embedding vectors.

Table 10.2 Advantages and disadvantages of embedding models.

Advantages	Disadvantages
Captures graph structure in compact form	May lose interpretability (vectors don't always explain relationships clearly)
Allows use of standard ML/Deep Learning (DL) algorithms	Fixed-size embeddings may miss finer graph details
Scales to large graphs (especially random walk-based)	Static embeddings (e.g., DeepWalk) don't adapt to graph updates
Can incorporate node features (with GNNs)	Hyperparameter tuning can be complex (walk length, context size, etc.)
Enables transfer learning across tasks	Not all models support inductive learning (e.g., Node2Vec is transductive)

They are essential in tasks like link prediction, community detection, and node classification.

In the neighborhood reconstruction of graph representation learning (GRL), similarity measures are used to estimate the strength or likelihood of connections between nodes, particularly when the graph is incomplete, noisy, or partially observed [4].

Its role in neighborhood reconstruction is to discover the unknown or partially missing true neighborhood of a node. It helps in reconnecting nodes that are structurally or semantically close, thereby enabling a more accurate and complete graph. They are often used in conjunction with embedding models or structural heuristics to decide which nodes should be connected in the reconstructed neighborhood. Other reasons for the importance of similarity measures are to handle missing edges by estimating likely connections in graphs where data is incomplete, to quantify node proximity to help in measuring closeness or relatedness of nodes based on features or neighborhoods, to support link prediction to predict future or missing relationships between nodes, and to enhance embedding models to validate or learn from embeddings by assessing node similarity in vector space.

10.2.3.1 Common Similarity Measures

1. Cosine Similarity

Cosine similarity is used when nodes are represented as feature or embedding vectors.

Formula

$$\text{CosineSim}(x, y) = \frac{f(x) + f(y)}{\|f(x) * f(y)\|}$$

where $f(x)$ and $f(y)$ are the vector representations of nodes x and y.

Example 10.6 Let $f(x) = [1,2], f(y) = [2,3]$

$$\text{CosineSim}(x, y) = \frac{1.2 + 2.3}{\sqrt{1^2 + 2^2}.\sqrt{2^2 + 3^2}} \approx 0.993$$

High value (close to 1), so nodes are directionally similar.

2. Jaccard Index

Jaccard measures are used to measure neighborhood overlap between nodes.

Formula

$$\text{Jaccard}(x, y) = \frac{| N(x) \cap N(y) |}{| N(x) \cup N(y) |}$$

where $N(x)$ and $N(y)$ are the neighbors of nodes x and y.

Example 10.7 Let $N(x) = \{a, b, c\}, N(y) = \{b, c, d\}$
$\text{Jaccard}(x, y) = 2 / 4 = 0.5$

3. Adamic–Adar Index

The Adamic–Adar Index is used to give higher weight to common neighbors with fewer connections.

$$\text{Adamic–Adar}(x, y) = \sum_{w \in N(x) \cap N(y)} \frac{1}{\log(N(w))}$$

10.2.3.2 Applications

In graph denoising, the measure removes spurious edges and infers missing ones by applying thresholds on similarity (e.g., cosine similarity or Jaccard index). In collaborative filtering/recommendation systems, this measure recommends items (nodes) based on neighbor similarity to the user's preferences using similarity scores. For graph completion, it estimates the likelihood of edge existence between nodes based on high similarity. This measure can be used in data imputation in biomedical graphs to infer missing interactions or attributes by comparing patient/gene embeddings using similarity metrics. It is helpful for new or sparsely connected nodes; similarity-based reconstruction helps bootstrap neighborhood structure.

10.2.3.3 Advantages and Disadvantages

Advantages and disadvantages of similarity measures is given in the Table 10.3.

Table 10.3 Advantages and disadvantages of similarity measures.

Advantages	Disadvantages
Simple and efficient: Easy to compute for small to medium graphs.	Scalability: May not scale well to large graphs without optimization.
Unsupervised: Does not require labels for learning.	Sparse graphs: Poor performance when neighborhood information is limited.
Interpretable: Scores are intuitive and explainable.	Feature ignorance: Traditional similarity scores (like Jaccard) may ignore node features or weights.
Generalizable: Works across domains (social, biological, etc.).	No learning: Fixed formulas lack adaptability—can't learn task-specific similarity patterns.
Enables transfer learning across tasks.	Not all models support inductive learning (e.g., Node2Vec is transductive).

10.3 Neighborhood Reconstruction Methods

10.3.1 An Encoder–Decoder Method

The concept of encoding and decoding graphs in the context of node embeddings has been evolving. The framework of encoding and decoding graphs involves mapping nodes to low-dimensional embeddings and using a decoder to reconstruct information about each node's neighborhood.

10.3.2 Factorization-Based Approaches

This includes methods such as Laplacian, one of the earliest factorization-based approaches introduced by Belkin and Niyogi in 2002, eigenmaps, and inner product methods, which optimize embeddings to capture node similarity based on adjacency or higher-order neighborhood information. Other methods such as graph factorization, GraRep, and Hierarchically Organized Predictive Experts (HOPE) have been developed more recently, with publications ranging from 2013 to 2016.

10.3.3 Random Walk Embeddings

It explores methods such as DeepWalk introduced by Perozzi et al. in 2014, who pioneered the use of random walks for learning node embeddings, and node2vec, proposed by Grover and Leskovec in 2016, which learns embeddings by capturing the statistics of random walks over the graph, enabling the modeling of node co-occurrence patterns.

10.3.4 An Encoder–Decoder Method

The encoder–decoder framework (Fig. 10.3) is widely used in GRL for neighborhood reconstruction, where the goal is to embed the nodes by collecting the local feature or graph structure information about each node and reconstructing the near neighbor nodes based on the information. This method is particularly effective for node classification, link prediction, and clustering tasks.

10.3.4.1 Encoder

Generally, the encoder is responsible for extracting features and converting input data into a latent (hidden) representation. It reduces the input vector representation from high dimensionality to low dimensionality while preserving important information. In GRL, an encoder is a function that transforms nodes, edges, or entire graphs into a low-dimensional vector space while preserving their structural and feature-based information.

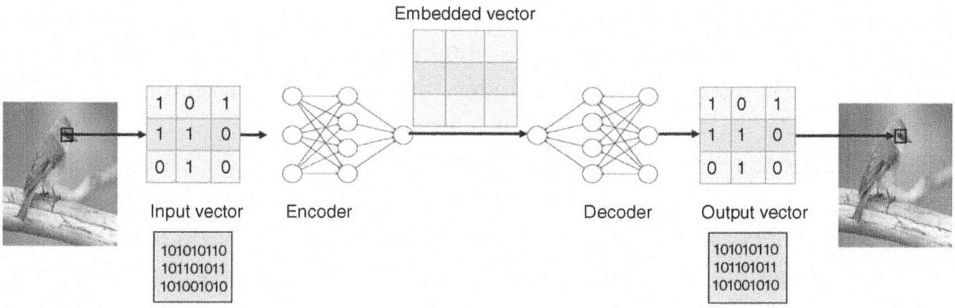

Figure 10.3 Encoder–decoder framework.

Consider a graph $G = \{V, E)$ where $v_i \varepsilon V$ and $e_i \varepsilon E$ as vertices and edges, respectively. The encoder function f_{ϕ} encodes the node feature vector represented as $\mathbb{R}^{mxn}$ and the encoder equation is

$$Z_{vi} = f_{\phi}(X, A)$$

where

Z_{vi} is the embedded vector for the node v_i vector.

f_{ϕ} is the encoder function.

X is the vector representation of node attributes/features.

A is the adjacency matrix, which represents connections within the graph.

Different types of encoders are used depending on the application and the types of graph data. Some of the encoders are as follows.

Graph Convolutional Encoders These encoders aggregate neighborhood information using message-passing techniques. They apply convolution-like operations on graphs to capture local node interactions. A graph convolutional encoder is a neural network component that uses GCNs to aggregate information from neighboring nodes and capture hierarchical structures within a graph [5]. The core equation for a GCN encoder is

$$H^{(l+1)} = \sigma(\widehat{A}\, H^{(l)} W^{(l)})$$

where

$H^{(l+1)}$ is the embedded vector at the current hidden layer. The encoded vector is obtained by aggregating the adjacency matrix $(\widehat{A})$ of node information and the encoded vector in the previous hidden layer $H^{(l)}$, along with the learnable weight matrix $W^{(l)}$ at the previous layer l. σ is the activation function used in the function.

GAT-Based Encoders (GAT-Based) GAT-based encoders [6] assign different importance (weights) to neighboring nodes using self-attention mechanisms, which allow a model to weigh the importance of different features in the input. Instead of treating all neighbors equally, they learn which neighbors contribute more information. The encoded vector Z_v is obtained by aggregating α, the attention coefficient between two neighboring nodes, and X, the feature vector of neighbor nodes along with W, a learnable weight matrix.

The self-attention mechanism is a key component in modern deep learning models, particularly in transformers (e.g., Bidirectional Encoder Representations from Transformers (BERT), Generative Pre-trained Transformer (GPT). It allows a model to weigh the importance of different words in a sentence when making predictions, improving performance in tasks such as machine translation, text summarization, and question answering.

$$Z_v = \sum \alpha XW$$

Autoencoder-Based Graph Encoders Autoencoders in GRL are unsupervised neural network architectures designed to learn compressed latent representations of nodes, edges, or entire graphs. The key idea is to encode graph data into a lower-dimensional space and then decode it back to reconstruct the original graph structure. This approach helps in capturing essential graph features while discarding noise or redundant information. The encoder transforms input graph data (nodes, edges, features) into a latent space representation. The encoder compresses the graph information that maps the input graph into a lower-dimensional embedding space. The equation is as follows:

$$Z = f_\theta(X, A)$$

where Z is the learned low-dimensional node representation and f_θ is a learnable encoding function.

10.3.4.2 Decoder

Generally, the goal of the decoder is to reconstruct or transform the encoded vector representation back to its original form or vector.

In GRL, the decoder in neighborhood reconstruction is responsible for reconstructing a node's local structure from its learned embedding. After the encoder compresses node and neighborhood information into a low-dimensional representation, the decoder attempts to restore the original neighborhood relationships, such as adjacency connections or feature similarities.

A common approach uses the inner product decoder, which estimates the probability of an edge existing between two nodes based on their latent embeddings.

Let the graph $G = (V,E)$ has nodes i and j. The decoder estimates the probability of an edge between nodes i and j by using the embedded nodes Z_{vi} and Z_{vj} and gives the output of the adjacency matrix of the original node information.

$$\widehat{Aij} = (Z_{vi}, Z_{vj})$$

The decoders used for reconstruction are inner product decoders that find similarity scores between latent embeddings to predict links, multilayer perceptron (MLP)-based decoders that use MLPs to model complex relationships, and recurrent decoders that apply sequential models for dynamic graph reconstruction.

10.4 Applications of Encoder–Decoder in Graph Learning

The encoder–decoder framework is widely used in GRL to process and analyze complex graph structures. The encoder compresses graph information into a meaningful latent representation, while the decoder reconstructs graph properties or generates predictions. This framework is applied across various domains, including link prediction, node classification, anomaly detection, graph generation, and recommendation systems.

10.4.1 Link Prediction

One of the most significant applications of the encoder–decoder model in graph learning is link prediction, where the goal is to predict missing or future connections in a graph. The encoder learns embeddings that capture node relationships, while the decoder reconstructs potential edges. This is particularly useful in social networks (suggesting new friends), biological networks (predicting protein-protein interactions), and e-commerce (recommending products based on user behavior). The decoder, often implemented as an inner product decoder, calculates the probability of an edge between two nodes using their latent representations.

10.4.2 Node Classification

In semi-supervised learning, encoder–decoder models help classify nodes based on their embeddings. The encoder extracts node features and structural information, while the decoder maps these embeddings to class labels. This is crucial in applications such as fraud detection (classifying suspicious transactions in financial networks), disease prediction (categorizing patients based on genetic data), and cybersecurity (identifying malicious network activity). GNNs with an MLP decoder are commonly used for this task.

10.4.3 Anomaly Detection

Graphs often contain irregularities, such as fraudulent transactions in financial networks or fake accounts in social media. Encoder–decoder models can detect these anomalies by learning a graph's normal patterns and identifying deviations. The encoder compresses node features into embeddings, while the decoder attempts to reconstruct the graph. If a node's reconstructed connections significantly differ from the actual structure, it is flagged as anomalous. Anomalies are identified by computing the reconstruction loss.

10.4.4 Graph-Based Recommendation Systems

Recommendation systems use graph learning to personalize user experiences by suggesting relevant content. In this setting, users and items are represented as nodes, and interactions (e.g., purchases, likes) are represented as edges. The encoder learns user preferences and item similarities, while the decoder predicts new user–item interactions. Techniques such as graph autoencoders (GAEs) and GNNs improve recommendations on platforms such as Netflix, Amazon, and YouTube.

10.4.5 Graph Generation and Completion

Encoder–decoder models also aid in graph generation, where the goal is to construct new graph structures based on learned patterns. This is particularly valuable in drug discovery, where models generate molecular graphs with desirable properties, and in network topology design, where missing connections in incomplete graphs are inferred. Variational GAEs are commonly used for this task, introducing a probabilistic component.

10.4.6 Knowledge Graph Completion

Knowledge graphs store structured relationships between entities (e.g., "Paris is the capital of France"). However, they often contain missing facts. Encoder–decoder models predict missing links by learning entity representations (encoder) and scoring potential relationships (decoder). This enhances search engines, chatbots, and AI assistants by enriching knowledge bases with inferred connections.

10.5 Case Study on Neighborhood Reconstruction

10.5.1 Case Study on Urban Road Network Reconstruction Using Neighborhood Inference

In many parts of the world, digital maps are either outdated or incomplete, especially in rural or rapidly developing urban regions. The major challenges are a lack of navigation systems, urban development planning, emergency response routing, and autonomous vehicle guidance. While Global Positioning System (GPS) trajectory data from vehicles and mobile devices is abundant, it is often noisy, sparse, and unstructured. Thus, the core problem is reconstructing accurate road network graphs from disorganized and partial Global Positioning System (GPS) trace data. The challenges are noise in Global Positioning System (GPS) data devices, which often record location data with slight deviations due to satellite signal loss, obstructions (e.g., buildings), low sampling frequency, and sparse coverage.

Some areas have fewer Global Positioning System (GPS) traces due to low population density or infrequent travel. **Nonuniform Sampling Rates [4]:** Devices may log positions at irregular time intervals, leading to difficulty in detecting turns, stops, or intersections. **Lack of Ground Truth**. No reliable map to compare against in many regions, especially in disaster-hit or remote areas. Ambiguity in road structure, complex intersections, multi-lane roads, or roundabouts can be difficult to infer without structured map data.

Biagioni and Eriksson (2012) proposed a graph-theoretic method to infer the underlying road network from Global Positioning System (GPS) traces. Each GPS point is treated as a node. Temporal or spatial adjacency (e.g., points within a time window or spatial proximity) creates edges between these nodes. This raw graph is noisy and redundant, so further steps are required. Nodes (GPS points) are grouped into spatial clusters using density-based clustering (e.g. Density-Based Spatial Clustering of Applications with Noise (DBSCAN)), forming road segments. Edges between clusters are inferred based on the sequence of GPS points, building a graph of road connectivity. For each node (or cluster), its neighborhood is analyzed to detect intersections (nodes with multiple outgoing connections), to reconstruct turns and connections between roads, and to identify dead ends or isolated paths. This stage is akin to building a graph neighborhood for each road segment, inferring how they connect in a broader network. The inferred graph is refined by aligning it with known geographic features (e.g., satellite images or partial maps) and smooth trajectories to match realistic road curvature.

The algorithm successfully reconstructed accurate and connected road networks, especially in areas where traditional maps were incomplete, in cities with rapid infrastructure changes, and for navigation applications in unmapped regions. The reconstructed graphs were used in open-source mapping tools such as OpenStreetMap and validated against official city maps where available.

10.6 Conclusion

In this chapter, we explored the concept and significance of neighborhood reconstruction within graph structures. We began by understanding the foundational idea behind neighborhood reconstruction and its essential role in recovering incomplete, noisy, or hidden graph relationships. The benefits of this process—such as improved link prediction, enhanced recommendation systems, and better community detection—were also emphasized. We examined core techniques such as matrix factorization, which is a powerful and foundational tool in graph learning, particularly useful for extracting latent node features, reconstructing missing graph structure, and enabling efficient downstream ML tasks. While newer methods such as GNNs offer more expressivity, matrix factorization remains relevant for its simplicity, interpretability in some cases, and computational efficiency.

Finally, we looked at an encoder–decoder-based method, which illustrates how deep learning can be used for this task. Overall, neighborhood reconstruction plays a critical role in enabling graph-based models to function effectively, especially in real-world scenarios where data is often partial or uncertain.

References

1 A. Hajiveiseh, S. A. Seyedi, and F. A. Tab, "Deep asymmetric nonnegative matrix factorization for graph clustering," *Pattern Recog*, vol. 148, 110179, 2024, doi: 10.1016/j.patcog.2023.110179.

2 Y. Zhang, "An introduction to matrix factorization and factorization machines in recommendation system, and beyond," *Information Retrieval*, 2022. https://arxiv.org/pdf/2203.11026.

3 V. T. Hoang, H.-J. Jeon, E.-S. You, Y. Yoon, S. Jung, and O.-J. Lee, "Graph representation learning and its applications: A survey," *Sensors (Basel)*, vol. 23, no. 8, p. 4168, 2023, doi: 10.3390/s23084168.

4 M. Marchand, K. Gallivan, W. Huang, and P. M. Van Dooren, "Analysis of the neighborhood pattern similarity measure for the role extraction problem," *SIAM J. Math. Data Sci*, vol. 3, no. 2, pp. 736–757, 2021, doi: 10.1137/20M1358785.

5 J. Wang, J. Liang, K. Yao, J. Liang, and D. Wang, "Graph convolutional autoencoders with co-learning of graph structure and node attributes," *Pattern Recogn*, vol. 121, 108215, 2022.

6 A. G. Vrahatis, K. Lazaros, and S. Kotsiantis, "Graph attention networks: A comprehensive review of methods and applications," *Future Internet*, vol. 16, no. 9, p. 318, 2024, doi: 10.3390/fi16090318.

11

Transfer Learning on Graph

In the previous chapter, we've explored graph alignment and matching. In this chapter, we will explore a new concept that is equally powerful, known as transfer learning on graphs. Imagine you've trained a model on one graph, and now you want to use that knowledge on a different but related graph. Instead of starting from scratch, transfer learning helps adapt what the model has already learned, saving both time and computational effort. In this chapter, we'll break down how transfer learning works in graph-based scenarios, why it's crucial for handling real-world networks, and the techniques that make it possible. Since transfer learning is an evolving trend in Graph Representation Learning (GRL), this chapter covers the topic of motivation of transfer graph learning (TGL), how transfer learning takes place, various strategies and types, adaptive and dynamic transfer learning, and its applications. This chapter also focuses on the benefits, along with the case studies and challenges of future trends.

11.1 Introduction

If one can learn to ride a bicycle, it is easier to ride the scooter without starting from scratch. People share their skills or knowledge with others to make the task easier and faster. Likewise, transfer learning is an evolving trend that involves the transfer of skills or knowledge from one task to another instead of starting from scratch. This chapter introduces transfer learning on graphs with its types and case studies.

Many machine learning models require vast amounts of labeled data to achieve high performance, which is often unavailable in specialized domains such as healthcare, astrophysics, or industrial applications. Collecting and annotating large datasets is time-consuming, expensive, and sometimes impractical. Models trained from scratch on small datasets often suffer from overfitting and fail to generalize to unseen data. Training large neural networks from scratch is computationally expensive and time-consuming, requiring substantial resources. Many tasks in machine learning share patterns, making it unnecessary to learn these patterns from scratch for each task. The transfer learning concept helps in providing solutions for these challenges.

Transfer learning is a machine learning technique that uses the knowledge or model obtained from one task in another related task without creating it from scratch. It minimizes the requirement for computational resources. It addresses data scarcity challenges. It improves the interpretability of models.

11.2 Overview of TGL

TGL is a technique in machine learning that transfers knowledge from one graph-based task or domain to another related graph-based task or domain. For example, in a conference author–publication graph scenario given in Fig. 11.1, where nodes are represented as authors and articles/papers and edges represent the authorship relationship. Transfer learning is used to predict the research progress of an author by using the knowledge obtained from the relevant journal author–publication graph.

Graphs often have sparse or incomplete data in certain domains. TGL enables robust predictions and inferences of incomplete data by incorporating knowledge from one domain (source graph) to solve sparsity in another domain (target graph).

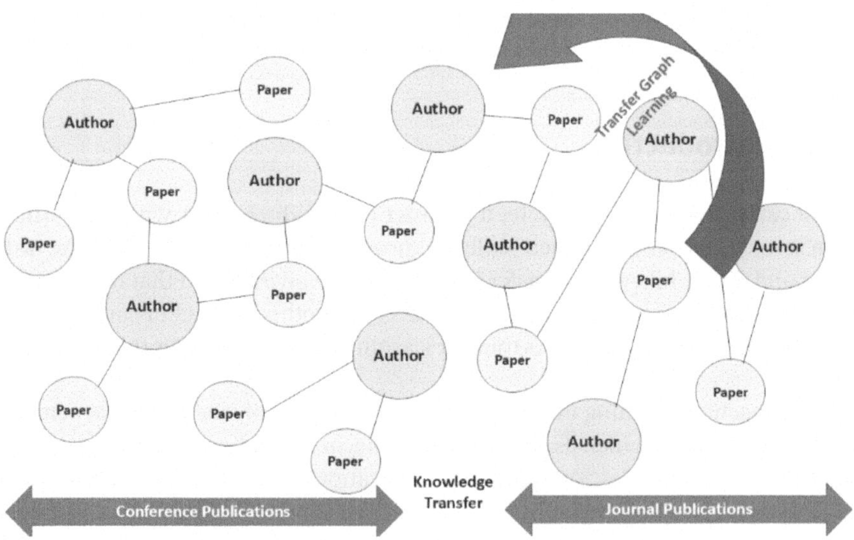

Figure 11.1 Model graph for transfer graph learning.

It allows for reusing existing knowledge across domains and tasks, addressing the growing demand for adaptable and resource-efficient AI solutions in diverse real-world applications. It allows the reuse of knowledge learned in one domain (source domain) to solve problems in another domain (target domain).

11.2.1 Key Features of TGL

Some of the key features of TGL include

- Transferring knowledge from one graph to another graph makes learning easier and faster.
- TGL establishes communication between nodes and edges across various graph domains.
- It works on two graphs: source and target graph structures.
- It reuses the pretrained models to optimize the learning process.
- It reduces the computational cost and time as it uses the transferred knowledge.
- It supports different types of graphs such as heterogeneous graphs and dynamic graphs.
- It uses graph aligning and matching methods to assess the similarity of the source and target graphs to transfer knowledge in a proper way.
- It maintains the performance of prediction in a situation where there is an insufficient amount of labeled data available for training a machine learning model.
- TGL is applicable in various real-time domains such as bioinformatics, fraud detection, recommendation systems, and natural language processing (NLP) for transferring the knowledge.

11.2.2 Benefits of TGL

- One significant advantage of TGL is its ability to speed up learning. Since the AI model has already been trained on a similar task, it can reuse that knowledge instead of starting from scratch. This also enhances adaptability as developing a new AI model from the ground up can be costly, time-intensive, and inconvenient when a task changes slightly. Instead, it's more efficient to repurpose an existing model that performs well for a similar task and fine-tune it for the new one.
- Another practical benefit of TGL is its potential to introduce innovative learning strategies. These strategies are particularly advantageous for industrial applications, offering faster and more cost-effective solutions. TGL compensates for the lack of annotated data in resource-constrained settings, making it invaluable in underexplored domains. It combines the power of graph-based representations with transfer learning methodologies, providing a powerful tool to address challenges across various disciplines.

11.2.3 The Need for TGL and Its Necessity

11.2.3.1 Need for TGLs

To transfer the knowledge between graphs effectively and to build a bridge between the graphs [1], TGL requires several key components:

1) A properly labeled source and target graph is needed.
2) Node features and edge similarity between the two graphs are essential for knowledge transfer.
3) Graph matching and alignment with the proper pattern to facilitate meaningful transfer.
4) The models trained for transfer learning must be adopted in both graphs.
5) Performance metrics to assess the effectiveness of knowledge transfer across graphs.

Graph-based data appears in various fields, including social networks, healthcare, drug discovery [3], and fraud detection. However, training graph models demands a significant amount of labeled data, which is costly and time-intensive to acquire. TGL mitigates this issue by transferring knowledge from a well-labeled source graph to a target graph, minimizing the reliance on large labeled datasets in the target domain.

11.2.3.2 Necessity of TGL

Some graphs lack labeled data, and it is difficult to train the deep learning models. They are known as low-labeled graphs. TGL transfers the knowledge from a well-labeled source graph to the low-labeled target graphs. TGL improves the performance of the graphs by using the models across similar graphs. To group the graphs having similarities in structure and pattern, TGL is a powerful technique, as it can transfer learned representations. Traditional graph models trained on one dataset may not generalize well to a new dataset. TGL enhances adaptability by transferring features and embeddings across related graphs. In real-world applications, graphs evolve over time (e.g., dynamic social networks, changing molecular properties). TGL helps models adapt to these shifts without retraining from scratch.

11.2.4 TGL vs GL

In many real-world applications, huge volumes of graph data are unlabeled, which gives less performance. It's a challenging process to obtain labeled graph data. These graph data can be obtained from a well-labeled graph by transferring knowledge to the unlabeled graph using TGL. Labeling requires expert knowledge, time, and resources, making it costly and impractical for large-scale datasets. Comparing TGL with traditional graph learning helps us understand how knowledge transfer improves learning efficiency, especially in low-data states. The key differences between the two approaches are:

1) Traditional Graph Learning: Requires large labeled datasets for training
   Transfer Graph Learning: Reduces labeled data dependency by transferring knowledge from a source graph
2) Traditional Graph Learning: Trains a model from scratch for each graph
   Transfer Graph Learning: Uses pretrained models or shared representations for adaptation
3) Traditional Graph Learning: Limited to a specific graph structure and dataset
   Transfer Graph Learning: Adapts knowledge to different but related graphs
4) Traditional Graph Learning: Works well in domains with abundant labeled graph data
   Transfer Graph Learning: Suitable for low-data scenarios, dynamic graphs, and cross-domain tasks
5) Traditional Graph Learning: Need high computational cost due to extensive data labeling and training
   Transfer Graph Learning: Need lower computational cost as pretrained knowledge reduces retraining efforts

11.3 Types of TGL

Depending on the relationships between tasks, availability of labeled data, nature of data, and domain similarity, TGL is divided into various types.

11.3.1 Inductive TGL

Inductive TGL (ITGL) is a form of transfer learning applied to graph-based data, where the source and target tasks differ. It involves transferring knowledge from one graph-based task to enhance the performance of a related task. By reusing embeddings, features, or model parameters, it enhances performance and generalization, making it particularly valuable in scenarios with limited labeled data.

11.3.1.1 Working Process of ITGL

Figure 11.2 shows the step-by-step procedure of ITGL for transferring knowledge from a source graph task to a related target graph task.

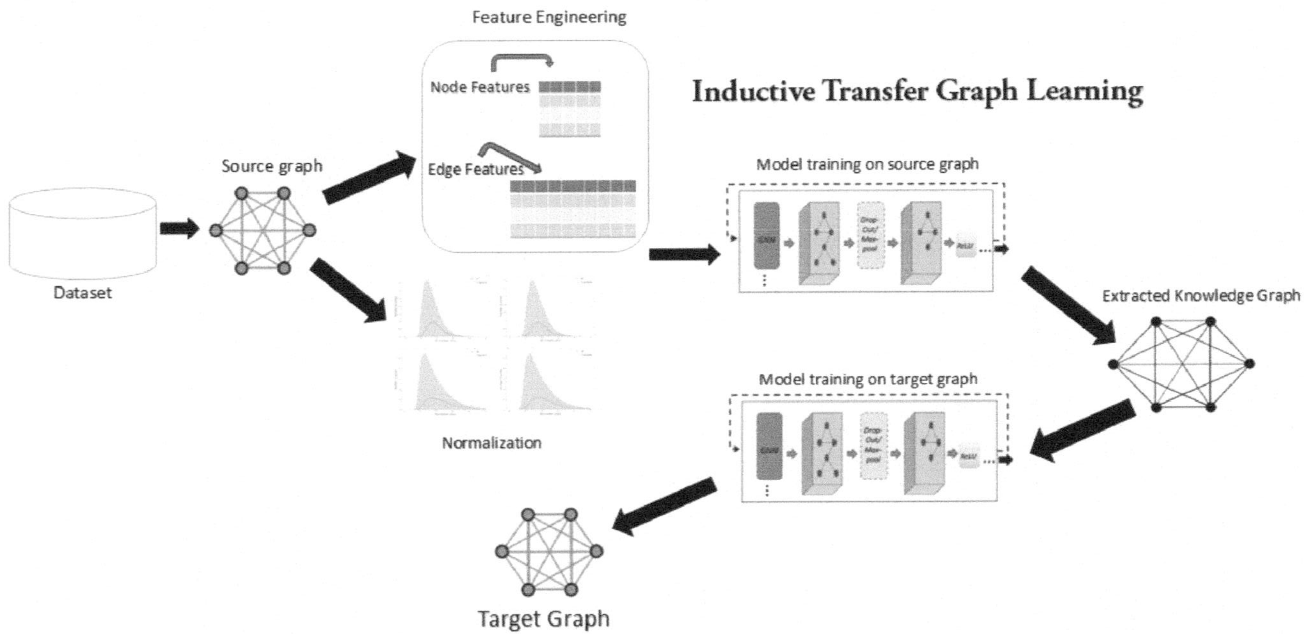

Figure 11.2 Working process of inductive transfer graph learning.

1) **Define Source and Target Tasks**
   - Consider two graphs, G_1 and $G_{2,}$ with tasks t_1 and $t_{2,}$ respectively. Let t_1 be the source task and t_2 be the target task. These two tasks can be similar or different. For example, in machine learning, node classification of users in a social network can be the source task $t_{1,}$ and link prediction of whether a connection occurs between two users in a social network can be the target task t_2. Nodes represent users, and edges represent friendships or interactions. Each node has features such as the number of followers, activity frequency, and average post likes.
2) **Construct Graph**
   - Represent data as graphs, including nodes, edges, and features. Nodes represent users, and edges represent friendships or interactions. Each node has features such as the number of followers, activity frequency, and average post likes.
3) **Preprocessing Step**

   This step focuses on preparing the graph data for analysis and model training, which involves feature engineering and normalization.
   - **Feature Engineering:** Generate or extract features for nodes and edges. For social networks, the extracted features for each user (node) are the number of followers, average posts per week, and average likes per post. The extracted features for each connection (edge) are the number of interactions between users (e.g., messages exchanged) and common friends (e.g., shared neighbors).
   - **Normalization:** Standardize features to ensure compatibility across tasks.
4) **Train Model on Source Task**
   - Use the source graph to train a graph-based model, such as a GNN. The inputs are node features, edge features, and graph structure. Training the model is done using a supervised learning technique, and the output is a trained model with learned embeddings, features, or parameters.
5) **Extract Transferable Knowledge**

   Extract knowledge from the trained source model, including node embeddings, model parameters, and feature representations. Transfer the extracted knowledge to the target graph.
6) **Train Model on Target Task**
   - Train the model using the target graph data such as node features, edge features, and graph structure of the target graph. Use supervised learning with the target task's labeled data, refining the transferred knowledge to adapt to the new task. A model is built for the target task.

11.3.1.2 Algorithm: GraphSAGE

Introduction GraphSAGE (graph sample and aggregate) is an inductive GNN framework designed to generalize to new graphs or nodes by learning node embedding functions based on node features and neighborhoods. Node embeddings transform high-dimensional, complex graph data into compact, computationally efficient representations. It maps nodes in a graph to a continuous vector space, where the position of each node reflects its structural and feature-based properties within the graph. These embeddings are low-dimensional numerical representations designed to capture the relationships and patterns in the graph, such as proximity, similarity, or connectivity.

GraphSAGE does not rely on fixed graph structures. Instead of processing the entire neighborhood of a node, GraphSAGE samples a fixed number of neighbors, improving scalability. It combines information from a node's sampled neighbors using differentiable aggregation functions (e.g., mean, pooling, or LSTM-based functions). The framework is adaptable to various tasks, such as node classification, link prediction, and clustering.

Algorithm

- Input: A graph $G = (V, E)$ with node features X.
- Output: Node embeddings $h_v \in R^d$, where d is the embedding dimension.

Steps

1) Neighborhood Sampling
   - For each node $v \in V$, take samples of the neighborhood $N(v)$ of v.
2) Aggregation
   - Aggregate the feature vectors of the sampled neighbors using a differentiable function (e.g., mean, LSTM, or pooling).
   - For node v, the aggregated features are

$$h_v^k = \text{AGGREGATE}\left(\left\{h_u^{k-1} : u \in N(v)\right\}\right) \tag{11.1}$$

   where h_v^k represents the embedding of node v at layer k.
3) Update Node Embeddings
   - Update the node embedding using its features and the aggregated neighborhood features:

$$h_v^k = \sigma\left(W^k \cdot \text{CONCAT}\left(h_v^{k-1},\ h^k{}_{\text{aggregate}}\right)\right) \tag{11.2}$$

   where W_k is a learnable weight matrix and σ is a nonlinear activation function.

4) Normalization
   Apply a normalization operation to the embeddings of nodes in the graph

$$h_v^k = \frac{h_v^k}{\left\|h_v^k\right\|_2}, \text{where } v \in V \tag{11.3}$$

   where $\|h_v^k\|_2$ is the Euclidean norm of the embedding vector.
5) Prediction
   - Use the final node embeddings for tasks (e.g., classification, link prediction) on unseen nodes or graphs.

11.3.1.3 Key Features and Benefits of GraphSAGE

1) **Inductive Learning:** GraphSAGE does not rely on fixed graph structures, making it suitable for dynamic or evolving graphs.
2) **Neighborhood Sampling:** Instead of processing the entire neighborhood of a node, GraphSAGE samples a fixed number of neighbors, improving scalability.
3) **Aggregation Mechanism:** It combines information from a node's sampled neighbors using differentiable aggregation functions (e.g., mean, pooling, or LSTM-based functions).
4) **Flexibility:** The framework is adaptable to various downstream tasks, such as node classification, link prediction, and clustering.

Benefits of GraphSAGE

- **Inductive learning:** It can generalize to unseen nodes (useful for dynamic graphs).
- **Scalability:** By sampling fixed-size neighborhoods, it can scale to large graphs.
- **Flexibility:** Supports different aggregation functions (mean, LSTM, pooling), allowing adaptation to different use cases.

11.3.2 Transductive TGL

Transductive TGL (TTGL) refers to a transfer learning paradigm applied to graph-based tasks where the source and target tasks are the same, but the source and target domains differ. The key distinction is that the target domain does not have labeled data, but the goal is to extract knowledge from the source domain to make predictions or extract insights directly in the target domain [2].

The main characteristics of TTGL are that the task remains identical across domains. The target domain lacks labeled data, and the focus is on transferring the model's understanding from the source domain to the target domain, so that the source and target domains share similarities.

11.3.2.1 Working Process of TTGL

The working process of TTGL is similar to ITGL but differs in defining the source and target.

1) **Define Source and Target Domains:**
   Define a graph dataset with labeled data and a related graph dataset without labels. In the social networks example, let the Twitter graph be the source domain: the nodes represent users on Twitter and the edges represent interactions such as mentions, retweets, or follows. The node features are the number of followers, frequency of tweets (activity level), and average likes on posts. The output from the source graph is detecting communities based on user interactions and activity patterns.
2) **Train the Model on the Source Domain:**
   Labeled data from the source domain is used to train a graph-based model (e.g., a GNN). The model learns to capture graph structure, node attributes, and relationships specific to the source domain. In the social networks example, the labeled data are the nodes in the source domain with community categories such as "Tech Enthusiasts," "Fitness Enthusiasts," and "Food Lovers."
3) **Model Training:**
   A GCN is trained on this labeled graph to predict community membership. The model learns patterns such as users with high activity frequency and follower count often belong to "Tech Enthusiasts"; and users with frequent mentions of fitness hashtags belong to "Fitness Enthusiasts."
4) **Extract Transferable Knowledge:**
   Node embeddings, feature representations, and model parameters are the knowledge to be extracted to apply in the target domain. The trained GNN on Twitter produces embeddings for nodes. These embeddings capture relationships such as similarity between users based on interactions and dense connections representing communities. A "Tech Enthusiast" node embedding might indicate strong ties to nodes with high follower counts and frequent tweets about technology. The GNN identifies important features for community prediction, such as a high follower count indicating popularity and frequent activity suggesting higher community participation. These representations can be applied to similar features in the Instagram graph. The GNN's trained parameters (e.g., convolutional layer weights) encode patterns learned from the Twitter graph. These weights can be reused to process the Instagram graph, assuming structural and feature similarity.
5) **Apply Model to Target Domain:**
   Directly apply the trained model to the target domain graph to predict outcomes (e.g., classify nodes or predict links).

11.3.2.2 Algorithm: Graph Convolutional Network with Domain Adaptation

The GCN-DA (graph convolutional network with domain adaptation) algorithm is designed for TTGL. It addresses the challenge of transferring knowledge across graphs from different domains while preserving the underlying graph structure. The core idea of GCN-DA is to adapt GCNs for domain adaptation, where the model is trained on a source domain and tested on a target domain, both sharing a related graph structure [4].

1) **Graph Convolution Networks**
   GCNs are used to aggregate and propagate information across the nodes of a graph, capturing structural relationships between nodes. The GCN-DA model employs a GCN to learn node embeddings for the source and target graphs.
2) **Domain Adaptation**
   In domain adaptation, the model is trained on one domain (source domain) and tested on another domain (target domain) with some shared or related graph structure. Domain adaptation aims to minimize the gap between the source and target domains so that the model can perform well on the target domain using the knowledge gained from the source domain. This is achieved through various techniques that help the model generalize across domain shifts.

The methods are feature alignment, where features of the source and target domains are aligned to make them similar, and instance weighting, where the instances from the source domain are re-weighted to emphasize the most relevant ones for the target domain, often using the similarity between source and target instances.

Algorithm

Inputs

Source Graph G_s and Target Graph G_t

- Consider $G_s = (V_s, E_s)$, where V_s is the set of nodes and E_s is the set of edges in the source domain, and $G_t = (V_t, E_t)$, where V_t is the set of nodes and E_t is the set of edges in the target domain.
- X_s: Node features for the source graph.
- X_t: Node features for the target graph.
- Y_s: Labeled node labels for the source graph (supervised labels).
- λ: A hyperparameter controlling the balance between the classification loss (this measures the difference between the model's predicted labels and the true labels of the source nodes) and the domain adaptation loss.

Output

- The model's prediction for the target domain's node labels.

Steps

1) **Input Processing**
   - Collect both the labeled source graph and the unlabeled target graph.
   - Normalize the adjacency matrices A_s or both source and target graphs.

     $\tilde{A} = D^{-1/2}AD^{-1/2}$, where D is the degree matrix.

2) **Graph Convolutional Layers for Feature Propagation**
   - **Source Graph Feature Learning**
     Apply the graph convolutional layers to the source graph data X_s to obtain node embeddings.

     $$H_s(L) = \sigma\left(\tilde{A}_s H_s^{(L-1)} W^{(L-1)}\right)$$

     - $H_s(L)$: Node representations after layer L for the source graph.
     - $\tilde{A}_s$: Normalized adjacency matrix for the source graph.
     - $W^{(L-1)}$: Learnable weight matrix at layer L−1.
     - Σ: Nonlinear activation function (e.g., ReLU).
   - **Target Graph Feature Learning:**
     - Similarly, apply graph convolutions to the target graph features X_t to learn node embeddings.

       $$H_t(L) = \sigma\left(\tilde{A}_t H_t^{(L-1)} W^{(L-1)}\right)$$

     - $H_t(L)$: Node representations after layer L for the source graph.
3) **Domain Adaptation Mechanism:**
   - **Domain Discriminator:** A domain discriminator is used to distinguish between node embeddings from the source and target domains. The goal is to make the model's node embeddings domain-invariant.
     - The discriminator D tries to classify whether an embedding h comes from the source or target domain.
     - The adversarial objective is $L_{\text{adv}} = -E[\log(D(H)]$, where $D(H)$ outputs the probability that the embeddings H belong to the source domain.
   - **Adversarial Training:** The goal is to minimize the domain discriminator's ability to classify the embeddings, which forces the model to learn embeddings that are indistinguishable between source and target domains.
   - The GCN part of the model tries to confuse the domain discriminator by producing similar embeddings across the source and target graphs.
4) **Classification Loss (for Source Domain):**
   - The GCN-DA model applies a classification loss on the source graph node labels:

     $$L_{cls} = \sum_{v \in V} I(v) \times \text{CrossEntropy}\left(f\left(H_s^{(L)}\right), Y_s\right)$$

where $f(H_s^{(L)})$ is the final node embeddings from the last layer L, $I(v)$ is an indicator function that selects labeled nodes in the source graph, and Y_s are the true labels for the source domain.

5) **Total Objective:**
   - The overall loss is a combination of the classification loss for the source domain and the adversarial loss to align the source and target embeddings.

$$L_{\text{total}} = L_{\text{cls}} + \lambda L_{\text{adv}}$$

   where λ is a hyperparameter controlling the trade-off between classification performance on the source domain and domain adaptation.

6) **Training:**
   - The model is trained using stochastic gradient descent (SGD) or other optimization algorithms to minimize the total loss L_{total}.
   - Both the graph convolution layers and the domain discriminator are updated during training.

7) **Inference on Target Domain:**
   - Once trained, the learned model is used to make predictions on the target domain's node embeddings. In the case of supervised tasks, the model can predict the labels for the target domain nodes. For unsupervised tasks, the embeddings for the target domain nodes can be used for clustering or further analysis.

11.3.2.3 Key Features and Benefits of GCN-DA

The key features of GCN-DA are

1) A graph is constructed to obtain the relationship between the source and target domain data samples.
2) GCN helps to transfer the labeled information from the source domain to the unlabeled target domain.
3) Aligns class-level semantics between domains rather than only marginal distribution.
4) Better preserves class identity across domains.

Benefits of GCN-DA

1) Achieves higher accuracy on target domain tasks compared to traditional domain adaptation methods.
2) Captures complex inter-sample relations using graph structure, leading to more generalized models.
3) Uses structural similarity in graphs to ensure better alignment and knowledge transfer.
4) Bridges the gap between source and target distributions, enabling better domain-invariant learning.

11.3.3 Heterogeneous Transfer Learning

The previous section explored the process of TTGL. TTGL deals with the transfer of knowledge within graphs of similar types. This leads to the challenge of transferring knowledge between graphs of different types. Heterogeneous transfer learning (HTL) highlights the limitations of transductive learning in handling diverse graph structures.

Definition
HTL is a TGL type that transfers knowledge between graphs that have different node and relationship types. For real-world domains where the graphs have diverse data, HTL bridges the gap between different domains by aligning feature spaces. Its purpose is to reduce labeled data dependency in the target domain.

11.3.3.1 Working Process of HTL

1) **Feature Transformation**
   - Aligns node and edge features between the source and target graphs.
   - Uses domain adaptation techniques such as adversarial training to match distributions.
2) **Graph Alignment**
   - Establishes relationships between heterogeneous graphs through entity mapping or meta-path learning.
3) **Knowledge Transfer**
   - Applies pretrained graph models from the source to the target graph.
   - Uses embedding-based techniques to transfer learned patterns.
4) **Fine-Tuning and Adaptation**
   - Adjusts the transferred knowledge for the target domain through fine-tuning.
   - Incorporates self-supervised learning when labeled data is scarce.

11.3.3.2 Algorithm: Heterogeneous Feature Augmentation

In this topic, you will learn about transferring knowledge between source and target domains that have different feature spaces (heterogeneous domains), and the target domain has limited labeled data. The idea is that heterogeneous feature augmentation (HFA) transforms heterogeneous feature spaces into a common augmented feature space, where a shared classifier can be trained. The idea is to augment the features such that the classifier can operate across both source and target domains effectively.

Algorithm Consider the source domain features as $X^S \in R^d$ and the target domain features as $X^T \in R^d$.

1) **Projection into Latent Space:**
   Learn two transformation matrices:
   - $P_S \in R_s^{d \times k}$
   - $P_T \in R_t^{d \times k}$

   To project both source and target features into a shared k-dimensional latent space.
2) **Augmented Feature Representation:**
   Construct augmented features for a sample:
   - For source:
   $$x^S = \begin{bmatrix} P_S^T \ x^S \\ x^s \end{bmatrix}$$
   - For target:
   $$X^T = \begin{bmatrix} P_T^T \ x^T \\ 0 \end{bmatrix}$$
3) **Classifier Training:**
   Train a linear classifier (like SVM) in the augmented space using the source domain's labeled data.
4) **Model Adaptation:**
   Iteratively update the projection matrices and classifier using an optimization objective that minimizes classification loss while aligning feature distributions.

11.3.3.3 Key Features and Benefits of HFA

Key Features of HFA

- Supports heterogeneous feature spaces.
- Uses shared augmented representations.
- Integrates representation learning and classifier training.
- Compatible with kernel methods.

Benefits of HFA

- **Domain-Invariant Learning:** Learns representations invariant to source–target differences.
- **No Assumption of Same Feature Space:** Works when domains use different types of features (e.g., image vs text).
- **Simple and Effective:** Easily integrated with SVMs or other linear classifiers.
- **Efficient for Small Target Labels:** Needs only a few labeled target samples to adapt.

11.4 Key Techniques in TGL

The types of TGL refer to different learning paradigms, such as transductive, inductive, and HTL, which define how knowledge is transferred across graphs. In contrast, techniques of TGL are specific methods or algorithms (e.g., domain adaptation, meta-path learning, adversarial training) used to implement the transfer process effectively. These techniques can be categorized into feature-based, structure-based, and hybrid approaches. Below are the key techniques used in TGL.

11.4.1 Feature-Based Transfer Techniques

Feature-based transfer techniques are techniques in TGL where the focus is on aligning feature representations between the source and target graphs. Instead of directly transferring nodes, edges, or labels, this method maps the feature space from one domain to another, ensuring that the learned features in the target graph are as similar as possible to those in the source graph. For example, in medical diagnosis, a disease prediction model trained on patient records from one hospital (source graph) is applied to another hospital (target graph) by aligning patient symptom patterns and test results.

Feature-based TGL helps in transferring knowledge when the source and target graphs have different distributions. It enables learning in graphs with limited labeled data by using knowledge from a well-labeled source graph. It also ensures that the feature distributions of both graphs align to improve model generalization. TGL works well with large-scale graphs where structure-based methods may be computationally expensive.

Figure 11.3 shows the process of feature-based learning, which involves feature extraction from both source and target graphs; feature transformation to map source features into a common feature space that aligns with the target. The methods used are principal component analysis (PCA), autoencoders and kernel methods, and feature alignment, which minimizes distribution divergence between source and target feature spaces using maximum mean discrepancy (MMD) or Kullback-Leibler Divergence (KL) divergence or adversarial learning. After these steps, a classifier is trained on the transformed features of the source

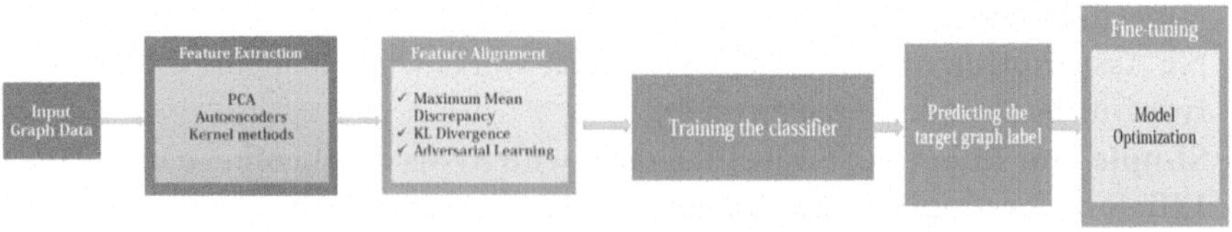

Figure 11.3 Flow of process of feature-based TGL.

graph. Prediction of the label for the target graph is done, followed by fine-tuning of optimizing the model using a small amount of labeled target data.

Feature extraction using embeddings from GNNs converts node features into compact vector representations while retaining their structural and relational properties. These embeddings facilitate transfer learning by capturing essential patterns from the source graph for effective adaptation to the target graph. Feature transformation using PCA in feature-based learning reduces the dimensionality of graph node features while retaining crucial variance. This ensures better alignment of feature distributions between the source and target graphs, enhancing transfer learning efficiency. Feature transformation using autoencoders in feature-based learning compresses graph node features into a lower-dimensional space while preserving essential patterns. The decoder reconstructs the data, enabling effective feature alignment between the source and target graphs for transfer learning. Feature transformation using kernel methods in feature-based learning projects graph node features into a higher-dimensional space, capturing intricate patterns. This improves feature alignment between source and target graphs, enhancing transfer learning performance.

Feature alignment with MMD in feature-based learning reduces the distribution disparity between source and target graph features. This ensures statistically similar transformed features, enhancing the effectiveness of transfer learning. Feature alignment using the KL divergence in feature-based learning quantifies the difference between source and target feature distributions. Reducing this divergence ensures better feature similarity, enhancing transfer learning effectiveness. Feature alignment using adversarial learning in feature-based learning utilizes a domain discriminator to reduce discrepancies between source and target features. This helps the model generate transferable representations, enhancing transfer learning effectiveness. Finally, training of the model and the prediction of the target graph label are employed.

Algorithm

Start

Step 1: Consider the source graph $G_s = (V_s, E_s, X_s)$, the target graph $G_t = (V_t, E_t, X_t)$, labels for source nodes Y_s, and output (target) graph predicted label as $\tilde{y}$.

Step 2: Compute node feature vectors X_s and X_t.

Step 3: Learn a transformation function f(·) using PCA, Autoencoders, or GNN-based embedding.

Step 4: Minimize the divergence $D(f(X_s), f(X_t))$.

Step 5: Train a classifier C on transformed source features.

Step 6: Apply C to predict labels $\tilde{y}$ for target nodes.

Step 7: If a few labeled target samples are available, update C for better generalization.

End

11.4.1.1 Transfer Component Analysis

Transfer component analysis (TCA) is a powerful technique of feature-based transfer learning. It transfers the knowledge from the source to the target graph by learning the shared feature space (features from different domains are mapped) among the graphs to reduce the distribution differences (variations in feature distribution between the source and target domains). TCA learns by identifying a common feature representation. TCA is based on kernel methods, which help project the data into a high-dimensional space, making it easier to align the feature distributions of the source and target domains.

The challenges in transfer learning are the discrepancy between source and target feature distributions. TCA mitigates this issue by minimizing the difference in statistical distributions using techniques such as MMD, ensuring that knowledge from the source domain can be effectively applied to the target domain. It retains the structural and geometric properties of data while transforming it into a new feature space. Kernel functions are used to map data into a higher-dimensional space, making it easier to find a shared feature representation between domains. This flexibility allows it to work well with both linear and nonlinear data relationships. TCA is widely used in image classification, text analysis, bioinformatics, financial forecasting, and healthcare. For example, in medical diagnosis, it can help transfer insights from a large dataset of labeled patient records to a new hospital's dataset with limited labels. Another example is transferring knowledge from a Twitter user graph to a Reddit discussion graph for sentiment analysis.

A. Mathematical Framework of TCA

The objective is to minimize the distribution discrepancy while preserving the structural integrity of the data. The objective function is to learn a transformation matrix that projects the original feature space into a new shared feature space, where the source and target distributions are aligned.

Let the source domain data be $X_s \in R^{d\times ns}$ with n_s samples and the target domain data be $X_t \in R^{d\times ns}$ with n_t samples. The combined data matrix:

$$X = [X_s, X_t] \in R^{d\times(n_s+n_t)},$$

where d is the feature dimension.

The MMD value is computed between source and target domains as

$$\mathrm{MMD}^2(X_s, X_t) = \left\| \frac{1}{n_s}\sum_{i=1}^{n_s}\phi(x_i) - \frac{1}{n_t}\sum_{j=1}^{n_t}\phi(x_j) \right\|^2$$

where $\phi(x)$ is the kernel-based feature transformation.

To capture complex patterns, TCA maps the original data into a high-dimensional space using a kernel function:

$$K = k(X, X),$$

where K is the kernel matrix (e.g., radial basis function [RBF] kernel or polynomial kernel).

$$k(x_i, x_j) = \exp\left(-\frac{\|x_i - x_j\|^2}{2\sigma^2}\right)$$

TCA solves the following optimization problem to find a transformation matrix A.

$$\min tr(A^{\top}XMX^{\top}A) + \lambda tr(A^{\top}A),$$

where M is the MMD-based domain discrepancy matrix, ensuring source and target alignment, λ is a regularization parameter to prevent overfitting, $\mathrm{tr}(\cdot)$ denotes the trace of a matrix.

The solution is obtained via eigenvalue decomposition

$$A = \arg\min tr(A^{\top}XMX^{\top}A)$$

B. Working Process of TCA

The step-by-step procedure for using TCA is shown using a flowchart in Fig. 11.4.

Step 1: Define the Problem and Input Source Domain Data and Target Domain Data.

Step 2: Kernel Mapping for Feature Transformation.

The kernel function commonly used is the RBF kernel.

Step 3: Learn Transfer Components by Minimizing Distribution Differences.

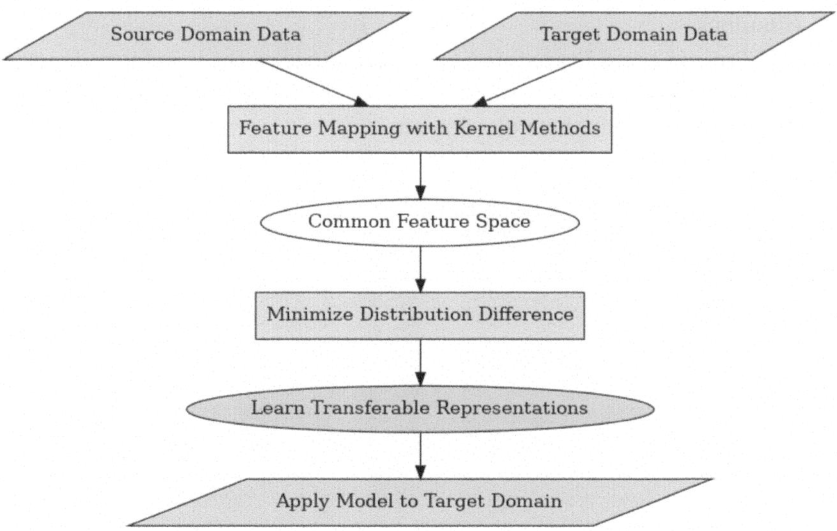

Figure 11.4 Working process of transfer component analysis.

Step 4: Solve the Optimization Problem Using Eigen decomposition or singular value decomposition to obtain the transformation matrix W.

Step 5: Train a Classifier on the Transformed Data.

- A classifier (e.g., SVM, decision tree, or neural networks) is trained on the transformed source domain. The trained model is then applied to the transformed target domain for prediction.

Step 6: Predict Target Labels and Evaluate Performance.

C. Advantages and Limitations of TCA

The key advantages and notable limitations of TCA are given in Fig. 11.5.

D. Example: Sentiment Analysis Across Domains

Consider a source domain labeled with movie reviews (positive/negative sentiment) and a target domain with product reviews, but without labels. The goal is to train a classifier on movie reviews and transfer the knowledge to classify product reviews.

1) **Feature Extraction:** The movie and product reviews are represented as word frequency vectors in a high-dimensional space.
2) **Kernel Mapping:** TCA maps both domains into a new feature space using a kernel-based transformation, aligning their feature distributions.
3) **Minimizing Distribution Differences:** TCA optimizes the feature representation by reducing the MMD between the movie and product review data distributions.
4) **Model Training and Transfer:** A classifier trained on the transformed movie review features can now be applied to classify product reviews effectively, even without labeled data in the target domain.

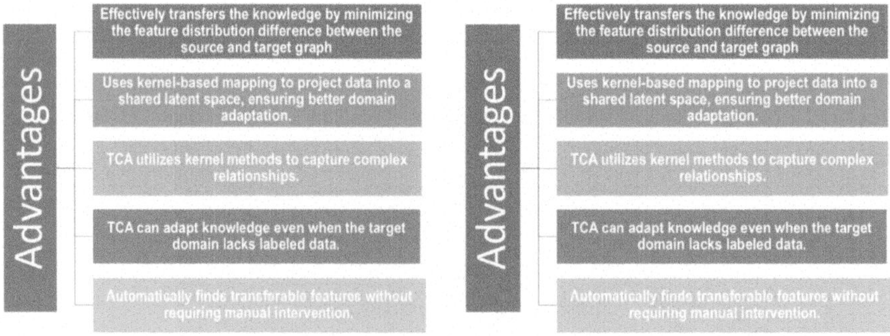

Figure 11.5 Advantages and limitations of TCA.

11.4.1.2 Domain Adversarial Neural Networks

In transfer learning, particularly domain adaptation, models trained on a source domain often face challenges when applied to a target domain due to distribution discrepancies. Traditional adversarial adaptation methods typically focus on aligning either the global (marginal) distributions or the local (conditional) distributions between domains, without considering their varying contributions to the adaptation process.

Domain adversarial neural network (DANN) is a novel approach in a feature-based transfer learning technique that uses adversarial training to extract domain-invariant features. By incorporating a domain discriminator, DANN ensures that the feature extractor learns representations that minimize distribution differences between the source and target domains, enabling effective knowledge transfer. DANN encourages the feature extractor to produce features that are indistinguishable across domains, thereby reducing distribution discrepancies. DANN helps adapt models trained on a labeled source domain to an unlabeled or differently distributed target domain. It explicitly reduces domain discrepancy, making transfer learning more effective in real-world applications such as sentiment analysis, medical imaging, and object recognition. By learning domain-invariant features, DANN ensures that the model can perform well on unseen data from different but related domains. DANN automatically aligns feature spaces through adversarial training, making it scalable and efficient for large datasets.

A. Mathematical Formulation of DANN

The idea is to reduce the difference between the source and target domains. The objective functions use two loss functions: one for the source domain and the other for the target domain. The key components in DANN are loss functions, a feature extractor that learns feature representations from both the source and target domains, a task-specific classifier that classifies the input samples based on learned features, and a domain discriminator that aims to distinguish whether the extracted features belong to the source or target domain.

Consider the source domain with fully labeled features and a target domain with some unlabeled features.

1) **Objective Function of DANN**

   The overall objective of DANN consists of two loss functions:

   - Task-Specific Loss (L_{task}): Ensures correct predictions on labeled source domain data.
   - Adversarial Domain Loss (L_{domain}): Aligns feature distributions between source and target domains.

$$\min \max L_{\text{DANN}} = L_{\text{task}}(F, C) - \lambda L_{\text{domain}}(F, D)$$

where F is the feature extractor, C is the task-specific classifier, D is the domain discriminator, and λ is a hyperparameter that controls the trade-off between classification and domain adaptation.

2) **Task-Specific Loss (L_{task})**
For a classification task, the model minimizes the standard cross-entropy loss on the labeled source domain data:

$$L_{\text{task}} = -\sum y_s \log\ C(F(x_s))$$

where (x_s, y_s) are the source domain samples and labels.

3) **Adversarial Domain Loss (L_{domain})**
To encourage domain-invariant feature learning, an adversarial loss is introduced using a domain discriminator. The discriminator D tries to distinguish between source and target domain samples, while F tries to fool D:

$$L_{\text{domain}} = -\sum \log\ D(F(x)) + (1-d)\log(1 - D(F(x)))$$

where $d = 0$ for the source domain and $d = 1$ for the target domain; D_s and D_t are source and target domain distributions.

4) **Gradient Reversal Trick**
To achieve adversarial learning, a gradient reversal layer is applied before the domain discriminator. The gradient reversal layer inverts the gradient during backpropagation.

$$\frac{\partial L_{\text{DANN}}}{\partial \theta_F} = \frac{\partial L_{\text{task}}}{\partial \theta_F} - \lambda \frac{\partial L_{\text{domain}}}{\partial \theta_F}$$

This ensures that the feature extractor learns representations that confuse the domain discriminator, making the source and target feature distributions more similar.

B. Working Process of DANN (Step-by-Step Methodology)

The key steps of the working process of DANN, as given in Fig. 11.6, are as follows:

Step 1: The input data (from both the source and target domains) is passed through a feature extractor (e.g., a deep neural network). The extracted features are then used for classification and domain discrimination.

Step 2: The extracted features from the source domain are passed to a label predictor to train a classifier. The classifier is trained using labeled source data.

Step 3: A domain discriminator tries to distinguish between the source and target domain features. A The gradient reversal layer is used to reverse the gradient from the domain discriminator to the feature extractor. This forces the feature extractor to learn domain-invariant features, making the model perform well on both source and target domains.

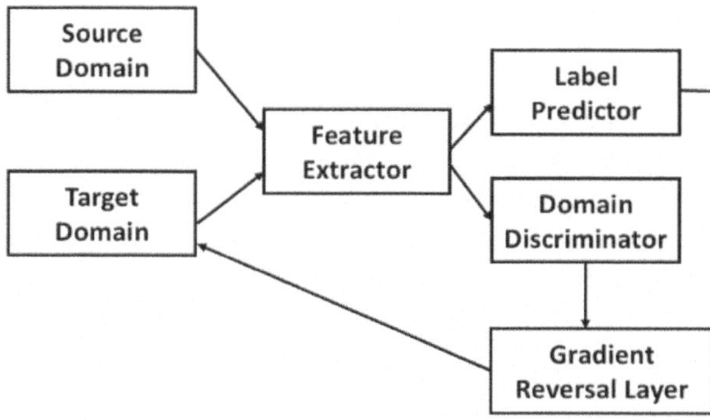

Figure 11.6 Working process of DANN.

Step 4: The graph is trained using both classification loss (for label prediction) and adversarial loss (for domain discrimination). The adversarial training ensures that the feature extractor learns domain-invariant representations, improving generalization on the target domain.

C. Example: Sentiment Analysis

Consider a sentiment analysis task where labeled English reviews (source) need to be adapted to unlabeled Spanish reviews (target).

1) The feature extractor learns text embeddings for both languages.
2) A task-specific classifier predicts sentiment labels using labeled English data.
3) A domain discriminator tries to distinguish between English and Spanish embeddings.
4) The adversarial training forces the feature extractor to learn embeddings that the discriminator cannot differentiate, leading to a domain-invariant sentiment model.

D. Advantages and Limitations of DANN

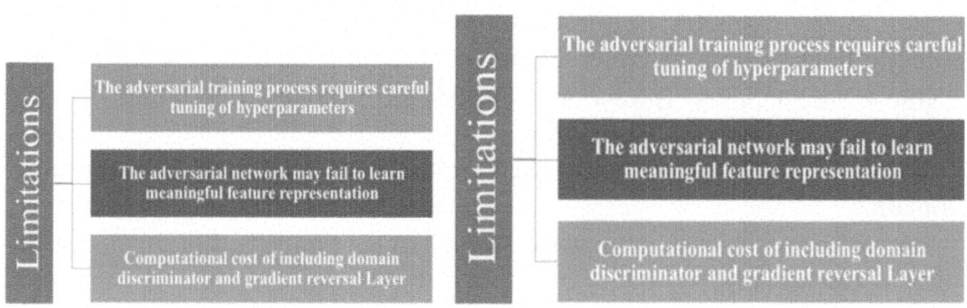

Figure 11.7 Advantages and limitations of DANN.

11.4.2 Structure-Based Transfer Techniques

11.4.2.1 Overview and Its Definition

We've explored feature-based transfer learning; let's move on to another approach, structure-based transfer techniques. Imagine you're moving to a new city. You don't just bring your personal belongings (features), but you also try to understand how the city is structured—its roads, neighborhoods, and transportation systems. This helps you navigate better, even though the environment is different. In the same way, structure-based transfer learning doesn't just transfer features from one domain to another but focuses on how data points are interconnected.

For example, think about social networks. If you switch from one platform (say Facebook) to another (say LinkedIn), your profile information (features) is important, as is your network of connections (structure). Structure-based techniques ensure that the relationships between data points are preserved and useful for effective learning across different domains.

In this section, we will explore how structure-based transfer learning works, its methodologies, and its real-world applications.

Definition Structure-based transfer learning is a powerful approach that preserves the structural patterns and relationships when transferring knowledge between domains. Rather than solely focusing on individual feature mappings, these techniques preserve the inherent data structure—such as graphs, hierarchies, or spatial relationships—to enhance generalization in the target domain.

11.4.2.2 Algorithm for Structure-Based Transfer Learning

Step 1: Consider source and target graphs as input, along with node features, edge features and relationships, and other structural features.

Step 2: Relevant structural features are extracted by node embedding, calculating edge weights, and relationship patterns.

Step 3: Align structural representations between source and target domains using techniques such as graph alignment (matching node/edge distributions), hierarchical mapping (preserving multi-level dependencies), and spectral embeddings for topology preservation.

Step 4: Transfer learned structural features from the source domain to the target domain.

Step 5: The model is trained on the target domain (graph) using adapted structural representations.

Step 6: Evaluate the performance of the transferred model using target domain data.

Example ***Fraud Detection in Financial Transactions***

Consider a source domain with one transaction data in one country, and the target domain represents the fraud detection applied in another country. Transactions can be represented as graphs, where nodes represent users, accounts, or merchants; edges represent transactions between entities; and features include transaction amounts, timestamps, and user profiles.

Applying Structure-Based Transfer Learning Step 1: Construct transaction graphs for both countries and define node features (e.g., transaction frequency, risk score) and edge attributes (e.g., transaction amount, time gap).

Step 2: Use GNNs to extract embeddings that capture relationships between users, merchants, and transaction behaviors. Identify patterns such as high-risk transaction clusters or frequent connections with flagged accounts.

Step 3: Apply graph matching techniques to align user–merchant interactions in the two domains. Use spectral embeddings to transform source domain node embeddings into a common feature space with the target domain.

Step 4: Transfer fraud detection rules and learned embeddings from the source domain to the target domain. Adjust for differences in transaction volume, currency, and fraud patterns.

Step 5: Train a fraud detection classifier using the adapted graph representations.

Step 6: Test the model on target domain transactions.

By transferring structural insights from the source to the target domain, the fraud detection model can detect fraudulent patterns even in the new environment, improving generalization and reducing reliance on labeled data in the target domain.

11.4.2.3 Flow Process and Its Diagram

Structure-based transfer learning uses various methods such as feature extraction and alignment for transferring the knowledge. The step-by-step flow process with mathematical representation is given below:

Step 1: The input to the process are two graphs, the source graph G_s and the target graph G_t, with features X_s and X_t and labels Y_s and Y_t.

Step 2: Next, methods such as embedding and spatial relationships are used for feature extraction.

Step 3: A similarity function is used to measure the relationship between the structures of the source and target graphs.

$$S(D_s, D_t) = \frac{1}{|X_s||X_t|} \sum_{i \varepsilon X_s} \sum_{j \varepsilon X_t} k(i, j)$$

where $k(i, j)$ is a kernel function measuring similarity.

Step 4: Structural Alignment via Feature Transformation.

- Transform source domain features to align with the target domain using structural transformation functions:

$$Xs' = f(X_s),$$

where $f(\cdot)$ is a mapping function.
Apply methods such as GNNs, manifold learning, or structural domain adaptation to preserve structural properties.

Step 5: Knowledge Transfer with Structural Constraints.

- Use a transfer learning function L_{trans} that minimizes distributional differences while maintaining structure:

$$L_{\text{trans}} = L_{\text{struct}}\left(X_s', X_t\right) - \lambda D\left(X_s', X_t\right)$$

where D is a divergence function (e.g., MMD, Wasserstein distance) and λ is a regularization parameter.

Step 6: Model Training and Optimization.

- Train a predictive model $h(\cdot)$ on the transformed source features

$$\min\ E_{(x,y)\in Ds}[L(h(x;\theta), y)]$$

Optimize using gradient descent, SGD, or the Adam optimizer.

Step 7: Adaptation and Final Prediction.

- Apply the trained model $h(\cdot)$ on the target domain

$$Y_t' = h(X_t)Y_t' = h(X_t)Y_t' = h(X_t)$$

- Fine-tune on target data if labeled data is available.

11.4.2.4 Meta-Path–Based Learning

Meta-path–based learning is a powerful structure-based transfer learning used in heterogeneous graphs to transfer knowledge, as it depends on structural relationships. Instead of relying on feature similarity, it captures meaningful relationships between domains using predefined meta-paths. A meta-path is a structured sequence that defines how nodes and edges are connected in a heterogeneous information network. It provides a meaningful context for capturing relationships.

Example of a Meta-Path in an Academic Network

Consider a graph with three node types: A (Author), P (Paper), and C (Conference). A meta-path like Author → Paper → Conference → Paper → Author

(APCPA) captures the relationship between two authors who have published in the same conference.

Meta-paths define specific sequences of node types and relationships in heterogeneous graphs, ensuring that structural patterns are maintained. It preserves relational information. It identifies common relationship patterns (meta-paths) across graphs. It uses random walks to generate sequences that capture these relationships. It helps in knowledge transfer where structural similarity is high. For example, recommend research collaborations by transferring knowledge from an academic citation graph to a social networking graph.

Working Process of Meta-Path-Based Transfer Learning Figure 11.8 shows the flow of the process in Meta-path-based transfer learning.

Step 1: Define the relationship between the source and target graphs and construct the relevant meta-paths.

Step 2: Using the embedding technique, transform the nodes into a vector representation and extract the features.

Step 3: Transfer learning across the two domains.

Step 4: Apply a classifier (e.g., neural networks, GNNs) on the transformed meta-path embeddings (target graph) for tasks such as node classification, link prediction, or clustering.

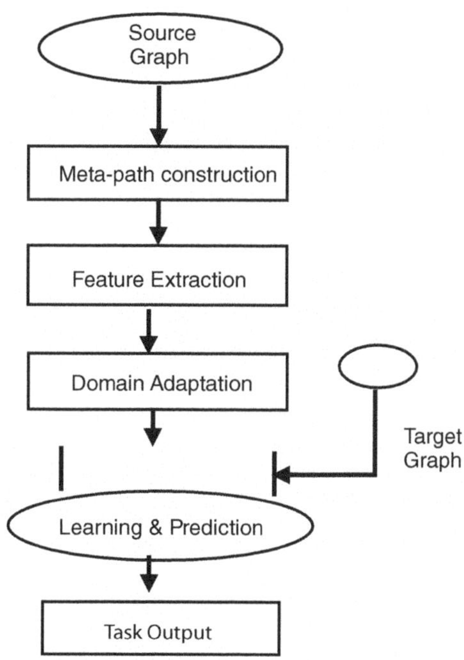

Figure 11.8 Flow of process in meta-path-based transfer learning.

11.5 Technique Comparisons

11.5.1 Inductive vs Transductive TGL

Inductive vs transductive TGL refers to two key settings in graph-based learning. While transductive learning makes predictions only on nodes seen during training,

Table 11.1 Inductive vs transductive transfer graph learning.

Inductive Transfer Graph Learning	Transductive Transfer Graph Learning
Inductive learning involves training a model using labeled data and then predicting the labels of unlabeled data.	Transductive learning trains on the entire dataset, including both labeled and unlabeled data, to predict the labels of the unlabeled points.
The trained model can be used directly for predictions without additional training.	Model may need to be retrained to incorporate the new data points.
Create a generalizable predictive model.	Does not create a generalizable predictive model.
This can efficiently label new test points as they become available with minimal computation.	This requires rerunning the algorithm each time a new test point is introduced, leading to higher computational costs.
Model is not exposed to the test data during the learning phase and is only provided with the training data for the learning purpose.	Model is exposed to both training and testing data sets in the learning phase itself.
Example: A decision tree classifier trained on a labeled dataset serves as a classic example. After training, the classifier can readily predict the labels of new, unseen data points.	An example is semi-supervised learning techniques, where the model uses the structure of the unlabeled data to enhance its performance on the specific unlabeled instances it is tasked with predicting.

Table 11.2 Feature-based transfer graph learning vs structure-based transfer graph learning.

Feature-based Transfer Learning	Structure-based Transfer Learning
Works on feature vectors	Works on structured data
Maps and aligns feature representation domains	Preserves and utilizes structural relationships
Used for image classification, text analysis	Social network analysis, knowledge graphs

inductive learning generalizes to completely unseen nodes or graphs. The difference is given in Table 11.1.

11.5.2 Feature-Based TGL vs Structure-Based TGL

Table 11.2 shows the difference between feature-based TGL and structure-based TGL.

11.6 Case Studies

Case Study 11.1

Enhancing Graph Anomaly Detection with Dual-Level Knowledge Distillation

Graph anomaly detection with graph transfer learning involves identifying unusual patterns or behaviors in graph-structured data by using knowledge from a related domain or graph. Instead of learning from scratch, the model transfers learned features—such as how people apply prior knowledge to solve new but similar problems. This is especially useful when labeled anomalies are scarce in the target graph. By using transfer learning, detection becomes more accurate and efficient across different but structurally related graph environments.

Graph anomaly detection is pivotal in identifying irregular patterns within graph-structured data, such as fraudulent activities in financial networks or malicious users in social platforms. However, acquiring labeled anomalies is often challenging due to their rarity and the high cost of manual annotation. This scarcity hampers the performance of traditional supervised learning models.

The authors introduce DualKD [5], a novel framework that uses transfer learning to enhance anomaly detection in graphs, especially under few-shot learning scenarios. The core idea is to distill knowledge from a well-trained teacher model to a student model, facilitating better generalization on limited labeled data. In the teacher model, training is done on an auxiliary dataset with ample labeled anomalies. They capture complex patterns and distributions of anomalies. The teacher model produces soft labels (probabilistic outputs) for the target dataset. These soft labels encapsulate nuanced information about data uncertainty and class distributions. It learns from the soft labels provided by the teacher model and aims to mimic the

(Continued)

Case Study 11.1 (Continued)

teacher's performance on the target dataset with limited labeled anomalies. It transfers fine-grained, local features from the teacher to the student and transfers high-level, global features, ensuring the student captures broader patterns.

Four benchmark datasets encompassing various domains are used to validate the model's robustness. And the metrics—precision, recall, F1-score, and area under the curve—are used to assess detection performance. DualKD consistently outperformed baseline models across all datasets. The student model, guided by the teacher, demonstrated enhanced generalization to unseen anomalies. DualKD exemplifies how knowledge distillation can bridge the gap between data-rich and data-scarce domains in graph anomaly detection. This algorithm is applicable to various sectors, including cyber-security, finance, and social network analysis, where anomalies are rare but critical.

Case Study 11.2

Transfer Learning in Biological Networks Using Geneformer

In network biology, predicting gene functions, interactions, and disease associations is challenging due to the scarcity of labeled data in specific contexts. Traditional models often struggle with generalization when data is limited, hindering advancements in understanding complex biological systems. The researchers developed Geneformer [6], a context-aware, attention-based deep learning model designed to address data scarcity in biological networks through transfer learning.

The key features of Geneformer are as follows: It was pretrained on a massive corpus of approximately 30 million single-cell transcriptomes, enabling it to learn general representations of gene expression patterns across various tissues and conditions, and possess self-supervised learning, which utilized a masked learning objective during pretraining to capture the underlying structure and hierarchy within gene networks without requiring labeled data. The pretrained model can be fine-tuned on specific downstream tasks with limited labeled data, such as predicting disease-associated genes or therapeutic targets.

Geneformer accurately predicted dosage-sensitive disease genes and their downstream targets using a context-aware in silico deletion approach. In a study on cardiomyopathy, Geneformer identified candidate therapeutic targets whose inhibition improved cardiomyocyte contraction in induced pluripotent stem cell (iPSC)–based models. Transfer learning with Geneformer reduces the need for extensive labeled datasets, accelerating research in network biology. The model's architecture allows it to be applied to diverse biological tasks, from gene function prediction to therapeutic target discovery.

This case study illustrates the power of transfer learning in overcoming data limitations within biological networks.

11.7 Conclusion

In summary, TGL is the process of transferring the knowledge from the labeled graph to the unlabeled graph. This chapter discussed the TGL's features and benefits. TGL is essential for overcoming data scarcity, reducing annotation costs, improving generalization, and handling evolving graph structures, making it a crucial technique in modern graph-based learning applications. HTL enables effective knowledge transfer across diverse graph structures, making it highly valuable in multi-domain applications such as bioinformatics, finance, and recommendation systems. By leveraging alignment techniques and feature transformations, HTL overcomes challenges posed by structural and feature heterogeneity in graphs.

TCA is a powerful feature-based transfer learning technique that enables cross-domain knowledge transfer by learning a shared latent feature space. By minimizing distribution differences while preserving essential data properties, TCA improves model adaptability and generalization, making it a crucial method in scenarios where labeled target data is limited.

DANN is widely used in domain adaptation for tasks such as medical image analysis, autonomous driving, and NLP, where labeled target data is scarce.

References

1 Andrey Gritsenko; Yuan Guo; Kimia Shayestehfard; Armin Moharrer; Jennifer Dy; Stratis Ioannidis, Graph transfer learning, 2021 IEEE Int. Conf. Data Mining (ICDM), Auckland, New Zealand, 07–10, December 2021.

2 Andrew Arnold, Ramesh Nallapati, William W. Cohen, A comparative study of methods for transductive transfer learning, Proc. 7th IEEE Int. Conf. Data Mining (ICDM 2007), Omaha, Nebraska, USA, October 28–31, 2007, Pages 77–82.

3 J. Vázquez, M. López, E. Gibert, E. Herrero, and F. J. Luque, "Merging ligand-based and structure-based methods in drug discovery: An overview of combined virtual screening approaches," *Molecules*, vol. 25, no. 20, p. 4723, 2020, doi: 10.3390/molecules25204723.

4 L. Guo, L. Tang, T. Chen, and L. Zhu, "DA-GCN: A domain-aware attentive graph convolution network for shared-account cross-domain sequential recommendation, In Thirtieth Int. Joint Conf. Artifi. Intell. {IJCAI-21},", 2021, doi: 10.24963/ijcai.2021/342.

5 L. Xuan, D. Cheng, L. Zhang, C. Zhang, and Z. Feng, "Few-shot graph anomaly detection via dual-level knowledge distillation," *Entropy*, vol. 27, no. 1, p. 28, 2025, doi: 10.3390/e27010028.

6 C. V. Theodoris *et al.*, "Transfer learning enables predictions in network biology," *Nature*, vol. 618, pp. 616–624, 2023.

Part IV

Emerging Trends with Case Studies

12

Graph Contrastive Learning

12.1 Introduction to Self-Supervised Learning

In Chapter 11, we explored transfer learning on graphs, highlighting how pretrained graph models can transfer knowledge from one domain or task to another. Transfer learning showed that graph neural networks (GNNs) can attain strong execution by transmitting structural and semantic information from source graphs to target graphs.

However, efficient transfer learning in graph-based systems critically depends on the value and generalization of learned representations. Traditional supervised learning methodologies frequently fall short since they depend on a huge volume of labeled data, which is costly and domain-specific. This issue has led to self-supervised learning paradigms that can obtain valuable, task-agnostic representations without manual annotation. In this chapter, we introduce the concept of graph contrastive learning (GCL), which focuses on obtaining knowledge through self-learning.

12.1.1 Definition With Example

Self-supervised learning (SSL) is a machine learning technique that creates its own supervisory signals (pseudo-labels) for the model to learn a useful representation. Labeling is done for the model to understand the structure and relationships within the data [1].

Example ***Predicting Missing Connections in a Social Network***
Let us consider a social network graph (Fig. 12.1) with nodes representing a person (John, David, Jerry, Dave, Frank) and edges representing a friendship connection.

The graph has only unlabeled data, which does not reveal whether the relationship (friendship) between two nodes (friends) is strong or weak, real or fake. Instead of relying on the labels, we can design a self-supervised task to help the model teach itself patterns in the data.

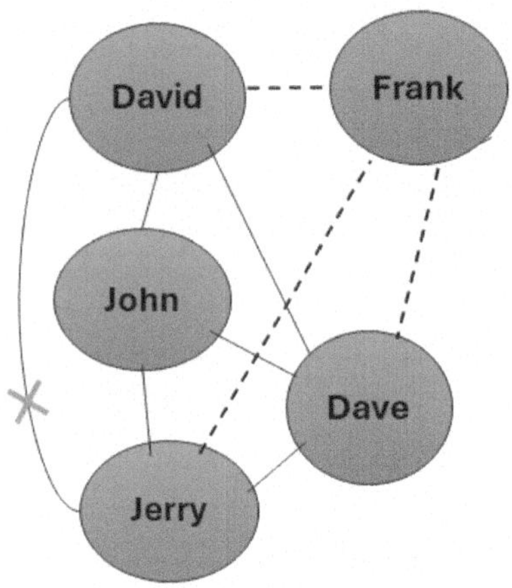

Figure 12.1 Social network graph.

12.1.1.1 Self-Supervised Task Idea: Predict Missing Links

1) Remove a few links. (In our example, remove the connection between David and Jerry.)
   The task is to predict whether there must be an edge between the two nodes (David and Jerry).
2) Three steps to be followed: the model must understand the nodes that are closely connected, the community structure form, and find which node pairs can communicate with each other.

2a) **Finding Whether the Nodes Are Closely Connected**
   If the nodes (David and Jerry) are not directly connected but share a common friend, John (David, John) and (John, Jerry), there is a high probability that (David and Jerry) should be connected.

2b) **Identifying Community Structure Form**
   Identify indirect paths. Given the graph shown in Fig. 12.2.
   An indirect path is a connection through other nodes.
   a) Path from David → John → Jerry (two-step path)
      So, there's one indirect path connecting David and Jerry.
   b) Add more paths
      Suppose we now also have another node in the community: Dave.
      Connections:
      - David ↔ John
      - David ↔ Dave
      - John ↔ Dave
      - John ↔ Jerry
      - Dave ↔ Jerry

Figure 12.2 Graph representing multiple indirect paths.

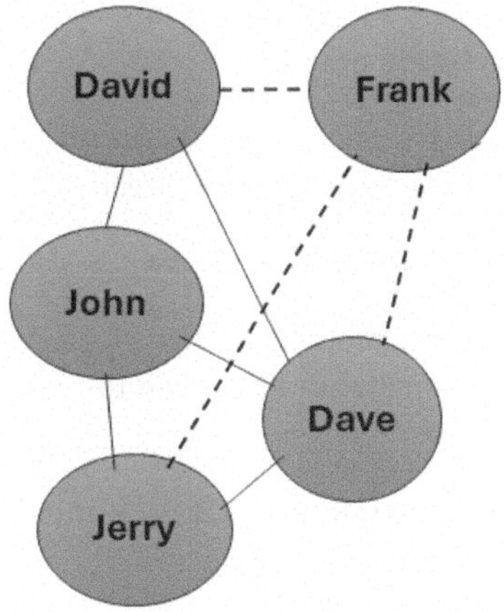

Now, David and Jerry are not directly connected, but they have multiple indirect paths:

1) David → John → Jerry
2) David → Dave → Jerry
3) David → John → Dave → Jerry

Since there are three different paths connecting David and Jerry, the model thinks:

> "David and Jerry are very likely to form a direct connection soon because nodes in a community often cluster together."

Multiple paths = strong evidence of community structure = likely direct connection.

2c) **Which Node Pairs Are Likely to Interact**

Nodes
David, John, Jerry, Dave
Connections (edges):

- David ↔ John
- John ↔ Jerry
- Jerry ↔ Dave

Step 1
Direct neighbors

- David's neighbor: John
- John's neighbors: David, Jerry

- Jerry's neighbors: John, Dave
- Dave's neighbor: Jerry

If we only count direct neighbors, David and Jerry seem unlikely to interact because they are not directly connected.

2d) **Latent Similarity**

Now, suppose we have feature information about nodes.

From Table 12.1, even though David and Jerry are not directly connected, they share:

- Same interests: Chess & music
- Same activity level: High

This latent similarity, which is shown in Fig. 12.3, signals that David and Jerry are likely to interact.

3) Model Inference

Table 12.1 Example for latent similarity.

Node	Interests	Activity Level
David	Chess, music	High
John	Chess, movies	Medium
Jerry	Chess, music	High
Dave	Movies, music	Low

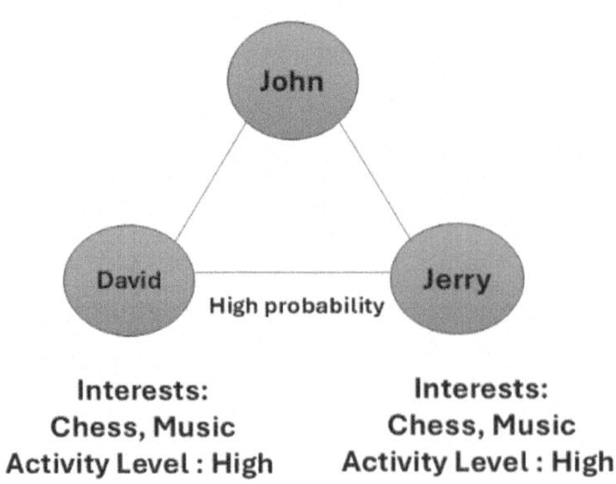

Figure 12.3 Latent similarity graph.

A self-supervised graph model could see patterns like

- Nodes with similar features and shared neighbors often form links.
- John connects to both David and Jerry.
- David ↔ John ↔ Jerry forms a two-step indirect path.
- Features: David ~ Jerry similarity = High.

Prediction

David ↔ Jerry → High probability

The model doesn't just look at neighbors. It learns that feature similarity + indirect paths make a link likely.

4) Graph Structure Learning

The model iteratively learns the graph structure without the labeled data.

12.1.2 Key Characteristics of SSL

- No need for label data. The model generates its own "pseudo-labels" from the data itself. For example, in a sentence like "The cat sat on the ______" the missing word ("wall") becomes a label automatically.
- Learning the patterns is done by using a pretext self-generated task. Then, the learned features are used for classification or prediction. For example, consider the pretext task as "Predict missing parts of an image." Then the prediction task is to identify the object in the image.
- SSL extracts hidden relationships and patterns within data. It uses contexts such as neighboring words in a sentence or adjacent pixels in an image to learn representations.
- The model learns generalized feature representations that work well across multiple tasks. These representations capture semantic meaning rather than specific task-based patterns.
- SSL works on text, images, audio, and graphs. For example, predicting a missing word in the case of text, predicting rotation or a masked region in the case of an image, and predicting missing edges or node features in the case of a graph.
- SSL efficiently utilizes large volumes of unlabeled data, which is easier and cheaper to collect. This makes it highly scalable for real-world applications.
- Learning goals such as contrastive learning and predictive learning are used, where contrastive learning distinguishes between similar and dissimilar pairs and predictive learning predicts one part of the data from another part.

12.1.3 Types of Self-Supervised Tasks

In SSL, models are trained using automatically generated labels derived directly from the data, rather than depending on human annotations or labeling. To accomplish this, the model performs specially designed pretext tasks that allow it to uncover hidden relationships, patterns, and structures within unlabeled data. These tasks help the model learn meaningful feature representations that can later be applied to tasks such as classification, prediction, and clustering.

The types of self-supervised tasks are generative tasks, contrastive tasks, predictive tasks, and clustering-based tasks.

12.1.3.1 Generative Tasks

The model is trained to reconstruct or generate parts of the data that are missing or intentionally hidden. By predicting missing information, the model learns to understand the underlying data structure and content, for example, predicting the missing word in a sentence using masked language modeling, which is a text-based system; hiding a part of an image and training the model to fill in the missing region using image in painting; and predicting missing segments in a speech recording using the audio completion technique.

Examples

1. Masked Language Modeling (Text Example—BERT)

BERT (bidirectional encoder representations from transformers) reads the text in both directions, from left to right and right to left, at the same time to understand the full context of a word based on the surrounding words. This can be done by using a probability distribution over all the words. Also, during the training phase, it adjusts weights to favor the true masked word. BERT uses the encoder part of the transformer to convert input text into contextual embeddings and a self-attention mechanism to understand the relationship between words in a sentence.

"The cat sat on the ________ and started to purr."

"The cat sat on the ________, looking out the window."

"mat" has the highest likelihood in the first example and "wall" has the highest probability for the second example.

2. Masked Autoencoders (MAE—Image Example)

This technique learns by masking (hiding) parts of an image and then trying to reconstruct (predict) those missing parts. The model learns global and local features of images and divides the images into patches (16 X 16 pixels each). Then, it randomly masks 75% of image patches and reconstructs them.

- Visible patches on the bird's head and tail.
- Masked patches with large empty gaps (e.g., wings, body).

The encoder looks only at the visible patches. It learns a compressed representation that captures the essence of what is visible, namely, color, texture, and shape clues. The decoder reconstructs the missing parts by learning.

"If the bird's head is blue and there's sky above, the missing patches below might be the bird's body and wings."

The reconstructed image is compared with the original image. Then the model's weight is updated based on the difference.

3. Audio Completion (Speech Example)
Audio completion is a generative self-supervised task where a model learns to predict the missing or masked part of an audio signal. Let us consider an example, "Good morning everyone," in audio form. The raw sound wave is converted into a spectrogram. Then, it randomly masks or removes a short portion of the audio. In our example, say we hide the sound corresponding to "morning." The sentence will look like "Good [mask] everyone." The encoder analyzes the unmasked parts such as "Good" and "everyone." It extracts contextual information such as rhythm, tone, speaker characteristics, and pronunciation style. This helps the model to understand what kind of sound or word should come next. The decoder uses the learned context to predict or reconstruct the missing audio portion. It generates a waveform or spectrogram pattern that matches the speaker's tone and the natural flow of the sentence. The reconstructed audio is compared with the original unmasked audio. The model's parameters are updated by finding the difference.

12.1.4 Application in Graph Domain

12.1.4.1 Node Attribute Masking and Link Prediction in Author Citation Graph

The author citation graph contains authors represented in nodes and who cites whose paper is represented as edges. Some of the node features are publication title, research area, and specialization. The task is to hide an author's profile information such as research area (node feature/attribute) and predict it using neighbors' information. For example, mask author A's research area. The model predicts it using the articles cited by author A.

For the link prediction problem, the model predicts whether there exists an edge between two authors. If authors A and C have similar topics and both cite author B's paper, then the model infers a high probability that A will cite C in the future.

Example
In Table 12.2, author A has not cited author D, but both cite author B. Through SSL, the model detects that authors A and D have the same research interest, and a new link from authors A to D is likely to appear.

Table 12.2 Author citation details.

Author	Research Topic	Citations
A	Artificial intelligence	Cited by B, C
B	Machine learning	Cited by A, D
C	Deep learning	Cited by A
D	Data mining	Cited by B

12.1.4.2 Recommendation System in Social Network Analysis

In a social network graph, the users are presented in nodes and associations between users (friendships, similar interests) are represented using edges. The node features are profile info, interests, etc. Some of the applications are predicting missing friendships or user interactions (link prediction), identifying similar users, or detecting fake accounts through structural similarity.

Example ***Friend Recommendation in a Social Graph***

Each user is a node, and each friendship is an edge. For link prediction, we mask some edges and train the model to predict if an edge should exist between two nodes based on the common neighbors, feature similarity, and friend-of-friends paths. In the next step, the model learns that David and Jerry are connected (refer to Table 12.3).

Other applications in social network analysis are community detection and user clustering, in which the model automatically identifies groups or communities with similar behavior or interests, identifying suspicious or automated fake accounts. For example, Twitter uses a graph-based learning model to detect bot networks that like each other abnormally, even without labeled bot accounts. Another application is sentiment and opinion analysis.

Table 12.3 Social network friend recommendation system.

User	Interests	Friends
David	Movies, music	John
John	Music, sports	David, Jerry
Jerry	Sports, fitness	John
Dave	Movies, fitness	—

Table 12.4 Payment network.

Node	Type	Description
A	Customer	Regular salary account
B	Merchant	Grocery shop
C	Merchant	Electronics store
D	Customer	Fraudster
E	Bank account	Money mule (used to transfer stolen funds)

12.1.4.3 Fraud Detection in Financial Transactions

The main idea is to detect suspicious users or abnormal transaction patterns. In modern financial systems, such as credit card transactions, money transfers, or online payments, fraud detection is done by self-supervised pretext tasks. For example, if account A frequently transfers amounts to account B, but suddenly transfers to a new account X, the model will detect it as an anomaly. In the node attribute masking system, the model predicts the missing attribute (usual spending amount) from the neighbor account.

Example ***Fraud in a Payment Network***
Transactions:

A → B: Rs. 2,000 (frequent, small payments)
A → C: Rs. 8,000 (occasional, electronics)
D → E: Rs. 50,000 (suspicious, large transfer)
E → C: Rs. 48,000 (immediate second transfer)

Observation:

From Table 12.4, the observation is

- Normal accounts (A, B, C) show *consistent*, repetitive transaction patterns.
- Fraud ring (D ↔ E ↔ C) forms a suspicious subgraph:
  - High-value transactions
  - Quick chain transfers
  - New or rarely seen accounts

12.2 Comparison with Supervised Graph Learning

Traditional supervised graph learning depends on labeled nodes that are labeled with a target value or class label. SSL does not depend on labeled nodes, but it directly gets the information from the graph structure itself. The comparison between supervised and SSL is given in Table 12.5.

Table 12.5 Difference between supervised graph learning and self-supervised learning.

Features	Supervised Graph Learning	Self-Supervised Learning
Input	Labeled graph	Unlabeled graph
Nature of supervision	Requires external supervision in the form of labeled data	Uses internal supervision (auto-generated)
Learning objective	Task-specific prediction	Representation Learning
Sensitivity	High with noisy labels	Low
Feature learning	Guided by labels	Data-driven and exploratory
Example	Node classification	Contrastive graph pretraining

12.3 Fundamentals of GCL

12.3.1 Motivation: Why Contrastive Learning for Graphs?

Traditional supervised and unsupervised machine learning techniques are not suitable for producing efficient models, as graph data are structured, complex, irregular, dynamic, and relational. Many graphs are unlabeled graphs used in bioinformatics, social media, transportation, and network security. Also, labeled graph usage is very low and inexpensive to obtain. There is an imbalance between labeled and unlabeled graphs.

Annotating or labeling the graph nodes is expensive in many applications. For example, labeling proteins in a molecular interaction network needs expert biochemical validation, and in financial transactions, labeling nodes is difficult as there is rare fraudulent behavior. Also, limited data sharing restricts access to labeled financial transactions. Capturing topological and semantic relations efficiently, creating robust, transferable embeddings suitable for diverse tasks, learning from unlabeled yet information-rich graph data, and providing a scalable graph network are needed. This leads to the development of SSL techniques.

SSL enables graph models to learn intrinsic structures and relationships directly from the data without human-provided labels. But, among various SSL approaches, contrastive learning has emerged as one of the most effective paradigms for graph representation learning.

Contrastive learning offers an effective method to learn graph representations without requiring labeled data. The main objective is to bring similar (positive) pairs of nodes, subgraphs, or entire graphs closer in the embedding space while pushing dissimilar (negative) pairs apart. GCL has become a self-supervised bridge between data abundance and label scarcity, making the model to generalize better across domains.

12.3.2 Key Components and Mechanism

Instead of explicit labeling, the GCL model learns by comparing the features or structures of neighborhood nodes and the community. The core components of GCL are anchor, positive and negative samples, encoder network, and contrastive objective function.

12.3.2.1 Anchor, Positive and Negative Samples

An anchor is defined as the reference data point (i.e., a node, subgraph, or entire graph) whose representation serves as the center of comparison. This anchor helps in finding out how similar the samples are or how different they are.

Example ***Social Network Graph***

In a social network graph, if we take node A as the anchor node, we want to understand how similar or different other nodes (people) are in relation to Alice based on her connections and attributes. Any node can be taken as an anchor.

Example ***Author Citation Graph***

In Fig. 12.4, the nodes {author A1, A2, A3, A4} are taken as anchors. If the A1 author node is taken as the anchor, which represents A1's publication and citation behavior.

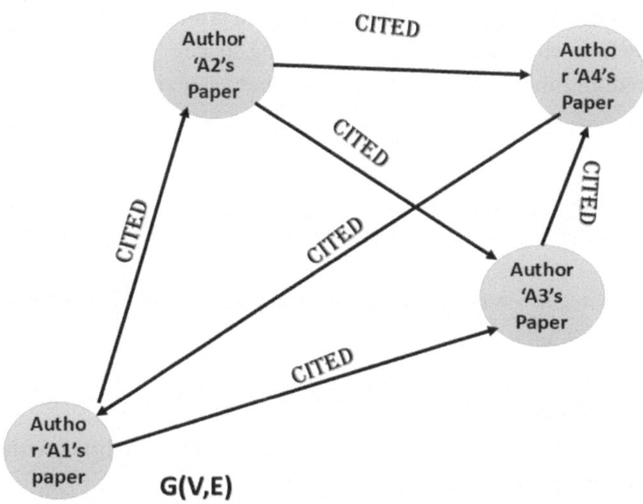

Figure 12.4 Core component example using author citation graph.

Positive Sample A positive sample is defined as another node that is semantically or structurally similar to the anchor. In other words, a node that has a similar property as the anchor node. It is also denoted as a node that has a similar community pattern.

Example ***Social Network***
For the anchor node A, a positive sample could be A's augmented version where some of her edges (friends) or attributes (profile details) are masked.

The model learns that despite such changes, both represent the same underlying person.

Example ***Author Citation Graph***
In an author citation graph, a positive can be

- An augmented view of A1's node (e.g., after masking some citation edges), or
- Another author node (e.g., A2) who frequently co-authors with A1 or is cited by the same community of researchers.

If A2 publishes in *machine learning conferences* and often co-authors with A1 or cites similar foundational papers, he forms a positive pair with A1.

The model learns that A1 and A2 are semantically similar within the research community.

Negative Sample A negative sample is not a similar node and is an unrelated entity that should be far away from the anchor in the embedding space.

It offers contrast, enabling the model to differentiate between similar and dissimilar samples.

Example ***Social Network***
In the same social network, B belongs to a different community and has no mutual connections with A.

Therefore, B serves as a *negative sample* for A; the model learns that their representations should be distinct.

Example ***Author Citation Graph***
A3, who publishes in *IoT* and has no citation overlap or co-authorship links with A1, becomes a negative sample.

The model should push A1's and A3's embeddings apart, learning that their research domains and citation networks differ.

12.3.2.2 Encoder Network

The encoder is a neural network model that transforms graph data into dense vector embeddings that capture both structural and node-level features.

In GCL, this is usually a GNN, such as

- GCN
- GraphSAGE
- GAT

Formally, given an input graph $G = (V, E)$, where V is the set of nodes and E is the set of edges:

$$h_i = f_\theta(v_i, \mathcal{N}(v_i))$$

where $\mathbf{h}_i$ is the embedding of node v_i, $\mathcal{N}(v_i)$ is the neighborhood of v_i, and f_θ is the GNN encoder parameterized by θ.

Example

In our social graph, the encoder processes each person's connections and features.

It learns that "A and B" have similar interaction patterns, resulting in closer embeddings in vector space.

In an author citation graph, each node represents an author, and each edge represents a citation or co-authorship link. Each node feature vector may include publication statistics, topic embeddings, or citation counts.

The encoder (GNN) processes this graph using message passing, where each author node updates its embedding based on its neighbors' information.

The encoder successfully maps similar authors (A1 and A2) closer in the embedding space, while distant authors (A3) are mapped farther apart.

These embeddings are then used in the contrastive objective to maximize agreement between related nodes.

12.3.2.3 Contrastive Objective Function (InfoNCE, JSD)

The contrastive objective defines how the model learns from comparisons between samples.

Its goal is to maximize similarity between positive pairs and minimize similarity between negative pairs.

Two common objectives are as follows.

a) **InfoNCE Loss**

The Info Noise-Contrastive Estimation (InfoNCE) loss is widely used in GCL frameworks such as Graph Contrastive Learning (GraphCL) and GRAph Contrastive lEarning (GRACE).

It measures how well the model can identify the positive sample among a set of negatives.

$$\mathcal{L}_i = -\log \frac{\exp\left(\frac{\text{sim}(h_i, h_i^+)}{\tau}\right)}{\sum_{j=1}^{N} \exp\left(\frac{\text{sim}\left(h_i, h_j^-\right)}{\tau}\right)}$$

where h_i: anchor embedding, h_i^+: positive embedding (augmented version of the same node), h_j^-: negative embeddings (different nodes or graphs), and τ: temperature parameter (controls the sharpness of the similarity distribution).

The numerator encourages similarity between anchor and positive pairs, while the denominator penalizes similarity with all negative samples.

b) **Jensen–Shannon Divergence–Based Loss**

Some models (e.g., Deep Graph Infomax) use Jensen–Shannon Divergence (JSD) to maximize mutual information between node-level and graph-level embeddings:

$$\mathcal{L}_{\text{JSD}} = \mathbb{E}_{\text{pos}}[\log D(h_i, s)] + \mathbb{E}_{\text{neg}}[\log(1 - D(h_j, s))]$$

where $D(\cdot)$ is a discriminator network estimating whether a node and a graph pair belong together and s represents a global summary vector of the graph.

This formulation helps the model align local (node-level) and global (graph-level) structures.

12.4 GCL Frameworks

The GCL framework is a self-supervised method that learns graphs by using similar (positive) and dissimilar (negative) samples. It aims to maximize agreement between different augmented views of the same graph while distinguishing it from unrelated graphs, enabling effective representation learning without labels. The components of GCL are graph encoder, graph augmentation, projection head, and contrastive objective [2] (Fig. 12.5).

12.4.1 Components

12.4.1.1 Graph Encoder

The main goal of the graph encoder is to transform a node or subgraph, or entire graph, into low-dimensional vector representations by gathering structural and feature information. The inputs are converted into vector embeddings. The input

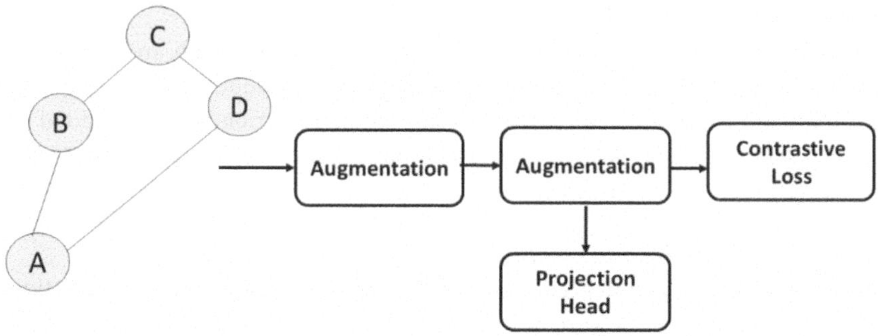

Figure 12.5 Graph contrastive learning frameworks with its components.

may be nodes or the entire graph. It captures both topological structure (connections) and node feature information. For example, in a social network, the encoder learns an embedding for each user based on their friendships and profile features.

Each node starts with an initial feature vector of information. Then the encoder aggregates the information from neighboring nodes based on their importance and frequent connections. It then updates each node's feature information. Finally, the embeddings capture global relational structure across the graph.

Example ***Author Citation Graph***
In the author citation graph, each node represents a citation and the node features may include publication o=count, h-index, specialization, and many more. During encoding, each author node collects information from neighboring authors' nodes it cites, or it is cited by some other author. After multiple layers, embedding becomes a context-rich representation that reflects both the research field and a similar pattern of publication. Authors working in similar domains or citing similar papers will have similar embeddings.

12.4.1.2 Graph Augmentation

Graph augmentation is the process of creating different "views" of the same graph by slightly altering its structure or features while still preserving its core meaning. Without augmentation, the model may overfit to one structure. Graph augmentation consists of three types, depending on what part of the graph is modified. The first type is structural augmentation, which focuses on changing the graph topology; feature-based augmentation, which modifies the attributes of nodes or edges while keeping the structure mostly the same; and the third type is semantic or contextual augmentation, which aims to preserve high-level meaning but change the context of the graph.

Example ***Social Network***

To perform graph augmentation, two different views of the graph are created as graph A and graph B. In graph A, a few users might be hidden, and in graph B, some connections might be slightly different, with a few friends' nodes added or deleted. The model receives both graphs as inputs. It learns to recognize that both graphs describe the same group of users.

Example ***Author Citation Graph***

When this graph gets augmented, one version might have a few missing citation links, as if some references were not recorded. Another version might have some topic data partially hidden, like removing keywords from paper titles. Even with these changes, the underlying semantic meaning remains the same. When both augmented graphs are fed into the model, the graph encoder learns to produce similar embeddings for the same author across both versions. The example is, if author A's citations to a few papers are missing in one version, the model still identifies A as a machine learning researcher because of the remaining connections and the similarity to others in the field.

12.4.1.3 Projection Head

After encoding, the embeddings are passed through a projection head. It maps embeddings into a new space where the contrastive loss is computed more effectively. This improves discrimination between positive and negative pairs.

Example

Two embeddings of the same author (from augmented graphs) are projected closer in this space.

12.4.1.4 Contrastive Objective Function

The contrastive loss ensures that positive pairs (same node or graph under different augmentations) have similar embeddings, and negative pairs (different nodes or graphs) have dissimilar embeddings. Common loss functions are InfoNCE Loss and NT-Xent Loss.

Example

If two papers belong to the same topic cluster, their embeddings should be close even if one's references are masked.

12.5 Conclusion

GCL helps the graph representations to learn from unlabeled data. By using the concept of SSL, GCL enables models to extract hidden relationships and structural semantics through the comparison of positive and negative samples derived from augmented graph views. In this chapter, we explored the components of GCL, and it is highly effective across domains.

Further Reading

1 L. Wu, H. Lin, C. Tan, Z. Gao, and S. Z. Li, "Self-supervised learning on graphs: Contrastive, generative, or predictive," *IEEE Trans. Knowl. Data Eng.*, vol. 35, pp. 4216–4235, 2021, doi: 10.1109/TKDE.2021.3131584.

2 Shuai, J., et al. (2022). A review-aware graph contrastive learning framework for recommendation. In: Proc. 45th Int. ACM SIGIR Conf. Res. Dev. Informat. Retr. New York, NJ: ACM, pp. 1283–1293.

3 X. Chen and S. Li, "A good view for graph contrastive learning," *Entropy*, vol. 26, no. 3, 2024, doi: 10.3390/e26030208.

4 Gao, T.; Yao, X.; Chen, D. Simcse: Simple contrastive learning of sentence embeddings. arXiv 2021, arXiv:2104.08821.

5 T. Chen, S. Kornblith, M. Norouzi, and G. Hinton, "A simple framework for contrastive learning of visual representations," in Proc. Int. Conf. Mach. Learn. (ICML), Vienna, Austria, PMLR 119, 2020, 2020, pp. 1597–1607.

6 T. Wang and P. Isola, "Understanding contrastive representation learning through alignment and uniformity on the hypersphere," in Proc. Int. Conf. Mach. Learn. (ICML), Vienna, Austria, PMLR, 2020 2020, pp. 9929–9939.

7 J. D. Robinson, C.-Y. Chuang, S. Sra, and S. Jegelka, "Contrastive learning with hard negative samples," in Proc. Int. Conf. Learn. Represent. (ICLR), ICLR, Addis Ababa, Ethiopia 2020.

8 L. Wu, H. Lin, T. Cheng, Z. Gao, and Stan Z Li., "Self supervised learning on graphs: Contrastive, generative, or predictive," *IEEE Trans. Knowledge Data Eng.*, vol. 35, 2021, no. 4, pp. 4216–4235, 2021.

9 Yanqiao Zhu, Yichen Xu, Qiang Liu, and Shu Wu 2021. An empirical study of graph contrastive learning. In *Proceedings of the Neural Information Processing Systems Track on Datasets and Benchmarks*, Joaquin Vanschoren and Serena Yeung (Eds.), Vol. *1*. Curran Associates, Inc. Published in NeurIPS Datasets and... 2 September 2021 Computer Science ArXiv. https://doi.org/10.48550/arXiv.2109.01116.

10 Y. Liu *et al.*, "Graph self-supervised learning: A survey," *IEEE Trans. Knowl. Data Eng.*, vol. 35, pp. 1–5900, 2022, doi: 10.1109/TKDE.2022.3172903.

11 S. Min, Z. Gao, J. Peng, L. Wang, K. Qin, and B. Fang, "STGSN–a spatial–temporal graph neural network framework for time-evolving social networks," *Knowl. Based Syst.*, vol. 214, 106746, 2021, doi: 10.1016/j.knosys.2021.106746.

13

Multimodal Graph Representation Learning

In Chapter 12, we discussed graph contrastive learning (GCL, which uncovers hidden information about data and uses it to classify it without labeled data. However, the data may come from different sources, such as text, images, videos, and numerical data. To capture complex data, we need to know about multiple data types and how to combine all the data types into a unified graph framework. Chapter 13 deals with multimodal graph representation learning (GRL), which focuses on combining multiple types of data into a unified graph framework. This approach enables a deeper understanding and more powerful representation of complex data.

13.1 Introduction to Multimodal GRL

The emerging area of research to solve the challenges of combining the different types of data is multimodal GRL. Multimodal GRL aims to combine various types of data into a unified graph structure, where each modality contributes unique semantic and structural information. By integrating these modalities, models can learn more comprehensive and meaningful graph representations. For example, in a social network graph, user posts (text), profile pictures (images), and interactive patterns (links) together describe relationships more accurately than any single modality alone.

Unlike traditional graph learning methods that process only one type of information, multimodal GRL integrates multiple data sources to capture both structural connections and semantic relationships. This leads to a more accurate representation of nodes and their interactions.

The process of multimodal GRL involves three steps. The first step is to represent different modalities as graph features; the second step is to fuse them into a common embedding space; and the third step is to learn unified representations using graph neural networks (GNNs) or contrastive methods.

The importance of using multimodal GRL is that today's real-world data is dynamic, and it comes from social media postings, sharing images, and interacting using links. Also, models trained on multimodal data give better learning and improve decision-making. Likewise, the machine learning (ML) systems mimic more like humans and become more intuitive and intelligent. Multimodal GRL improves many real-world tasks in diverse applications.

Example ***Social Network***

Facebook has become a crucial social media platform for information sharing, communication, and community building. It connects people with similar patterns globally. Business people analyze their business using Facebook, one of the vital social media components.

In the Facebook environment, each user is considered a node in the graph. Friendships, followers, likes, or comments are represented as edges. Each node has different types of modalities such as posts, comments as text, profile picture, shared photos, and stories as images, and location, time, and likes as metadata. Traditional models work with relationships only. However, multimodal GRL learns from various types of data. It learns from postings, interests, visual patterns, and content. The final output is a learned embedding vector that improves recommendations, content meaning, and user experience.

13.2 Types of Modalities in Graph Data

Modality refers to the different types of data or input formats. There are different types of data, such as text modality, image modality, audio modality, video modality, structured modality, and spatial modality.

13.2.1 Text Modality

The inputs given to the model will be in text format (words, sentences, documents). It helps the model to understand the semantic relationships in the graph. In a graph, text is represented in numerical form by using an embedding technique. Natural language processing (NLP) is used for the entire process of text representation. The text is broken into words or tokens. The tokens are represented as vectors by using pre-trained models such as Word2Vec, GloVe, or BERT. The next step is to combine all word vectors to get a single node text embedding. Once the text embeddings are attached to nodes, GNNs process them along with structural connections. Text modality works on learning semantic similarity and structural similarity.

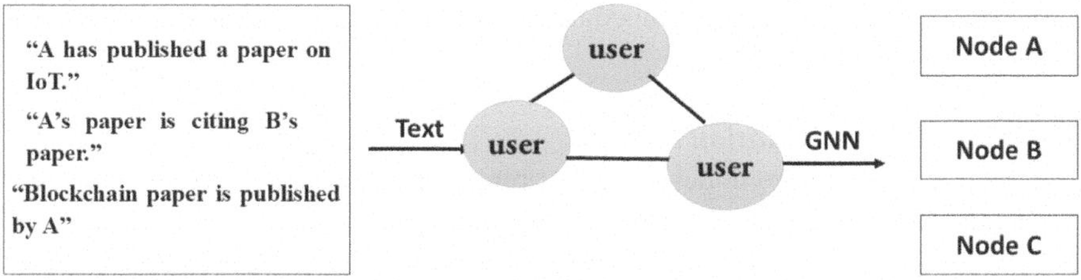

Figure 13.1 Text modality in author citation graph.

Example ***Author Citation Graph***

Nodes represent research papers, authors, and paper titles. Edges denote the citation relationship. Paper titles, author names, and abstracts are text modalities.

Consider the text:

"A has published a paper on IoT."

"A's paper is citing B's paper."

"Blockchain paper is published by A."

The first statement is represented as the author's name in node A; the second statement represents the author's paper in node B; and the third statement represents the paper title. These texts are given as inputs to the graph shown in Fig. 13.1.

The graph structure shows that each node is a user and the edges show their social connections. Text features from each user are converted into embeddings and attached to their respective nodes. This is then processed by GNN using textual and structural information to learn node representations (Node A, Node B, Node C), which can then be used for tasks such as recommendation, community detection, or interest prediction.

If two papers have a similar title, the text embeddings will be close in vector space even if they are not directly connected in the citation graph. Then, GNN is used to learn the relationships by using the connections and also by using the text meaning.

13.2.2 Image Modality

Image modality refers to photos, figures, diagrams, or any other image-based information. In a social media network example, people upload profile pictures or post pictures. These are the image modalities. In a graph, nodes are represented as users, and edges are represented as tags, likes, and comments. The image modalities are profile photos, shared images, etc. The model helps to identify visual similarities, like people posting similar kinds of images or styles.

The images are given as inputs. CNN or Vision Transformers (ViT) are used to extract visual features. Then the embedding model converts the image into a dense numerical vector. This image embedding becomes a feature of the corresponding node in the graph.

Example ***Author Citation Graph***
Consider a graph where nodes represent research papers/authors and edges represent citation relationships. Each paper node contains images such as figures, charts, and experimental results as images. Assume we have two research papers:

1) Paper A includes CNN architecture diagrams
2) Paper B includes transformer architecture visualizations.

Even if both papers don't cite each other directly, their image embeddings may be similar, showing that they discuss related methods. After generating image embeddings, the model combines them with text and structural information. Fusion techniques such as early fusion, late fusion, or attention-based fusion combine image and text embeddings before graph learning.

Some of the benefits of image modality are richer node representation, improved classification/clustering, enhanced similarity detection, help identifying figures copied, and supporting cross-domain learning.

13.2.3 Audio Modality

This refers to speech or sound data associated with the node. Sound-based data includes music, environmental sounds, or any acoustic signals. These sounds carry meaningful information about nodes and relationships in a graph. Audio reveals emotion, tone, rhythm, or speaker voice that text or image cannot capture. When integrated into a graph, they help models learn richer multimodal representations. Audio adds a temporal and emotional layer to the graph's understanding.

Example ***Social Media Network Graph***
Today's social media platforms, such as Instagram Reels, TikTok, and YouTube Shorts, use texts, images, and audio content. This audio content plays a vital role in understanding the user's interests, content similarity, and interaction dynamics.

Nodes represent user videos, reels, and voice clips, and edges represent the relationships such as "follows," "likes," "shares," and "comments."

Background music, speech, or sound effects are the audio modality. Each audio is collected from posts and converted to a feature representation using models such as VGGish, YAMNet, or Wav2vec 2.0. Then, attach the audio embedding with the nodes and construct a graph. Finally, a GNN learns patterns between the nodes.

13.3 Data Fusion Techniques in Multimodal GRL

13.3.1 What Is Data Fusion?

Data fusion refers to the process of combining data or information from various sources of different data types or modalities to produce a unified and richer representation that improves learning and decision-making. The data types may be text, images, audio, video, numerical data, etc. In multimodal GRL, the graph is represented by nodes with different features from different modalities. For example, in a social network (Facebook), the nodes are considered as users, products, and posts, and the features of each node have modalities such as text (captions, comments), images (profile pictures, product photos, posts' pictures), audio (background music, comments through speech), and video.

Data fusion merges all these diverse modalities into node embedding, so that the graph models can learn from these embeddings and decisions can be taken based on the knowledge gained from the model.

13.3.1.1 The Importance of Data Fusion

- To give a description about the text and an interpretation about the images.
- To use images or voice to clarify the unclear text.
- To transform heterogeneous information into a unified, robust representation.
- To improve the performance of the model for recommendation and classification.
- To discover the interaction between modalities.

13.3.2 Data Fusion Techniques

There are three main categories in data fusion in multimodal learning:

A) Early Fusion
B) Intermediate (Joint) Fusion
C) Late Fusion

13.3.2.1 Early Fusion

Early fusion happens during the input level before being fed into the model. Raw or preprocessed features from different modalities are combined into a single vector for each node.

Consider a social network graph as an example, each node represents a user or a post. Each node has features from different modalities, such as user posts, comments as text, profile picture, or post photo as image, voice message as audio, and links between users as a graph. These features are merged/fused into a vector before being used by the GNN model for learning.

Let X_t, X_i, and X_a be the text features, image features, and audio features. Then, early fusion is denoted by

$$X_f = f\,(X_t \,||X_i||\, X_a) \tag{13.1}$$

where X_f is the input node feature to the models.

Working Process The step-by-step process of the early fusion technique is shown in layers (Fig. 13.2).

Step 1. Input Modalities Layer

The top layer has three different types of input data such as text, image, and audio modalities.

Each represents a different source of information associated with a node in the graph. Each modality is first converted into a numerical vector representation called an embedding using suitable feature extractors.

Step 2. Feature Fusion Layer

This layer is the middle layer called fusion concatenation/fusion. All the extracted features from different modalities are aligned (normalized/projected)

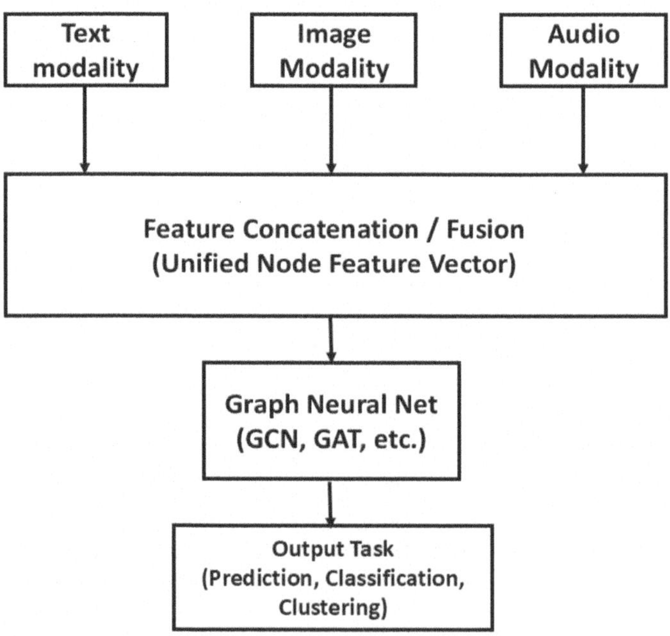

Figure 13.2 Early fusion working process.

to a common dimensional space called latent space. Then they are fused through a linear combination. This fused vector now represents all available information about the node into a single, unified representation.

At this stage, the multimodal information is merged early before any graph learning takes place, allowing the model to learn combined representations.

Step 3. GNN Layer

After fusion, the fused node features are passed into a GNN. This is represented by the middle layer "Graph Neural Net (GCN, GAT, etc.)."

Each node is represented by its fused multimodal vector. The GNN then performs message passing or graph convolution to learn how nodes influence each other through edges (relationships) and how multimodal information interacts across the graph structures.

Step 4. Output Layer

The bottom layer is "Output Task (Prediction, Clustering, Classification etc.)," which represents the final stage of the multimodal graph learning process. After the GNN processes the fused features, the resulting embeddings are used for various downstream tasks such as node classification, link prediction, community detection, and recommendation systems.

Advantages:

- Simple and computationally efficient.
- Captures correlations between modalities early.
- Easy to implement in graph models.

Disadvantages:

- If one modality is noisy, it can affect the entire fused representation.
- Fixed fusion may not handle missing modalities.
- Doesn't consider cross-modal attention or weighting.

13.3.2.2 Intermediate (Joint) Fusion

In this method, each modality is processed first separately to extract features. Then they are fused at a later intermediate stage of the model, during the GNN process. It is called "Joint" fusion because it is not done once, but instead gradually allows each modality to interact while preserving its unique presentation.

Early fusion fuses all the modalities to be fused into one vector at the beginning. This may lead to the loss of information for later analysis. So, intermediate or joint fusion is needed as it fuses the modalities during the middle process of the model.

Working Process The step-by-step process of the Early Fusion technique is shown in layers (Fig. 13.3).

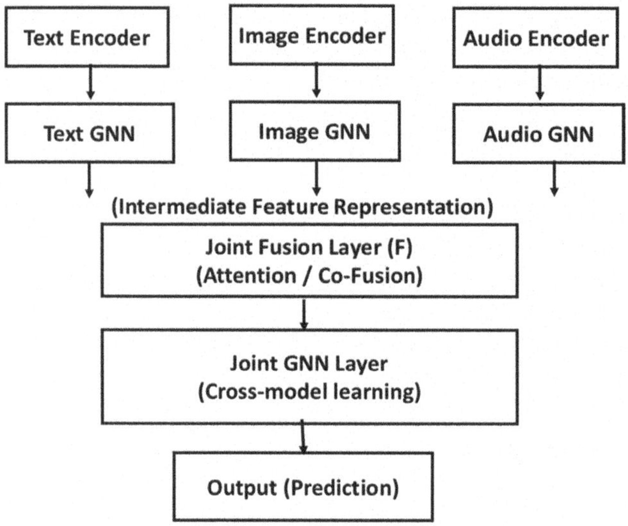

Figure 13.3 Intermediate fusion working process.

Step 1 Input Layer (Separate Modality Encoders)

From the diagram, we see that each modality is fed into its own encoder to extract the features of its type. Text encoders such as BERT/Glove are used on the text input and create text embedding. Similarly, images are used by encoders (ResNet) to create image embedding, and audio inputs are used by encoders (CNN) to create audio embedding. This shows that separate vectors are created for each modality. Each embedding preserves the semantics of each modality.

Step 2 Modality-Specific Graph Layers

Each modality has its own graph, and these graph undergoes GNN propagation independently:

$$H_T{}^{(l)} = \mathrm{GNN}_T\left(H_T{}^{(l-1)}, A_T\right) \tag{13.2}$$

$$H_I{}^{(l)} = \mathrm{GNN}_I\left(H_I{}^{(l-1)}, A_I\right) \tag{13.3}$$

$$H_A{}^{(l)} = \mathrm{GNN}_A\left(H_A{}^{(l-1)}, A_A\right) \tag{13.4}$$

where $H_M{}^{(l)}$ is the feature matrix for modality M at layer l and A_M is the adjacency matrix for that modality's graph. Each feature matrix is given as input to the next layer.

Step 3 Intermediate Fusion Layer

At this stage, the separate embeddings are jointly fused, and the fusion takes place between GNN layers. The fusion function F combines embeddings as

$$H_{\text{joint}}{}^{(l)} = F\left(H_T{}^{(l)}, H_I{}^{(l)}, H_A{}^{(l)}\right) \tag{13.5}$$

Equation 13.5 concatenates or fuses the feature matrix of each modality (text, image, and audio). Fusion also includes attention-based weighting (learning is done based on the attention of each modality); co-attention networks, where text and image attend to each other; and bilinear pooling, which captures multiplicative interactions between modalities.

Step 4 Joint GNN Propagation

Joint GNN layers are used to operate on the fused multimodal graph. Each fused component undergoes another set of processes using the GNN function

Step 5 Output Layer

The joint embeddings are used for node classification, link prediction, and community detection.

Advantages

- Learns complex inter-modal interactions.
- Can give more weight to informative modalities.
- Works well with partially missing data.

Disadvantages

- More computational cost.
- Requires careful design and tuning.

13.3.2.3 Late Fusion (Decision-Level Fusion)

In this layer, each modality acts in its own way independently, and finally, its outputs are combined. In this layer, the features are not fused; only the outputs are fused. The decisions or predictions taken are fused at this final stage. For example, in the author citation graph, each node represents a user or a paper, and edges represent citations or co-authors. Each paper includes text and images such as figures, charts, or diagrams. To predict the similarity among the papers, the text and image modalities work independently with GNN functions working on the adjacency matrices and embeddings. Finally, the prediction is fused. If a paper's abstract discusses deep learning and its images contain neural network diagrams, both models predict "AI category," and when the output from both modalities is fused, they also confirm the same. When compared to other fusion methods, this layer merges only the decisions or final representations.

Working Process The step-by-step process of late fusion is given in Fig. 13.4.

Step 1 The Input Process

Each text modality, image modality, and audio modality is given as input to the text encoder, image encoder, and audio encoder, respectively. For example, in the author citation graph, the abstract is the text modality, the figures are the image modality, and the citation pattern is the graph modality. Each of these modalities provides unique information.

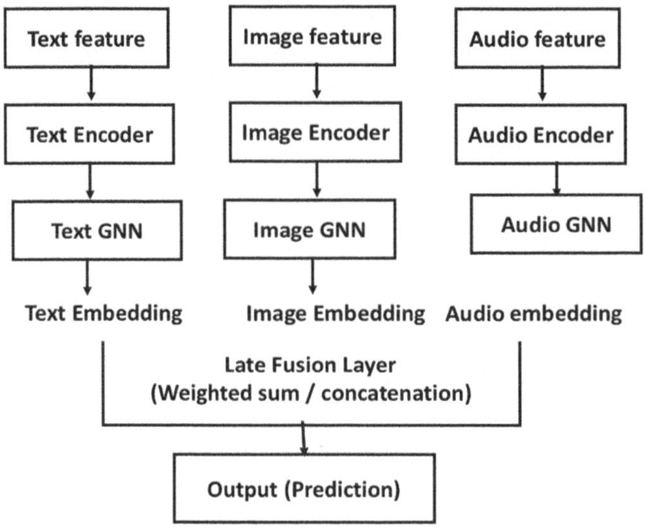

Figure 13.4 Late fusion working process.

Step 2 Independent Modality Processing

Each node's text is fed into a text encoder. Likewise, other modalities feed their inputs to their encoders. The output from this stage is the embedding vector (text embedding, image embedding, or audio or graph embedding).

Consider three independent embeddings per node as Z_T, Z_I, Z_A, and Z_G.

Step 3: Independent Learning Stage

Each modality can be trained separately, and they produce modality-specific models with outputs (embeddings). The output is the probabilities of prediction.

$$P_T = F_r(X_T), P_I = F_I(X_I), P_A = F_A(X_A), \text{and } P_G = F_G(X_G)$$

Step 4 Fusion Stage (Late Fusion)

Now, at this step, the separate outputs are combined. The different methods to combine the embeddings are (a) weighted average fusion, (b) concatenation + meta classifier, and (c) stacking.

Step 5 Decision Output Stage

The fused outputs are final classification, final embedding, or graph-level prediction. If the task is paper classification, the late fusion model will predict the topic label such as "GNNs" based on combined evidence from text, image, audio, or graph.

Advantages

- Modularity, robustness, interpretability, easy to add/remove modalities, works well when modalities are asynchronous or missing.

Disadvantages

- Misses deep cross-modal feature interactions (less expressive than joint fusion).
- Can be suboptimal when modalities strongly complement at the feature level.
- Might require careful probability calibration and normalization of representations before fusion.

13.4 Applications

13.4.1 Autonomous Vehicles

Autonomous vehicles are also known as self-driving cars without drivers. The system uses sensors for capturing its environment and for navigating without any human intervention. The technologies used are artificial intelligence (AI), ML, and computer vision. Using a perception system, they collect the raw data from sensors such as cameras, LiDAR, GPS, and ultrasonic sensors. This system will identify the lanes, pedestrians, and obstacles. GPS is used to determine the exact position of the vehicle. Controlling the entire system and decision-making is done using AI models automatically. The problem is to predict the traffic flow on roads.

13.4.1.1 Graph Representation

Consider an autonomous vehicle graph G with nodes {Sensors, Vehicles} and edges {Roads, Communication Links}.

13.4.1.2 Modalities

- Image/Videos: camera feeds
- Signal: LiDAR, radar data
- Text/Metadata: GPS coordinates, timestamps

Image/video modalities are used to detect objects such as pedestrians, other vehicles, traffic lights, and bumps on roads. Point cloud (3D) modalities from LiDAR are used to estimate the distance or depth. Radar modality taken from radio sensors is used to detect motion and speed during a change in the climate. Text modalities taken from road instruction and navigation maps are used for planning the route. Finally, noises from the environment, sound from sirens, and horns are the audio modalities to give awareness of the environment.

13.4.1.3 Working Process of the Multimodal GRL

Step 1: Multimodal Data Collection

All the modalities discussed above are collected by the autonomous vehicles.

Step 2: Feature Extraction for Each Modality

Each sensor's data is processed by a specialized feature extractor, such as an encoder, to produce an output of a feature vector. For extracting features from images, CNN or ResNet, or vision transformer can be employed, and the output might be visual feature vectors of objects in the road.

After this stage, every sensor produces an output of feature embedding.

Step 3: Multimodal Fusion

All modalities' feature vectors are combined (fused) into a unified node representation using a fusion technique.

Step 4: GNN Processing

GNN learns the high-level representation after fusing takes place in the graph. Each node updates its features based on information from neighborhood nodes, simulating how objects influence each other. For example, if a vehicle in front slows down, the next vehicle node receives this signal through the graph edges and decelerates. GNNs process the graph to perceive, reason, and make safe driving decisions in real time (Fig. 13.5).

13.4.2 Agriculture—Pest Detection Network

Agriculture is the essential sector in real-world applications. Many research areas in agriculture are crop health monitoring, yield prediction, pest detection, irrigation management, fertilizer recommendation, weather impact assessment, and supply chain optimization. Agriculture depends on data from heterogeneous

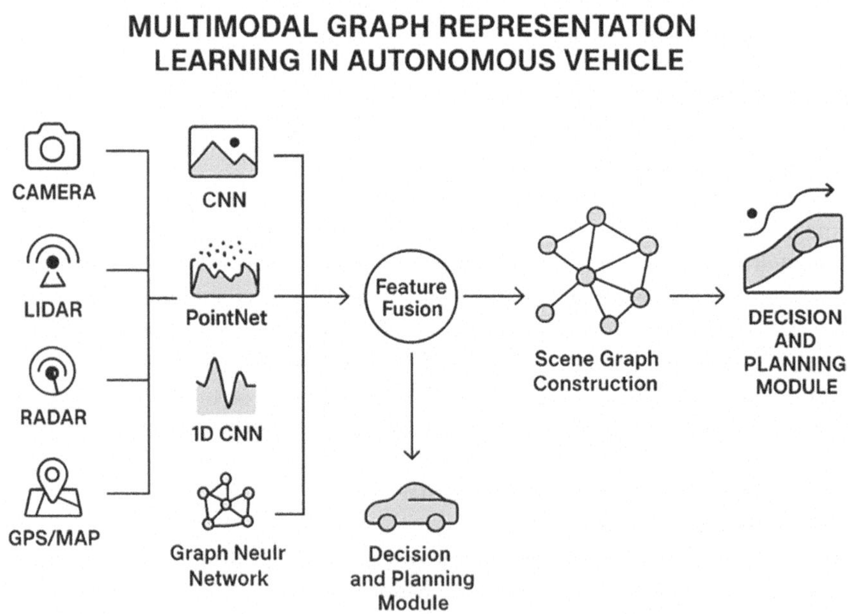

Figure 13.5 Autonomous vehicle's multimodal graph pipeline.

sources such as satellite images, soil sensors, weather data, crop reports, and text descriptions from farmers or experts.

The pest detection network uses multimodal GRL to identify diseases affecting plants. The graph is used to find the relationship between different farms, crop types, and environmental conditions. If pests are detected in a field node, the graph can predict the likelihood of the spread of the disease to neighboring nodes based on the connectivity. This helps the farmers take early preventive actions, reducing crop damage.

13.4.2.1 Graph Representation

Consider a graph with farms, crop fields as nodes and neighboring farms and irrigation connections as edges.

13.4.2.2 Modalities

- Images are the modalities taken from the satellite or drone.
- Sensor data are the numerical/signal modalities taken from the soil moisture, temperature, humidity, rainfall, and pH.
- Texts are the modalities taken from farmers' logs and weather reports.
- Graph structures are the modalities taken from spatial or relational links between farms, regions, or sensors.

13.4.2.3 Working Process of the Multimodal GRL

Step 1: Multimodal Data Collection

All the modalities discussed above are collected. Different types of agricultural data are collected.

Step 2: Feature Extraction for Each Modality

Images of pest shapes and leaf damage are the features preprocessed using CNN. Text data and sensor data are encoded into numerical features. Special data are converted into graph nodes and edges to represent the relationship between locations. These features are standardized for fusion.

Step 3: Multimodal Fusion

This step has three techniques, and based on the merging of features, vital information interacts and produces meaningful output.

Step 4: GRL

GNN or GAT learns embeddings for each node by aggregating multimodal information from neighboring nodes. The model captures the relationship between crop type and pest occurrence, and pest spread details.

Step 5: Prediction and Decision Support

The ML model performs pest detection by identifying the presence and type of pest, forecasting pest outbreaks in nearby nodes, and visualizing high-risk farm zones (Fig. 13.6).

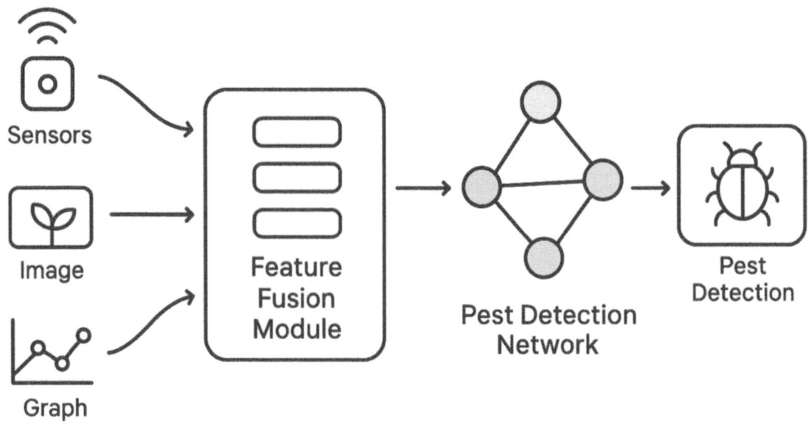

Figure 13.6 Pest detection network multimodal graph pipeline.

As shown in Fig. 13.6, multimodal GRL is pest detection that combines all the modalities to analyze pest patterns and detect the pest diseases that affect the crop and farms.

13.5 Conclusion

Heterogeneous complex data are handled by multimodal GRL. All the modalities are integrated, and the information are used for producing the output. By combining the modalities through effective data fusion techniques, this model enhances the accuracy of graph-based learning. This approach captures not only deeper structure but also relationships and improves the performance in various domains. The case study taken in this chapter is the pest detection network in agriculture and autonomous vehicles. Intelligent decisions can be made by AI models.

Further Reading

1 A. Bordes, N. Usunier, A. Garcia-Duran, J. Weston, and O. Yakhnenko, "Translating embeddings for modeling multi-relational data," in *Advances in Neural Information Processing Systems 26*, C.J.C. Burges, L. Bottou, M. Welling, Z. Ghahramani, and K.Q. Weinberger, Eds. Lake Tahoe, Nevada: Curran Associates, Inc., 2013.

2 L. Yankai, L. Zhiyuan, S. Maosong, L. Yang, and Z. Xuan, "Learning entity and relation embeddings for knowledge graph completion. In 29th *AAAI Conf. AI*, Austin, Texas USA, January 25–30, 2015,", pp. 2181–2187, 2015.

3 Hatem M S, Teresa B, Iryna G, and Stefan R. 2018. A multimodal translation-based approach for knowledge graph representation learning. In 7th Joint Conf. Lexical Comput. Semantics, New Orleans, Louisiana, June, 2018, 225–234.

4 Karen Simonyan and Andrew Zisserman. 2014. Very deep convolutional networks for large-scale image recognition. arXiv preprint arXiv:1409.1556.

5 Q. Wang, Z. Mao, B. Wang, and L. Guo, "Knowledge graph embedding: A survey of approaches and applications," *IEEE Transac. Knowl. Data Eng.*, vol. 29, no. 12, pp. 2724–2743, 2017.20 September 2017

6 H. Zhou, X. Zhou, Z. Zeng, L. Zhang, and Z. Shen. "A comprehensive survey on multimodal recommender systems: Taxonomy, evaluation, and future directions", arXiv preprint arXiv:2302.04473.

14

Demystifying Graph Embeddings and Industrial Applications

14.1 Introduction

A graph is a popular mathematical structure primarily consisting of two main things: nodes (alternatively termed vertices) and edges that expound the relationships between the connected nodes. Nodes represent people, places, products, processes, etc., while edges articulate the usable relationships between these nodes. Graphs carry the unique ability to explicitly and exemplarily model and store these relationships. Unravelling the hidden yet beneficial relationships is a serious target for the data science team in any business behemoth and start-up. Thus, graphs are trumpeted as the most flexible and futuristic data structure for accurately representing and visualizing large-scale interconnected systems.

Graph analytics is for precisely detecting complex and hidden patterns using graph algorithms and extracting context to do comprehensive analytics. Graph representation learning (GRL) is a prominent activity to fasten graph analytics. In other words, learning effective graph embeddings for nodes, edges, and the total graph is imperative to derive sustainable business value from graph data. Generating graph embeddings is invaluable and indispensable for methodically simplifying and speeding up graph analytics. Another noteworthy transformation is the systematic leverage of groundbreaking machine and deep learning (ML/DL) models and agents on graph-structured data to rewardingly uncover hidden patterns and intricate relationships. Thus, AI-powered graph data analytics is being proclaimed as the way forward for availing all the expressed initial benefits. This chapter discusses the significance of graph embeddings and their industry use cases.

14.2 The Importance of Graph Representation

A graph is a powerful and promising data structure comprising two significant constructs: nodes (vertices or entities) and edges (links) that establish a valuable linkage between nodes. That is, edges can exhibit the relationships that exist and emerge among the graph entities. Graphs mathematically represent networks. We come across various networks in our everyday life (personal, professional, and social). Graphs guarantee an optimized and organized representation of network components. We are well-accustomed to the city route map. Other popular graphs/networks include city transportation networks, air flight routes, social networks, recommendation systems, molecular structures, etc. Graph theory is a hugely popular mathematical subject that deals with creating value out of graphs. We have networks of subject matter experts and even fraudsters, world cities, international supply chains, etc. Graphs have the strength to capture and encode the gist of complicated networks of relationships. Pioneers and pundits say graphs are the most influential and impactful tool for methodically representing and deeply analyzing interconnected information. A molecule can be represented as a small, sparse, and static graph, whereas a large, dense, and dynamic graph could represent a social network.

The graph paradigm is being widely used in real-world situations. The social network illustrates relationships between users. The web is the world's largest graph, establishing connections between web pages, services, and applications. Other popular graphs include supply chain networks, etc.

In the digital era, millions of microservices, billions of connected devices, and trillions of digitized elements interact purposefully and generate a massive quantity of multi-structured data. To make sense of such big data, graphs have become an indispensable tool for efficient data encoding, manipulation, and visualization. An optimal graph representation is important for readily acquiring value from digital data. That is, graph-structured data is pronounced as a more efficient representation for knowledge discovery and dissemination. Precisely speaking, efficient graph representation techniques are the most important contributing factor to the tremendous success of the graph paradigm.

14.3 Making Sense Out of Graph-Structured Data

As mentioned above, graphs are a deeply studied data structure that describes different object relationships. Most real-world data and problems (personal, social, and professional) can be represented and articulated through graphs. If any complex problem can be optimally represented using a formal and flexible structure, the problem and solution complexities can be drastically curtailed.

Graphs can represent the nanotubes that are used in nanoelectronics. In the case of chemical graph theory, the edges represent the chemical bonds that connect the compound's atoms, and the nodes represent the atoms themselves. In bioinformatics, biological networks represent the molecular structure of proteins. Thus, multiple domains immensely benefit from all the distinct advancements in the graph domain. Recently, with more business domains embracing the graph concept, the graph-structured data size has grown tremendously. Therefore, appropriate mechanisms are being rolled out to facilitate data scientists and graph theory researchers to work on graphs effectively. The techniques and tools for graph data processing, mining, and analytics to extract actionable insights in time look extremely promising. Problems such as fraud detection in banking and recommendation systems on streaming data are neatly solved through graph analytics.

The real challenge is decisively analyzing graph structure and relationships embedded for knowledge discovery and dissemination. Graph analytics needs a considerable amount of processing power and memory capacity. Therefore, graph embedding has attracted much attention, as it can transform a high-dimensional graph into a continuous, dense, and low-dimensional vector space. Of course, vectors preserve the original graph structure and features. There is no loss when graph nodes and edges are converted into vectors.

Graph data can be ingested into the ML/DL algorithms. This training results in ML/DL models that can perform classification, regression, clustering, etc. Another contribution is the much-insisted AI explainability and interpretability. AI models on graph-structured data can tell why they have made such a decision. Therefore, besides encoding real-world and real-time data in graphs, making sense of graph-structured data is essential through pioneering graph data analytics methods.

14.4 Delineating AI Model Engineering Steps

AI model engineering is a top activity as high-quality AI models are developed, deployed, and improved across business domains. AI models are to automate and accelerate business operations. In short, AI algorithms, enabling frameworks, automated tools, software libraries, best practices, integrated platforms, and AI accelerators in AI-centric processing units collectively speed up high-performing AI models' realization. Like microservices repositories (private and public), we now go into the era of AI model repositories. IT divisions of enterprising businesses, IT organizations, AI start-ups, independent software vendors, Global Capability Centres, etc. are upskilling their talent forces to bring competent AI models. Thus, AI model engineering methodology continuously advances to make AI models penetrative and pervasive.

Now that the agentic AI paradigm is becoming mainstream, there is a gradual transition from AI models to AI agents. Thus, the AI agent engineering process is getting sufficiently strengthened with the ready availability of agentic frameworks.

It is common knowledge that feature selection and optimization are vital for AI model engineering. Input data gets processed to arrive at a collection of features. The idea is that a feature set gives a meaningful and compact representation of the original dataset. The curated feature set helps in producing AI models. There are several AI algorithms (ML/DL) enabling the realization of competent AI models that are then evaluated for their performance, optimized through a host of techniques such as pruning, quantization, and knowledge distillation and then taken to production environments such as clouds (private, public, hybrid, and edge) through any standardized MLOps tool.

Once an AI model is deployed in any production environment, the model is meticulously and minutely monitored and observed to detect any degradation. There are robust monitoring and observability platform solutions to continuously capture all kinds of performance metrics, operational data, security, scalability, and health condition data. By leveraging AI-powered data analytics (batch and real-time processing), any performance drift and degradation of AI models can be proactively and preemptively detected and addressed with all the clarity and alacrity. That is, it is mandatory to maintain performance to gain the loyalty of consumers. The different phases of any AI model-building activities are illustrated below.

AI model engineering →, model evaluation →, model optimization →, model deployment →, model upgrade

Fortunately, the tool ecosystem is growing rapidly, so many manual activities are compactly automated, speedily resulting in breakthrough AI models and agents.

14.5 Graph Embeddings

14.5.1 The Need for Graph Embeddings

AI model engineering traditionally happens on tabular structured datasets. However, replicating the same on graph data comes with many challenges. Experts insist on formulating a simplified representation of graph data. Researchers have embarked on unearthing a strategically sound solution that guarantees meaningful representations of graphs. The concept of embeddings is being celebrated as the way forward to address the above-mentioned challenges and concerns. Graph embeddings have the ingrained capability to learn the graph representation that unwaveringly maintains the original graph structure. Formally speaking, embedding is a mapping function that transforms a discrete graph into a continuous space. Experts say this function must be learned and applied to the graph. A graph is the input to the function, resulting in a feature set [1]. This feature set is the input for an AI algorithm (ML/DL). Thus, a competent AI model can be made and deployed. Creating handcrafted feature sets is an error-prone and complicated task.

Graph representation vectors, alternatively termed graph embeddings, transform complex graph structures into numerical vectors. Advanced AI models can perform efficient analytics on vectors, helping to detect deeper relationships and hidden patterns within the graph.

Graph representation illustrates how a graph is stored and managed in memory. Analyzing complicated graphs/networks using conventional mechanisms is neither straightforward nor simple. Creating graph embeddings is recommended as the most favored and flavored approach for empowering data scientists, researchers, and AI engineers in their everyday assignments. That is, deeper and more decisive graph analysis can be accomplished mathematically by mapping graph nodes, edges, or even graphs to continuous vector spaces. The widely discussed graph analytics toward knowledge discovery is hugely enabled through graph embeddings. Several benefits are associated with the approach of graph embeddings.

Graph embeddings can help extract functional patterns and relationships hidden in graphs. ML/DL algorithms can be trained on graph embeddings (feature sets) to produce powerful AI models. Embeddings distill complex graph structures into simple numerical representations. Such dimensionality reduction leads to fewer computational resources being required.

Embedding vectors encode semantic and structural details. Vectors give low-dimensional and compact graph representations stored in a vector space. Graph embeddings optimize complicated graph structures as vectors. These vectors are generally real-valued and dense. They theoretically capture the essence of a node's position and role within the graph. Such a mapping brings many advantages, as illustrated elsewhere.

14.5.2 Knowledge Graph Embeddings

The main aim of knowledge graph (KG) embeddings (KGEs) is to represent entities/facts and their relationships in a KG using low-dimensional and dense vectors. As reported earlier, these vectors represent a continuous feature space and preserve the graph's intrinsic structure and semantics. As KGs (domain-specific and agnostic) are typically large enough to be comprehensive and cognitive in their offerings, such vector generation and representation enable optimized storage, accurate information retrieval, untangling hidden relationships, and faster inferencing. As conventional graphs show, generating vectors for entities and relationships is accomplished through an encoding scheme. A scoring function is also designed to verify and validate the facts. Finally, an optimization algorithm is employed to accurately learn the embeddings by minimizing a loss function over the training data.

In short, the entities and relations in the KG can be represented as embedding vectors in semantic space. These embedding vectors can be used to predict relationships between entities. Thus, KGE techniques empower AI engineers and data scientists to build and deploy high-end ML models and agents with heightened accuracy in their obligations.

There are a few KGE approaches, and we will discuss them in this section.

The first approach is triplet fact-based representation learning models. These models learn entity and relation embeddings from the observed facts in the KG. The facts are represented as triplets (h, r, t), where h is the head entity, t is the tail entity, and r is the relationship between h and t. These fact-based models first capture the structure and patterns within the triplets and generate embeddings. There are a few variants, such as tensor factorization-based, neural network (NN)-based, and translation-based models.

1) **Tensor factorization-based** models represent a KG as a three-way tensor (head entities, relations, and tail entities). Each element in the tensor tells the presence or absence of a triplet (h, r, t) in the KG. The idea is to decompose a large and sparse tensor into embeddings (low-dimensional vector representations).
2) **NN-based models** leverage different NN architectures to learn expressive embeddings for entities and relations. These models are becoming popular as they can deeply capture complex patterns and dependencies in the KG.
3) **Translation-based models** interpret relations as translations operating on entity embeddings. The point is that the tail entity embedding should be close to the head entity and the relation embedding. The distance between the translated head and tail entities determines the scoring function. Researchers have developed several models.

The second approach is to use description-based representation learning models. In addition to the triplet structure of the KG, these models use external data sources such as textual descriptions of entities and relations. This combination helps arrive at informative embeddings. These models are being subdivided into textual description-based and relation path-based models.

1) **Textual description-based models** incorporate textual information associated with entities and relations to enhance the quality of the embeddings.
2) **Relation path-based models** consider multi-hop relation paths in the KG to capture complex relationships between entities. These models simplify reasoning over longer distances in the graph.

There are a few mission-critical applications of KGEs. As articulated above, KGs have extreme advantages when surmounting language models. As we all know, many language models exist, such as large, small, vision, and multimodal. Domain-specific language models are being produced and released for wide use. KGs explicitly empower language models to generate contextually coherent and cogent responses. KGs assist in identifying context information, which is then fed into language models that plunge into response generation with all the sagacity, alacrity, and clarity. The other widely expressed applications include link prediction, triplet classification, question and answering, and recommendation systems.

KG completion (KGC) predicts missing links. KGs suffer from incompleteness. KGs, sometimes termed multi-relational heterogeneous graphs, are primarily static. However, many facts about the KGs have changed over time. Researchers are proposing appropriate methods showing improved prediction results by incorporating the temporal validity of facts.

As inscribed above, complex systems are being modeled as graphs of interconnected nodes. Biological systems are also represented as graphs of interconnected biological entities. There are graph exploratory methods to perform different analytical and predictive activities on such graphs. The challenge is that these methods support high predictive accuracy, and hence, they are not scalable. Therefore, new approaches (KGE models) have emerged for modeling and mining graphs. These models innately guarantee high scalability and predictive accuracy. They learn low-rank vector representations of graph nodes and edges. Research publications illustrate how KGE models are an excellent tool for biological KGs.

Neurological disorders, such as Alzheimer's and Parkinson's diseases, and mental disorders, such as depression and anxiety, need to be addressed through competent technologies. As research on diseases is gaining momentum, the amount of medical data is also equally growing. The accumulation of data is seen as a positive thing. With the ready availability of data, researchers and inspired minds can explore the ways and means that aid in slicing and studying data intensely. Physicians, surgeons, and specialists can precisely extract and utilize the information in their assignments.

A KG, an organized representation of facts, is a powerful tool for extracting the correct and relevant knowledge from large amounts of data. KGs are portrayed as a proven, promising, and potential mechanism for studying neurological and mental disorders.

For more information on KGEs, visit https://medium.com/@EleventhHourEnthusiast/a-survey-on-knowledge-graph-embedding-approaches-applications-and-benchmarks-894b53563cba.

14.5.3 The Advantages of Graph Embeddings

Node embeddings are calculated for each node and stored to simplify querying. Edge embeddings represent connections between nodes. Edge embeddings are derived from node embeddings and stored similarly. Graph-level embeddings represent entire subgraphs or the entire graph and facilitate graph-wide analytics.

Several graph databases are stuffed with the ability to store and search embedding (vector) data. With graph embeddings stored in a database, it is possible to perform nearest-neighbor searches. Such searches return the graph embeddings that articulate the graphs that are similar in structure. Experts say that the graph embeddings can include links to their corresponding graphs. This link enables the easy retrieval of the source graphs.

Consider a graph for bank customers. We can submit a query asking the graph database to retrieve the 10 graph embeddings similar to those of a particular customer. This method helps identify fraudulent identities faster and more accurately. Traditionally, it is all about searching for individual bits of customer and transaction data to find fraudsters.

As inscribed above, graph embeddings simplify graph analytics, emitting actionable insights for correct decision-making. Graph embeddings can also further enhance graph functionalities.

- **Capturing interconnectedness to bring additional value**—Graph embeddings can encapsulate the relationships encoded in a graph. This optimal encapsulation can considerably enhance the power and value of graph analytics in extracting deeper and decisive insights.
- **Enhanced capabilities through ML/DL**—Essentially, graph relationships are transitioned into vectors to accomplish bigger and better things. Such a transition opens up fresh possibilities and opportunities. Graph embeddings are a bridge and booster between graph-structured data and AI algorithms. A dazzling array of ML/DL operations can be applied to graph data by converting graph relationships into vectors.
- **Dimensionality reduction**—Graphs can be high-dimensional, as each node potentially relates to many other nodes. Graph embeddings can reduce this to a lower-dimensional space. This reduction uses reduced computational resources and improves the contributions of the ML/DL models.

Thus, the idea of graph embeddings has brought a tectonic shift in setting up and sustaining sophisticated AI systems. There are a few algorithms and libraries to create graph embeddings that have the ingrained strength to preserve the structural properties of the graph even with lower-dimensional vectors. Each node in a graph gets mapped to a vector of real numbers. There are two requirements. Nodes close in the graph must have similar embeddings (proximity preservation). Second, nodes that play similar roles in the graph must have similar embeddings (structural equivalence). Many futuristic applications can be envisaged and accomplished through the smart leverage of graph embeddings.

14.5.4 Graph Embedding Applications

A graph can represent protein interactions, road networks within and across cities, citation networks, social networks, chemical bonds, etc. With the faster maturity and stability of graph embedding techniques and tools, many applications are being envisaged and implemented. Graphs support AI to support human-like capabilities. Experts continuously explore and expound fresh applications that leverage graph embeddings. In this section, we will discuss the key applications of graph embeddings.

Node classification is the process of automatically identifying and assigning the correct target label to each node in a graph. In a social network, it is like identifying user preferences or demographic details for each user based on his or her connections. Graph embeddings come in handy here.

14.5.4.1 Clustering

This is another application that helps group specific nodes within a graph into clusters based on certain criteria. For example, two nodes are grouped if they are within a specific distance from each other. Ultimately, clustering forms subgraphs or communities that share or serve helpful information. In social networks, clustering specifically helps in community formation.

14.5.4.2 Anomaly Detection

This is to identify nodes, edges, or subgraphs that are outliers. This capability facilitates the timely detection of fraud or whether a certain attempt is a security attack.

Recommendation systems for e-commerce or content platforms—Any similarity between user and item embeddings can be used to make personalized recommendations.

Information retrieval—With a graph representation of documents and web content, information retrieval to extract context details is hugely simplified. Context details are more accurately obtained by integrating RAG and KGs. Furthermore, identifying similar entities helps accelerate the formation of KGs.

Link prediction is to predict additional edges to be established in a graph. Link prediction helps in the deeper analysis of graphs/networks. Several domain areas such as social networks, bioinformatics, cybersecurity, and e-commerce are systematically analyzed using link prediction. In short, graph embeddings bring the power to capture both local and global graph structures, making predictions more accurate and comprehensive. Graph embeddings are being pronounced as a versatile tool for accomplishing a variety of modern AI applications [2]. Fresh capabilities can be embedded in versatile, state-of-the-art AI systems by translating graph information into vectors. Complex and interconnected information can be tackled relatively easily by graph embeddings. The concept of graph embeddings has laid a stimulating and sparkling foundation for visualizing disruptive and transformative applications.

14.5.5 Types of Graph Embeddings

The phenomenon of graph embeddings is all set to become the de facto way to identify similar items in large billion-vertex graphs. Typically, the goal is to extract node-, edge-, or graph-level features to understand the network's topology. Then, these features are used to train and create classical AI models (ML/DL models) for prediction tasks. Feature engineering is a challenging and important step in the AI model engineering process. Designing features that effectively represent the graph's nodes and relationships is time-consuming. This needs domain expertise. Creating handcrafted features is highly time-consuming. Automated tools such as AutoML can produce AI models directly from the feature set. However, the automated model generation is beset with several challenges. Through their vast experience, AI engineers derive suitable AI models that satisfy the model performance metrics. To overcome this problem, the concept of node embeddings is stated as an automated solution. There are a few techniques to create graph embeddings. Let us start with the concept of node embedding.

As per AI leaders, graph embeddings can map the information stuffed in graphs into a flexible format (vectors) that is easy to manipulate through mathematical operations. Also, vectors are computationally efficient. Experts point out that graph analytics happens at three levels (node, edge, and graph). As expressed above, creating graph embeddings is the way forward to facilitate graph analytics. There are different techniques to generate embeddings for the above three levels. In this section, we will discuss them in detail.

14.5.5.1 Node Embeddings

An embedding vector corresponding to each node in the graph must be generated. The beauty here is that the embedding vector can mimic and maintain the graph representation and structure. Embeddings have the power to guarantee this: nodes near a graph are to have their vectors near each other.

An embedding is formally defined as a mapping from an input space to an output space, typically a lower-dimensional space. A 3D vector can be mapped to a 2D vector. In the case of graphs, a node embedding takes a node in a graph and creates a vector. Such a mapping results in several interesting use cases such as kNN similarity graph construction, link prediction, and node classification.

A city transportation network typically consists of all the major junctions within a city area. The idea is to learn node embedding for each junction using a GNN. As per the experts, the steps involved here are indicated as follows:

- Data preparation involves collecting information about each junction, including its geographical coordinates and intersection.
- Graph construction—The graph captures the connections and relationships between city junctions.
- Node features—Additional features can be incorporated for each junction. With more features, capturing detailed and decisive context information is hugely simplified.
- Node embedding learning—We can train a GNN on this freshly created city transportation graph to learn node embeddings. The GNN takes the graph structure and the node features as input and performs NN operations to learn the relationships in the data.
- Loss function—A loss function measures the difference between the desired and predicted node embeddings. It helps identify and move similar junctions closer in the embedding space.
- Optimization—It is all about fine-tuning the GNN iteratively to generate embeddings with all the relevant details of each city junction.
- Node embedding interpretation—By analyzing the embeddings of each junction, it is possible to pinpoint clusters of similar junctions based on various transportation-related characteristics. The embeddings can also be used as inputs for tasks such as predicting traffic patterns and recommending optimal routes.

Thus, the node embeddings help capture the city's transportation features. Once features are engineered and optimized, deeper analytics are sped up to uncover actionable insights that can enable transportation planning, articulate the infrastructure utilization levels, and enhance the travel experience for city residents.

Nodes represent research papers. Each paper cites specific other research papers. Edges formally represent this linkage between research papers. Node embeddings predict the class of nodes in a graph. One more example is as follows. There is a citation graph. Forecasting the topics of each research article in the graph is necessary. This is a link prediction use case.

In short, node embeddings represent each node in the graph as unique, low-dimensional vectors. Node embedding algorithms compute low-dimensional vector representations of nodes in a graph.

Node2Vec is a famous implementation of the node embedding technique. GraphSAGE is another popular one, which focuses on aggregating information from a node's local neighborhood to arrive at its embedding. Experts say that GraphSAGE can tackle large graphs by sampling fixed-size neighborhoods for each node during training.

In short, node embeddings (vectors) encode each node in a graph as a low-dimensional vector. This vector typically captures all the valuable information in the graph. The vector embeddings are supplied as the viable input to AI models that can learn meaningful and decision-enabling embeddings for nodes. These embeddings have the intensity and sagacity to capture and articulate the context details.

14.6 Edge Embedding Techniques

We discussed node embeddings above. Now, we jump into edge embeddings. Herein, all the edges in graphs are mapped into low-dimensional vectors. These vectors are to capture the relationships and their attributes neatly.

Here, an embedding vector is generated for each edge in the graph. These embeddings learn the edge attributes provided by the graph. In a social network, nodes are typically linked through edges based on different attributes such as age, location, and education. Edge embeddings aid in link prediction, articulating that a particular pair of nodes should have an edge connecting them.

14.6.1 Graph Embeddings

This is to generate an embedding vector representing each graph. Large graphs have many subgraphs. Each subgraph would have its corresponding embedding vector accurately representing the graph structure. Embeddings can capture a graph's structural and semantic information. KGEs are vector representations of entities and relationships in a KG. KGEs are mainly used to predict missing links and enable advanced ML/DL tasks.

Graph Embedding Techniques—These techniques primarily target the entire graph. Graph embedding algorithms transform graphs into a lower-dimensional vector space while maintaining structural information and node relationships intact. Graph embeddings enable advanced ML/DL tasks. Embeddings also simplify graph visualization and analysis. More details can be found at https://linkurious.com/graph-embeddings/.

1) **Factorization-Based Techniques**
   - **Graph Factorization**—In this method, the connections between vertices are represented as a matrix, which is factorized to arrive at a graph embedding.
   - **Laplacian Eigenmaps:** This method leverages a quadratic penalty function on the distance between embeddings to preserve node dissimilarity.
2) **Random Walk-Based Techniques**
   - **DeepWalk**—This GNN type uses language models to learn embeddings of vertices in a graph. This is a method leveraging random walks to

learn embeddings. There are a few critical applications, too. DeepWalk is helpful in network classification and anomaly detection. In addition, embeddings learned through this method can predict the likelihood of edges between nodes. The DeepWalk technique is scalable and, hence, can handle large-scale graphs. This method consumes comparatively few computational resources and can generalize well to unseen data (https://medium.com/@anhtuan_40207/paper-review-deepwalk-online-learning-of-social-representations-6aefac08c47).

DeepWalk first generates a set of random walks starting from each node in the graph. Each random walk is a sequence of nodes that starts at a particular node and moves to one of its neighbors at each step. These random walks capture the local structure of the graph and provide a way to learn representations of nodes that capture their relationships with nearby nodes. More details are found on this page (https://medium.com/@tejpal.abhyuday/deep-walk-and-node2vec-graph-embeddings-faf02d369442).

> Given a graph and a starting point, we randomly select a neighbor of the starting point. We continue this process by selecting the current point's random neighbors and moving on. This sequence of points visited in this manner constitutes a random walk on the graph (https://medium.com/@taunkdhaval08/graph-representational-learning-creating-node-and-graph-embeddings-25915b5a5aca).
>
> DeepWalk treats the graph as a "network of paths." These generate sequences of nodes by simulating random walks. The model Word2Vec then helps in learning embeddings.

- **Node2Vec** is a scalable feature learning algorithm for graphs, and this is to capture the structural information of graphs by learning embeddings of nodes. Node2vec leverages the random walk approach and uses biased walks rather than random walks to generate and learn embeddings—Node2Vec aids in exploring graph neighborhoods. Node2Vec fulfils proximity preservation and structural equivalence. Node2Vec, being a versatile tool, contributes to solving a wider range of real-world applications.
- **LINE**—LINE learns node embeddings by preserving both first-order and second-order proximities in the graph. This is an algorithmic framework for embedding very large-scale information networks. It suits various networks, including directed, undirected, binary, or weighted edges. This is based on a research paper (https://arxiv.org/abs/1503.03578).

- **Graph2vec**—This is for graph classification by focusing on learning the embeddings of entire graphs.

3) **DL-Based Techniques**

There are a few key mechanisms to generate graph embeddings with the help of DL algorithms and approaches. This section explains how DL methods come in handy in generating graph embeddings.

GNNs—There are research publications expounding the contributions of GNNs in generating graph embeddings with more accuracy. As indicated above, graph embeddings are numerical representations (vectors). Embeddings can be derived for nodes, edges, or even entire graphs. Embeddings are gaining momentum as they can neatly capture the structural and semantic information of graphs or their components (nodes and edges). Structural information means that the embeddings capture the graph's structure and linkage. Semantic information means the embeddings capture the content associated with nodes and edges. Embeddings are generally dense and low-dimensional vectors. Due to the lower-dimensional nature, analyzing embeddings is pretty easy and fast. Embeddings enable the accomplishment of many downstream tasks, such as link prediction and node classification.

GNNs are a special type of NN exclusively designed to handle and make sense of graph-structured data. GNNs are proficient in learning node and edge representations by aggregating information from neighboring nodes and edges. Node embeddings are the vector representations of every node in the graph. Edge embeddings capture relationships between nodes. Graph embeddings are derived by aggregating the embeddings of nodes and edges.

Matrix Factorization—Recommendation systems are important for many business domains. Product recommendations are essential for online shopping, and content and cinema recommendations are important for entertainment. Personalized recommendations enhance the user experience considerably. For recommendations, collaborative and content-based filtering methods are effective [3]. However, researchers have articulated advanced techniques, such as matrix factorization and DL-based models, that can significantly improve recommendation accuracy.

Matrix factorization can decompose the user–item interaction matrix into lower-dimensional matrices. This decomposition captures latent factors that represent user preferences and item characteristics. Matrix factorization can handle sparse data efficiently and capture latent features such as user preferences and item attributes.

For recommendation systems, autoencoders can capture complex patterns in user–item interactions. DL models can extract nonlinear relationships and tackle large datasets. DL models are beneficial for large-scale datasets with nonlinear relationships.

GCNs can learn graph embeddings by iteratively aggregating information from a node's neighbors. GCNs conceptually empower CNNs to work on graph data. The primary operator in CNNs is convolution. In GCNs, the convolution operator is used on graph data. Typically, CNNs process images and other Euclidean data, whereas GCNs process graph data. GCNs use a sequence of convolutional layers to aggregate information from a node's neighbors. Each layer in a GCN learns parameters/weights. This process can learn a rich representation of each node of the graph. The final GCN output is a set of node embeddings. That is, a corresponding vector represents each node. Nodes pass information via edges. Such an arrangement empowers GCNs to learn global context.

GCNS are undoubtedly a type of GNN. GraphSAGE is a popular GCN framework that uses a neighborhood aggregation approach to learn node embeddings. GraphSAGE is efficient for large graphs.

GraphSAGE takes a different approach. Instead of learning individual embeddings, this learns a function to generate embeddings. The process involves aggregating features from a node's local neighborhood to derive the node's embedding. There are several established aggregating functions to combine neighbor information. This method can capture and express important structural information in a compact format.

According to the experts, GraphSAGE is hugely helpful for large-scale graphs. This method can generate embeddings for unseen nodes, a unique capability for managing dynamic graphs.

There are applications of graph embeddings learned by GCNs. By learning a node's features and neighbors, GCNs can predict which class a node belongs to. That is, GCNs can predict labels by categorizing users in a network. Similarly, by understanding a graph's structure and node features, GCNs can classify a complete graph. GCNs can also tell whether two nodes have to be linked. GCNs calculate the similarity level between embeddings to predict missing edges by recommending friends.

Take a social network in which nodes represent users. Each user has features such as occupation, age, and hobbies. Edges represent friendships. A GCN can generate embeddings for each user in the network by capturing personal, social, and professional details from his or her friends and aggregating them. These embeddings come in handy when recommending fresh friends. GCNs incorporate the graph's topology and are ideal for recommendation systems, social network analysis, etc.

GATs have the innate strength to learn from graph-structured data. As inscribed above, many real-world problems are encoded and solved through graphs. In the exciting LLM era, KGs occupy a prime slot. Attention is the primary mechanism GATs use to assign different weights to the nodes and edges of a graph. Different weights are assigned based on the importance of nodes and edges for a given task. Thus, GATs capture the features of nodes and edges of the graph. There are blogs, research papers, and technical articles illustrating the uniqueness of GATs, an important GNN category. In this section, we will look into some of the prominent use cases of GATs.

- **GATs for Recommendation Systems**—GARec (https://arxiv.org/pdf/2201.05499) is a recommendation system (recommending specific items to users) that uses the attention mechanism along with a spatial GCN on a recommendation graph to extract embeddings for users and items. By learning the features of users and items comprehensively, GATs in association with GCN constitute next-generation recommendation systems.
- **Sentiment Analysis**—A paper titled "Graph-Based Attention Networks for Aspect Level Sentiment Analysis" discusses using a DL model that leverages GNNs and GATs to analyze sentiment based on different aspects [4].

  Fraud detection is important as frauds have become common and illegal across industry verticals. Fraudsters often use sophisticated techniques not to be caught. Graph-structured ODE is the complex relationship between users, products, and transactions. A research paper, "Improving Fraud Detection via Hierarchical Attention-based Graph Neural Network," describes the smart leverage of attention to address fraud detection.
- **Drug Discovery:** Graph-based attention is handy for capturing the complex and dynamic interactions between drugs and targets. Such an arrangement helps predict the binding affinity of drug candidates. A paper, "Meta-Learning With Graph Attention Networks for Low-Data Drug Discovery" (https://ieeexplore.ieee.org/document/10059171), introduces a new approach combining an Heterogeneous Graph Attention Network (hGAT) with meta-learning techniques. This addresses the challenge of finding promising drug molecules with specific properties.
- **Malware Detection**—Malware attacks are becoming sophisticated these days, and hence, there is a renewed focus on stringent malware detection mechanisms. Here is a paper titled "HAWK: Rapid Android Malware Detection through Heterogeneous Graph Attention Networks" (https://arxiv.org/pdf/2108.07548), which employs a novel malware detection framework using heterogeneous GATs to address this problem.

  A HIN is a special GNN. Researchers have shown that HIN's application domains are growing steadily. The Internet of Things (IoT) and cybersecurity fields are adopting HIN beneficially by exploiting relational semantic information before embedding it into representation vectors.

In the case of malware detection, if App1 and App2 share permission SEND_SMS while App2 and App3 share permission READ_SMS, HIN can capture the implicit semantic relationship between App1 and App3. Such an implicit relationship cannot be well-articulated by feature engineering methods. HIN-based modeling is powerful because malware developers cannot hide such implicit relationships.

However, HINS are primarily static networks. Therefore, the authors have developed HAWK, a novel Android malware detection framework with a GRL model and HIN.

- **Time Series Anomaly Detection**—This is a well-known process. Now, it gets extended to multimodal data. Multimodal time series (MTS) anomaly detection is widely used to monitor multimodal data emitted by IoT devices, sensors, business workloads, and IT systems. The current MTS techniques cannot pinpoint spatial–temporal correlations between univariate time series of various modalities. To address this limitation, there is a research paper, "MST-GAT: A Multimodal Spatial–Temporal Graph Attention Network for Time Series Anomaly Detection" (https://arxiv.org/pdf/2310.11169). This uses a multimodal GAT (M-GAT) and a temporal convolution network. M-GAT uses a multi-head attention module and two relational attention modules to model modal correlations explicitly.

Thus, the heightened power of GATs is being experimented with and expounded as a viable solution for several everyday problems.

Graph Autoencoders (GAEs)—Autoencoders are unsupervised learning models leveraged for specific use cases such as representation learning, dimensionality reduction, and feature engineering. Autoencoders consist of two components. First, an encoder compresses input data into a lower-dimensional latent representation. The second component is a decoder for reconstructing the original data from the learned latent representation. The input data for autoencoders can be textual and visual.

GAEs are a popular NN model class that works on graph data. GAEs can learn semantic representations of graph data. GAEs comprise an encoder that captures a graph's topological structure and node details. The result is a latent graph representation. On the other hand, a decoder reconstructs the graph from the latent representation. GAEs are distinctively designed to handle graph data.

VGAEs are a type of GAE that incorporates variational inference techniques to learn a probabilistic latent representation of graph data. VGAEs further enforce the latent representation to match a prior distribution. Such an arrangement helps produce new graph structures, and thereby, the robustness of the learned representation can be further improved.

GAEs are a research focus area within GNNs for generating graph embeddings. Existing GAE models overlook node representations and fail to capture contextual node information within the graph data. This results in poor embeddings. A group of researchers has proposed the ensemble GAE (E-GAE) models (for clustering and link prediction by Chengxin Xie and others). This model utilizes the ensemble random walk GAE, the random walk GAE of the ensemble network, and the GAE to generate three node embedding matrices. Then, these techniques are combined using adaptive weights to reconstruct a new node embedding matrix. This method addresses the problem of low-quality embeddings.

Researchers have made a few noteworthy advancements in the GAE domain. Research scholars and scientists have proposed different techniques to improve the performance of GAEs. By smartly leveraging GAEs, DeepMind can develop more accurate and efficient models for complex biological systems. GAEs are being experimented with for molecular graph analysis, image clustering, and link prediction tasks.

14.7 Applications of Graph Embeddings

As discussed above, graphs are presented as a powerful, amenable, and next-generation data structure for comprehensively representing, visualizing, and analyzing complicated and multimodal data. Many real-world applications are being efficiently tackled through the power of graphs. With graph embeddings gaining popularity, the interest in graph engineering and analytics is gathering momentum. Many business domains are trying to exploit the distinctions of graph data for knowledge discovery. Besides applying traditional analytical methods to graph-structured data, there is an enhanced focus on leveraging the advancements in AI. Experts and exponents articulate many fresh opportunities and possibilities by methodically using advanced AI models and agents on graph data. Graph AI is, therefore, acquiring special significance these days [5]. Especially in the language model era, the contributions of KGs are certainly and rapidly growing. There are certain limitations to large and small vision and multimodal language models. The key challenges and concerns of NLP, understanding and generation (NLP/U/G) tasks can be nullified by leveraging KGs.

Graph embeddings have various applications, including biological networks, ML, and knowledge representation. They are used for tasks such as network compression, visualization, clustering, link prediction, node classification, and KGC.

Graph embeddings detect relationships between genes and diseases in biological networks. They assist in drug discovery and help in understanding protein functions. Graph embeddings also aid in social network analysis, optimization of transportation networks, and fraud detection in financial services. Protein interaction networks can be transformed into graph embeddings. Graph-structured biological data with embeddings enables new drug discovery.

Graph embeddings facilitate more profound insights into the graph structure, connectivity, and relationships. Graph embeddings help to capture interactions within graphs. As written above, graph embeddings help detect special-purpose communities, predict user behavior, and identify important nodes in social networks. The accuracy of recommendation systems is bound to increase significantly with the smart leverage of graph embeddings. Online businesses increasingly rely on sophisticated recommendation systems to improve user experience substantially. KGs are being extensively built and used across industry verticals. Graph embeddings help to accrue many KGs. Entity linking and computing semantic similarity levels are enabled through graph embeddings. In biological networks, protein-to-protein interactions are being understood and used.

Graph embeddings help detect fraud in the financial services domain. They empower root cause analysis to find performance bottlenecks in computer networks. Anomaly/outlier detection is another widespread use case enabled by graph embeddings.

14.7.1 Graph Embeddings Challenges

Enabling algorithms and tools simplifies the process of generating effective graph embeddings. However, according to experts, creating accurate graph embeddings involves a few critical challenges. In this section, we will focus on the prevailing and perpetual challenges.

- **Scalability**—Creating accurate embeddings is not challenging, as graphs are enormous and highly complex. Solving real-world problems through large-scale graphs is seen as a critical challenge that can be surmounted through path-breaking technologies and tools.
- **Heterogeneity**—Besides multiplicity, graph heterogeneity is a barrier for graphs to shine as problem-solvers. With heightened multiplicity and heterogeneity, graph complexity is bound to go up sharply.
- **Sparsity**—Many nodes may go without any connectivity. That is, such graphs are termed sparse. This poses the challenge of accurately representing the graph's structural information in graph embeddings. Researchers have proposed breakthrough techniques to generate effective embeddings. Adversarial and inductive learning methods are recommended to surmount the problem of sparsity.

As known widely, the explainability and interpretability of AI decisions are vital for boosting users' confidence in AI models and agents. There are ways and means of being exposed to the transition from block boxes to gray and white boxes. For multifaceted real-world problems, the fear of high graph complexity emerges. Thus, complex mitigation mechanisms are being solicited to empower the graph technology to be penetrative and pervasive. Multimodal graphs are essential for insightfully tackling many new-generation problems. Graph embeddings are indispensable for learning many valuable things from graph-structured data. Untangling hidden connections between nodes is one of the foremost cases of use in graph embeddings.

Deep GRL—As we have been discussing, GRL is to encode high-dimensional sparse graph-structured data into low-dimensional dense vectors effectively. In the existing graph embedding methods, the embedding vectors of interconnected nodes can still maintain a relatively close distance. This is to preserve the structural information between the nodes in the graph. However, this is suboptimal for a few reasons. Traditional methods have less model capacity, which limits the learning performance. The techniques primarily rely on unsupervised learning techniques, which are incompatible with the recent learning paradigms.

With DL's tremendous success, deep GRL is gaining the attention of many these days. Deep GRL offers a slew of advantages over traditional methods. Researchers have developed a series of breakthrough techniques for deep GRL. Wei Ju and the team have written a research paper titled "A Comprehensive Survey on Deep Graph Representation Learning" that explains state-of-the-art deep GRL methods.

14.8 Conclusion

Learning graph representations is an important and computationally intensive task for availing all the initially expressed benefits of graph-represented data. Learning graph representations is all about creating efficient embeddings (vectors) for each node, edge, and entire graph. Rather than working on graph components directly, it is pretty easy, fast, and helpful to work on graph embeddings stored as vectors in a vector space. Several purpose-specific and agnostic use cases are being envisioned and implemented through graph embeddings. Besides leveraging traditional graph algorithms and data analytics methods, the trend is that advanced AI models and agents are being increasingly trained on graph embedding data. ML/DL and reinforcement learning algorithms are applied to graph-structured data to envisage and engineer highly competent, resilient, robust, and sophisticated AI models.

We have discussed many advancements in graph network architectures, such as GCNs, GNNs, and GATs, to make sense of graph-structured data. This chapter discusses many industrial use cases. With the seamless and spontaneous integration between AI and graphs, a new powerful concept of graph AI emerges and evolves fast to cater to complicated problems and bring forth sophisticated solutions to elevate human society substantially.

References

1 I. Makarov, D. Kiselev, N. Nikitinsky, and L. Subelj, "Survey on graph embeddings and their applications to machine learning problems on graphs," *PeerJ Comp. Sci.*, vol. 3, p. e357, February, 2021, doi: 10.7717/peerj-cs.357.

2 T. Tao, W. Qianqian, Y. Ruan, X. Li, and X. Wang, "Graph embedding with similarity metric learning," *Symmetry*, vol. 15, no. 8, p. 1618, 2023, doi: 10.3390/sym15081618.

3 V. T. Hoang, H.-J. Jeon, E.-S. You, Y. Yoon, S. Jung, and O.-J. Lee, "Graph representation learning and its applications: A survey," *Sensors*, vol. 23, no. 8, p. 4168, 2023, doi: 10.3390/s23084168.

4 Ihab Moudhich, Abdelhadi Fennan, Graph embedding approach to analyze sentiments on cryptocurrency, February 2024, *Int. J. Electric. Comp. Eng. (IJECE)* 14(1), 690, pp. 690–697, DOI:10.11591/ijece.v14i1.

5 P. Goyal and E. Ferrara, "Graph embedding techniques, applications, and performance: A survey," *Knowl.-Based Syst*, vol. 151, no. 1 , pp. 78–94, 2018, July.

15

Knowledge Graph Foundation, Techniques, and Its Case Studies

As data is spread across in huge global network, gathering information and finding relationships among them is tedious and complex. We need a data structure to organize the data simply and make it convenient for use. We have already seen that a graph is a mechanism to organize the data in a well-defined manner and to gather the information and find relationships among the data. Currently, the data structure that is powerful and can handle a complex set of data is the knowledge graph (KG) [1]. In this chapter, we discuss on the history and evolution of KGs, their techniques, and their applications in various domains.

15.1 Introduction to KG

15.1.1 History and Evolution

Before learning about the knowledge graph, we must know how it evolved and who is responsible for bringing in the new idea of the knowledge graph. In this topic, we know about the reasons behind its boom and its importance. The flowchart of the evolution is shown in Fig. 15.1. Around 1990s, Tim Berners-Lee proposed Semantic Web to transform the web from a collection of linked documents to a web of linked data that machines can understand and process intelligently. The Semantic Web aimed to create a machine-readable web, enabling automated agents to perform reasoning and integration across different data sources. The main idea of the Semantic Web is to give meaning (semantics) to web content. Structured data is used to define relationships among entities. The machines will learn to understand, infer, and reason over web data. This overcomes the traditional way of using the web, which is built for humans with HTML pages easy to read but hard for machines to interpret. For example, a webpage might say: "Delhi is the capital of India." But to a computer, it's just a string of text—there's no built-in understanding of what "Delhi is the

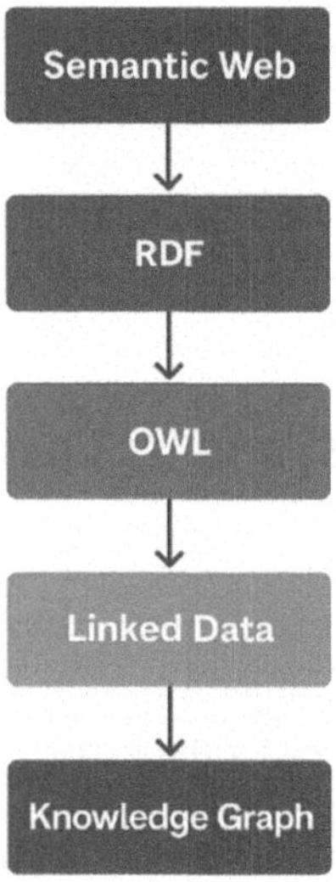

Figure 15.1 Flowchart showing the evolution.

capital of India" means, or what "Capital of" implies. To bridge this gap between human-readable and machine-understandable data, we needed a set of formal, structured standards. That's where the building blocks came in.

Resource Description Framework (RDF) was introduced in 1999 to create a common data model for expressing facts as machine-readable statements—a data model to describe information in the form of triples (subject, predicate, object). For example, the sentence "Delhi is the capital of India" can be written as triples (Delhi, istheCapitalof, India). This forms a graph structure, allowing data to be linked across the web. RDF forms the backbone of how knowledge is structured and represented in early semantic systems. RDF Schema (RDFS) was introduced in 2000 as an extension of RDF that adds basic schema-level constructs (such as class hierarchies and properties). RDF alone doesn't define the types of entities or relationships—we need semantics such as class hierarchies and constraints. It provides basic vocabulary for declaring classes (e.g., place, Country), specifying relationships between them (e.g., istheCapitalof), and defining inheritance. So now, a machine can know: "Delhi is the Capital of India." This adds semantic meaning to the raw triples in RDF.

RDF provides a basic framework to represent data as triples, but it cannot define rich semantics, such as class hierarchies, constraints, and logical relationships between concepts. To overcome these limitations, ontology languages such as RDFS and later Web Ontology Language (OWL) were introduced. They add the necessary structure and meaning by defining types, relationships, and rules, enabling machines not only to store data but also to reason and infer new knowledge from it. In 2004, OWL was introduced—a more expressive schema language for defining rich ontologies. It enables class hierarchies, property restrictions (e.g., cardinality), and logical axioms. OWL made it possible to do reasoning and inference over data.

After OWL was introduced in 2004, the theoretical and structural foundations for representing complex knowledge were in place. However, despite having powerful tools such as RDF, RDFS, and OWL, real-world adoption was limited—mainly because most data remained isolated, without practical strategies for interlinking or publishing it on the web. To solve this, the Linked Data Movement led by Tim Berners-Lee emerged as a practical step during 2010 toward realizing the Semantic Web. It focused on simple, actionable principles for publishing and connecting data using existing standards (RDF, uniform resource identifiers [URIs], HTTP), thereby transforming theoretical models into a decentralized, machine-readable web of interlinked data. The key projects are DBpedia, which extracts structured data from Wikipedia using RDF; FOAF (Friend of a Friend), a vocabulary to describe people and relationships; and LOD Cloud (Linked Open Data Cloud), which is a visualization of interlinked datasets (e.g., government data, bibliographic data, life sciences).

While the Linked Data Movement focused on publishing and interlinking open structured data on the web, it lacked widespread usability, scalability, and real-time application for end users. In 2012, Google introduced the KG to address these gaps by organizing information into entities and relationships that could enhance search results with semantic context and factual understanding. This marked a shift from merely linking data to using it intelligently—enabling personalized, contextual, and enriched experiences for users.

Then, Tech giants such as Microsoft (with Satori), Facebook (with their social graph), and LinkedIn (with their economic graph) all started building their own massive knowledge graphs. "In recent years, Knowledge Graphs have become a core part of AI and machine learning (ML). Instead of just storing information, we now learn patterns from the graph—using techniques like Graph Neural Networks and Knowledge Graph Embeddings."

15.1.2 Definition and Core Concepts

A KG is a powerful data structure that organizes information into a graph format, where nodes represent entities (e.g., people, places, concepts) and edges represent relationships between them. KGs combine semantic technologies and graph theory to model complex, interlinked knowledge, enabling machines to purpose, gather, and learn hidden patterns in data.

A KG is a structured representation of real-world knowledge as shown in Fig. 15.2, where entities (things) are connected by relationships (edges), and these connections are organized according to a formal ontology. It captures both factual

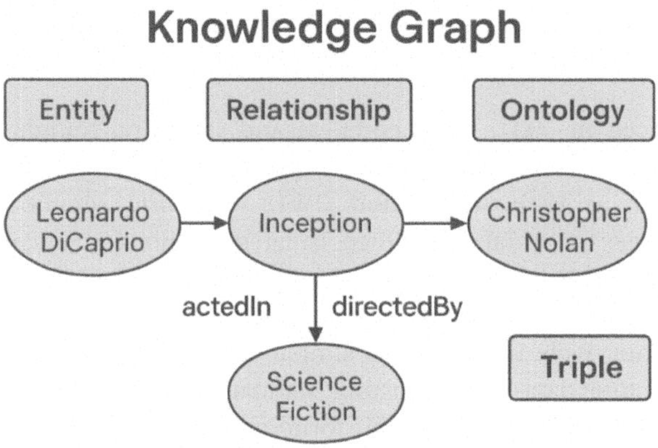

Figure 15.2 Knowledge graph representation of entities, relationships, and ontology.

information and semantic meaning, allowing machines to understand, query, and reason over the data.

In its simplest form, a KG is composed of triples:

(subject, predicate, object)

Example:

(Mahatma Gandhi, isBornIn, India)

The Author Citation Knowledge Graph shown in Fig. 15.3 visually represents the relationships between prominent researchers and their contributions across domains such as Generative Adversarial Networks, Healthcare, Renewable Energy Sciences, and Cybersecurity. Entities such as authors (e.g., Ian Goodfellow, Geoffrey Hinton, Fei-Fei Li) and research papers are connected by semantic relationships such as cites, writes, and works on. This graph helps trace citation flow, thematic connections, and interdisciplinary collaborations, highlighting how knowledge propagates and evolves within and across scientific communities.

15.1.2.1 Core Concepts

1. Entities (Nodes)

Entities represent real-world objects or concepts. Each entity is a node in the graph. For example, "Mahatma Gandhi is born in India"—Mahatma Gandhi (Person) and India (Location). Entities can be Named entities (with unique identifiers) or Literal values (e.g., dates, numbers, text).

2. Relationships (Edges)

Relationships describe how two entities are connected. They are represented as directed edges in the graph. Each relationship has a type (predicate), defining the nature of the link. In (Mahatma Gandhi, isBornIn, India), "isBornin" is the predicate for relationship between two entities.

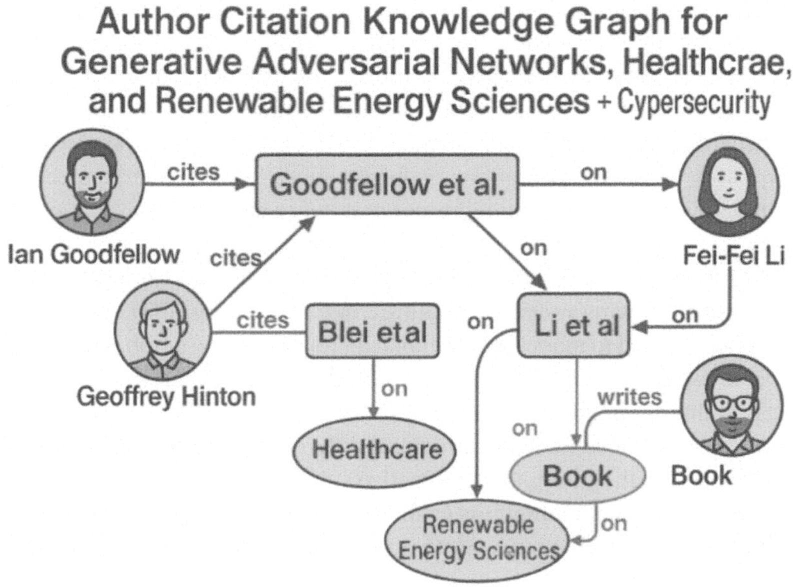

Figure 15.3 Author Citation Knowledge Graph.

3. Ontology (Schema/Vocabulary)

Ontology is the blueprint or schema of a knowledge graph. It defines the classes (e.g., Person, Country, Company), Properties (e.g., isBornin, hasBirthPlace, directedBy), and Domain and range (what types of entities can be connected by a relationship). Ontologies help ensure consistency and semantic clarity in the graph.

Example ontology

<Class, Property, Domain/Range>

Class:

Person

Property

isBornIn (Domain: Person, Range: Location)

4. Triples (Subject, Predicate, Object)

A triple is the fundamental unit of data in a knowledge graph. Each triple asserts a fact or relation, for example, triple ("Mahatma Gandhi," "isBornIn," "India"). Triples are often stored in RDF databases (triple stores) and queried using SPARQL.

15.1.3 Difference Between KGs and Traditional Databases

As the volume and complexity of data continue to grow, the limitations of traditional data storage and retrieval systems have become increasingly apparent.

Conventional relational databases have long been the backbone of structured data management, offering reliable storage, query capabilities, and transactional integrity. However, they are primarily optimized for well-defined, tabular data with rigid schemas. In contrast, many modern applications—ranging from intelligent search engines and recommendation systems to biomedical research and enterprise knowledge integration—require a more flexible, interconnected, and semantically rich approach to represent and query data. This has led to the rise of KGs.

KGs go beyond rows and columns. They represent data as a network of entities and relationships, allowing systems to capture context, meaning, and connections that are implicit or hard to model in traditional databases. Using graph structures, they enable more natural modeling of real-world domains and support advanced reasoning, making them ideal for handling complex and evolving datasets. This chapter explores the conceptual and structural differences between KGs and traditional databases, highlighting their respective strengths, limitations, and areas of applications. By understanding this evolution, we gain insights into why KGs have become foundational to modern data-driven systems. The difference is given in tabular format [1] in Table 15.1.

Traditional databases are ideal for structured, transactional operations where relationships are simple and schema is fixed. KGs works well in complex, evolving domains where entities and relationships are dynamic, interconnected, and semantically rich—such as research citation networks, biomedical ontologies, and knowledge-based AI.

Table 15.1 Difference between knowledge graph and traditional databases.

Feature	Knowledge Graph (KG)	Traditional Database (RDBMS/SQL)
Data Model	Graph-based (nodes and edges) using triples or quads	Table-based (rows and columns)
Schema	Schema-flexible (ontology-driven)	Rigid schema (predefined table structure)
Semantic Understanding	High—supports semantics and reasoning via ontologies	Low—semantics must be encoded manually
Relationships	Directly modeled as edges	Represented via foreign keys or join tables
Query Language	SPARQL (semantic queries across graphs)	SQL (relational queries)
Data Integration	Easily integrates heterogeneous and linked data	Requires manual ETL and schema alignment

15.2 Construction of a KG

The construction of a KG is a multi-stage process that involves the transformation of raw data into a structured, semantically rich network of interconnected entities and relationships. This is shown as the flowchart in Fig. 15.4.

The process begins with knowledge acquisition, where data is collected from diverse sources—ranging from structured databases and spreadsheets to semistructured formats, such as XML or JSON, and unstructured text, such as webpages, research articles, and social media content. This raw information forms the foundation for extracting meaningful knowledge.

The next critical step is entity extraction, typically performed using NLP techniques. This involves identifying named entities such as people, organizations, locations, and dates from unstructured or semistructured text. Advanced named entity recognition (NER) models, often powered by deep learning, can recognize complex and domain-specific terms. Once the entities are extracted, entity linking (EL) or disambiguation ensures that these entities are matched to a unique,

Figure 15.4 Multi-stage process of a knowledge graph.

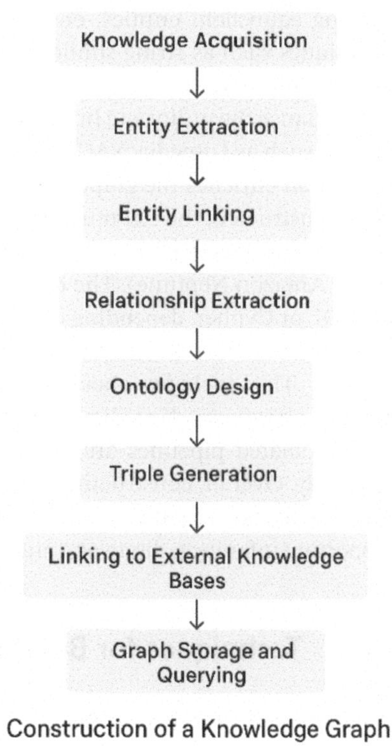

canonical representation. For example, the name "Apple" could refer to the technology company or the fruit, and EL resolves such ambiguities using contextual clues and external knowledge bases (KBs) such as Wikidata.

Following entity recognition and linking, relationship extraction identifies the semantic connections between entities. This step may involve rule-based pattern matching, supervised ML, or more sophisticated neural approaches that learn from context. For example, from the sentence "Alan Turing developed the Turing Machine," the KG would extract a triple like (Alan Turing, developed, Turing Machine). These extracted entities and relationships are then mapped to a formal structure, which requires designing an ontology—a conceptual schema that defines the classes, properties, and constraints of the domain. Ontology development is crucial for maintaining consistency and enabling reasoning over the graph.

Once the schema is defined, triple generation takes place, where information is encoded in the form of subject–predicate–object triples. These triples form the backbone of the KG, providing a flexible, graph-based structure to represent complex information. However, duplicates and variations often arise, making entity resolution a necessary step. This involves de-duplicating entries and merging equivalent entities, ensuring the integrity and accuracy of the graph. Techniques such as string similarity, rule-based matching, or ML can be used to perform this task.

To enhance the utility and interoperability of the KG, it is often linked with external KBs such as DBpedia, YAGO, or domain-specific ontologies. This Linked Data integration enriches the graph with additional facts and contextual information. Once constructed, the KG must be stored using appropriate technologies such as RDF triple stores (e.g., Blazegraph, Virtuoso) or property graph databases (e.g., Neo4j, Amazon Neptune). The data can then be queried using languages such as SPARQL or Cypher, depending on the underlying model.

Finally, a robust KG requires continuous evaluation, validation, and maintenance. This includes checking for data quality, schema consistency, and logical correctness. Periodic updates are essential to reflect new knowledge, and automated pipelines are often developed to ingest and process new data efficiently. Overall, constructing a KG is a complex but highly rewarding process that transforms disparate data into a coherent, intelligent system capable of supporting inference, discovery, and decision-making.

15.3 Techniques for Building a KG

Building a KG includes various precise techniques that transform raw data into structured, semantically meaningful graphs. These techniques are essential for extracting knowledge from unstructured sources, aligning it with a defined ontology, and enabling reasoning and advanced querying.

15.3.1 Named Entity Recognition

NER is a technique in NLP that focuses on identifying and classifying specific elements within unstructured text into predefined categories. These elements, known as named entities, typically include names of people, organizations, locations, products, dates, time expressions, monetary values, percentages, and other key contextual markers. The primary goal of NER [2] is to extract structured information from textual content, making it easier for machines to understand and analyze.

Also known as entity extraction, chunking, or entity identification, NER plays a crucial role across various domains of AI, particularly in ML, deep learning, and neural networks. It is widely applied in real-world applications such as chatbots, sentiment analysis, recommendation systems, and intelligent search engines. Industries such as healthcare, finance, human resources, education, and social media analytics leverage NER to transform large volumes of unstructured data into actionable insights.

15.3.1.1 Working Process of NER in NLP

NER is a fundamental task within the domain of NLP. It involves the automatic identification of real-world entities embedded in unstructured text and classifies them into predefined categories such as Person, Organization, Location, Date, Time, Money, Percentage, and others. NER transforms raw textual information into structured data by detecting and labeling these significant entities, making the content more interpretable and machine readable.

The process of NER typically begins with text preprocessing, where the input text is cleaned by removing punctuation, special characters, and other noise and often converted to lowercase for normalization. The text is then tokenized, meaning it is split into individual words or tokens. This is followed by part-of-speech (POS) tagging, which assigns grammatical roles (such as noun, verb, or adjective) to each token, providing syntactic context for further analysis.

In the feature extraction phase, various linguistic and semantic features are captured to inform the NER model. These features may include the shape of the word (such as capitalization patterns and digits), POS tags, distributed word representations or embeddings (e.g., Word2Vec, GloVe, or BERT), and contextual information from surrounding words. These features help the model learn patterns that distinguish named entities from regular text.

Once features are extracted, the NER model application phase begins. In this step, an ML or deep learning model—trained on annotated datasets—processes the input tokens and assigns each one a label based on its role. These labels typically follow formats such as B-PER (Beginning of a Person entity), I-LOC (Inside a Location entity), or O (Outside of any named entity). These labels help the model construct structured representations from the text.

Finally, in the entity classification step, the labeled tokens are grouped and categorized into complete named entities. The model aggregates adjacent tokens with the same entity label and produces a structured output that includes both the named entity and its associated type. For example, the phrase "New York City" would be identified and classified as a Location.

Example

Input Sentence:

"Sundar Pichai is the CEO of Google, which is headquartered in Mountain View."

NER Output:

"Sundar Pichai" → PERSON

"Google" → ORGANIZATION

"Mountain View" → LOCATION

15.3.2 Entity Linking and Disambiguation

Entity linking and entity disambiguation (EL and ELD) is a critical step in the pipeline of KG construction and NLP. After NER identifies and classifies entities (such as names of people, places, or organizations) in unstructured text, the next task is to connect those mentions to real-world entities in a structured KB such as Wikidata, DBpedia, YAGO, or Freebase. This process is what EL handles, while disambiguation ensures that each mention maps to the correct entity, especially when multiple possibilities exist [3].

15.3.2.1 Purpose of EL and ELD

The core objective of EL is to move from surface-level mentions in text (e.g., "Apple") to a unique, canonical representation of the entity in a structured knowledge source (e.g., Apple_Inc vs. Apple_(fruit)). This ensures that machines interpret and process textual references unambiguously.

It is essential for downstream tasks such as

- Semantic search
- Question answering systems
- Personal assistants (e.g., Siri, Alexa)
- Recommendation systems
- Text enrichment for KG population

15.3.2.2 Step-by-Step Working Process of EL

1) Candidate generation: The system identifies all possible entities from the KB that a mention might refer to. For instance, for the mention "Jaguar," it might retrieve
   - Jaguar (animal)
   - Jaguar Cars
   - Jacksonville Jaguars (NFL team)
2) Contextual analysis: The algorithm analyzes the surrounding context of the mention in the sentence or document. Contextual words such as "drive," "engine," or "luxury" may point toward the car brand, while "jungle" or "endangered species" could indicate the animal.
3) Candidate ranking and disambiguation: Using a combination of statistical methods (TF-IDF, cosine similarity), neural models (BERT-based encoders, entity embeddings), and KG features (popularity, type consistency) the candidates are ranked by relevance, and the top match is selected.
4) Linking to KB: The selected entity is then linked via a unique identifier from the KB, often through a URI (e.g., http://dbpedia.org/resource/Jaguar_Cars), ensuring consistency and reusability across systems.

15.3.2.3 Example of Disambiguation

Consider the sentence: "The Jaguar leaped silently through the jungle."

- The mention "Jaguar" could refer to an animal or a car.
- The context contains "leaped," "silently," and "jungle"—these strongly suggest the animal.
- The system disambiguates this mention and links it to Jaguar_(animal) in the KB.

  Now, in a different sentence:
  "The new Jaguar comes with a hybrid engine and advanced navigation."

- Here, "engine" and "navigation" strongly suggest a vehicle.
- Thus, the correct link is Jaguar_Cars.

15.3.3 Relation Extraction

Relation extraction (RE) is a crucial task in NLP and KG construction, focused on identifying and extracting semantic relationships between recognized entities in unstructured text. After entities such as people, places, or organizations are detected through NER [4], RE establishes how these entities are connected—for example, whether one person authored a book, was born in a location, or is affiliated with an organization. These relationships are often expressed as binary triples of the form (subject, relation, object), and they become essential components of a knowledge graph.

15.3.3.1 Step-by-Step Working Process

The working process of RE typically starts after named entities have been identified. The first step involves analyzing the syntactic and semantic structure of the sentence to determine the possible relationships that may exist between entities. This can be done using a variety of techniques. Pattern-based methods rely on predefined linguistic rules or regular expressions (e.g., "X discovered Y" → discovered(X, Y)). These methods are fast but limited in scope. Supervised ML approaches involve training classifiers on annotated datasets where entity pairs and their relationships are labeled. These models learn patterns from features such as word tokens, POS tags, dependency parses, and syntactic paths between entities. More recently, deep learning models, particularly those based on transformers (such as BERT), have shown state-of-the-art performance by automatically capturing contextual dependencies and sentence-level semantics without extensive feature engineering.

For example, consider the sentence: "Marie Curie discovered radium."

Here, the entities "Marie Curie" and "radium" are already recognized. The task of RE is to identify the semantic relationship between them—namely, "discovered." This yields the relation triple:

(Marie Curie, discovered, radium)

Such extracted relationships can then be stored in a knowledge graph, enhancing the structured understanding of textual information.

RE plays a vital role in domains such as biomedical research (e.g., extracting gene–disease interactions), scholarly publishing (e.g., identifying author–publication relations), and digital assistants (e.g., understanding user intent through relation cues). As a bridge between unstructured text and structured knowledge, RE significantly contributes to automated reasoning, question answering, and intelligent information retrieval systems.

15.3.4 Ontology Engineering

Ontology engineering [5] is a foundational process in KG construction and Semantic Web technologies that focuses on systematically creating and managing ontologies—formal representations of knowledge within a specific domain. The core purpose of ontology engineering is to define a shared schema or structure that organizes how entities, their attributes, and their interrelationships are represented and understood. Unlike raw data or unstructured information, ontologies introduce a semantic layer that enables both humans and machines to interpret and reason over complex domains with clarity and consistency.

The process of ontology engineering begins with domain modeling, where experts identify the key entity types (classes), their attributes (properties), and the relationships (object properties) between them. For example, in a university domain, one might define a class called "Person" with properties such as name, birthdate, and affiliation. This entity could be linked to another class, such as "University," via a relationship such as worksFor. Similarly, the ontology might define a "Student" as a subclass of "Person" and specify constraints such as cardinality (e.g., a student can enroll in multiple courses, but each course must have at least one instructor).

Once the conceptual schema is defined, ontology engineers often use ontology languages such as RDFS and OWL to formally represent these structures. These languages support logical reasoning and classification, enabling advanced capabilities such as inferring subclass relationships, validating data, or answering complex queries through SPARQL. Tools such as Protégé, TopBraid Composer, and OntoStudio are widely used for designing, visualizing, and validating ontologies.

For instance, consider the knowledge triple:

(Marie Curie, worksFor, University of Paris) Here, "Marie Curie" would be an instance of the "Person" class, "University of Paris" would be an instance of the "University" class, and "worksFor" is the defined relationship between them. The ontology ensures that such a relationship is meaningful within the domain's structure.

Ontology engineering is essential for ensuring semantic interoperability, data integration across systems, and knowledge reuse, particularly in domains such as healthcare, finance, education, and scientific research. It underpins the logic and consistency of knowledge graphs and enhances the effectiveness of AI applications by providing a structured framework for reasoning and inference.

15.4 Representation and Storage

In the previous topic, we've now walked through how a KG is constructed—from extracting entities and relations to building ontologies. But once the KG is built, the big question is: how do we represent and store it efficiently?

15.4.1 Introduction to Representation and Storage of KGs

Once a KG is constructed—complete with extracted entities, relationships, and ontological structure—the next critical step is its representation and storage. This phase determines how the graph will be organized, stored, accessed, and queried efficiently for downstream applications such as search, reasoning, recommendation, and analytics [6].

KGs are typically represented in a graph-based data model, where information is structured as nodes (entities) and edges (relationships). The most common and foundational format is the RDF triple, which expresses data as a combination of subject–predicate–object. This representation is both human readable and machine interpretable, making it ideal for semantic web technologies. To support practical use at scale, KGs must be stored in specialized graph databases or triplestores. These databases are optimized for graph traversal and semantic querying. Depending on the application requirements, either RDF-based systems (e.g., Apache Jena, Virtuoso) or property graph models (e.g., Neo4j, Amazon Neptune) are employed. The choice of storage model influences not only the efficiency of data retrieval but also the capabilities of integration, reasoning, and data analytics.

In short, the representation and storage layer forms the backbone of any operational KG, enabling structured data to be utilized intelligently and meaningfully across various domains.

15.4.2 RDF Triples and SPARQL

15.4.2.1 RDF Triples: The Foundation of Semantic Representation

RDF is a W3C standard designed to represent structured information about resources in the form of triples. RDF triples are a data representation format used in KGs, expressing facts as subject–predicate–object statements (e.g., *Marie Curie – discovered – radium*). An RDF triple is a simple, yet powerful data model that encodes knowledge as a statement consisting of three parts:

- Subject – the entity being described
- Predicate – the property or relationship
- Object – the value or target entity of the property

This structure forms a directed graph where nodes represent entities and edges represent the relationships or properties between them.

Example ***RDF Triple***

<Marie_Curie> <discovered> <Radium>

This can be interpreted as: Marie Curie discovered Radium.

In RDF:

Entities and properties are represented using URIs to ensure global uniqueness. Objects can be either another URI (another resource) or a literal value (such as a string, number, or date).

Formal Structure

(Subject, Predicate, Object)

RDF triples provide the structural basis for storing knowledge in graph format and facilitate data sharing across diverse systems, especially in the Semantic Web and Linked Data contexts.

15.4.2.2 SPARQL: Querying RDF Data

Once data is stored as RDF triples, it needs to be queried efficiently [7]. This is where SPARQL (SPARQL Protocol and RDF Query Language) comes in. SPARQL is the standard query language for retrieving and manipulating RDF data, much like SQL is for relational databases.

SPARQL allows users to

- Query specific patterns of triples (similar to "select where" in SQL)
- Filter results based on conditions
- Join related triples
- Create or update RDF data
- Perform federated queries across multiple datasets

Basic SPARQL Query Example SELECT ?scientist ?discovery WHERE {?scientist <http://example.org/discovered> ?discovery .}

This query retrieves all scientists and their discoveries by matching triples with the predicate <discovered>.

Features of SPARQL

- Pattern matching over RDF graphs
- Support for optional and union queries
- Filters for data constraints (e.g., numerical comparisons, regex)
- Aggregation functions (e.g., COUNT, AVG)
- Subqueries and nesting

Table 15.2 Comparison of RDF triples and SPARQL.

Feature	RDF Triples	SPARQL
Purpose	Data representation	Data querying and manipulation
Structure	Subject–Predicate–Object	SQL-like query syntax
Example	(Marie_Curie, discovered, Radium)	SELECT ?x WHERE {?x <discovered> <Radium>}
Tools/Usage	RDF databases, Linked Data	SPARQL endpoints, semantic applications

SPARQL queries can be executed on SPARQL endpoints, which are interfaces provided by triplestores or RDF databases such as Virtuoso, Blazegraph, or Apache Jena Fuseki.

15.4.2.3 Comparison: RDF Triples vs SPARQL

Comparison between RDF Triples vs SPARQL based on purpose is given in Table 15.2

15.5 Case Studies of KG

15.5.1 Supply Chain Management Using KG

Traditional supply chain networks face challenges related to inefficient transportation logistics, limited real-time visibility, and lack of dynamic responsiveness. These inefficiencies often lead to higher operational costs and delayed deliveries. A critical gap exists in uncovering hidden city-to-city relationships within transportation networks, especially where direct connections do not exist. There is a need for a more intelligent and adaptive approach that can identify latent connections and optimize logistics routes using graph-based techniques.

This case study explores how KGs, integrated with graph neural network techniques, can transform supply chain logistics by uncovering hidden relationships between cities. Modern supply chain management faces persistent challenges, including inefficient transportation routes, lack of real-time visibility, and the inability to dynamically adapt to changing conditions. Leveraging big data, AI/ML, and cloud-based collaboration, this approach employs node embeddings to represent city attributes in a latent space and utilizes a graph attention network (GAT) to learn complex dependencies between nodes for link prediction. The system demonstrates that the predicted links—representing new or previously unconsidered routes—often offer lower costs compared to existing direct links. These newly identified pathways create efficient and transparent supply chain flows by connecting source cities with optimal intermediate hubs. The outcome supports strategic urban planning, enhances transportation efficiency, and contributes to cost-effective logistics management.

15.5.1.1 Introduction

This work aims to optimize supply chain management by leveraging graph-based algorithms and KG technologies. The core objective is to enhance operational efficiency, reduce logistics costs, and enable smarter decision-making across complex supply chain networks. By applying graph algorithms, the system models real-world supply chain interactions as interconnected entities and relationships—providing real-time visibility, agility, and responsiveness critical to modern logistics.

Supply chain management faces a broad spectrum of challenges, including inventory control, demand forecasting inaccuracies, transportation inefficiencies, unreliable suppliers, and the growing need for transparency and real-time monitoring. Moreover, with the global emphasis on ethical sourcing and sustainability, organizations must also address environmental and social responsibilities while managing risks such as financial disruptions, geopolitical tensions, and operational uncertainties.

Current research in supply chain management is increasingly multidisciplinary, integrating insights from logistics, operations research, information systems, AI, and sustainability. One major area of focus is the incorporation of digital technologies—such as blockchain for traceability and AI/ML for predictive analytics—to build intelligent, adaptive, and transparent supply chains. These technologies help organizations anticipate demand shifts, optimize route planning, and detect anomalies in real time.

In parallel, sustainability and ethics are taking center stage. Emerging frameworks now assess environmental footprints, reduce waste, and support circular economy practices. Social sustainability is also gaining traction, with emphasis on responsible labor practices, human rights, and diversity within global supply networks.

To address these multifaceted challenges, this case study adopts graph representation learning methods—specifically node embedding and GATs—to uncover hidden logistics patterns and predict potential connections between locations. These insights enable the design of more efficient routes, connect cities indirectly through cost-effective paths, and, ultimately, foster more resilient and optimized supply chain systems.

15.5.1.2 Methodology

This methodology focuses on optimizing travel routes between cities by minimizing transportation costs, using a graph-based approach implemented with the NetworkX library in Python. In this model, each node represents a city, and each directed edge corresponds to a transportation route with an associated cost.

The process begins by constructing a directed graph where transportation costs are embedded as edge attributes. To identify the most cost-efficient route between two cities, the method leverages NetworkX's shortest_path function, which calculates the path based on the lowest cumulative cost rather than distance or number of hops. A custom function is used to compute the total cost of a selected path by summing the cost values of all connecting edges. The algorithm then identifies the optimized path as the one with the minimum total cost between the source and destination cities. If such a path exists, it is returned along with its corresponding cost details.

To assess the effectiveness of the predicted paths, two evaluation metrics are employed:

- Hits@k: Measures the accuracy of the predicted path by verifying whether the correct path (or its segments) is found within the top-k ranked options.
- Mean reciprocal rank (MRR): Evaluates the ranking performance by computing the reciprocal of the rank at which the first correct city appears in the list of predicted cities.

Together, these metrics provide insights into both the precision and relevance of the predicted routes. This methodology thus offers a structured, data-driven approach to optimizing supply chain transportation networks, ensuring cost-effective connectivity between cities while enabling performance evaluation through well-established metrics.

15.5.1.3 Approach

The approach employs graph analytics and visualization using Python's NetworkX library to analyze transportation data. It begins by importing route information from a CSV file into a Pandas DataFrame, which includes details such as source cities, destination cities, travel costs, and product categories.

Using this data, a directed graph (DiGraph) is constructed in NetworkX, where

- Nodes represent cities.
- Edges represent directed transportation routes, annotated with attributes such as travel cost and product type.

Once the graph is built, the code calculates important node-level features such as in-degree and out-degree, which indicate how many connections a city has coming in or going out. At the graph level, it computes metrics including

- Total number of nodes and edges
- Average transportation cost across all routes.

These statistics provide a foundational understanding of the network's structure and flow dynamics.

For visualization, the graph is rendered using Matplotlib. Node sizes are scaled according to their degree (connectivity), while edge labels display the associated transportation cost. The resulting visualization helps intuitively interpret network structure, identify key hubs, and highlight cost-heavy routes.

15.5.1.4 Evaluation Metrics Used

- Hits@k and MRR are evaluation metrics used to assess the effectiveness of the optimized path generated between two cities. Hits@k measures the proportion of correct cities in the optimized path when considering only the top-k cities, where k is a predefined value.

- It calculates the ratio of correctly predicted cities in the optimized path to the total number of cities in the actual path, up to the specified top-k value. MRR calculates the reciprocal rank of the first correctly predicted city in the optimized path. It measures the average of the reciprocals of the ranks of the first correctly predicted city across multiple queries.
- These evaluation metrics provide insights into the accuracy and ranking performance of the optimized path compared to the actual shortest path between the two cities.

Visualization of KG Figure 15.5 illustrates that the the graph shows the optimized travel routes. This optimized routes are used to find out the optimized path.

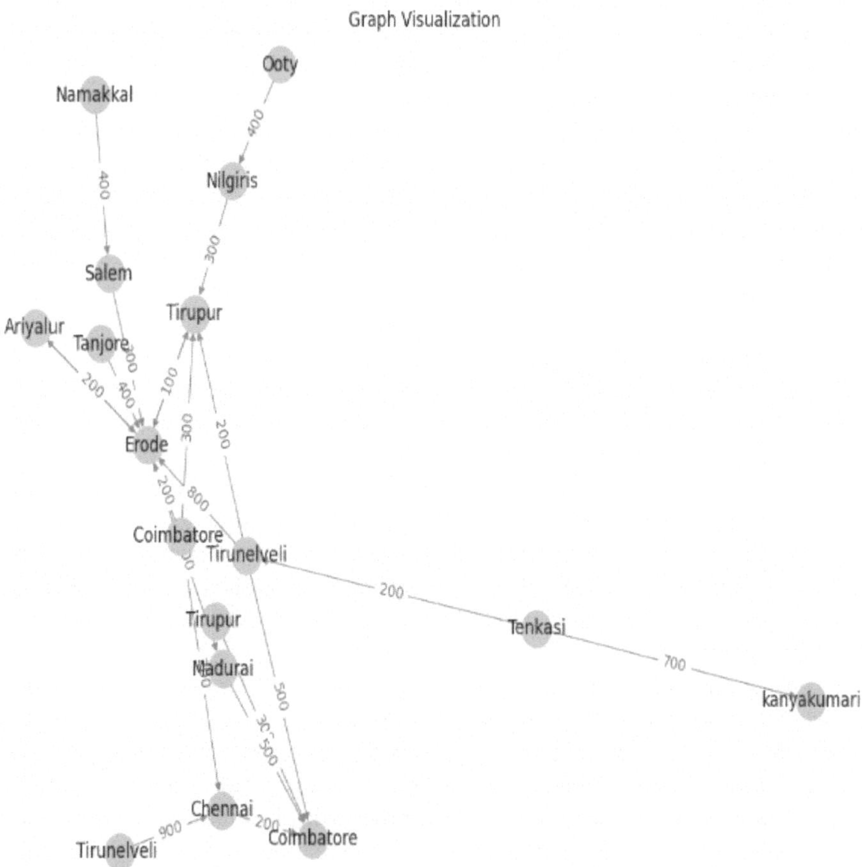

Figure 15.5 Supply chain knowledge graph showing optimized travel routes.

15.5.1.5 Result

```
Total Cost: 1000
Optimized Path:['Ooty', ' Nilgiris', Tirupur', 'Erode', 'Ariyalur']
Hits@5: 1.00
MRR: 1.00
```

15.5.2 DRKG: A KG Approach to Drug Repurposing for COVID-19

The COVID-19 pandemic has underscored the urgent need for efficient drug discovery strategies, with drug repurposing (DR) emerging as a promising approach to accelerate treatment identification. This chapter presents the development of the Drug Repurposing Knowledge Graph (DRKG)—a comprehensive biological knowledge graph that integrates data from multiple biomedical databases and recent COVID-19 literature. DRKG is designed to predict novel interactions between genes and chemical compounds, focusing on inhibiting pathways related to COVID-19 host proteins. The chapter details techniques used to construct and refine the graph, including methods to filter out noninformative nodes and links. It also explores the use of graph ML models and KGEs to support DR tasks. Evaluation results demonstrate the ability of DRKG to identify potential drug candidates, some of which are currently in clinical trials. By making the DRKG, learned embeddings, and source code publicly available, this work highlights the potential of graph-based approaches to expedite drug discovery for emerging infectious diseases.

15.5.2.1 Introduction

The COVID-19 pandemic has underscored the critical need for rapid and cost-effective drug discovery approaches to combat emerging infectious diseases. Traditional de novo drug development is both time-consuming and expensive, often requiring 10–15 years and significant financial investment to bring a new drug to market. In light of these challenges, DR—the strategy of identifying new therapeutic uses for existing drugs—has gained substantial attention. This approach leverages the shared molecular mechanisms across different diseases, enabling faster deployment of treatments by bypassing early-phase drug development stages.

Recent research efforts have focused on optimizing DR by integrating existing knowledge about drugs, their molecular targets, and disease pathways. Among these efforts, KGE techniques have emerged as powerful tools. KGE models generate compact vector representations of entities and relationships in a knowledge graph, which can then be used for various tasks, including link prediction, knowledge graph completion, and drug recommendation. These techniques help uncover previously unknown associations, thereby facilitating the identification of promising drug candidates.

This work introduces the construction and application of the DRKG—a unified and comprehensive biological knowledge graph designed specifically to support COVID-19-related DR. The DRKG consolidates data from multiple biomedical sources, such as DrugBank, GNBR, and STRING, alongside curated information from recent COVID-19 research publications. It is structured to predict novel interactions between genes and chemical compounds, with a special focus on biological pathways associated with host responses to SARS-CoV-2 infection.

To extract meaningful insights from the DRKG, we apply advanced KGE models to learn semantic representations of entities and relations. These embeddings are then employed to identify potential repurposable drugs for COVID-19. Our findings highlight several drugs—currently under clinical investigation—that emerge as strong candidates for repurposing.

The following sections of this chapter detail the methodologies used for DRKG construction, embedding generation, and evaluation of repurposing outcomes. We also present a comparative analysis between the predictive capabilities of the DRKG and its individual source databases, reinforcing the value of an integrated knowledge graph approach in accelerating drug discovery.

15.5.2.2 Methodology

Data Collection and Integration The methodological process begins with aggregating biomedical interactions from a diverse range of publicly available databases, including DrugBank, GNBR, STRING, IntAct, and DGIdb, as well as bibliographic sources. To ensure interoperability, all biological entities are mapped to a unified identifier space, facilitating cross-database linking. Following integration, data is rigorously filtered to eliminate noisy or redundant nodes and edges. The result is the DRKG, comprising 97,055 entities across 13 distinct entity types, and 5,869,294 relational triplets spanning 107 relation types. COVID-19-specific genes and proteins, curated from recent scientific literature, are incorporated to enhance domain relevance.

Knowledge Graph Embedding To enable predictive learning, the DRKG is embedded using state-of-the-art KGE techniques. Specifically, the Translating Embedding (TransE) model is employed to learn vectorized, low-dimensional representations of entities and relations. These embeddings, with a dimensionality of 400, encode the semantic and structural information inherent in the graph. The quality of these embeddings is validated through downstream analytical tasks, establishing a foundation for link prediction and DR inference.

DR Through Relation-Specific Link Prediction The central objective of this methodology is to identify potential drug candidates for COVID-19 by predicting novel interactions. Two predictive tasks are formulated:

- Direct drug–disease interaction prediction
- Inference of gene–drug interactions where the gene is linked to COVID-19 pathophysiology

Using TransE, link prediction is conducted on these relational pathways. The resulting predictions are benchmarked against known clinical trial data to identify repurposable drugs with empirical support.

Graph Structure Quality Assessment To ensure the structural integrity of the DRKG, a detailed graph analysis is conducted. This includes:

- Measuring the percentage overlap of triplets among different edge types.
- Assessing the consistency of predicted neighbors across relation types using TransE.
- Evaluating the scoring function output for each triplet, which serves as a proxy for embedding effectiveness and relational coherence.

Embedding Similarity and Visualization To evaluate semantic consistency, entity and relation embeddings are analyzed using t-distributed stochastic neighbor embedding (t-SNE) for dimensionality reduction and visualization in 2D space. Additionally, cosine similarity metrics are computed:

- Within the same entity category (intra-class similarity)
- Across different categories (inter-class similarity)

This analysis reveals how well the embeddings capture intra-type consistency and inter-type diversity, which is critical for effective link prediction and interpretability.

Edge Score and Link Confidence Evaluation The final component involves analyzing the distribution of edge scores derived from the TransE model. These scores indicate the model's confidence in predicted interactions. Furthermore, cross-relation similarity analysis is conducted to understand the transferability and generalizability of the learned relations. This aids in assessing the robustness of the embedding model in identifying novel drug candidates across different interaction types.

15.5.2.3 Approach Used

Comprehensive Data Collection and Integration

- A multi-source strategy was adopted to compile a wide array of biological interactions from publicly available databases, such as DrugBank, GNBR, STRING, IntAct, and DGIdb, along with literature-curated COVID-19 data.
- Biological entities were systematically mapped to a unified ID space, facilitating seamless integration and consistent linkage across heterogeneous sources.

- Rigorous filtering procedures were employed to remove noisy or redundant links and entities, leading to the construction of a high-quality DRKG enriched with COVID-19-relevant components.

Utilization of Advanced KGE Models

- State-of-the-art KGE techniques were applied to transform the DRKG into low-dimensional vector representations, enabling computational modeling of semantic relationships.
- The TransE model was specifically utilized to learn embeddings that preserve relational structure, optimizing 400-dimensional vectors for all entities and relations.
- The effectiveness of the embeddings was validated through qualitative and quantitative analysis, confirming their ability to capture biologically meaningful interactions within the DRKG.

15.5.2.4 Proposed Methodology

Innovative DR Framework

- A novel methodology was devised to address the urgent need for COVID-19 therapeutics by leveraging the DRKG for predictive tasks.
- Two core prediction tasks were defined: (i) identifying direct associations between disease and drug entities and (ii) uncovering interactions between gene entities and drugs that inhibit disease-relevant pathways.
- The TransE KGE model was employed to learn relational patterns and infer potential DR candidates, with a special focus on those undergoing clinical trials.

Rigorous Graph Structure Evaluation

- A comprehensive analysis was performed to assess the structural soundness and informativeness of the DRKG.
- Metrics such as the proportion of overlapping triplets across edge types and predicted neighborhood similarities were used to evaluate relational coherence.
- The model's scoring function performance was further analyzed to validate the quality of the learned embeddings, offering insights into their robustness and suitability for downstream drug discovery tasks.

15.5.2.5 Implementation Procedure

KGE with TransE

- **Model Description:** The TransE model is employed to learn low-dimensional vector representations for entities and relations in the DRKG. TransE operates under the principle that for a valid triple ⟨*head, relation, tail*⟩, the embedding of the head entity added to the relation vector should be close to the tail entity in vector space.

- **Objective:** To generate 400-dimensional embeddings for all entities and relations in the DRKG, enabling meaningful relational inference and downstream predictive tasks.

Optimization and Preprocessing Pipeline

a) **Candidate Drug Filtering**
   - Food and Drug Administration (FDA)-approved drugs were selected from DrugBank as candidate entities.
   - Molecules with a molecular weight below 250 Daltons were excluded to avoid low-complexity compounds less likely to be viable drug candidates.

b) **Target Disease Identification**
   - The study focuses on coronavirus-related diseases (Severe Acute Respiratory Syndrome (SARS), Middle East Respiratory Syndrome (MERS), Severe Acute Respiratory Syndrome COVID-19 (SARS-CoV-2)) as the core targets for repurposing, aligning with the COVID-19 research objective.

c) **Task Formulation and Prediction**
   - Two predictive tasks were formulated:
     1. Direct prediction of links between disease and drug entities.
     2. Indirect prediction via gene–drug interactions where the genes are implicated in COVID-19-related pathways.
   - The trained TransE embeddings were utilized to score and rank candidate drug links for these tasks.

d) **Validation with Clinical Trial Data**
   - Predicted drugs were cross-referenced with ongoing and past clinical trials for COVID-19.
   - This comparison served as an empirical validation of the model's predictive capacity.

e) **Embedding Optimization and Drug Ranking**
   - Pretrained embeddings were leveraged to compute confidence scores for candidate drugs.
   - Drugs were ranked based on their vector similarity scores to disease or gene entities, with higher scores indicating stronger repurposing potential.

f) **Comparative Analysis with Source Databases**
   - The performance of the DRKG was benchmarked against models trained on individual databases (GNBR, DrugBank, DGIdb).
   - This comparison confirmed the superior predictive strength and completeness of the unified DRKG over isolated knowledge sources.

15.6 Conclusion

This chapter covers the path of the evolution of KG with its history and discusses the concepts of the knowledge graph. The core concepts of entities, relationships, ontology, and triples are discussed with the illustration of a few examples of the knowledge graph. NER, EL, RE, and ontology engineering were the techniques focused on with their working process. The procedure and flow of the process of constructing, representing, and storing the knowledge graph are elaborated in one of the sections of this chapter. Finally, the case study on KG in supply chain management and DR for COVID-19 were elaborated with the approaches, methodologies, and evaluation using the tools of KG.

References

1 S. Ji, S. Pan, E. Cambria, P. Marttinen, and P. S. Yu, "A survey on knowledge graphs: Representation," *Acquis. Appl*, 2020, doi: 10.48550/arXiv.2002.00388.

2 B. Jehangir, S. Radhakrishnan, and R. Agarwal, "A survey on named entity recognition — datasets, tools, and methodologies," *Nat. Language Process. J.*, vol. 3, 100017, 2023, doi: 10.1016/j.nlp.2023.100017.

3 Q. Li *et al.*, "Improving entity linking by introducing knowledge graph structure information," *Appl. Sci*, vol. 12, no. 5, p. 2702, 2022, doi: 10.3390/app12052702.

4 K. Detroja, C. K. Bhensdadia, and B. S. Bhatt, "A survey on relation extraction," *Intell. Syst. Appl*, vol. 19, 2023, doi: 10.1016/j.iswa.2023.200244.

5 R. Iqbal, M. A. A. Murad, A. Mustapha, and N. M. Sharef, "An analysis of ontology engineering methodologies: a literature review," *Res. J. Appl. Sci., Eng. Technol*, vol. 6, no. 16, pp. 2993–3000, 2013, doi: 10.19026/rjaset.6.3684.

6 K. Sun *et al.*, "Relational structure-aware knowledge graph representation in complex space," *Mathematics*, vol. 10, no. 11, p. 1930, 2022, doi: 10.3390/math10111930.

7 C. Ranichandra Dharmara and B. K. Tripathy, "Optimisation of SPARQL queries over the RDF data in the cloud environment," *Int. J. Adv. Intell. Paradig*, vol. 24, no. 3/4, pp. 428–439, 2023.

16

Graph Representation Learning in Wireless Communication and Tourist Movement Analysis

Recent advancements in graph representation learning (GRL) have opened new avenues for solving complex real-world problems that involve relational and structured data. As traditional machine learning (ML) models often struggle with graph-structured inputs, GRL offers a powerful framework for embedding nodes, edges, and entire subgraphs into vector spaces that preserve graph topology and semantics. This capability is transforming domains such as communication networks, urban planning, healthcare, and social behavior analysis. In this chapter, we explore the versatility of GRL through two diverse yet graph-intensive case studies: one in wireless communication, focusing on optimizing network performance using graph-based methods, and the other in tourist movement analysis, where social media and points of interest (POI) data are modeled as graphs to uncover patterns of tourist behavior in Jaipur, India. These case studies illustrate the broad applicability of GRL in extracting meaningful insights from complex networked data.

16.1 A Graph-Theoretic Framework for Analyzing Tourist Flows from Social Media Data

This section explores the applications of graph-based algorithm techniques in various real-time domains. It presents a data-driven analysis of POIs in Jaipur, India, utilizing advanced data science techniques to uncover meaningful patterns and insights. The dataset comprises detailed attributes, including POI names, categories, entry fees, visitor demographics, and geographic coordinates. To analyze this data, we employ clustering, network analysis, and ML methods. Additionally, feature engineering is used to enhance model performance in predicting the priority classification of POIs, with the ultimate goal of supporting strategic tourism planning and decision-making.

16.1.1 Introduction

Jaipur, often referred to as the "Pink City," is a renowned tourist destination in India, celebrated for its architectural marvels, heritage sites, and vibrant cultural landscape. To optimize tourism experiences and improve infrastructure planning, it is essential to understand how different POIs function and interact [1]. This work uses data science techniques to analyze and interpret tourism patterns based on POI characteristics in Jaipur. By integrating visitor trends, category-based segmentation, and spatial data, the analysis provides actionable insights that can inform tourism management and policy development. The dataset comprises comprehensive information on a variety of POIs located in Jaipur. Each record includes attributes such as the POI name, type or category (e.g., historical site, museum, religious place), entry ticket price, demographic distribution of visitors (domestic vs. international), and latitude/longitude coordinates. During preprocessing, missing or inconsistent values are identified and addressed to ensure data quality and integrity. This structured dataset serves as the foundation for applying analytical models and extracting insights relevant to tourist behavior and POI classification.

16.1.2 Methodologies

16.1.2.1 Data Preprocessing

The initial stage involves cleaning and preparing the dataset for analysis. This includes handling missing or inconsistent values and transforming categorical variables into numerical representations using appropriate encoding techniques, ensuring the data is suitable for modeling and analysis.

16.1.2.2 Clustering Analysis

To identify spatial patterns among POIs, clustering algorithms such as K-means and DBSCAN [2] are applied using the geographic coordinates (latitude and longitude) of each location. These methods help group POIs with similar locational attributes, revealing clusters of popular or related tourist spots.

16.1.2.3 Network Analysis

Using NetworkX, graph-based methods are implemented to explore relationships between POIs. Edges are constructed based on geographic proximity, and structures such as minimum spanning trees are generated to uncover optimal connectivity paths among POIs, providing insights into tourist flow and accessibility.

16.1.2.4 Feature Engineering with Weisfeiler–Lehman Algorithm

Graph-based feature extraction is performed using the WL color refinement technique. This method encodes the local neighborhood structure of each POI within the graph, enriching the feature set for downstream ML tasks.

16.1.2.5 ML with GNNs

A GraphSAGE model—an inductive GNN architecture—is trained to predict the priority category of POIs. The model leverages structured features including ticket pricing, visitor demographics, and spatial relationships, enabling accurate classification of POIs based on their importance and usage patterns.

16.1.3 Approach Used

Data Exploration: The dataset is explored to understand the distribution of POIs across different categories and their geographic distribution. The data distribution is given in Fig. 16.1.

Clustering and Visualization: Clustering techniques are applied to group POIs based on geographic proximity, and the results are visualized using maps and Voronoi diagrams in Fig. 16.2.

Network Analysis: NetworkX is used to analyze the network structure of POIs, including proximity edges and minimum spanning trees. Graph of tourist spots (POIs) with proximity edges is shown in Fig. 16.3.

16.1.3.1 Feature Engineering

Features are engineered from graph representations of POI relationships using WL color refinement.

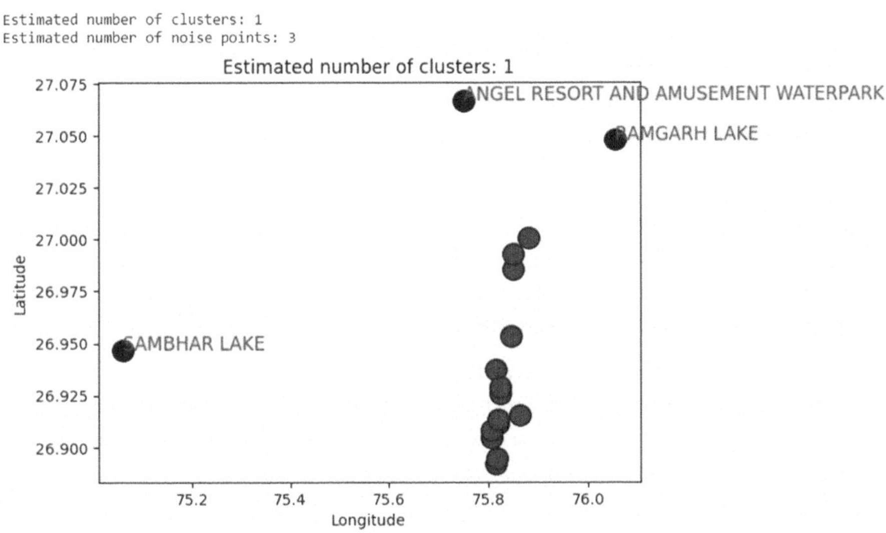

Figure 16.1 Data exploration of tourist POIs.

```
POI: AMBER PALACE, Cluster: 2
POI: CITY PALACE JAIPUR, Cluster: 5
POI: ELEFANTASTIC ELEPHANT FARM, Cluster: 2
POI: ALBERT HALL MUSEUM (CENTRAL MUSEUM), Cluster: 5
POI: NAHARGARH FORT, Cluster: 5
POI: BIRLA TEMPLE JAIPUR, Cluster: 5
POI: JAL MAHAL, Cluster: 2
POI: CENTRAL PARK JAIPUR INDIA, Cluster: 5
POI: ANOKHI MUSEUM OF HAND PRINTING, Cluster: 2
POI: GOVIND DEVJI TEMPLE, Cluster: 5
POI: MOTI DOONGRI GANESH TEMPLE, Cluster: 5
POI: SAMBHAR LAKE, Cluster: 3
POI: GALTAJI, Cluster: 5
POI: STATUE CIRCLE, Cluster: 5
POI: ZOOLOGICAL GARDEN JAIPUR, Cluster: 5
POI: ANGEL RESORT AND AMUSEMENT WATERPARK, Cluster: 6
POI: RAMGARH LAKE, Cluster: 4
```

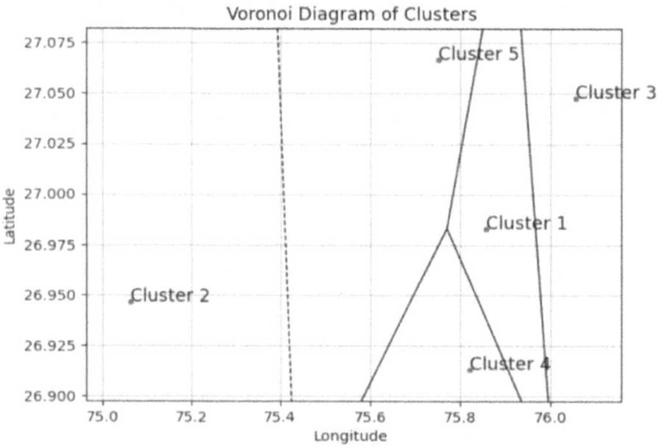

Figure 16.2 Visualization of grouping POIs into clusters.

16.1.3.2 ML Modeling

GraphSAGE is trained on the features extracted from POI graphs to predict priority categories for the POIs.

16.1.4 Inference

This work focuses on clustering tourist attractions in Jaipur based on their geographical proximity and visualizing these groupings through interactive mapping. Several key insights emerge from this approach:

- **Geospatial Clustering of Attractions:** Using agglomerative hierarchical clustering on the geographical coordinates of attractions, the project identifies natural groupings based on spatial closeness. Attractions situated near each other are systematically grouped into coherent clusters, reflecting geographic accessibility.
- **Interactive Cluster Visualization:** The clustered data is rendered on an interactive map using the Folium library. Each attraction is marked, and cluster

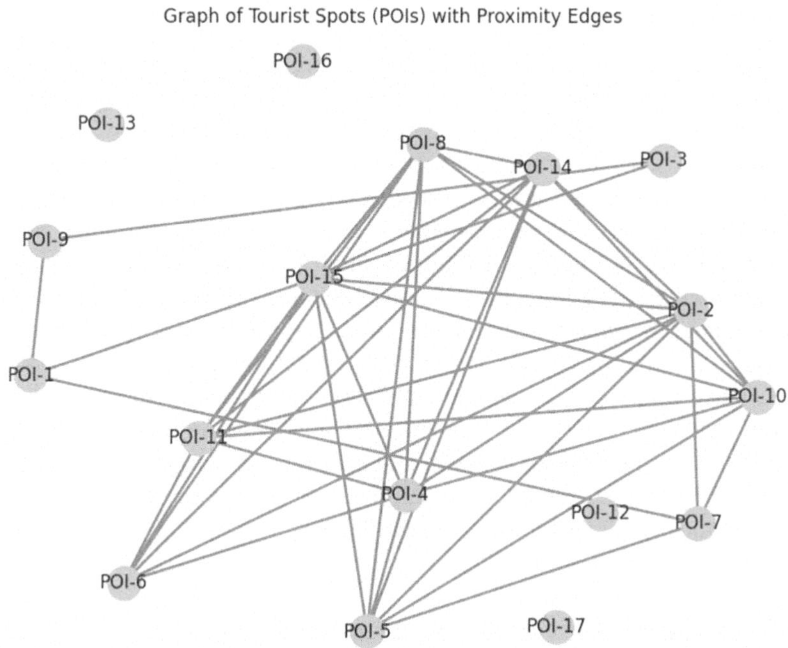

Figure 16.3 Graph of tourist spots (POIs) with proximity edges.

membership is visually distinguished by color-coding. This enables users to intuitively understand the spatial organization and density of attractions across Jaipur.

- **Tourism and Urban Planning Insights:** The visualized clusters offer actionable insights for stakeholders such as tourism departments and city planners. They can identify zones with high attraction density for targeted resource deployment, infrastructure development, or visitor flow management and detect underdeveloped regions for potential growth.
- **Thematic Interpretation of Clusters:** Each cluster may reflect a thematic connection—such as historical sites, religious landmarks, or recreational areas—based on proximity. This provides contextually relevant groupings that can inform thematic tour development and tailored promotional strategies.
- **Customizable Clustering for Strategic Flexibility:** The model supports parameter tuning, including the number of clusters, allowing users to explore alternative configurations based on specific goals or stakeholder preferences. This adaptability enhances the model's practical value in scenario-based planning and tourism optimization.

16.1.5 Conclusion

This study presents a holistic analysis of POIs in Jaipur, India, using advanced data science methodologies to uncover spatial patterns, relationships, and predictive insights. Beginning with rigorous data preprocessing to manage missing values and encode categorical variables, the study employed clustering algorithms such as DBSCAN and K-means to group geographically proximate POIs, illuminating tourist movement patterns and potential travel routes. Network analysis using NetworkX highlighted inter-POI connectivity, revealing central hubs and optimal itineraries. Feature engineering through WL color refinement enhanced graph-based representations, capturing intricate relational characteristics. Leveraging GraphSAGE, a GNN model, the project developed a robust predictive framework to classify POIs based on attributes such as ticket prices, visitor demographics, and location. The integrated approach not only deepens understanding of tourist behavior and POI interactions but also provides actionable insights for stakeholders to improve tourism planning, marketing strategies, and the overall visitor experience in Jaipur.

16.2 Knowledge-Driven Graph Learning for Next-Generation Wireless Networks

The rapid proliferation of smart devices and the resulting explosion of data in fifth-generation (5G) wireless communication networks have intensified the need for effective data processing and intelligent network management. While current research predominantly emphasizes upper-layer application data and transmission optimization—often relying on Monte Carlo simulations—the intrinsic relationships within wireless network data remain underexplored. This study addresses this gap by constructing a domain-informed knowledge graph rooted in wireless communication protocols and expert insights to capture endogenous intelligence in wireless networks. We present a novel methodology for modeling core network data from 5G/Beyond-5G (B5G) testbeds by learning graph representations through a GCN-based framework. This model supports unsupervised node classification and anomaly cause identification within the network. Experimental evaluations on both proprietary and public datasets reveal that our approach significantly outperforms baseline models such as VGAE and ARVGE in classification accuracy, demonstrating its effectiveness in enhancing the interpretability and intelligence of wireless communication systems.

16.2.1 Introduction

The advent of 5G mobile networks has revolutionized communication, significantly enhancing connectivity and service quality for users. However, the proliferation of smart terminals has increased the complexity of wireless communication networks, rendering traditional model-driven approaches inadequate for efficient network design and optimization. Simultaneously, the enormous volume of data generated by access terminals presents new opportunities for data-driven intelligence to optimize and manage wireless networks. A critical challenge, however, lies in the underutilized portion of this data—referred to as underlying data—which is difficult to incorporate directly into conventional AI algorithms due to its raw and unstructured nature.

Current research in intelligent wireless communications predominantly focuses on performance optimization—such as channel allocation and cache placement—using simulated data generated through Monte Carlo methods. While effective to some extent, these approaches often overlook the semantic structure and latent relationships embedded within the actual wireless communication data fields. Additionally, the lack of accessible, real-world wireless communication datasets has led to an overreliance on synthetic data, limiting the practical applicability of many proposed algorithms.

Understanding and utilizing real-world wireless data effectively requires a deep comprehension of communication protocol structures and the interdependencies among data fields. Due to the technical complexity and heterogeneity of wireless protocols, both experts and nonexperts face challenges in translating this knowledge into actionable insights. This necessitates the development of tools that bridge the gap between protocol knowledge and data-driven models.

KGs have emerged as powerful tools for representing and integrating structured knowledge through entities and relationships. By leveraging KGs in the context of wireless communication, it becomes possible to transform complex, low-level data into interpretable, high-level knowledge. This not only supports the visualization and understanding of data relationships but also enables advanced downstream tasks such as network optimization and fault diagnosis.

Motivated by the absence of existing wireless data knowledge graphs and the potential of KG-based learning, this study introduces a comprehensive knowledge graph constructed from core wireless network data. Furthermore, we propose a novel KRL model that combines GCNNs with GANs within a graph autoencoder framework. Our model achieves superior performance in unsupervised node classification and demonstrates high accuracy in relation prediction, offering a valuable foundation for tasks such as anomaly detection and network optimization in next-generation wireless systems.

16.2.2 Methodology

16.2.2.1 GAN Without GCN

Data Loading The code starts by loading the input data from a CSV file named "input.csv" using pandas' 'read_csv()' function into a DataFrame named 'df.'

Data Preprocessing

- Categorical variables are converted into numerical variables using one-hot encoding, except for columns "ID," "State," "Area," "NetworkName," and "NetworkType."
- The numerical features are then normalized to ensure all features are on the same scale. This is done to prevent any particular feature from dominating the training process due to its larger magnitude.

Generator Model Definition ('build_generator()') This function defines the architecture of the generator model. It takes two arguments: 'latent_dim,' the dimensionality of the input noise vector, and 'output_shape,' the number of features in the dataset. The generator starts with a fully connected layer of 128 units with ReLU activation function followed by another fully connected layer of 256 units also with ReLU activation. Next, a dense layer with 64 units and ReLU activation is added to preprocess the input for the GCNN. The data is then reshaped to fit the input shape required by the GCN.

A 1D convolutional layer with 64 filters, kernel size 2, and ReLU activation is added for the GCN layer. The output is flattened and passed through a final dense layer with 'output_shape' units and sigmoid activation function, which generates the synthetic data.

Discriminator Model Definition ('build_discriminator()') This function defines the architecture of the discriminator model. It takes 'input_shape' as an argument, representing the number of features in the dataset. The discriminator begins by reshaping the input data to fit the shape required by the GCN. A 1D convolutional layer with 64 filters, kernel size 2, and ReLU activation is added for the GCN layer. The output is flattened and passed through two fully connected layers with 128 and 1 unit(s), respectively, both with ReLU and sigmoid activation functions, making a binary classification (real or generated).

GAN Model Definition ('build_gan()') This function defines the architecture of the GAN, which combines the generator and discriminator. The discriminator is set to be nontrainable during the training of the GAN to prevent it from being updated when the generator is trained. The GAN takes noise vectors as input and outputs the discriminator's prediction on the generated data.

Training the GAN ('train_gan()') This function trains the GAN model. It iterates through the dataset in batches, where each batch consists of real data samples and noise samples. For each batch, the discriminator is trained first on both the real and generated data with corresponding labels. Next, the generator is trained using the GAN model, with misleading labels (zeros) to encourage the generator to produce data that the discriminator classifies as real. The losses for both the generator and discriminator are recorded for each epoch. The function returns the generator and discriminator losses throughout the training process.

Model Training Finally, the GAN model is trained by calling 'train_gan()' function with the defined generator, discriminator, GAN, dataset, and other parameters. This entire process aims to train a GAN to generate synthetic data that closely resembles the real data while fooling the discriminator into classifying it as real.

16.2.2.2 GAN with GCN

Data Loading and Preprocessing The code starts by loading the input data from a CSV file named "input.csv" using pandas' 'read_csv()' function into a DataFrame named 'df.' Categorical variables are converted into numerical variables using one-hot encoding, except for columns "ID," "State," "Area," "NetworkName," and "NetworkType."

The numerical features are then normalized to ensure all features are on the same scale. This is done to prevent any particular feature from dominating the training process due to its larger magnitude.

Graph Structure Conversion The next step involves converting the preprocessed data into a graph structure. An adjacency matrix is created with dimensions '(num_features, num_features),' where 'num_features' represents the number of features in the dataset. The matrix is initialized with ones and the diagonal elements are set to zero ('np.ones((num_features, num_features)) - np.eye(num_features)') to ensure that each feature is connected to every other feature, except itself.

Generator Model Definition ('build_generator()') This function defines the architecture of the generator model. It takes 'latent_dim' as an argument, representing the dimensionality of the input noise vector. Two inputs are defined: 'noise,' representing the random noise vector, and 'input_data,' representing the real data samples. The noise vector is passed through two dense layers with ReLU activation functions to preprocess it. The real data samples are passed through a GCN layer ('GCNConv') with ReLU activation, using the adjacency matrix as input. The output of the GCN layer is flattened and passed through a dense layer with sigmoid activation to generate the synthetic data.

Discriminator Model Definition ('build_discriminator()') This function defines the architecture of the discriminator model. An input is defined, representing the data samples (real or generated). The data samples are passed through a GCN layer ('GCNConv') with ReLU activation, using the adjacency matrix as input. The output of the GCN layer is flattened and passed through two dense layers with ReLU activation functions. The output layer consists of a single unit with sigmoid activation, indicating the probability that the input data is real.

GAN Model Definition ('build_gan()') This function defines the architecture of the GAN, which combines the generator and discriminator. The discriminator is set to be nontrainable during the training of the GAN to prevent it from being updated when the generator is trained. Two inputs are defined: 'noise' (random noise vector) and 'input_data' (real data samples). The generator generates synthetic data using both noise and real data as input, and the discriminator predicts the authenticity of the generated data.

Training the GAN ('train_gan()') This function trains the GAN model. It iterates through the dataset in batches, where each batch consists of real data samples and corresponding noise samples. For each batch, the discriminator is trained first on both the real and generated data with the corresponding labels.

Next, the generator is trained using the GAN model, with misleading labels (ones) to encourage the generator to produce data that the discriminator classifies as real. The losses for both the generator and discriminator are recorded for each epoch. The function returns the generator and discriminator losses throughout the training process.

Model Training Finally, the GAN model is trained by calling 'train_gan()' function with the defined generator, discriminator, GAN, dataset, and other parameters.

16.2.3 Approach

This study adopts a GAN [3] framework integrated with GCNs to generate synthetic data from a structured dataset. The process begins by importing data from a CSV file, followed by preprocessing steps that include one-hot encoding of categorical variables and normalization of numerical features to ensure consistency and model compatibility.

A graph structure is then constructed from the dataset using an adjacency matrix, representing relationships between data instances. This graph representation serves as the foundation for applying graph-based learning techniques in subsequent stages. Two core models are defined using the Keras Functional API: the generator and the discriminator. The generator accepts random noise vectors and real data samples as inputs. It processes the noise through a dense layer and applies GCN layers to the structured data to produce synthetic samples. The discriminator, in contrast, is designed to differentiate between real and synthetic data. It takes either real or generated samples as input, passes them through GCN layers, and outputs a prediction, indicating the authenticity of the sample.

A composite GAN model is then created by combining the generator and discriminator with the discriminator's weights frozen (nontrainable) during the generator's training to ensure stable adversarial learning. The training process proceeds in an alternating manner: in each iteration, the discriminator is updated using a batch of real and generated samples, while the generator is updated to produce data that the discriminator misclassifies as real. Throughout training, losses from both the generator and the discriminator are monitored and recorded across epochs to track performance and convergence. Finally, both models are compiled with suitable optimizers and loss functions, and the entire GAN architecture is trained using a custom training loop that orchestrates data batching, alternating updates, and performance tracking (Figure 16.4).

16.2.4 Experimental Evaluation

From Fig. 16.5, we infer that GAN with Conv-layers brings out the lowest amount of loss as 0.297722.

16.2.5 Conclusion

As we conclude, the model is well trained with two neural networks. Generators and discriminators are used to process the latent space data and produce the original data. We conclude that GAN framework integrated with GCNs gives improved result than using other GAN variants.

16.3 Applications of GRL in Wireless Networks and Urban Tourism

GRL has emerged as a powerful technique to model complex, structured data in diverse domains, including wireless network communication and urban tourism analytics. In wireless communication networks, GRL is applied to model the

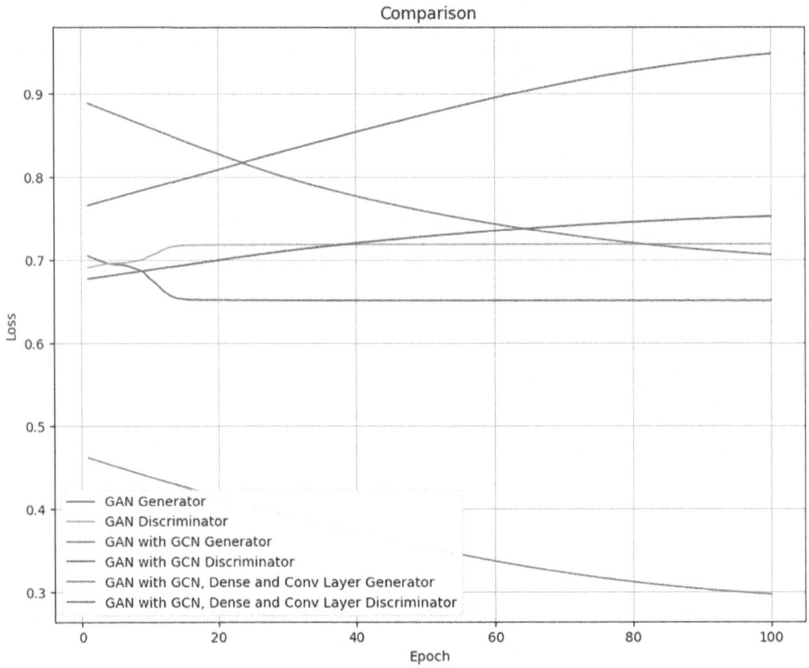

Figure 16.4 Comparative analysis using GAN and its variants.

	GAN-Generator	GAN-Discriminator	GAN GCN-Generator	GAN GCN-Discriminator	GAN GCN Conv-Generator	GAN GCN Conv-Discriminator
0	0.650393	0.718484	0.562907	0.750412	0.302849	0.939525
1	0.650715	0.718309	0.562639	0.750589	0.302136	0.940522
2	0.650388	0.718487	0.562377	0.750761	0.301444	0.941493
3	0.650697	0.718319	0.562124	0.750928	0.300773	0.942436
4	0.650350	0.718508	0.561878	0.751090	0.300123	0.943352
5	0.650700	0.718317	0.561639	0.751248	0.299493	0.944242
6	0.650376	0.718494	0.561407	0.751401	0.298884	0.945106
7	0.650697	0.718318	0.561183	0.751549	0.298293	0.945944
8	0.650335	0.718516	0.560964	0.751693	0.297722	0.946757

Figure 16.5 Epoch execution for different models.

intricate topologies and relationships among base stations, access points, and data packets. By learning low-dimensional representations of network entities from graph-structured data, GRL enables tasks such as network anomaly detection, traffic prediction, dynamic routing optimization, and spectrum allocation. It enhances the ability to predict faults and trace root causes in large-scale 5G and beyond-5G infrastructures by capturing dependencies across spatial and temporal dimensions.

In the domain of urban tourism, particularly in analyzing POIs in cities such as Jaipur, GRL facilitates the understanding of spatial, social, and semantic relationships among tourist locations. POIs and their visitor interactions are modeled as graphs where nodes represent locations and edges denote proximity, shared visitor patterns, or transportation connectivity. GRL techniques such as GNNs or GraphSAGE help uncover hidden patterns in tourist movements, recommend optimal tour paths, and predict high-priority attractions based on features such as ticket price, visitor demographics, and geographic clusters. Such applications support smart tourism, enabling city planners and tourism boards to design more efficient, personalized, and sustainable travel experiences.

16.4 Other Areas of GRL Applications

16.4.1 Healthcare and Biomedical Informatics

16.4.1.1 Application

GRL is widely used in drug discovery, disease–gene interaction prediction, patient similarity networks, and medical knowledge graph completion.

16.4.1.2 Drug Discovery

Molecules are naturally represented as graphs, with atoms as nodes and chemical bonds as edges. GRL enables learning representations of these molecular graphs to predict properties such as toxicity, solubility, or binding affinity to a target protein [4].

16.4.1.3 Drug Repurposing

Knowledge graphs such as DRKG encode known relationships among diseases, drugs, and genes. GRL helps in learning embeddings to infer missing links (e.g., a drug treating a new disease).

16.4.1.4 Patient Graphs

In EHRs, patients can be modeled as nodes connected based on clinical similarity. GRL helps in predicting disease risk, readmission likelihood, and personalized treatment paths.

16.4.2 E-commerce and Recommendation Systems

16.4.2.1 Application

GRL enhances recommendation engines by capturing user–item interaction graphs and their contextual relationships.

16.4.2.2 User–Item Graphs

Users and items are nodes, and their interactions (clicks, purchases, ratings) are edges. GRL enables learning rich embeddings that capture user preferences and item similarities.

16.4.2.3 Session-Based Recommendations

GRL can model short-term user behavior sessions as graphs and generate real-time, context-aware recommendations.

16.4.2.4 Social Influence Modeling

Incorporates user social network graphs to account for peer influence in purchasing decisions.

16.4.3 Financial Fraud Detection

16.4.3.1 Application

GRL aids in detecting fraudulent activities in banking, insurance, and financial transactions.

16.4.3.2 Transaction Graphs

Entities such as users, devices, accounts, and transactions form heterogeneous graphs. GRL helps in identifying suspicious patterns or accounts that deviate from normal behavior.

16.4.3.3 Anomaly Detection

By modeling temporal financial activities and their relationships, GRL can detect sudden spikes or atypical paths that may indicate fraud or money laundering.

16.4.3.4 Link Prediction

Useful in identifying hidden collusion or unauthorized access patterns by predicting likely but unobserved links in a network.

16.4.4 Cybersecurity

16.4.4.1 Application

GRL is used in intrusion detection, malware classification, and attack path prediction in networked systems [5].

16.4.4.2 Network Graphs

Hosts, IP addresses, and communication logs are represented as nodes and edges. GRL models this topology to identify potential threats.

16.4.4.3 Attack Graphs

Graphs representing sequences of potential attacks (like privilege escalation paths) are used to proactively strengthen system defenses.

16.4.4.4 Code Graphs

Source code or binaries can be transformed into abstract syntax trees or control-flow graphs. GRL helps in detecting vulnerabilities or malware signatures.

16.4.5 Social Network Analysis

16.4.5.1 Application

GRL helps in community detection, influence maximization, and misinformation tracking.

16.4.5.2 Community Detection

Learns embeddings that group users based on behavior or interactions.

16.4.5.3 Fake News and Bot Detection

User–post interaction graphs are used to identify coordinated misinformation campaigns or bot-like behavior.

16.4.5.4 User Profiling

Combines content and structural features to model user behavior, interests, and influence in a network.

16.4.6 Traffic and Smart Transportation

16.4.6.1 Application

GRL supports route optimization, congestion forecasting, and public transit planning.

16.4.6.2 Traffic Graphs

Roads/intersections as nodes and traffic flows as edges. GRL helps in predicting congestion and recommending alternate routes.

16.4.6.3 Multimodal Networks

Incorporates different modes of transport (bus, metro, rideshare) into a unified graph to improve multimodal journey planning.

16.4.6.4 Dynamic Graphs

Real-time GRL models help in reacting to changes in traffic patterns due to events or accidents.

16.4.7 Natural Language Processing

16.4.7.1 Application

GRL enhances semantic understanding in tasks such as question answering, text classification, and knowledge graph completion.

16.4.7.2 Knowledge Graph Embedding

GRL learns vector representations of entities and relations for tasks such as entity linking and relation extraction.

16.4.7.3 Document Graphs

Sentences or concepts in a document can be modeled as graphs. GRL captures context and co-occurrence to improve document classification and summarization.

16.4.7.4 Dialogue Systems

Models dialogue turns and dependencies as graphs to generate coherent and context-aware responses.

16.4.8 Supply Chain and Logistics

16.4.8.1 Application

GRL enables efficiency improvements in inventory management, demand forecasting, and transportation logistics.

16.4.8.2 Supply Network Graphs

Entities such as suppliers, warehouses, and distribution centers are nodes. GRL helps in identifying bottlenecks and optimizing logistics paths.

16.4.8.3 Demand Graphs

Products and customer demands form graphs where GRL predicts future trends or disruptions.

16.4.8.4 Risk Management

Models interdependencies to predict cascading failures due to supplier delays or transportation issues.

16.4.9 Energy Systems and Smart Grids

16.4.9.1 Application

GRL supports predictive maintenance, load forecasting, and energy distribution optimization.

16.4.9.2 Grid Graphs

Power generation units, substations, and consumers form a graph. GRL models the energy flow to detect outages or optimize distribution.

16.4.9.3 Sensor Networks

GRL processes readings from IoT devices across the grid to detect anomalies and predict equipment failures.

16.4.9.4 Renewable Integration

Helps manage variability in solar/wind power through better modeling of supply–demand patterns.

16.5 Conclusion

This chapter presented a comprehensive exploration of graph-based representation learning techniques across two distinct yet data-rich domains: urban tourism and wireless communication networks. By analyzing POIs in Jaipur, India, using social media data, we demonstrated how graph–theoretical methods can effectively capture and visualize tourist flow patterns, enabling deeper insights into spatial clustering, connectivity, and urban mobility behavior. In parallel, we addressed the challenges of managing complex, high-dimensional wireless communication data in 5G networks by leveraging knowledge graphs and advanced GNNs. Our approach showcased how knowledge-driven graph learning can uncover latent relationships within protocol data, enabling efficient node classification, anomaly detection, and network optimization. Together, these case studies highlight the versatility and power of GRL as a unifying framework for intelligent data interpretation, decision-making, and system optimization in both physical and digital infrastructures. As the volume and complexity of networked data continue to grow, GRL is poised to play a transformative role in enabling smart cities, adaptive communication systems, and data-driven governance.

References

1 Z. Khan, Z. Khan, B.-G. Lee, H. K. Kim, and M. Jeon, "Graph neural networks-based framework to analyze social media platforms for malicious user detection," *Appl. Soft Comput*, vol. 155, April, p. 111416, 2024.

2 F. Andriyani and Y. Puspitarani, "Performance comparison of K-Means and DBScan algorithms for text clustering product reviews," *Sinkron: Jurnal dan Penelitian Teknik Informatika*, vol. 7, no. 3, 2022, doi: 10.33395/sinkron.v7i3.11569.

3 A. Aggarwal, M. Mittal, and G. Battineni, "Generative adversarial network: An overview of theory and applications," *Int. J. Informat. Manag. Data Insights*, vol. 1, no. 1, 2021, doi: 10.1016/j.jjimei.2020.100004.April

4 M. S. M. Shahrizan, Z. H. A. Aziz, and H. Katas, "Fluid gels: A systematic review towards their application in pharmaceutical dosage forms and drug delivery systems," *J. Drug Deliv. Sci. Technol*, vol. 67, January, 2022, doi: 10.1016/j.jddst.2021.102947.

5 L. F. Sikos, "Cybersecurity knowledge graphs," *Knowl. Informat. Syst*, vol. 65, no. 9, pp. 1–21, 2023, doi: 10.1007/s10115-023-01860-3.

Index

a

activation function 181, 184, 198, 204, 223, 226, 263
acyclic graphs 6
adamic-adar index 76, 261
adam optimizer 294
adjacency matrix 14, 44, 45, 55, 66, 67, 71, 242, 263, 329
adjacent node 17, 223
adversarial domain loss 289, 290
adversarial learning 284, 285, 290, 395
adversarial objective 280
aggregate function 192, 225
aggregation functions 190, 192, 194, 276, 277, 373
anomalous subgraph 25
anomaly detection 22, 46, 74, 236, 265
artificial intelligence 16, 22, 32, 34, 223, 310, 331
attention pooling 162–164, 179
auc-roc 101
audio modality 322, 329
autoencoder-based graph encoders 264
autoencoders 224, 230, 264, 284, 285, 308, 350, 353
autonomous vehicles 267, 331, 332, 334

b

bag of nodes 58
betweenness 33
betweenness centrality 37, 41–43
bidirectional encoder 264, 308
bi-fan motif 51
bilinear pooling 329
binary matrix 68
bioinformatics 25, 108, 124, 176, 200, 203, 228, 237, 238, 251, 286, 299, 312, 338, 345
biological
  knowledge graph 378
  networks 13, 265, 354
  systems 34, 354
biomed central 31
biomedical ontologies 364
bipartite
  graph 10, 11
  motifs 20, 21
blockchain 375
b-per 368
brain network analysis 24
breadth first search 22

c

cat-GNN model 188
centrality measures 33, 36, 38, 59

central node 19, 20, 37
chain motifs 20, 21, 50
chronic diseases 118
citation
  behaviors 11
  graph 10, 12, 13, 15, 22, 57, 58
  links 10
  network 13, 16, 50, 51
  patterns 11
classification 46, 59, 64, 101, 327
clique motif 51
closed triangle 46, 48, 50
closeness 33
closeness centrality 37–41, 43
cluster community 55
clustering 15, 22, 59, 67, 76, 277, 327, 387
clustering coefficient 33, 46–48, 50, 52, 57
communication networks 22
community
  associations 14
  detection 22, 26, 27, 68, 74, 115, 310, 327, 329
  structures 46, 56, 78
complete graph 9, 125, 226, 253, 260, 266, 351
computed tomography 108
computer vision 5, 181, 238, 245, 331
connected graph 9, 17, 110, 148, 164
contrastive learning 109, 244, 245–248, 303, 307, 312
ContrastPool 178, 179
convolution neural networks 153
cosine similarity 260
crystallography 25
CT scans 24
cybersecurity 17, 25, 91, 265

d

data
  fusion 325, 334
  integration 236, 364, 366, 371
  mining 34, 150, 310
  model 360, 364, 372
decision support systems 5, 92, 149
decision tree 99, 288, 296
decoder 224, 228, 230, 264, 265, 309, 353
deep
  asymmetric NMF 254
  GRL 356
  learning 14, 31, 207, 310, 337
  neural network 290
DeepWalk 14, 29, 30, 109, 256, 348
degree
  centrality 33, 37, 39, 44
  matrix 69, 71, 110, 111, 226, 280
degree-based node sampling 129
demystifying graph embeddings 337
dense graphs 6, 83, 117, 143, 153
depth first search 22, 257
diagonal matrix 69–71, 111
differentiable pooling 171
Diffpool 171–173
digital technologies 375
dimensionality reduction 14, 341, 344, 353, 380
directed graph 6, 15, 35, 53
discriminative network embedding 31
distance minimization 241
divergence function 294
domain adversarial neural network 289
domain discriminator 280
domain-invariant learning 283
drug discovery 352
drug-drug interactions 189
drug repurposing 120, 378
drug repurposing knowledge graph 378
DYGCN 221

dynamic GNNs 216, 217, 220
dynamic graph 219
dynamic node classification 221

e
eccentricity 33, 35
edge
  bundling 83
  classification 102, 106
  embedding 185, 343, 348, 350
  sampling 137–139
egograph 33, 46, 48, 50
ego neighborhood 19
eigen decomposition 288
eigenvalue decomposition 287
eigenvector 33, 110–113, 185
eigenvector centrality 37, 43, 45
embedding vector 330
encoder-decoder
  framework 262
  models 266
entity linking 355, 365
Euclidean distance 243

f
Facebook 26–28, 45, 49, 325
face recognition 23
feature
  alignment 279, 284, 285
  engineering 14, 229, 275, 346, 353, 370, 385–387, 390
  extraction 14, 285, 288, 331, 333
  information 14, 59, 306, 316, 317
  learning 245, 312
  transformation 287, 294
  vector 65, 296, 317, 331, 332
feature-based transfer learning 292
feedforward motif 51
flat pooling 155, 156, 165, 167, 178–180
four-node graphlets 21
fraud detection 17, 25, 103, 241, 293, 311
fuzzy C-means 91

g
gated recurrent units 195
Geneformer 298
generative pre-trained transformer 264
global
  alignment 239
  overlap measures 78
  pooling 193
Graclus pooling 168
gradient
  boosting 59
  descent 294
  reversal trick 290
graph
  aligning 271
  alignment 235, 237, 240, 241, 246–248, 282, 292
  analysis 7, 22, 126, 185, 235, 255, 341, 354, 380
  analytics 339
  attention networks 14, 183, 199, 352, 374
  augmentation 316, 317
  autoencoder 109, 224, 266
  classification 107, 108, 121, 194
  clustering 14
  clustering coefficient 56
  connectivity 14, 15, 17
  contrastive learning 303, 315, 321
  convolutional encoders 263
  convolutional networks 14, 102, 153, 279
  convolution layer 197, 199
  data 14, 15, 25, 95, 100, 101, 106, 123, 155, 183, 191, 198, 208, 224, 227, 248, 250, 251, 263, 264, 272, 339
  density 33, 53

graph (*contd.*)
  eccentricity 53, 54
  embedding 30, 108, 241, 330, 354
  encoder 109, 316
  factorization 348
  feature extraction 197
  isomorphism 237
  Laplacian 111
  machine learning 100
  matching 236, 237, 293
  modularity 54, 55
  neighborhoods 18, 73, 92
  neural network 14, 68, 100, 242, 303, 322
  pooling 153, 235
  recurrent neural networks 211
  representation learning 3, 33, 73, 237, 260, 269, 337, 385
  sparsification 14
  structures 13, 15, 34, 339
  theory 14, 15
  traversal 22
graph-based
  applications 25
  learning 46, 70, 166, 208, 232, 299, 310, 334, 395
  models 23, 30, 208, 278
  neural networks 23
  representations 23, 271, 390
graphlets 19, 21, 64
graphsage 14, 102, 103, 258, 276, 277, 315, 390
grarep 262
Gromov-wasserstein distance 243

h

healthcare
  industry 4
  sector 4
heatmaps 82, 83
heterogeneous
  feature augmentation 282
  graph 13, 83, 85, 86
  transfer learning 282
hierarchical
  graph 12
  manner 12
  pooling 166, 178
  structures 6
histogram matching 63
histograms 62
homogeneous graph 12, 13
homophily 56
hyperedge 11
hypergraph 11
hypergraph convolution layer 223
hypergraph neural network 223

i

i-loc 368
image embedding 330
image modality 322, 323, 329
image segmentation 23
incident matrix 66, 67
inductive learning 277
inductive learning methods 355
InfoNCE loss 315, 318
info noise-constrastive estimation 315
input
  data 14, 188, 230, 262, 290, 326, 340, 353
  graph 14, 59, 107, 128, 136
interconnected data 5
internet of things 223, 352
inverse square root 70

j

Jaccard
  coefficient 105
  measures 260

Jaccard similarity measure 75, 76
Jensen–Shannon divergence-based loss 316

k

Katz index 78, 79, 95
kernel
  function 287, 293
  mapping 287, 288
kernel-based feature transformation 286
k-hop neighborhood 18, 143
k-mean clustering 111
k-means 91
knowledge
  discovery 338, 354
  graph 85, 359, 361, 363, 378
  graph fusion 241
knowledge-based AI 364
Kullback-Leibler divergence 284

l

label propagation 63
label propagation algorithm 109
Laplacian 33
  Eigenmaps 348
  matrix 66, 69
latent similarity 306
layer-wise neighborhood sampling 147
learning management systems 149
learning process 14, 202, 271, 327
LinkedIn 26, 27, 28, 45, 49
link prediction 14, 15, 22, 65, 74–76, 87, 101, 104, 194, 205, 228, 265, 277, 310, 329, 374, 378
local
  alignment 240
  connectivity 46–48, 50, 64, 81
  neighbors 18
  overlap measures 75
LOD cloud 361
logistic regression 30
long-short-term memory 195
loss functions 226, 318
Louvain algorithm 109

m

machine learning 6, 58, 61, 249, 275, 310, 322
  algorithms 66
  models 14, 25, 59, 67, 385
malware detection 352
Markov chain 71
Masked autoencoders 308
materials science 25
Matplotlib 376
matrix factorization 268, 350
maximum mean discrepancy 184
max pooling 160–164, 171, 175, 178, 184
mean pooling 158–160, 163
medical imaging 24
message passing 202
meta-path-based
  adjacency matrix 88
  learning 294
MinCutPool 177
minimum cut pooling 177
MLP layers 194
model
  deployment 184, 340
  engineering 339, 340, 346
  evaluation 340
  optimization 340
modularity 53, 56, 72, 116, 151, 330
modularity score 56
ModulePred 31
molecular orbitals 24
motifs 19, 20, 33, 35, 46, 50
multigraph 6, 8, 9

multimodal
  data 322, 331, 333, 353, 354
  fusion 332, 333
  graph 321, 327, 329, 334, 356
  GRL 333, 334
multiple edges 6, 8, 9

n
named entity recognition 365
natural language processing 271, 322
neighborhood
  connectivity 34
  nodes 17, 18, 19
  overlap 73, 74
  reconstruction 249, 251
  relationships 14
  sampling 142, 143, 145, 149, 150, 219, 276, 277
  structures 22, 95, 125, 258
neighboring nodes 18, 19, 22, 44, 45, 62, 67, 75, 102, 190, 192, 197, 200, 225, 250, 256
network
  analysis 6, 76, 387
  connectivity 78
  routing 22
neural network 30, 288, 329
neural network models 14
node
  centrality 36, 37
  classification 15, 22, 46, 65, 67, 87, 194, 205, 275, 277, 329
  clustering 109, 229
  degree 18, 35, 36
  embeddings 74, 82, 276
  sampling 126
Node2Vec 14, 29, 106
node-edge relationships 66
node-link diagrams 82
nonadjacent nodes 20
non-grid-structured graph 15
nonlinear activation function 186, 276, 280
normalization 275
normalized Laplacian matrix 69
NT-Xent loss 318
nuclear magnetic resonance 25

o
objective function 286
object recognition 23
ontology engineering 370, 371
ordinary differential equation 218
outlier
  detection 355
  nodes 82

p
PageRank 33, 35, 45
PageRank-based similarity 78, 81
parallel edges 8
path-based methods 65
pathfinding 22
pathfinding algorithms 37
PathSim 88
pattern
  classification 23
  matching 373
  recognition 23, 236
planar graph 10
points of interest 385
prediction 59, 327
predictive modeling 22
principal component analysis 284
protein-protein interactions 24, 265
PubMed Central 31

q
quantitative structure-activity relationship models 24
quantum chemistry 24
query language 364

r
random forest 59, 189
random walk 66, 81, 135, 143, 145, 146, 148, 255–257
random walk-based sampling 135
random walk neighborhood sampling 145, 146
RBF kernel 287
RDF schema 360
RDF triples 372
recommendation systems 22, 207, 266, 268, 310, 327
rectified linear unit 226
recurrent neural networks 182
recurrent subgraph 19
region of interest (ROI) 178
relational learning 100
relation extraction 369
ReLU activation function 392, 394
research communities 16
resource allocation index 77
routing networks 19

s
SAGPool 176
sampling probability 130
satellite images 333
schema language 360
self-supervised
  learning 303
  tasks 307
semantic web 359
semantic web technologies 370
semi-supervised learning 265
sentiment analysis 352
sigmoid activation function 392
signature verification systems 23
similarity measures 259
SimRank 78–81, 95
singular value decomposition 288
skip-gram 256
snowball sampling 134
social
  behavior analysis 385
  interactions 26
  media 17, 18
  network analysis 24, 61, 166, 310
  network graph 61, 310, 313
  networks 13, 22, 26, 27, 28, 42, 48, 49, 322, 325, 351
soft clustering methods 90
soil sensors 333
SPARQI 363, 364, 366, 373
sparsity 355
spatial learning 216
spatial-temporal fusion 216
spatial-temporal graph 215
spatiotemporal GNNs 211
spectral clustering 109, 110
spectral similarity measures 78
square matrix 66
square motifs 20, 21
star graphs 63
star motifs 20, 21, 50
stochastic gradient descent 257
stratified node sampling 13, 133
structural
  alignment 294
  neighborhood 19
  patterns 20, 50
  relationships 14, 74
structure-based transfer learning 292
subgraph 19, 48
subgraph sampling 148
sum pooling 156
supervised GML 101
supervised graph learning 311
supply chain
  management 374
  networks 374
  optimization 332
SVM 59

t

telecommunication networks 19
temporal
  edge sampling 141, 142
  GAT 220
  Learning 212
text embeddings 322
TF-IDF 369
Top-k pooling 168, 169
Transductive TGL 277
transfer component analysis 286
transfer graph learning 269, 273
transfer learning 270
transfer learning function 294
transformation matrix 288
transition matrices 33, 70, 71
traveling salesman problems 17
trees 6
triangle
  graph 10
  motifs 20, 21, 51
t-SNE 84
twitter 26–28, 45
twitter graph 278
two-star motifs 20, 21

u

undirected graph 7, 8, 15, 53, 67, 257
uniform node sampling 127
unnormalized Laplacian matrix 69
unsupervised deep learning 230

v

variational autoencoder 229
variational graph autoencoder 231
Venn diagram 81
VGGish 324
video
  analysis 23
  modality 322
virtual assistants 23
vision transformers 323

w

Wasserstein distance 294
Wav2vec 324
weather data 333
web crawling 22
web ontology language 360
web ranking 79
weighted edge sampling 138, 139, 141
weighted graphs 6, 8
Weisfeiler–Lehman 33, 386
WL Kernel 61, 63, 78
Word2vec 322

y

YAMNet 324

Wiley The manufacturer's authorized representative according to the EU General Product Safety Regulation is Wiley-VCH GmbH, Boschstr. 12, 69469 Weinheim, Germany, e-mail: Product_Safety@wiley.com.

Printed and bound by CPI Group (UK) Ltd, Croydon, CR0 4YY

28/07/2026

02179781-0002